NEW YORK CITY
THE BRONX
W 155th St.
Harlem River Dr.
W 145th St.
HARLEM
W 125th St.
7th Avenue
Lenox Avenue
Broadway
Henry Hudson Pkwy.
MANHATTAN
Park Avenue
2nd Avenue
1st Avenue
Central Park
Amsterdam Ave.
E 106th St.
Hudson River
UPPER WEST SIDE
W 81st St.
5th Avenue
E 96th St.
UPPER EAST SIDE
E 84th St.
Triborough Bridge
Lincoln Center
Broadway
Park Avenue
3rd Avenue
2nd Avenue
E 79th St.
E 66th St.
1st Avenue
Central Park St.
Lincoln Tunnel
10th Avenue
9th Avenue
E 57th St.
QUEENS
W 42nd St.
Times Square
Avenue of the Americas
Museum of Modern Art
12th Avenue
Rockefeller Center
Queensboro Bridge
W 34th St.
8th Avenue
5th Avenue
Chrysler Building
E 42nd St.
MIDTOWN
United Nations
Queens Midtown Tunnel
NEW JERSEY
9th Avenue
7th Avenue
Broadway
E 34th St.
Empire State Building
W 14th St.
E 23rd St.
West Side Highway
Greenwich Village
E 14th St.
Hudson St.
Bleeker St.
Holland Tunnel
Broadway
Avenue D
LOWER WEST SIDE
Broome St.
Little Italy
E Houston St.
East River
Canal St.
LOWER EAST SIDE
Chinatown
Bowery
Williamsburg Bridge
Freedom Memorial
Castle Garden
FDR Drive
Brooklyn Bridge
Manhattan Bridge
ELLIS ISLAND
Brooklyn Battery Tunnel
LIBERTY ISLAND
Statue of Liberty
BROOKLYN
MANHATTAN
THE BRONX
NEW JERSEY
QUEENS
BROOKLYN
STATEN ISLAND

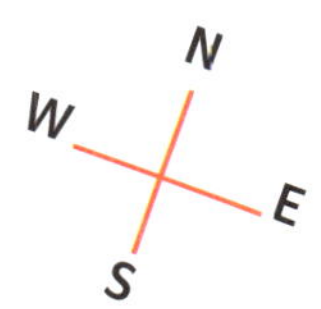

1. Name five boroughs in New York City.
2. Which river is to the west of Manhattan?
3. Which airport is nearest to the Bronx?
4. How many bridges are there across the East River? Name two of them.

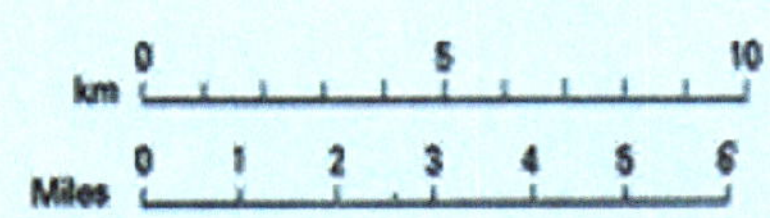

Orange **Line**

Erweiterungskurs 4

Herausgeber: Dr. Frank Haß

Ernst Klett Verlag
Stuttgart • Leipzig

Orange Line 4 Erweiterungskurs für Klasse 8 an differenzierenden Schulen

Herausgeber: Frank Haß, Kirchberg
unter besonderer Mitwirkung von Harald Weisshaar, Bisingen

Autorinnen und Autoren: Holly De Marco, Cambridge; Elizabeth Rutledge, München;
sowie Wolfgang Hamm, Marktredwitz und Christian Wunsch, M.A., Neumarkt (Oberpfalz) (Dead on the roof?); Rolf W. Roth, Idar-Oberstein (Lost in the USA);
unter Mitwirkung von Hamida Aziz, Tübingen; Sheila McBride, Stuttgart

Beratung: Anette Christiani, Dortmund; Ulf Degen, Braunschweig; Susan King-Köcher, Kassel;
Margitta Kuty, Greifswald; Heike Parma, Halver; Annegret Preker-Franke, Bielefeld

Zusatzmaterial für Schülerinnen und Schüler zu diesem Band:

Workbook mit Audio-CD und Lernsoftware	978-3-12-547648-6
Lernsoftware Einzellizenz	978-3-12-547644-8
Workbook mit Audio-CD	978-3-12-546048-5
Vokabellernheft	978-3-12-547575-5
Fit für Tests und Klassenarbeiten	978-3-12-547583-0
Action UK! Fotostory: Go, Greg, go!	978-3-12-585337-9
Action UK! Fotostory: Meeting a star	978-3-12-585338-6

1. Auflage **ISBN** 978-3-12-547541-0 1 10 9 8 | 2017 16 15 14

1. Auflage **ISBN** 978-3-12-547641-7 1 13 12 11 10 9 | 2018 17 16 15 14

Alle Drucke dieser Auflage sind unverändert und können im Unterricht nebeneinander verwendet werden.
Die letzte Zahl bezeichnet das Jahr des Druckes.

Redaktion: Susanne Frehoff M.A.; Cornelia Schaller, Lektorat editoria, Fellbach
Herstellung: Ulrike Wursthorn

Umschlaggestaltung: Koma Amok, Stuttgart
Umschlagfoto: Getty images, Fotografin: Clarisa Leahy
Illustrationen: Christian Dekelver, Weinstadt (Karte hinten); Joachim Krüger, Korntal (Karten vorne);
David Norman, Meerbusch; Sylvia Wolf, Wiesbaden; Steffen Wolff, Düsseldorf.
Wir danken Anne-Kathrin Praßler für die Bereitstellung ihrer Zeichnungen (S. 92/93).
Reproduktion: Meyle + Müller, Medien-Management, Pforzheim
Druck: Stürtz GmbH, Würzburg

Printed in Germany
ISBN 978-3-12-547541-0 (fester Einband)
ISBN 978-3-12-547641-7 (flexibler Einband)

9 783125 475410

9 783125 476417

Welcome back to Orange Line!

Nach drei Jahren Englischlernen mit Orange Line kommt nun der vierte Band.
Vieles wirst du wieder erkennen, aber manches ist auch anders.
Hier ein kurzer Überblick, um Bekanntes aufzufrischen und auf Neues einzustimmen:

In den fünf **Units** (Kapiteln) erfährst du viel Interessantes über die USA – Land und Leute.
Band 4 hat folgende Unit-Teile (einige davon erkennst du auch gleich wieder):

Check-in	Neue Wörter und Landeskunde
Language	Sprache und Grammatik
Everyday English	Nützliche Redewendungen und Ausdrücke
Get fit!	Fertigkeitstraining
Overheard	Hörverstehen
Facts and fiction	Erlebnisse und Geschichten
Wordwise	Alles rund ums Wort!
Check-out	Prüfe, ob du alles verstanden hast
Skills in action	Weitere Fertigkeiten
Try it out!	Testaufgaben

In **Extras** findest du diese Projekte:
A 'reader' project
A 'homepage' project
A 'special days' project
A history project (x 2)
Nach den Extras folgen **Mediation and communication** und **Grammar** (Grammatikanhang) mit vielen Beispielen, Regeln, Tipps und Übungen.
Am Ende des Buches findest du den Teil **Vocabulary** (Vokabelliste). Hier kannst du alle neuen Wörter nachschlagen und lernen.
Das **Dictionary** (Wörterbuch) listet die Vokabeln alphabetisch auf. Es ist auch zum Nachschlagen gedacht, wenn du einmal ein Wort vergessen hast.

Alles klar? Dann auf geht's nach New York …

Erläuterungen:

Let's talk	Lasst uns reden
Let's listen	Lasst uns zuhören
Let's look	Lasst uns nachschauen
Role play	Verschiedene Rollen übernehmen
For my folder	Für meine Sammelmappe
Mixed bag	Eine kontrastive Übung
Cloze text	Ein Lückentext
Detective work	Neue Grammatikregeln entdecken

Diese Teile sind auf den Begleit-CDs (Langversion) enthalten.
Diese Übungen sind besonders knifflig.
Partnerarbeit
Gruppenarbeit
Diese Übungen kannst du machen, sie können aber auch wegfallen.

▶ Tipp zum Vokabellernen ▶ Tipp zur Grammatik ▶ Tipp mit Redemitteln

WELCOME
TO Fabulous
LAS VEGAS
NEVADA

HOLLYWOOD

Unit 1 I ♥ New York City

1 In the background: Lakes in Central Park, Manhattan, from the top of the Empire State Building

1 A big city

a) *What do you know about New York City? Start a mind map for your folder. Continue it as you go through the unit.*

b) *Look at photo 1. What can you see? Describe the photo in two or three sentences. Perhaps your mind map can help you.*

L1, 1–5

2 Let's listen: Out and about

a) *Listen. Where are the people? Match each scene with a photo.*

b) *What do you find out about the places in the photos?*

2 The Statue of Liberty
3 In the foreground: A jogger on Brooklyn Bridge
4 Kids with kickboards on steps, in Brooklyn
5 Neon lights, stores and theaters on Times Square, Manhattan

DID YOU KNOW?

- More than 8 million people live in New York City. Over a third were born outside the US.
- It has five boroughs: Manhattan, Brooklyn, Queens, the Bronx and Staten Island. They are on the map at the front of your book.
- Each borough has neighborhoods. One of the most famous is Chinatown in Manhattan. The hub of Manhattan is Times Square.
- Native Americans (Mohawks) helped to build Manhattan's skyscrapers, like the Empire State Building.
- The Statue of Liberty in New York Harbor is a symbol of freedom. A famous island in the harbor is Ellis Island, where millions of immigrants landed.
- Central Park is huge! It has lakes, playgrounds and lots of fields for ball games. It is the safest public park in any city in the US.

3 Let's talk: A New York City quiz (→ p. 4/ex. 1)

a) *Read the fact box and write questions for a partner.*

b) *Close your books and answer each other's questions.*

A: Which Native Americans helped to build Manhattan?
B: That's easy. It was the … .
A: Right. Now it's your turn.
B: OK. Who landed …?

4 For my folder: Central Park (→ p. 4/ex. 2)

Find out more about events in the park. Use the Internet.

The **simple past** is for actions in the past.
... who **landed** at Ellis Island ... .
Some **didn't eat** for weeks.

The **past perfect** is for actions before past actions.
After they **had landed** at Ellis Island, ...
Some **hadn't eaten** for weeks, when they ... . → G1–3

US immigration

Most of the twelve million immigrants who landed at Ellis Island didn't want to leave their homes. They emigrated to escape from famine, poverty, war and oppression. Today there is a museum on the island.

1620 1640 1660 1680 1700 1720 1740 1760 1780 1800 1820 1840 1860 1880 1900

1626
Dutch immigrants founded New Amsterdam.

1630
The Dutch bought Little Oyster Island from Native Americans.

1664
After the English had taken the town from the Dutch, they named it New York.

1785
When Samuel Ellis had bought the island from the Dutch, he named it Ellis Island.

Early immigrants

1820
The numbers of immigrants started to rise. They sailed to New York and landed at Castle Garden, Manhattan.

1845
There was a famine in Ireland and millions of Irish started to leave on ships to New York. The journey was terrible. After they had been seasick for five days, many of the passengers were more dead than alive. Some hadn't eaten for weeks when they arrived.

1892
They closed the immigration station in Manhattan and opened one on Ellis Island. The first immigrant was a young Irish girl called Annie Moore.

1900 1910 1920 1930 1940 1950 1960 1970 1980 1990 2000 today

1910
An Italian immigrant wrote, "Some had left the end of a ball of yarn with someone on land. As the ship moved farther and farther out to sea, the balls unwound. When the yarn had run out, all you could see were the long threads in the air behind the ship."

1921
The US started quotas for immigrants from Eastern Europe. A Polish woman had a baby on a British ship from Belgium. When she landed on Ellis Island, the Polish, British and Belgian quotas had just run out. The officials there said, "You can stay, but not your baby." There was little hope for the baby but one man had an idea. "The ship was late," he said, "and the baby was early. So the baby is American."

1954
They closed the immigration station on Ellis Island.

1960
In the 1960s the journey for immigrants got better and better as planes started to bring them to airports in the US.

1978
The US started a quota for immigrants from all over the world. Today most people who immigrate into the US come from Mexico, the Philippines, India and China.

The museum on Ellis Island

1 The journey to the US (→ p. 5/ex. 3)

Look at the timeline on page 10 and read the texts. Find Ellis Island on the map at the front of your book. When did these things happen? Make sentences.

Example: **In 1892** they closed the immigration station in **Manhattan**.

1. … they closed the immigration station in … .
2. … the English gave the city of New York its … .
3. … they closed the immigration station on … .
4. … Samuel Ellis named it … .
5. … the Dutch founded New … .
6. … they started quotas for … .
7. … there was a famine in … .
8. … immigrants started to fly to … .

2 At Ellis Island (→ p. 5/ex. 4; p. 6/ex. 5, 6; p. 7/ex. 7)

a) *Use the past perfect to complete these sentences.*

1. After the immigrants … (*to land*) at Ellis Island, they waited in the immigration hall.
2. They were often still weak because they … (*to be*) seasick on the journey.
3. Many … (*not/to eat*) for days when they went onto the ship
4. Some … (*to leave*) their own country to escape from oppression and they still felt tired or sick.
5. After the doctors … (*to check*) them, they sent them to an official, who asked them a lot of questions.

b) *Use the simple past or the past perfect and complete the sentences.*

In 1921 the US … (*to start*) quotas for many countries. Before this date officials often … (*to send*) back old, sick people. After 1921 they … (*to start*) to send healthy, young immigrants home by ship because the quota for their country … (*to run out*). Others … (*to be*) luckier. They … (*not/to have to*) go back because the quota for their country … (*not/to run out*). After they … (*to show*) their money to the officials, they … (*to leave*) Ellis Island.

3 Let's talk: Pros and cons

What do you think it's like to be an immigrant? Look at the text and the pictures again. Make a list of the pros and cons. Discuss them in your group.

Giving an opinion
Yes, but … .
I think/don't think … .
I agree/don't agree because … .

4 For my folder: Internet research on immigration (→ p. 7/ex. 8)

Choose one of the groups of immigrants from the timeline and find out more about them. Where did they come from and why?
Write a short report and present it to the class.

DIEGO'S DELI

Coffee to go	$2.60
Coffee to go & Danish or cupcake	$4.60
Empire State Breakfast pancakes with maple syrup, eggs, sausage, bacon, potatoes, bagel or toast and coffee	$7.49
Big sandwiches cream cheese or egg, two slices of bacon, pastrami or turkey with lettuce, tomato and French fries	$5.95
Milkshakes strawberry, cherry, banana	$2.90

THE MANHATTAN MONSTER

José has a vacation job in his uncle's deli in New York City. It's his first day.

1 A deli menu

a) *Look at the menu on page 12. Match the pictures with the food words on it. Example:* Number 1 is … .

b) *What kind of snack bars have you got in your town? What can you eat there? What's different from Diego's Deli?*

a cent

a dime (10 cents)

2 Role play: At Diego's Deli (→ p. 8/ex. 9)

a) *Read the 'The Manhattan Monster' on page 12. Choose a part and practise it in your group.*

b) *Act it in front of the class.*

c) *Change the highlighted words. Write new dialogues and act them.*

a dollar ($ 1 = 100 cents)

3 Let's talk: Something for lunch (→ p. 8/ex. 10)

Now order something to eat and something to drink at the deli.

A: Hi! I'd like a … and a …, please.
B: Would you like it with or without …?
A: …, please.
B: OK. That's … dollars and … cents, please.
A: Here's … . Give me … and you can keep the change.

a nickel (5 cents)

a quarter (25 cents)

L1, 6 4 Let's listen: Our Manhattan Monster

a) *Look at the photo. What do you think is in this Manhattan Monster?*

b) *Now listen to a girl who is talking about a Manhattan Monster. Make a grid like this and complete it.*

Steps	What?	How much/many?
1. 2. …	bread … …	11 slices 1 small packet …

c) *Use the photo and your grid and write down how she and her friend made their sandwich. Start like this:* First they took eleven slices of bread. After they had done that, they … .

5 For my folder: My favourite recipe

Think of your own recipe for a sandwich. Write a list of what you need. Add instructions. Find a photo or draw a picture of the sandwich.

READING SKILLS

Writing notes on a factual text

You write notes to prepare for a presentation, a test, or a talk on a topic.

1. Read the text and find out what it is about.
2. If you don't understand a sentence, look up unknown words.
3. Note all the important facts. You can do this in different ways:

a) A list

Chinese New Year
a Chinese festival
big event
...

b) A mind map

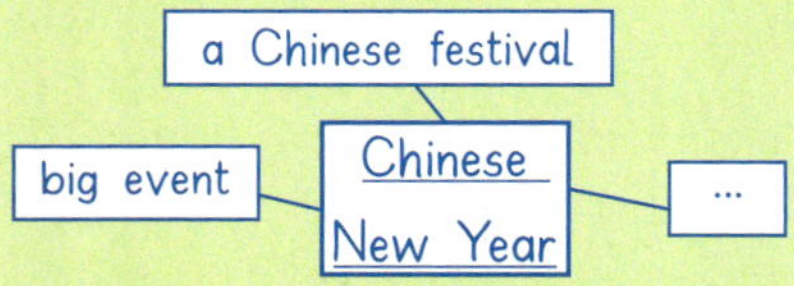

c) A grid

...	...	...

4. Compare your notes again with the text. Is everything right?

1 A factual text (→ p. 9/ex. 11)

a) *Read the text and use the skills box. Write notes (either as a list, a mind map or a grid).*

Chinese New Year

Chinatown in New York City is the largest Chinatown in the US. This busy neighborhood, which is full of candy stores, fruit and fish markets and restaurants, lies on the lower east side of Manhattan. Its population (around 100,000) is mostly Chinese but other groups, such as Puerto Ricans, live there, too. Today Chinatown is a popular place with New Yorkers and tourists, too. If you visit New York City in January or February, you can take part in the biggest Chinese event of the year: Chinese New Year. They also call it the Spring Festival because it takes place at the beginning of spring in the Chinese calendar.

Not many people know how the festival started and there are different, very old stories about this. One is that an old man saved a village from a monster. He told the people there to put up red paper decorations in the windows and doors because the monster was scared of this color. They also began to use fireworks because they thought that the noise could frighten monsters and horrible ghosts away. But Chinese New Year is not just decorations and fireworks. There are lots of events that go on for three to five days. There is a big parade with people who dress as huge dragons and dance in the streets. Some dragons are a hundred feet long! In the Chinese tradition dragons

are strong, friendly animals that always bring good luck.

One part of the tradition is a special family meal on the night before the New Year. On the next morning they give each other presents. For three days most stores and businesses are closed so that people can visit all their friends and family.

As with other New Year traditions, activities at Chinese New Year are also a symbol of new beginnings.

b) *Did you use a mind map/list/grid? Compare your notes. Did you all have the same points?*

c) *Use your notes and present 'Chinese New Year' to the class.*

,7–9 1 Let's listen: Sidewalks, mansions and skyscrapers (→ p. 10/ex. 12)

a) *Every week DJ Ray from 'Sunrise NY' chats with people in Central Park.*
Today he is talking to a house-sitter, a Mohawk steelworker and a sidewalk painter.
Which do you think is which and why?

1

2

3

b) *Now listen to the interviews and write notes.*

c) *Use your notes and answer the questions.*

1. Which parts of New York are the people from?
2. What do they like about their job?
3. What is not so good about their jobs?
4. Which job do you like best? Why?

0–11 2 Sounds: British or American English? (→ p. 10/ex. 13, 14)

a) *Listen to the words.*

b) *Now listen to the sentences. Which speaker is American and which one is English?*

1, 12 3 A song: I love New York

(Madonna/Stuart David Price © Neue Welt Musikverlag)

I don't like cities but I like New York
Other places make me feel like a dork[1]
Los Angeles is for people who sleep
Paris and London, baby, you can keep
Chorus[2]:
Other cities always make me mad
Other places always make me sad
No other city ever made me glad except[3] New York
I love New York

If you don't like my attitude[4] then you can F off[5]
Just go to Texas, isn't that where they golf[6]
New York is not for little pussies who scream[7]
If you can't stand the heat[8] then get off my street
Then get off my street

Answer the questions.

1. Which cities does she sing about?
2. How does she feel about New York?
3. How does she feel about the other cities?
4. What can people do who don't agree with her?

[1]dork [dɔ:k] – *Langweiler*, [2]chorus ['kɒrəs] – *Refrain*, [3]except [ɪk'sept] – *außer*, [4]attitude ['ætitju:d] – *Einstellung*, [5]to F off [ef 'ɒf] – *verschwinden*, [6]to golf [gɒlf] – *golfen*, [7]pussies who scream ['pʊsiz hʊ: 'skri:m] – *Angsthasen, die schreien*, [8]to stand the heat [ˌstænd ðə 'hi:t] – *die Aufregung ertragen*

L1, 13–17

Dead on the roof?

A "Welcome on our tour of New York City. I'm Frank, your pilot. It's a fine day and it's nice and cool in our helicopter. So just sit back and relax – and enjoy the spectacular views!"

A few minutes later the engine roared and the helicopter took off. Kim and Brandon were two passengers on the flight. They were from Texas and it was their first time in New York – and their very first trip in a helicopter. So they were both very excited. They sat just behind the pilot so they could get a good view and ask questions.

B "Wow! Brandon, look!" shouted Kim over the noise of the engine. "There's the Statue of Liberty. It looks so big from here!"

"Yeah, and isn't that Ellis Island over there?" asked Brandon. He had a strange feeling in his stomach but he tried not to think about it.

"You're right. Immigrants landed there in the past. OK, folks, we're turning back now to fly over Greenwich Village."

"Oh, that's where all those actors and stars live, right?" said Kim.

"Yeah, and it also has a lot of really good restaurants and delis. In fact that's where my favorite deli 'Shake-A-Break' is, and believe me, they make the best milkshakes in Manhattan! Oh, yes, and there are loads of tattoo shops in the Village, if you're into that sort of thing."

"No, thanks," Brandon answered. "But maybe we'll try out that milkshake place." But when he thought about milkshakes, he began to feel sick.

"Brandon, are you OK?" asked Kim. "Yes, I think so. Yeah, I'm fine," answered Brandon and tried to smile at his girlfriend. Then he turned to the pilot.

"Hey, Frank, what are those smaller houses down there?"

C "That's Little Italy – that's my home. I've lived there all my life and I love it," he said. Then he flew the helicopter over Manhattan with its huge skyscrapers and other tall buildings. "What's that flat blue roof down there?" one of the other passengers suddenly asked and pointed to the right.

Brandon looked down.

"I bet that's not a blue roof. It's a swimming pool! Look, there's a woman in a swimsuit in a chair and she's waving!" he said. He waved back although she probably couldn't see them in the helicopter.

"Yes, there are all kinds of things on the roofs of skyscrapers in New York. Over there is a block of apartments with a big roof garden. Now everybody, look to the left in front of us: I'm sure you all know what that is!" said Frank.

"The Empire State Building!" answered Kim in a loud voice. "I must get a snapshot!"

As she took the picture, she saw something flash at the side of the building. Two men were cleaning windows! At that height!

Brandon saw them, too, and thought, "It's almost 100° F out there. I'm already dizzy. I couldn't do that job to save my life!" And something turned in his stomach.

D "Hey, what's that?" Kim shouted suddenly as she grabbed Brandon's arm. "Someone is lying there on the roof of that skyscraper!"

"Where?" asked Brandon.

"Over there, to the left of the Empire State Building. He isn't moving," she answered, worried. "Oh, yes. I can see him now. But what's that next to the man? It looks like a gun," Brandon said excitedly.

"Perhaps he's dead," Kim whispered.

She leaned forward to tell the pilot. "Frank, look, there's someone on top of that roof."

"Yes, you're right. I'll try to get nearer," he said.

"Can you land on that skyscraper?" Kim asked.
"Well, only if it's a real emergency ..."
"This is an emergency!" shouted Brandon. He had forgotten all about his stomach now.
"I should tell the cops," said Frank.
"But it could be too late!" said Kim.
"OK, I'll tell the cops. Then I'll land on the roof if it's not too difficult," said Frank.

E The pilot flew in circles round the skyscraper. Then he went down slowly and landed on the roof. He switched the engine off and turned to the passengers.
"Now, all of you," he said. "Please, don't follow me. You know, it could be dangerous."
Frank opened the door and walked towards the man. Brandon and Kim, who were too excited to stay in the helicopter, got out and waited. Frank touched the man's arm.
"Hey, mister, what's up?" he asked.
But the man didn't move.
"He isn't dead, is he?" Kim shouted.
"No, he isn't. I think he just fainted. It's the heat. I mean, it's quite hot, even for July.

Could one of you, please, get him some water?"
Kim found a bottle in the helicopter and brought it to Frank. Brandon followed her. Frank put a little water on the man's face. Slowly the man opened his eyes but he didn't speak. Frank gave him some water to drink. Brandon looked at the man's clothes. They were blue.
"I think he's a workman," he said. "Perhaps he just wanted to repair something up here."
"Yeah, you're right. Look, here's his 'gun'," Kim laughed. "It's an electric drill!"

1 Before you read: Can you guess?

a) *Read the title and look at the picture. Which of these clues are correct?*

1. The story takes place in a city.
2. The passengers are on a plane.
3. There's someone on a roof.
4. They land in Central Park.
5. Three people want to attack someone.

b) *Correct the clues that you think are wrong.*

2 The story so far

Read parts A to C and answer the questions.

1. Why were Kim and Brandon excited?
2. What was the weather like on that day?
3. What did Frank tell them about Greenwich Village and Little Italy?
4. What did they see on the roofs?
5. What did Kim take a snapshot of?
6. How did Brandon feel in the helicopter?

3 Suddenly ... (→ p. 11/ex. 15)

Read parts D and E. Where do you find out the following information? Example:

Kim saw something that she didn't expect.
That's line 69: Kim said: Hey, what's that?

1. Brandon thought there could be some action.
2. Frank wanted to get a better look.
3. Frank didn't usually land on roofs.
4. The two didn't follow Frank's instructions.
5. The man on the roof was not dead.
6. The man was not dangerous.

4 For my folder: And then ... (→ p. 11/ex. 16)

Write your own ending for the story.

5 Role play: The whole story

Imagine you are Kim or Brandon. How did you feel on the trip? Talk to a friend about it.

1 A quiz: London or New York City?

a) *Read each sentence. Is it about London or New York City?*

1. There was a <u>terrible fire</u> in 1666.
2. The city has got <u>five boroughs</u>.
3. There's an <u>island</u> with a museum on it.
4. You can see a famous <u>clock</u> from a <u>capsule</u>.
5. There's a famous <u>tower</u> which is over 900 years old.
6. You can see a big <u>statue</u> of a woman with a torch.
7. There's a very rich and famous <u>family</u> in a palace.
8. It's got a <u>huge park</u> with lakes and fields, e.g. for baseball.

b) *What are the names of the things which are underlined?*

c) *Now write more quiz sentences for your partner.*

2 In a picture (→ p. 12/ex. 17)

a) *Find the opposites of these words in the box on the right.*

inside · above · in front of · on the left · at the top · in the foreground · under

behind • below • on the right • on top of • in the background • at the bottom • outside

b) *Use the words to describe the picture in exercise 1.*

3 Let's look: A tourist's day

a) *Look at the map and the pictures. What did the tourist do/see/visit and when? Make a timeline.*

time	place
8:00	Hotel Rome in ...

b) *Use the timeline and say what he did in New York. Start like this:*
At eight o'clock he ate breakfast in his hotel in … . At … .

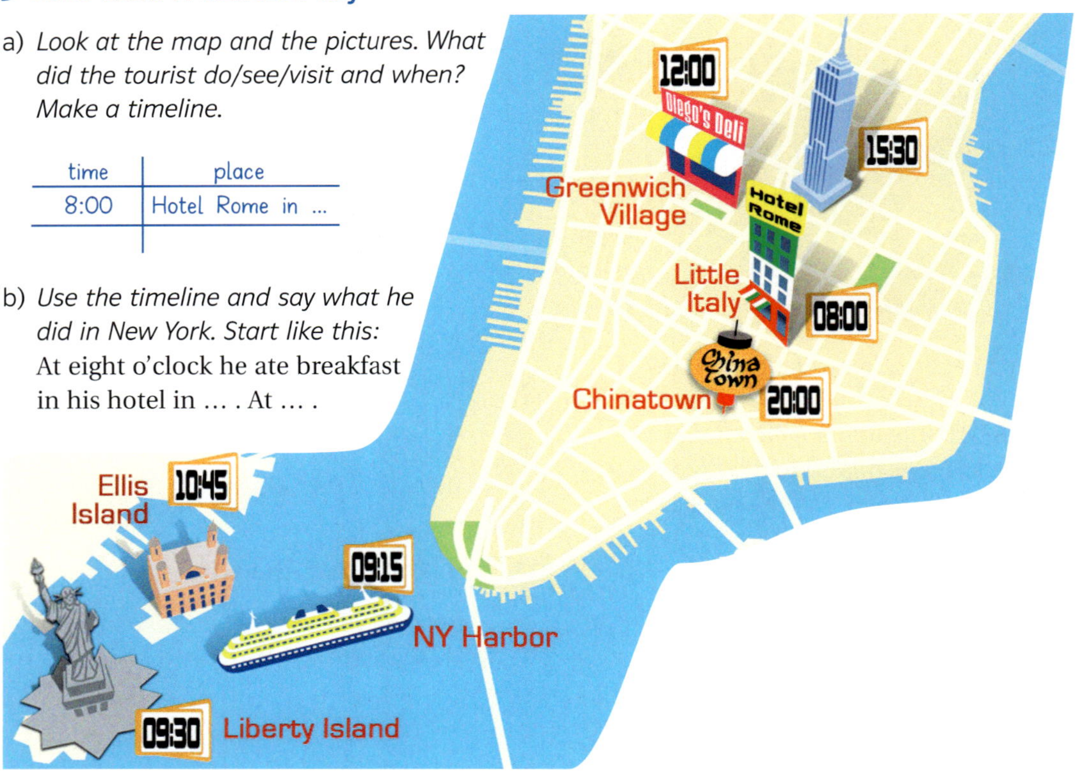

4 They have different words! (→ p. 12/ex. 18)

a) *Find the American words for the underlined words and phrases and rewrite the sentences.*

1. I love fish and chips.
2. There are a lot of flats in that building.
3. Yes, I can help you.
4. It was the best café in the world!
5. I like the colour *(Spelling!)* of your T-shirt!
6. There was big trouble in the park, so someone called the police.
7. Which neighbourhood *(Spelling!)* is better, Greenwich Village or Manhattan's East Side?
8. We can visit New York in the summer holidays.
9. Lots of boats sail out of this harbour *(Spelling!)*.
10. What's your favourite *(Spelling!)* ice-cream?

b) *Put the words in a grid and add the German meaning.*

AE	BE	German
...	chips	...
...	...	...

5 Different prices

a) *How much do these things cost in London, New York and Berlin? Check how many dollars there are in a pound and in a euro. Compare the prices.*
Start like this: The mobile in London **is more expensive than** the mobile in New York. The mobile in New York is **cheaper than** the mobile in London.

 1	 2	 3	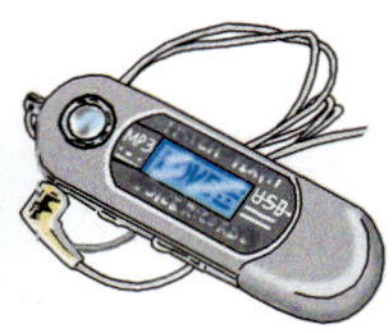 4	 5
£ 27.50 $ 39.35 € 44.99	£ 39.99 $ 49.95 € 57.50	£ 34.99 $ 149.15 € 92.10	£ 41.00 $ 69.99 € 39.95	£ 8.99 $ 9.49 € 11.00

b) *Imagine you are in New York. What change do you get out of 100 dollars for each of the things?*
Example: 1. I get 60 dollars and 65 cents (two quarters, a dime and a nickel).

6 What's the word?

Find the right word and complete the sentences.

1. A person who moves to another country because life at home has become difficult is an ... .
2. When they get to the new country, they have to go through ... .
3. The first immigrants from Europe travelled to the US by ... .
4. If you are ..., this means you get sick on a ship.
5. Many Irish people decided to go to the US because there was a ... .
6. The ... that were in the air behind the ship were from balls of yarn.
7. Today a lot of people who ... into the US come from Mexico.
8. The number of people who can come to the US from one country is called a ... .

1 A day in NYC (simple past → G1) (→ p. 13/ex. 19)

a) *What did/didn't three visitors – Tom, Dick and Harry – do on their trip to NYC? Write sentences.*

- ✔ eat at a deli
- ✔ climb to the top of the ESB
- ✘ walk through Central Park
- ✘ ride on a kickboard
- ✔ take lots of photos
- ✘ buy souvenirs
- ✔ visit Chinatown
- ✘ write postcards
- ✔ go to Ellis Island
- ✘ fly in a helicopter

b) *Imagine you spent a day in New York. What did or didn't you see/do/visit? What was good and what was bad? Start like this:* We saw lots of places. But we didn't … because … .

2 Yesterday in Central Park (simple past → G1/past perfect → G2) (→ p. 13/ex. 20)

a) *Look at the pictures. What happened yesterday in Central Park?*
Example: 1. The police **took away** two young men.

1 to take away

2 to play

3 to lie down

4 to pick up

5 to lose

6 to eat

b) *Match each picture below with a picture from a).*
Example: 1.-E Before that the two young men **had jumped into** the lake.

A to land

B to feel

C to throw

D to find

E to jump into

F to escape

3 Mixed bag: The history of Central Park (simple past or past perfect → G3) (→ p. 13/ex. 21)

Fill in the right forms of the verbs and find out more about the park.

Before they (*to come*) to the US, many immigrants (*to live*) in the country. After they (*to be*) in New York for a year or two, they (*to start*) to miss the trees and fields of home. They also (*to want*) a place for their families, a park where their children (*can*) play or do sports. After officials (*to argue*) for about three years, they finally (*to decide*) where to put it. After they (*to draw*) the plans, they (*to talk*) to people who (*to live*) in the area which they (*to choose*). After the people (*to leave*) their homes, workers (*to destroy*) their houses and (*to start*) to work on the park project. They (*to change*) a huge area in the middle of Manhattan into a beautiful park. 20,000 workers (*to work*) on the area which is now called Central Park. This (*to be*) the first public park in the US. Work on the project (*to start*) in 1858 and it (*to take*) eight years to finish it.

4 Cloze text: Day one in NYC! (→ p. 14/ex. 1)

Find the missing words and use them in the text.

When Kim and Brandon arrived (1) New York City, (2) were really surprised. The buildings were (3), even taller than they had (4). There were (5) of people everywhere and the noise of the cars was terrible. It was really (6) so all they wanted to do was to go to their hotel room and have a (7). Then after they (8), they felt much better. They left their hotel and took a tourist bus through Manhattan (9) they saw famous things like the Empire State (10) and Central Park. After they (11) in the park, they went back to their (12). In the evening they (13) supper in a little restaurant in Greenwich Village. They still (14) their friends and family at home but they had already (15) to understand why so many people (16) New York.

expected | huge | crowds | in | hot | they | shower | had rested | ate | where | love | Building | had walked | hotel | missed | started

NOW YOU CAN

- ✓ use the past perfect for actions. → *Talk about five things that happened after you had done something stupid.*
- ✓ talk about events in the past. → *Find out about the history of your town. Write notes and use them to give a short talk.*
- ✓ talk about food and order it. → *Write a short menu for your favourite food and order it.*
- ✓ compare American English (AE) and British English (BE). → *Write down three words which sound different and three which look different in AE and BE.*

From East to West

Eva Gorzalkowski wrote in a woman's magazine about how she came to the US.

My name is Eva Gordon. I immigrated into the US 20 years ago. My real name is Gorzalkowski. But I changed it because no one could spell it! It's a Polish name.

I was born in a small town in the south of Poland in 1972. I wasn't the best student[1] at school but I was good at Maths and languages. I learnt Russian and English.

It was my dream to go to America and live there. I hated our small town. America was my idea of a happy future.

When I was 18, my English teacher told me about a job in London. Her daughter[2] was married to an American who worked there and they had three very young children. They needed an au-pair[3]. I wrote to them at once and they offered me the job. It took a few months to organize my visa[4] and work permit[5] because Poland wasn't in the EU[6] at that time.

I spent a really happy time with them. So when they moved to LA a year later, I was really sad. But at least I found a new job – this time in a company in England.

Six months after they had left, I got a letter from the husband[7]. His company was looking for people with language skills. He said I should write to them. I went for an interview[8] in London and the company offered me a job in LA. But I had to wait to get my Green Card[9] – as you all know, you can't live and work here legally[10] without it. And that's when I met my Polish husband, Jaroslaw. He worked in the same office.

We decided to marry. I thought he could come out to LA with me, but it wasn't as easy as that. They told me that he needed an immigrant visa. He had to stay in England. He couldn't even visit me in the US! I had to travel back to Britain to see him. Four years after we married, he got his visa and moved to LA.

[1]student ['stju:dnt] – *Schüler/Schülerin,* [2]daughter ['dɔ:tə] – *Tochter,* [3]au-pair [ˌəʊ'peə] – *Kindermädchen,* [4]visa ['vi:zə] – *Visum,* [5]work permit ['wɜ:k ˌpɜ:mɪt] – *Arbeitserlaubnis,* [6]EU [ˌi:'ju:] – *Europäische Union,* [7]husband ['hʌzbənd] – *(Ehe-)Mann,* [8]interview ['ɪntəvju:] – *hier: Vorstellungsgespräch,* [9]Green Card ['gri:n ˌkɑ:d] – *unbefristete Aufenthaltserlaubnis,* [10]legally ['li:gəli] – *rechtmäßig*

A Reading

Read the text and complete the sentences.

a. Eva was born in	1 the US.	2 Poland.	3 Russia.
b. She worked in London as	1 an au-pair.	2 an actress.	3 a teacher.
c. Later she got a job	1 in LA.	2 in Russia.	3 in Poland.
d. She couldn't work in the US without	1 a visitor's visa.	2 a Green Card.	3 a husband.
e. She married	1 her teacher.	2 in England.	3 in LA.

B Language

Read the sentences. How does Eva say them in her article?

a. I came to the US 20 years ago.
b. No one could say it or write it.
c. My dearest wish was to go to the US.
d. I needed some months to get a visa.
e. He had a job in the same company.

C Listening

Listen to what Eva told a reporter and do the exercise.

a. Name two reasons why Eva is happy in the US.
b. Name two problems which some immigrants have.
c. What often happens to immigrants without a Green Card from Mexico?

D Mediation and communication

An immigrant to Germany is talking to a US immigrant. Answer his/her questions.

Immigrant: Was genau ist eine Green Card?
You: …
US immigrant: If you are an immigrant to the US and you want to work and live there, you must have a Green Card.
You: …
Immigrant: Warum immigrieren Leute in die USA?
You: …
US immigrant: Many come to find work or because they want a better future for their children.
You: …

E Writing

1 Skills

Make a timeline of Eva's life between Poland, England and the US.

2 Writing

Use your timeline from exercise 1. Imagine you are Jaroslaw. Write about what happened to you as an immigrant. Write 5–6 sentences.

Unit 2 A new school year

Home | Curriculum | Clubs&Activities | Students | Parents

PARADISE VALLEY
High School (PVHS)

CLUBS & ACTIVITIES

BREAKING NEWS

YEARBOOK CLUB
- first meeting
- last year
- plans for this year

SPORTS CLUBS
- football
  - dates for games
  - practice
- baseball
  - dates for games
  - practice

HOMECOMING CLUB
- cheerleaders
  - tryouts
- dance
- parade/rally

OTHER CLUBS
- video club
- hip hop club

Breaking news! Breaking news! Breaking news!

Make a Difference Day:
8th Grade students win prize.

At the beginning of the month the school organized a 'Make a Difference Day' for all classes. Each class did projects or activities which helped other people. There was a prize for the best project: a class trip to a theme park!

Click here to find out more.

The winners!

BLUE EAGLES

1 A school website

a) *What clubs are there at Paradise Valley High School? What do you find out about them on the website?*

b) *Look at 'Breaking news'. What could 'Make a Difference Day' be? What kind of projects do you think that they do on this day?*

c) *Do you have anything like this at your school? If yes, what do you do then?*

L1, 19 2 Let's listen: Make a Difference Day

a) *Listen to an interview with students who took part in this project. Were you right with your guess in exercise 1?*

b) *Listen again.*

1. What did Mr MacDonald's class and the other class do on the day?
2. Which idea won the competition?
3. What did one father give them?

1

2

3

3 Website info (→ p. 17/ex. 1)

Look at the pictures and match them with the texts below from the website.

Have you already guessed who is in the picture? Well, it's Sandra from Mr MacDonald's 8th Grade. Here, of course, she's pledging allegiance to the flag as we all do in class every morning. But notice the big difference: Every class now has a brand new American flag!
A

This year's 8th Grade back-to-school dance is in the second week of school. So the cheerleaders choose the homecoming queen this week. Remember: The lucky girl goes to the dance with the captain of the school football team. And don't forget: Everybody wears formal dress at the dance. So, please, no jeans and no T-shirts! And you just have enough time to practice ballroom dancing.
B

Cheerleaders are our greatest supporters at all the school games. When they chant, wave their pompoms and dance, they make every event more colorful and exciting. There are tryouts this week, where the sports teachers choose the best girls for this year's cheerleader team.
C

4 For my folder: American schools (→ p. 17/ex. 2)

a) *Make mind maps, one for each topic.*
Put these together in a cluster.
Add more words as you go through the unit.

b) *At the end of the unit present American schools to your class.*

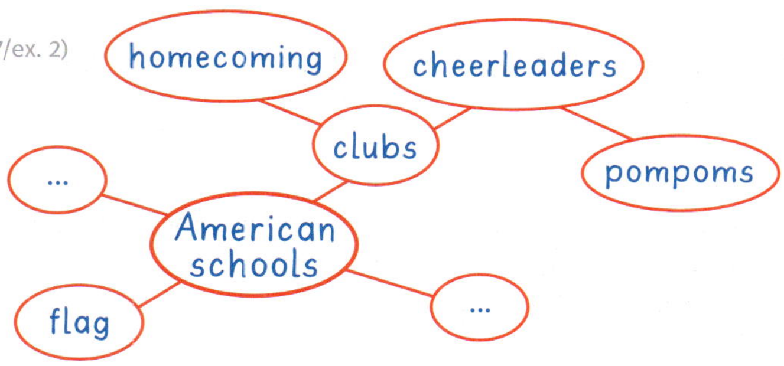

You use the present perfect
1. when you talk about a past action and link it with the present.
   … some of you **have** <u>already</u> **been** … . (You **now** know something about it.)
   But our … club **hasn't started** <u>yet</u>. (**Now** we want to plan the first meeting.)
2. in questions with 'ever'.
   … **have** you <u>ever</u> **visited** … ?

→ G4

School yearbooks

A student at PVHS is telling you about school yearbooks on the Internet:

"I'm sure some of you have already been to the US. But have you ever visited a high school here? Well, if not, you probably haven't heard about yearbooks. A yearbook has lots of photos of important people and events which have happened during the year: who got a prize, who dated who at the homecoming dance, etc. It's a lot of work! But luckily, our English teacher has promised to help us this year. The best thing to do is to have a look at a yearbook! But our 8th Grade Yearbook Club hasn't started yet. Next week is our first meeting – so I haven't got any material to show you. But have a look at these pages from last year's yearbook. And, of course, when we've finished our new one, you can download your favorite page!"

1 Let's talk: About yearbooks (→ p. 18/ex. 3, 4)

a) *Read the text above. What is a yearbook? Explain it to your partner.*

b) *Look at the text again and make sentences about yearbooks.*

Some of you But You probably It tells you about events which But luckily our English teacher The 8th Grade Yearbook Club	+	has hasn't have haven't	+	promised to help us this year. started yet. already been to the US. you ever visited a high school here? heard about yearbooks. happened during the year.

c) *Has your class ever made a yearbook? If you want to, look on pages 24/25 for ideas.*

2 Plans for a yearbook (→ p. 19/ex. 5)

What have the students already done? What haven't they done yet?

Example: 1. Sue and Larry **have already planned** … . 2. Brad **hasn't** … .

<u>Sue and Larry</u>	<u>Brad</u>
✔ plan the yearbook	✘ edit all the photos
✘ collect lots of jokes	✔ write a report about homecoming
✘ finish a diary of events	✔ find a title for the yearbook
✔ interview the students	✔ take photos of cheerleaders
✔ organize adverts	✘ think up captions

Home | Curriculum | Clubs&Activities | Students | Parents

PARADISE VALLEY
High School (PVHS)

School Rules!

- Absent students should make sure that the school gets an absence slip. The slip should arrive before the absence or (if the student is sick) on the first day they are absent. Students must not sign the slip. Only a parent or other adult may do this.
- All students may wear their own clothes but they must not wear anything with adverts for alcohol, drugs, or tobacco or which shows that they belong to a gang.
- No student may bring a gun or knife to school.
- The school is a smoke-free zone. Students must not smoke on the way to and from school, in school or at any school activities.
- Students should go to the toilet during recess. In an emergency they may leave a class but they should get a permission slip from their teacher.
- All students who are late should go to the school office. They must not go straight to their lessons.
- Students with a problem may contact teachers 30 minutes before the first period, during morning recess, at lunchtime or 30 minutes after school.

3 Rules to remember (→ p. 19/ex. 6; p. 20/ex. 7–9)

a) *Make sentences. Use the words in the lists.*
Example: **Absent students should** make sure that the school gets an **absence slip.**

Absent students	+	may	+	absence slip
Sick students		must not		first day
A parent or other adult		should		sign
Students				clothes
All students				adverts
No student				gun or knife
Students who are late				school office
Students with a problem				teachers

▶ They **should** make sure … .
All students **may** wear … .
Students **must not** sign … .
→ G5

b) *What about rules at your school?*
What is the same and what is different?
Make two lists.

4 A cartoon: Back to school

1. Who do you think is in the tree?
2. Where should he or she be?
3. What must the woman not do?

© Tim Dolighan, Dolighan Cartoons

5 A game: What rule is it?

Invent a rule. One of you starts to draw it.
Can the other groups guess your rule?

The art of dating ...

So you like someone and you want to go out with him or her: Well, you have to ask for a date! And – as we all know – there are very clear rules about how to date. If you do it wrong, you could get 'no' for an answer. But even if it's 'yes', you can make terrible mistakes. OK, you want to take your date to the movies or you still don't have a date for the homecoming dance. Well, you better learn quick! And to help you – here are some dating survival tips:

Be direct.

Don't take too long.

Don't be late! And say something nice ...

... but don't overdo it.

Do something together ...

... which you both like!

If it was a good date:

If it wasn't so hot, you must still end the date politely:

1 How to do it!

a) *Look at the article from a school magazine. Read the introduction and answer the questions.*

1. What may you do if you like someone?
2. Why should you be careful?
3. When could the tips be helpful?

b) *Read the tips. What should you do when you are dating? What mustn't you do?*

2 The most difficult thing

What is the most difficult thing for you when you want a date? Use the box to help you. Example:
The most difficult thing for me is meeting his/her … .

making the first move • asking for a date • planning … • meeting … • talking about my feelings • knowing what to wear/say/…

.1, 20 3 Let's listen: Making the first move (→ p. 21/ex. 10)

a) *Listen to the dialogues. Who wants to date who? Match the names of the students.*
Example: Tyler wants to date … .

Brad · Tyler · Larry · Charlie · Ron · Stu

Nina · Terri · Sue · Paula-Jo · Tammy · Rebecca

b) *Listen to the dialogues again. Make a list of phrases for dating.*

4 Role play: Dating (→ p. 21/ex. 11)

Imagine you and your partner are the people in one of the scenes in the dating tips. Write a short dialogue and act the scene. Be polite! Don't say 'no' in a hurtful way. You can use the phrases from exercise 3 b).

5 Let's talk: Questions

a) *Imagine you have a date with a boy or girl from the US: Can you understand what he/she asks? What are the highlighted AE words in BE? Use the words in the boxes to help you.*

Do you go to a high school?
What grade are you in?
What do you do at recess?
Would you like to go to the movies with me?

How many students are there?
When will you graduate?
Do they play football at your school?
Should I come over to your apartment?

pupils · break · American football · flat · comprehensive school · cinema · year · leave school

b) *Find answers to the questions and make mini dialogues with your partner.*

LEARNING SKILLS

Keeping a 'mistakes.doc'

With a 'mistakes.doc' you can record all the mistakes which you make in English. Then you can work out a plan of how to avoid them. You can use a note book or a computer.

1. Start a diary for mistakes. For four weeks collect all your mistakes in a list.
   Write down the correct words or sentences and underline what you got wrong.
2. Look at your list of mistakes.
   Which mistakes do you often make?
3. Ask your teacher for tips or exercises which can help you to avoid these mistakes and improve your English.

My mistakes Week ...

Spelling:

...

Grammar:

...

1 Comparing schools in the UK and the US (→ p. 22/ex. 12)

a) *Read the text and make a list of the 18 mistakes in it. Correct the words.*

In the UK puipils leave primary school and than go in a comprehensiv or grammar school in the age of 11 (Year 7). They can leave at 16.
If they passed their GCSE exams, they can do two more years in the upper school, where they can make A-levels.
In the US most studence are graduating from elementary school and go to a middle school (6th to 8th Grade).
Then they move to a hi school (9th to 12th Grade). Sum may leave school at 16, but in many states they must stay at school untill they are 18. Students must make school tests each year.
Most students in the US go to publick schools. In the UK a public school is a privat school. And theirs another diffrence. In the UK a student go to college or university and only students can graduate.

b) *Write a text about your own school. Ask a partner or your teacher to check your text.*

c) *Discuss your mistakes. Then put them with their corrections into your 'mistakes.doc'. Use the check list on page 120.*

1, 21 1 Let's listen: Attention, please! (→ p. 23/ex. 13)

Robotics Club • lockers • homecoming rally • the video wall • girls' soccer • homecoming parade

a) *Before first period at Paradise Valley High School there are often announcements.*
Listen and say what each announcement is about. Give a time.
Example: Announcement 1 is about … . You can/must go to … **any day** … .

b) *Read the sentences. Listen again and write notes.*
Then correct the sentences.

1. Students can use the wall for paintings.
2. The homecoming queen can perform at the rally.
3. Sports teachers can take part in the homecoming parade.
4. Grade 9 girls who are interested in soccer should go to Room 520.
5. If you need a locker just put your things in an empty locker.
6. The Reporters' Club has its first meeting on Friday.

c) *Which club do you find interesting? Why?*

1, 22 2 Sounds: PVHS cheerleader chants (→ p. 23/ex. 14, 15)

a) *Listen to the chants and practise them in groups.*

PVHS

Yes! Yes! P – V – H – S!
We're the best! P – V – H – S!
Yes! Yes! P – V – H – S!
Nothing less! P– V – H – S!

P – V – H – S!
Eagles score!
P – V – H – S!
Let's have more!
Go, Eagles! Go!

Let it begin! – Let's fight! – Let's win!
Eagles are fair –
But Eagles dare!
So you take care!

PVHS

PVHS

b) *Write a chant for your school/club. Present it to the class and decide which is best.*

1, 23 3 A song: First date

(Tr. L. Barker/Th. DeLonge/M. Hoppus © EMI Music Publishing Germany GmbH & Co. KG)

In the car I just can't wait,
to pick you up on our very first … .
Is it … if I hold your hand?
Is it wrong if I think it's lame[1] to dance?
Do you like my … hair?
Would you guess that I didn't know what to …?
I'm too … of what you think
You make me … so I really can't eat.
Let's go, don't …, this night's almost over.
Honest[2], let's make this … last[3] forever[4]
Forever and ever, let's make this last forever (2x)

a) *Read the song text. What could the missing words be?*

b) *Listen and find the missing words.*

c) *How does the singer feel? Why?*

[1]lame [leɪm] – *blöd*, [2]honest ['ɒnɪst] – *ehrlich*, [3]to last [lɑ:st] – *dauern*, [4]forever [fə'revə] – *für immer*

Sharleen

Miles

Alysha

Jay

Cal

Tyler

Donna

L1, 24–27

Homecoming dance

A "Just imagine, Tyler: There I am at work in the café down in the mall," said Miles, – and suddenly Sharleen is right in front of me. She smiles sweetly and says 'Hi, Miles. A coffee for Donna and a latte for the Queen you're taking to the homecoming dance on Saturday!' "

"No, Miles, you're kidding! Girls!" said his older brother and shook his head.

"Man, was I embarrassed! I didn't know where to look!" said Miles.

"But Miles, I thought you'd already asked her to the big event," said Tyler.

"Well, yeah, I wanted to, but –," said Miles, unhappily.

"OK, cheer up. It isn't the end of the world." Then, to change the subject, Tyler asked, "Well, what about clothes? Have you sorted out that problem yet?"

"Don't worry about that, bro'. I've got loads of clothes. But I have other problems like – dancing! Yuk! I mean, can't someone else start up the dance?"

"No, definitely not. You know that only the football captain and the homecoming queen can do that. That means you and Sharleen, so forget it: You won't get out of that one! Come on! Let me show you a few steps."

B At football practice on Monday the players were talking about the dance. Cal was happy because Alysha had said yes. "What about you, Miles," he asked. "Did you ask Sharleen for a date?"

"Yeah," said Miles, "but everybody knows that Sharleen and I have to go together – so what's all the fuss about?"

"You're right, Miles," added Jay. "I'm going with Donna. But they're all the same. They're all girls, aren't they?"

"OK," said Cal. "But Alysha is special. She should be queen. Why did they vote for Sharleen? She just likes posing, I'd say."

"But, Cal, maybe Sharleen is just better at cheerleading," said Miles. "That's what this queen thing is about, you know."

He had to speak for his date, although Cal could be right: Alysha was definitely a kinder person. But why were they all just hanging around and talking when they should be training?

"OK, guys," said Miles, in his captain's voice, "we're here to get some football practice, not to waste our time on gossip about girls. Come on, time to warm up!"

C "Donna, we just have to go back to the store," said Sharleen. "These shoes don't match my dress at all. I told you they're the wrong color!" She threw them back into their box.

"OK, I'll come," said Donna. "But take the dress, too, this time! And I'm meeting Jay at the juice bar after practice, so let's be quick."

Later at the juice bar Sharleen suddenly whispered, "Don't look now, but it's that awful Alysha over there."

"But Alysha is really nice" said Donna.

"Oh, no! She's coming to the bar. I'm going! Oh, can you pay for my drink?" Sharleen picked up her bag and left.

"Hi, Donna. Sharleen left in a hurry," said Alysha.

"Yeah. I should be honest with you. She's still angry that you didn't come to her pool party." Alysha was surprised.

"How strange: Just before we voted for our queen, Sharleen invited all the girls to a party. But not me, her big rival! And now she's angry because I didn't come?!"

D The light from hundreds of lanterns filled the hall. The flowers on the tables and the decorations on the walls looked fantastic.
"The organizers did a great job," said Miles.
Sharleen didn't say anything. She was trying hard not to look at Miles's jacket. The arms were much too short. Why wasn't he in a suit like the others?
Miles had forgotten until the last minute to check his clothes. He had a good shirt and black trousers, and he had found a jacket that he had last worn in spring. That'll be OK, he had thought.
The band played a slow song. Miles knew he had to dance with Sharleen now. Cal and Alysha came onto the dance floor, too.
Miles stepped on Sharleen's foot three times. The fourth time she shouted, "Hey, clumsy, got lead in your shoes?" She pushed him away and turned to a table with drinks.
"Sharleen, I'm –," he started to explain.
As quick as fire Sharleen turned around with a glass of cherry juice in her hand.
Alysha, who was standing near Miles, walked in front of him.
"No, Sharleen, don't!" she cried.
But it was too late. The juice missed Miles but landed all down the front of Alysha's dress.
Donna, Jay, Cal and some others stood around them.
Miles took off his jacket, put it over Alysha's shoulders and said quietly, "I'm sorry, Alysha. Cal, come on, we should take Alysha home."
"I'm coming with you, too, Alysha," said Donna, "but just wait a moment, please."
She turned to Sharleen. "I know now that you tried to fix the vote. You said Alysha didn't want to come to your stupid party but you lied: She didn't even know about it. You never invited her. Enjoy your homecoming, you mean queen, – without us!"

1 Before you read: Couples

a) *Make groups. Choose one of the people in the pictures and describe him/her.*

b) *Who will your person go to the homecoming dance with? What do you think?*

c) *Read the story. Were you right?*

2 Before the big day

a) *Read parts A–C again. Find out:*
- *who is in each part.*
- *who has got a date with whom.*
- *what they're talking about.*

b) *What do you find out about Miles?*

3 At the dance

a) *Read part D. Match the phrases with the people and make sentences.*

1. danced with Alysha
2. said Sharleen lied
3. stepped on Sharleen's foot
4. threw juice at Miles
5. got juice all over her dress
6. had to dance to slow music

Miles | Sharleen | Cal | Alysha | Donna

b) *Put the sentences in the right order to get a summary for part D.*

4 The characters (→ p. 24/ex. 16)

Match the characters with the words.

Miles Sharleen Alysha Donna	mean • clumsy • kind • angry • nice • surprised • honest • helpful • friendly

5 Role play: The next day (→ p. 24/ex. 17)

a) *Later Donna tells Tyler about the dance. What do they say? Write a dialogue.*

b) *You and your partner are Donna and Tyler. Act the dialogue.*

1 School words

a) *Make a grid with the three headings British schools, American schools and German schools. Put the words from the box under the right heading(s).*

baseball • pupil • Make a Difference Day • own clothes • Grade 8 • American football • cheerleaders • school uniform • Year 8 • holidays • student • football • vacation

b) *Add to your grid where you can.*

2 Let's look: Ready for the homecoming dance?

It's almost time for the homecoming dance. Look at the two pictures. What has/hasn't Miles done? And what about Sharleen? Use the box for help.

1

2

dyed hair • put on jacket • bought flowers • cleaned shoes • put tickets in wallet • chosen jewellery • put on dress • done hair • collected Sharleen • packed evening bag

3 Kids at Miles's school (→ p. 25/ex. 18)

a) *The kids at Miles's school like doing different things. What do they love/hate doing? Use the words in the box.*
Example: 1. Jay **loves gossiping** but Miles … .

wearing a suit | gossiping | posing | shopping | dating | ballroom dancing

1. Jay ☺ Miles ☹
2. Sharleen ☺ Alysha ☹
3. Jay ☺ Miles ☹
4. Tyler ☺ Miles ☹
5. Donna ☹ Sharleen ☺
6. Miles ☹ Sharleen ☺

b) *What about you? What do you love/hate doing?*

4 Messages from the dance (→ p. 25/ex. 19)

Three students wrote text messages from the dance. Rewrite their messages with long forms. The words in the box can help you.

1

HI CUZ. GR8 DECO + MUSIC! BUT HOQU CAME LATE AS ALWAYS. POOR MILES! CAN U IMAGINE? HOQU THRU CHERRY JUS AT HIM BUT IT LNDD ON AL'S DRESS! MORE L8ER. LUV BRENDA

2

hey sis, u were right bout sharl. she fixt vote. big scene here! ali, donna, cal + miles have left dance. wot will sharl do nxt?!!!! bye mariya

3

Hi, Ted, hope ya leg is ok. Ya not missing much, only Al's dress full of red jus. Sharl thru it. Just stupid girls' fight about sth. cud b Miles! Leroy

juice • cousin • your/you're • could • love • homecoming queen • landed • decorations • next • fixed • threw • something

1 On Make a Difference Day (present perfect → G4) (→ p. 26/ex. 20)

a) *What have the students already done? What haven't they done yet? Write sentences.*

Sharleen	Cal + Alysha	Miles
✔ buy paper	✔ collect old books	✔ buy paint
✔ make cards	✔ repair the covers	✔ borrow ladder
✔ draw pictures	✔ wash old plates	✘ clean windows
✘ write text	✘ write prices on them	✘ paint wood
✘ make envelopes	✘ fix broken toys	✘ take back ladder

b) *Which projects do you think they did?*

2 Things they should do (present perfect → G4) (→ p. 26/ex. 21)

a) *The students at Paradise Valley should do a lot of things. What haven't they done yet?*
Example: 1. Tyler **hasn't taken** a shower **yet**.

1 Tyler 2 Terri 3 Paula-Jo + Tammy 4 Sue 5 Brad + Larry 6 Stu

b) *What should you do this week? Have you done it yet? Write three sentences.*
Start like this: 1. I should **organize** …, but I **haven't organized … yet**.
2. I should …, but … .

3 Different school rules (modals → G5) (→ p. 26/ex. 22)

a) *Read the e-mail which a PVHS student wrote to her exchange partner and complete it. Use 'should', 'may' or 'must not'.*

Hi Kate,

You will be my exchange partner next month. Our class teacher said we … write an e-mail to our partner and tell him or her about our school. I have read your school rules. We have some different rules so I think I … tell you about them. You probably know that we haven't got a school uniform. You … wear your own clothes if you want to. But you … wear T-shirts with adverts on them for things like drugs and alcohol. You … wear jewellery at school but you … smoke in school or on the way to school. There are some other rules but you … worry about them until you are here. Oh and I … tell you about the homecoming dance. Dress is formal so you … bring a long dress with you.

Bye! Terri

b) *Kate should/may/must not do some things in the American school. What does she tell her friend?*

4 Cloze text: A great start to the year (→ p. 27/ex. 1)

Find the missing words and use them in the text.

The year (1) well with a great (2) dance. It was a real (3) and we would like to (4) all parents and friends who (5) . You can see photos of the (6) captain and his queen if you click on 'HOMECOMING ➜ Photos'. A few days (7) the dance we had the (8) tryouts where they (9) twenty girls for the team. In October the school (10) a Make a (11) Day. The first (12) went to students in (13) 8. They won the (14) with a garden project. After that in November Grade 7 (15) performed their play *The* (16) *of Oz*. If you went, then I'm sure that you (17) with us that it was a great show. Now for some future plans: The PTA is planning a fair in February. If you would like to (18) us, please send an e-mail to the (19) at the end of this report.

thank | Difference | helped | chose | agree | football | homecoming | prize | started | organized | cheerleader | address | students | competition | Grade | Wizard | help | success | before

NOW YOU CAN

✓ talk about schools in the US.	→ *Describe an American school.*
✓ say what you have/haven't done.	→ *Which three things have/haven't you done today.*
✓ use 'should/may/must not' for rules.	→ *What rules do you have at home?*
✓ date an American boy or girl. ☺	→ *Date a partner. Where can you go on the first date?*
✓ keep a 'mistakes.doc'.	→ *Write a mistakes.doc for this page.*

1 What is a debate[1]?

One of the most popular clubs in American high schools is the Debate Club.
Look at the picture and the texts and explain to your partner what happens there.

2 The texts (→ p. 28/ex. 1, 2)

Plan a debate. The skills box can help you.

WRITING/SPEAKING SKILLS

1. Agree in your group on a motion.
2. Choose a chairperson.
3. Speakers should write down their arguments for or against the motion.
4. The audience should write notes while the speakers are speaking.

1. Agree on a motion, for example: "American schools are more dangerous than German schools". Use the phrases to help you.

▶ I'd like to suggest … .
How about … ?
I think we should … .
I think that's a good/bad/… idea.
Let's vote on it. Who's for/against … ?

2. Choose a chairperson. What should he/she do and when? Write a list. The phrases can help.

▶ Good morning/afternoon/… .
Our motion for today's debate is … .
Speakers for/against the motion are … .
…, it's your turn. You may speak now.
The results[6] of the vote are … for and … against the motion.

3. Choose some speakers. Collect arguments for and against your motion. Use the collage[7] on the opposite page. Write sentences. You can use some of the phrases in the box.

▶ I agree/don't agree with … .
In my opinion … .
I think it is a prejudice[8] to say that … .
The facts tell a different story.

[1]debate [dɪ'beɪt] – *Debatte,* [2]discussion [dɪ'skʌʃn] – *Diskussion,* [3]motion ['məʊʃn] – *Thema,* [4]chairperson ['tʃeəˌpɜːsn] – *Vorsitzende/r,* [5]to introduce [ˌɪntrə'djuːs] – *einführen, vorstellen,* [6]result [rɪ'zʌlt] – *Ergebnis,* [7]collage [kɒ'lɑːʒ] – *Collage,* [8]prejudice ['predʒədɪs] – *Vorurteil*

Are American schools more dangerous than German schools?

Staff and agencies — Guardian Unlimited

Eighteen killed in German school shooting[1]

Friday April 26, 2002

Students and parents wait near the Gutenberg high school in Erfurt, Eastern Germany. Photo: AP

Sammlung von verbotenen Waffen im Rahmen der Aktionswoche „Waffenfreies Bremen – Zeichen gegen Gewalt" der Polizei Bremen Foto: Polizei Bremen

A 14-year-old girl student at a high school in Pasadena wounded[2] another girl with a knife in the cafeteria of their school. She was fed up because the other girl bullied her.

April 16, 2007
Blacksburg, Virginia

A 23-year-old student, Cho Seung-Hui, killed two students. Two hours later he killed 30 more and wounded fifteen. He then killed himself.

Between Jan. 2000 and April 2007 there were 23 shootings at schools and colleges in the US. There were four shootings at schools in Germany during this time.

Kids film bullying with phones

Parents and teachers at a middle school in Germany met last night to see what their kids are using their phones for: They attack and bully other kids and film them.

[1]shooting [ˈʃuːtɪŋ] – *Schießerei*, [2]to wound [wuːnd] – *verletzen*

Part-time jobs

1

2

3

4

L1, 28–30

A Listening

1 Part a)

Look at the photos above. Listen to part a) and match each photo with a name: Jason, Marie, Carly or Ramon.

2 Part b)

Listen to part b) and find the correct answers about Ramon.

a. He got a bike	1 for his birthday.	2 from his dad.	3 from a company.
b. He has a job	1 in the company.	2 in a bike store.	3 in a deli.
c. He has to	1 ride bikes.	2 test bikes.	3 deliver parts of bikes.
d. He gets	1 five dollars a day.	2 15 dollars an hour.	3 five dollars an hour.

3 Part c)

Listen to part c). Which of these facts is true and which is false[1]?

a. Marie looks after kids.
b. Jason's dad says a few extra dollars is more important than basketball.
c. Jason gets money from his dad if he works around the house.
d. Carly has a part-time job in a deli.
e. She thinks it's better to have a job outside in the real world.
f. Her mum doesn't want her to work part-time.
g. Ramon's uncle thinks he needs to relax.

4 All parts

Listen to parts a), b) and c). The names in these sentences are mixed up[2]. Correct them.

a. The friends are waiting for Carly.
b. Jason is always tired in class.
c. Marie has to get up at 6 on Saturdays.
d. Ramon's dad won't let him have a job.
e. Carly gets 50 dollars a month.
f. Marie meets lots of interesting people.
g. Jason wants to go home and work.
h. Ramon has to be home at 5 o'clock.

B Speaking

1 Role play

You are talking to an American kid about part-time jobs. Answer his/her questions.

American: What do kids in Germany do when school finishes?
You: …
American: Do you get pocket money? How much? Do you have to do jobs at home?
You: …
American: Can you have a part-time job while you are still at school?
You: …
American: What sort of jobs can kids do?
You: …

2 Reporting

What do you think Jason tells his dad when he gets home?
Start like this: Dad, I met Ramon in the park this afternoon. We wanted to … .

C Writing

1 Skills

Collect words and phrases about part-time jobs in a mind map.

2 Writing

"Kids shouldn't work while they are at school."
What do you think? Write 35–40 words.

[1]false [fɔːls] – *falsch*, [2]to mix up [mɪks‿ˈʌp] – *durcheinander bringen*

Unit 3 Our smart world

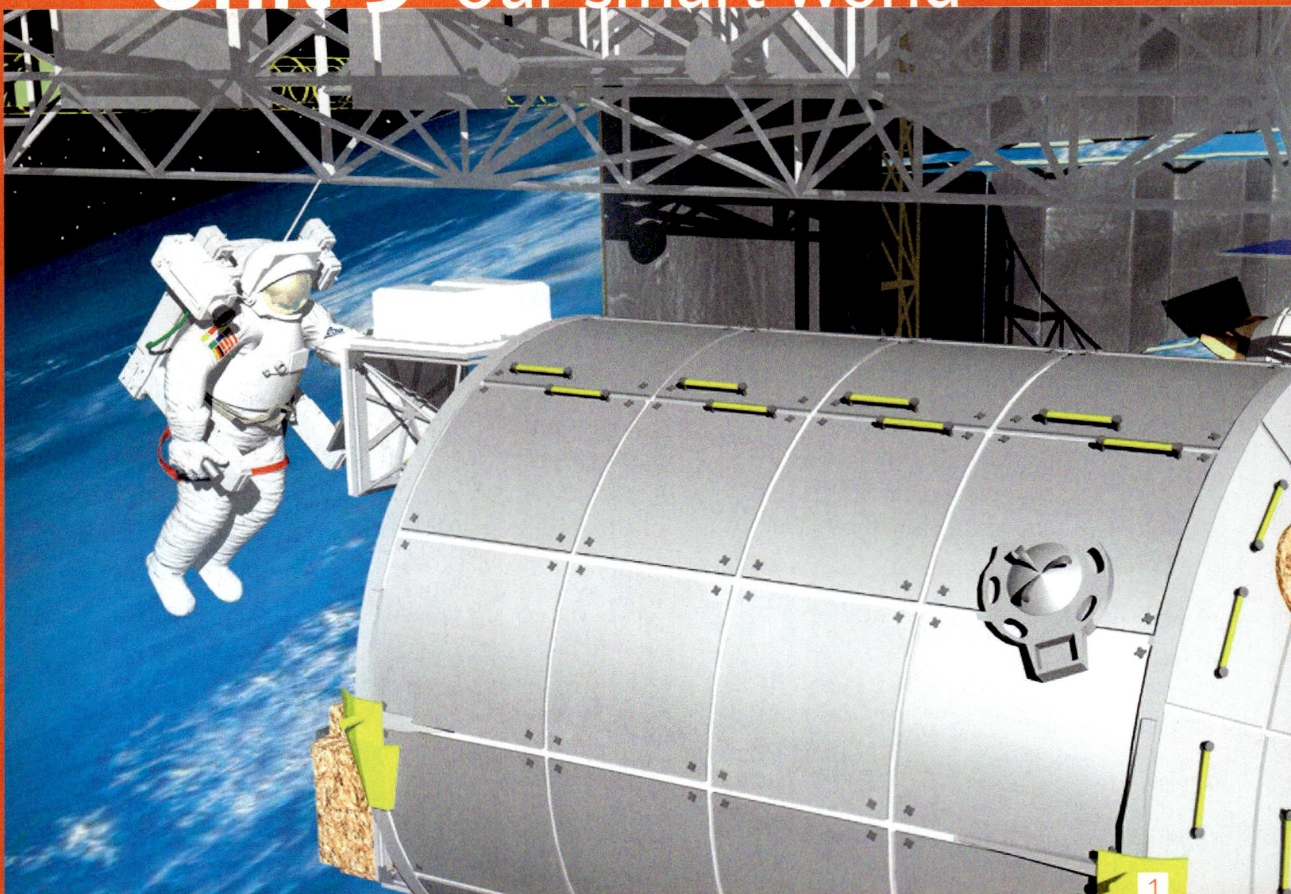

1 A space station

1 Space work

Look at photo 1. What can you see? What is happening? You can use the 'words' box.

WORDS

(outer) space [ˌaʊtə 'speɪs] – *Weltraum*
space station ['speɪs ˌsteɪʃn] – *Wetltraumstation*
astronaut ['æstrənɔ:t] – *Astronaut/in*
the Earth [ðiː 'ɜːθ] – *die Erde*
to control [kən'trəʊl] – *leiten, führen, überwachen, kontrollieren*
scientific equipment [saɪən'tɪfɪk ɪ'kwɪpmənt] – *wissenschaftliche Ausrüstung*

2 Space technologies (→ p. 29/ex. 1)

a) *With the help of the photos and the fact box make a 'space technology' cluster. The phrases in the box can help you.*

b) *Put your cluster in your folder and add to it as you work through the unit.*

send back signals
help drivers
use two screens
wear space suits
save lives

L2, 1 ## 3 Let's listen: Radio reports

Now look at all the photos again. Listen and match each report with one of the photos.

Example: The first report is about … so I think it goes with photo … .

2 A tractor with GPS ploughs rows in a field.

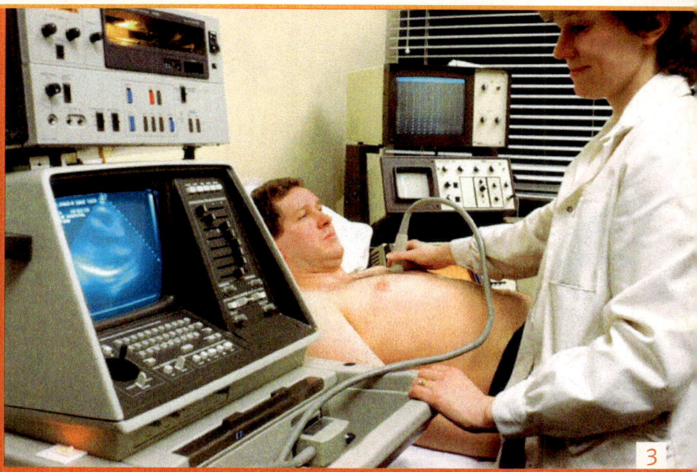

3 A doctor monitors a patient with a pacemaker.

4 Virtual reality computer game

5 A robot checks luggage.

DID YOU KNOW?

Many of today's inventions are spin-offs from space research projects:

- The US space agency, NASA, monitored its astronauts in space with pacemakers. Doctors now use them to monitor patients. Burglar alarm systems, which monitor homes, also come from this technology.
- Scientists operate robots with remote control. They can explore planets which are too hot, cold or dangerous for humans in space. They can also do dangerous jobs on the Earth, e.g. defuse bombs.
- With VR (virtual reality) equipment astronauts needn't leave their spaceship. They can fix it from inside. In VR games you can leave your world and visit one which only exists in your computer.
- Scientists can't launch a shuttle in a storm. They use satellites (GPS) to forecast the weather. Modern farmers also use GPS and they know: If their rows aren't straight, then their GPS isn't working.

4 For my folder: Inventions (→ p. 29/ex. 2)

a) *Think about other inventions which make life easier, safer or more fun for us. Write a list.*

b) *Talk to your grandad, grandma or an older person. Which of the inventions in part a) did they not have when they were your age?*

How intelligent is your home?

High-tech homes are also called 'smart' homes or intelligent homes. In homes like this everything is done by remote control. Imagine you and your family are spending a day in the country. It's getting dark. Your dad sends a text message to your apartment in the city. The lights are switched off and on a few times so that any burglars are frightened away. Then the refrigerator is checked and a list of food is written. You want to cook pancakes for breakfast tomorrow. You must stop at the shopping mall on the way home. Pictures of all the rooms are sent by cameras. Everything looks OK. But there's water under the bathroom sink. Is it leaking? Or did you leave the plug in and forget to turn off the faucet? Just as your parents start to panic, the water is turned off. The plug is removed so that the water can run away, and the floor is dried.
Imagine another scene: Your dad sends a message but the lights aren't switched off and on, so the burglars aren't frightened away. But he can't see them because the cameras aren't operated. The water isn't turned off and the plug isn't removed. Later you arrive home and find that the apartment is flooded. Burglars have stolen all your electrical equipment. They have even taken the washing machine and the tumble dryer! And the refrigerator is empty.

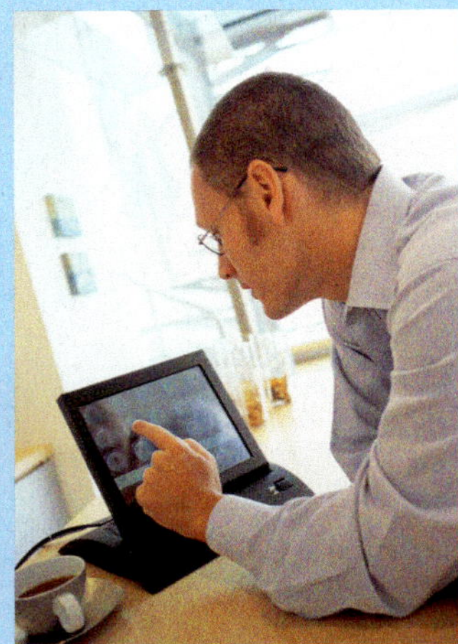

You see, smart homes are only smart if they have electricity. If this is cut off, then even intelligent homes have problems. And every winter in the US there are lots of blackouts.

1 How 'smart' are they really?

a) *Read the text and say what is correct.*

1. Smart is another word for intelligent.
2. All smart homes are in the country.
3. Burglars don't like 'smart' homes.
4. Cameras send pictures to your cell phone.
5. Electricity is important for a 'smart' home.
6. They never have blackouts in the US.

b) *Would you like to live in an 'intelligent' home? Why or why not?*

2 Detective work: Find the rule (→ p. 30/ex. 3)

1. Look at these sentences from the text above. How would you translate them?

   High-tech homes are also called 'smart' homes … … everything is done by remote control.

2. Look for more examples from the text and make a list.
3. Make a rule about how you form sentences like these.

→ G6

3 When things go wrong

a) *Choose five verbs and make sentences that follow your rule.*

b) *Now write sentences about what happens when everything goes wrong in a smart home.*
Example: The lights aren't switched … .

4 'High-tech' everywhere (→ p. 30/ex. 4; p. 31/ex. 5, 6)

▶ are/aren't switched on **by** …
is/isn't forecast **by** …
→ G6

a) *In our high-tech world we often can't see how things are done.*
How are the things in the pictures done: by computer/by GPS/by … ?
Example: 1. Street lights **are switched on by** computer. The weather **is** … .

1 to switch on/computer

2 to forecast/GPS

3 operate/remote control

4 send/satellite

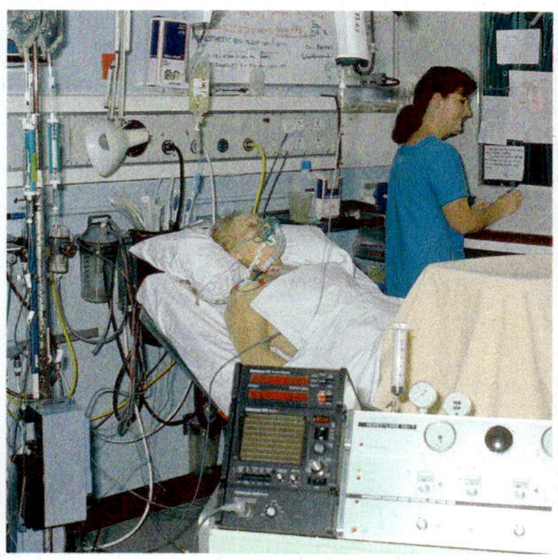

5 to monitor/computer

6 to build/robots

b) *Say what happens if something goes wrong.*
Example: 1. The street lights **aren't** … .

5 Let's talk: It's all done by … (→ p. 32/ex. 7, 8)

Talk to a partner about what is or isn't done by remote control/satellite/GPS/… in your home.

▶ What is done by … in your home?
The burglar alarm …, and … .

6 For my folder: My smart room/house/school/…

a) *Design a 'smart' place. Think about things which you would like technology to do.*

b) *Present your place to the class. Say what is done there by computer/… .*

c) *Discuss whose place is the 'smartest'? Put the nicest places on the wall of your classroom.*

1 In a motel room (→ p. 33/ex. 9)

a) *What are these objects?* *Example:* Number 1 is a … .

switch • socket • remote control • shower • refrigerator • lamp • curtain • microwave • hairdryer • plug • battery • light bulb • faucet • adaptor • bathroom sink • cord

b) *Find the word.*
Example: 1. You can find it in the wall near a TV, lamp, etc. – That's a **socket**.

1. You can find it in the wall near a TV, lamp, etc.
2. You use it to dry your hair.
3. You get water if you turn it on.
4. You can change the TV channel with it.
5. You can keep food and drinks in it.
6. If it's dark, you can switch it on.
7. You can wash your hands here.
8. Here you can cook food.

c) *Match these words with the things in the picture and make sentences.*
Example: You put a **plug** into a socket.
You find a **plug** on a … . You need a **battery** … .

plug | battery | cord | adaptor | switch | curtain | light bulb | …

2, 2–3 2 Let's listen: Problems in the motel

a) *Write sentences about problems with each piece of equipment.*

light bulb • cord • plug • battery • faucet • hairdryer • bathroom sink	is dripping • is leaking • is dead • is missing • is damaged • isn't working • is broken

b) *Listen to the sounds. Each person is using one of the things in the picture of the motel room. Which piece of equipment is it?*

c) *Listen again. There are clues in what the people say. Were you right?*

3 Role play: I'm afraid there's something wrong with ...

You ring the motel reception desk. Your partner answers the phone.
Tell him/her what is wrong. Ask him/her to send someone to fix it. Be polite.

4 Instructions for use (→ p. 33/ex. 10, 11)

a) *Read the instructions. Which pieces of equipment do you think they come from?*

Before you use it, read the instructions on the packet. Keep the door closed when you are using this equipment. Close the door when you have switched it off. This equipment is for food only. Never use it to dry your dog or shoes. Clean it carefully after you have used it.

A

This equipment can be dangerous if you use it in a bathroom. Never use it while you are under the shower. Do not use it if the cord is damaged. Take the plug out of the socket when you have finished. Do not leave the cord where someone can have an accident.

B

Do not put hot food in here. Food should be cold before you put it on a shelf. Please clean it at once if a bottle leaks or if you drop some food or drink in it. Do not put heavy things on top of it. Always keep the door closed. If it is too loud, please call this number: 6845723.

C

b) *Write instructions for another piece of equipment which you often use. Can your partner guess what it is?*

5 Let's talk: I can't live without it

Your group has €100. What piece of equipment would you buy? Why? Discuss in your group.

I can't live without a ... .
I'd like to buy a ... because ... .
We need a ... . We can watch/... with it.
I think a ... is useless/more useful/helpful because ... .

GROUP SKILLS

When you are doing group work, these things are important:

- Agree on what you want to do. → You can collect ideas in mind maps, clusters or lists. Decide in your group what you want to use. Follow your plan. Check the results for mistakes.
- Plan steps together. → Decide in the group who should do what. Who should lead the group? Who should collect ideas, information and materials? Who should write the texts? Who should do the layout? Who should present the results to the class? Who keeps an eye on the clock?
- Work together with the others in your group. → Be polite to others. Everyone in the group should have a chance to say something. Let him or her finish speaking. Check the list of classroom phrases at the back of your book if you need help. Read the task in your group.

1 What could make your life easier? (→ p. 34/ex. 12–14)

a) *A group of high school students had to think of an idea/invention that could make their lives easier. Read the text. Look up the new words in a dictionary.*

More sleep, less stress!

We all know how hard it can be to get to school on time. But with our fantastic new idea you can stay in bed longer and have less stress in the mornings. And this is how you do it: It's Monday. The voice alarm on your cell phone rings and says "Monday, Monday, …". But don't worry. Your smart phone 'knows' exactly what classes you have today and, in fact, on every day of the week. So listen as you pack your bag. Of course, you always keep your textbooks in the same order on your shelf (subjects from A–Z). And you use a good system of color codes so you can grab the right ones quickly even if you're still half asleep. Five minutes later your alarm goes off again. This time it says: REMEMBER YOUR SNACK! GET IT FROM THE FRIDGE NOW! THEN GO TO THE BATHROOM. Your favorite song on your phone's MP3-player is just the right length for these tasks but it ends with a loud warning sound. You still have enough time for your breakfast with 2–3 songs of your choice, plus a voice recording that says: NOW BRUSH YOUR TEETH. THEN GET THAT SCHOOL BUS!

b) *Plan your own invention. It can be a crazy one.*
- *Search the Internet for ideas (under 'chindogu' or 'crazy inventions').*
- *Choose four to five ideas.*
- *Then decide who wants to work on which idea. Make groups.*
- *Plan your steps with the help of the skills box.*

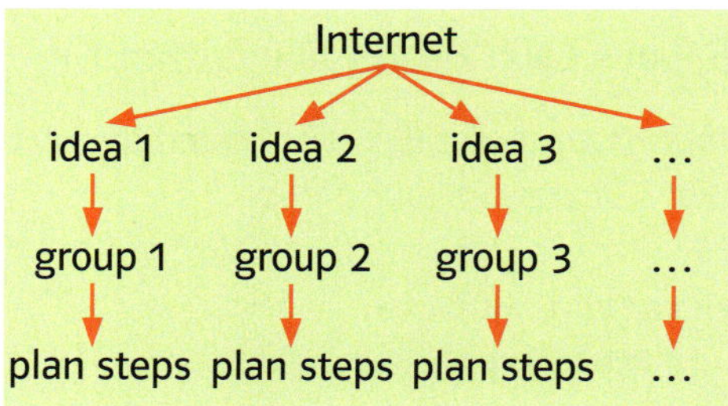

c) *Present your invention to the class.*

2, 4–6 1 Let's listen: High-tech tractors, cars and dolls! (→ p. 35/ex. 15, 16)

a) *In our high-tech world many jobs have changed. Look at the photos. Which jobs do these people do – car mechanic, … ? How important is high-tech for these jobs?*

1

2

3

4

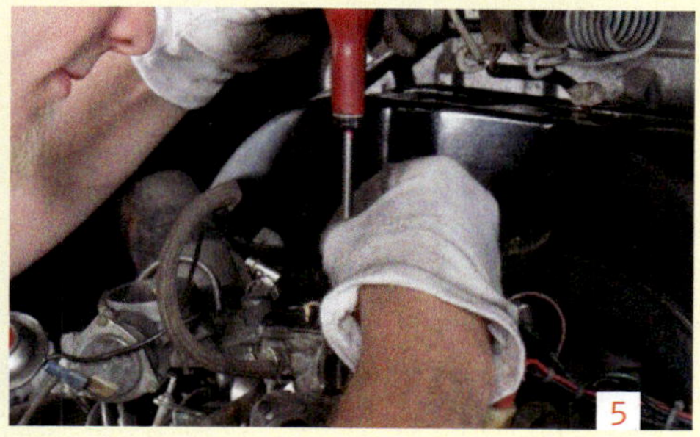
5

b) *Listen to three of the young people in part a). Which job do they do?*

c) *Listen again. What has changed in their jobs? Make a grid and add to it.*

job	in the past	today
car mechanic	hard work	…
…	…	…
…	…	…

d) *Which of the jobs would you most like to do? What are the advantages/disadvantages?*

L2, 7 2 A poem: News from near Alpha Centauri[1] (→ p. 35/ex. 17)

(Sheila McBride)

Please stop sending messages and signals
And we must say it was all an awful bore.[2]
We landed near Las Vegas on vacation
Don't even try to hear us any more[3]

Were the worst that we have seen in outer space.
The motel was like something from the Stone Age
And the programs that we saw on television
With plugs and sockets all around the place

Why don't you try another solar system[4]
So there isn't any reason[5] to make contact[6]
We cannot understand your point of view[7]
We're sure there's someone out there just for you.

a) *Before you listen: Put the lines in the right order.*

b) *Listen to the poem. Were you right?*

c) *Answer the questions.*
1. What is Alpha Centauri?
2. Who is the poem from?
3. Who do you think they are talking to?
4. Do they like the Earth? Why/why not?

[1] Alpha Centauri ['ælfə sən'tɔ:ri] – *Name eines Sterns,* [2] bore ['bɔ:] – *eine langweilige Sache,* [3] not … any more [ˌeni 'mɔ:] – *nicht mehr,* [4] solar system ['səʊlə ˌsɪstəm] – *Sonnensystem,* [5] reason ['ri:zn] – *Grund,* [6] to make contact [ˌmeɪk 'kɒntækt] – *Kontakt aufnehmen,* [7] point of view [ˌpɔɪnt‿əv 'vju:] – *Ansicht*

L2, 8–10 Alien worlds

A young New York cop is discovered by a secret police agency: the MiB. Before he can say 'Neuralizer', he has become a new agent, Agent J! The only problem is that he has no idea about the work they do. He doesn't even know what a neuralizer is! (You don't know either? Well, read on …)

Agent J gets his uniform – a black suit and dark glasses – and starts to learn about the job. He (and we) find out that large numbers of aliens live on the Earth but they are kept 'under cover' and are controlled by the MiB. So if someone actually notices an alien, then 'Zap'! – his or her memory is erased by an agent with a piece of equipment that looks like a large pen. Yes, you got it: a Neuralizer.

It's Agent J's bad luck that he becomes an MiB agent just when some horrible aliens ('bugs') come to Earth from another planet and begin to make big trouble.

Agent J is following one of these bugs that now looks just like a human. It has got something that doesn't belong to it and that could be dangerous to the lives of us all! So stay in your seats for a few hours of fun and suspense!

I remember my first day in New York. There was a heat wave. It was even hotter than back home in India. There I had lived in the mountains. I had a tourist visa but very little money and I had nowhere to sleep. Then I found a job in the kitchens of a big restaurant and I also got a place to sleep – on the floor in an old factory where one of the other kitchen workers lived. We worked in the basement so there were no real windows. It was hotter than in hell!

We workers spoke English but we couldn't really understand each other as we all came from different countries. And most of us were without papers. We never saw the customers upstairs. We worked long hours at night and slept through the day. The money was really bad but it was better than nothing. Then one evening I got a terrible toothache. Dentists are expensive and I had no social security number so I told my boss. What did he do? He threw me out into the street. I was a big risk because I was illegal.

It was night. I walked the streets and tried to forget my tooth.

My thoughts went back to India where political trouble and bands of robbers had made life dangerous. Now I was in America but my life here was no better. In the middle of a big city full of strange people, illegal, in pain, without money, I felt all alone, – a real 'alien'! Then my luck changed: A couple came over to me. I'm sure I looked awful because the man asked if he should call an ambulance.

I told them about my toothache. And you won't believe it: The woman was a dentist! She fixed my tooth and then they helped me to find another job.

Now I'm 'legal' and things are better but I still often feel like an alien here.'

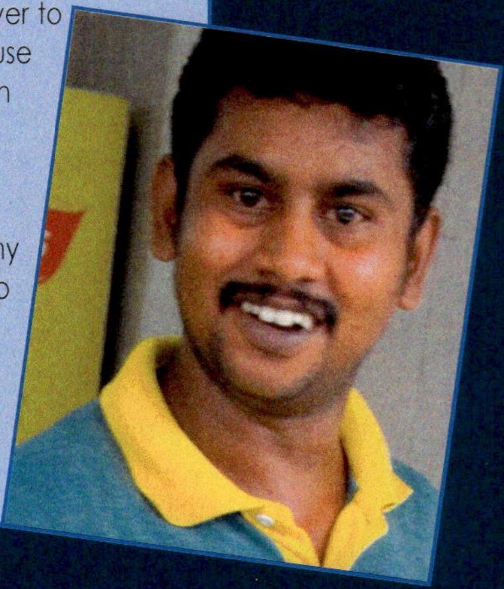

In the early evening of March 13, 1997 thousands of people across Arizona and Phoenix noticed something strange in the sky. They described it as a huge, V-shaped object with large lights on it. It was one to two miles across.
The first reports came in around 7 p.m. from people who saw it in the northwest of Arizona. It moved from there towards Phoenix. It flew very near the town of Prescott. Air traffic controllers at Phoenix International Airport and the crew of a plane reported it, too. It moved over the city towards the Valley of the Sun and then disappeared. Local people took photos or videos of the object and many called the police, TV stations or newspapers. The story was on TV that evening and in local newspapers the next day. Investigators asked questions and collected information.

Almost a year later they told people that the lights were flares from a plane. But this didn't explain the whole story.
Why did the flares stay in the air for so long – almost 4 hours? And how was it possible that people from Nevada to Tucson, a distance of more than 300 miles, saw them? Flares do not travel, they simply fall to the ground. Was the UFO in fact a spaceship from a planet near Alpha Centauri with aliens on board?

1 Before you read: The photos

What can you see in the photos?

2 Fact or fiction? (→ p. 36/ex. 18, 19)

a) *Read the texts. Did the stories really happen? What do you think? The photos and the sort of text can help you.*

b) *Match a heading with each text.*

NYC alien • Agents and aliens • Alien lights?

3 A group puzzle (→ p. 36/ex. 20)

a) *Form groups of three in which each of you reads a different text. Make a mind map for 'alien' from your text. Explain your mind map to the others in your group.*

b) *Now form 'expert' groups in which each of you has the same text. Find definitions for all the new words in it and write them down for the other groups.*

c) *What has your group found out about the aliens in your text? What makes it/him/them an alien/aliens? Present your ideas to the class.*

4 For my folder: An alien story

What films/stories about aliens do you know? Choose one and write about the alien(s) in it.

Remember: It helps to think of:
Who? What? Where? When? Why?
You can write notes in a cluster, a mind map, a list or a grid.

1 Topics (→ p. 37/ex. 21)

a) *Which word is the odd man out in each list?*

space shuttle	VR games	bathroom sink	water	microwave
astronaut	drums	plugs	elephant	bed
burglar	pacemakers	to switch on	soap	remote control
to launch	GPS	blackouts	mirror	tractor

b) *Find headings for the lists of words and add more words to your lists.*

c) *Write a short text (three or four sentences) about one of the topics which you find interesting. Say what you know about it and why you find it interesting.*

2 Let's look: A crazy motel room (→ p. 37/ex. 22)

a) *Mr Fox gets this motel room. What ten things are in the wrong place? Where are they?*

b) *Mr Fox phones the manager and tells him what is wrong. Write a short dialogue. Say what is missing/broken/damaged/dripping/leaking/burnt/dead.*

3 Definitions: Different high-tech jobs

a) *Start a grid like this on high-tech jobs. Add four more high-tech jobs from this unit.*

Who?	What?	Where?	What else?
scientists …	forecast the … …	on Earth …	satellites …

b) *Use your grid and make sentences about the different people.*
Example: 1. Scientists forecast the weather on Earth. They use … .

4 New technologies

a) *Look at the pictures. What can you see?*

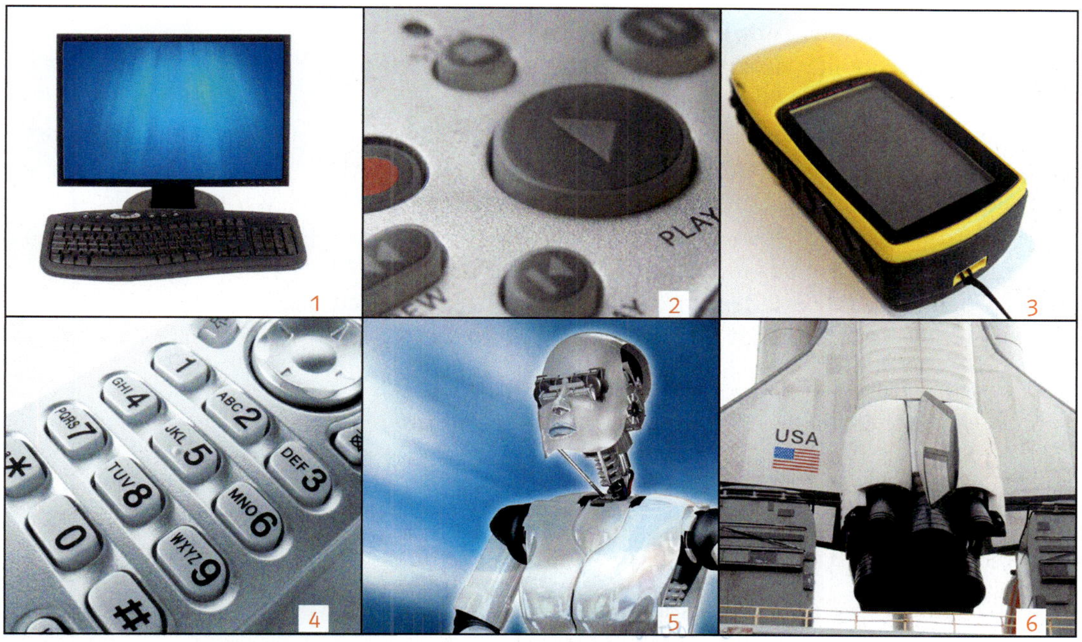

b) *Find activities which go with the objects which you can see.*
Example: 1. Computer: send e-mails, do your homework, play games, …

5 What could it be? (→ p. 37/ex. 23)

a) *Read the clues and find the words. They are all in Unit 3.*

1. a station where you can't catch a train
2. equipment that space scientists use
3. a suit that you don't wear to a dance
4. a phone that can send messages
5. a wave that isn't in the ocean
6. glasses that you can't drink from
7. a ship that can't travel on water
8. it could be a man or woman

b) *Write clues for these words: docu soap, cupboard, greenhouse, traffic jam, timetable.*

1 Short forms (passive forms → G6) (→ p. 38/ex. 24)

a) *Use 'is'/'are' with the right verb form.*
Example: 1. AE **is spoken** in all American states.

1. AE (*to speak*) in all American states.
2. NASA (*to write*) on shuttles.
3. Strange objects in the sky (*to call*) UFOs.
4. The astronauts (*to show*) on TV.
5. The letters VR (*to use*) for the words 'virtual reality'.
6. Agent J (*to discover*) in the film MiB.
7. Shuttles (*to launch*) by US scientists.
8. The weather (*to forecast*) with the help of GPS.

b) *Think of two or three more short forms. Use them in sentences with a passive form.*

2 Every year (passive forms → G6)

a) *What is wrong in these sentences from a newspaper article? Use isn't'/'aren't'.*
Example: 1. That's wrong. The US **isn't** hit every year by police.

1. The US is hit every year by **police**.
2. These storms are first noticed by **trees which fall on their cars**.
3. The path of a storm is then drawn by **the strong winds**.
4. TV stations in the storm area are contacted by **flash floods**.
5. Towns in the path of the storm are given a warning by **experts**.
6. Children are often sent home from school by **the TV stations**.
7. People are told to stay inside by **terrible storms**.
8. But many drivers are killed every year by **teachers**.
9. And often bridges are destroyed by **the national weather stations**.
10. Large numbers of buildings are damaged by **phone**.

b) *Write the correct article.*
Start like this: The US is hit every year by **terrible storms**.

3 Your own robot (passive forms → G6) (→ p. 38/ex. 25)

Read the text. Put the right passive forms into the sentences.

Thanks to technology a lot of work in homes today **isn't done** (*not/to do*) by people. It … (*to do*) by machines. Clothes … (*not/to wash*) in enormous pots on a fire. They … (*to wash*) in washing machines. And they … (*not/to put*) outside to dry – they … (*to dry*) in a tumble dryer. But in a real smart home most of the jobs … (*not/to do*) by the people who live there. They … (*to organize*) by a robot. Imagine! Your clothes … (*to put away*) while you are at school. Your football boots … (*to clean*) and your bike … (*to fix*) by your robot. The TV … (*not/to switch on*) by him. That … (*to do*) by remote control. But all the other jobs like shopping or cooking … (*to do*) by your robot. Some of you may say that these things … (*to do*) by someone already. You don't need a robot. Your mum or dad is your robot. You're lucky!

4 Things that are done ('by' with passive forms → G6) (→ p. 38/ex. 26)

a) *Write sentences in the passive form. Use 'by' to stress the 'by' agent (people, machines, …).*
Example: 1. Doctors **monitor** the astronauts.
The astronauts **are monitored** by … .

1. Doctors monitor the astronauts.
2. Scientists plan experiments.
3. Assistants check the scientific equipment.
4. The astronauts practise VR activities.
5. High-tech companies design special clothes.
6. Cooks make special meals.
7. Guards watch TV screens.
8. Weathermen forecast the weather.

b) *What happens if there is a blackout?*
Start like this: The astronauts **aren't** monitored by … .

c) *Think of two or three more things that are done by people with high-tech machines.*

5 Cloze text: The new boy (→ p. 39/ex. 1)

a) *Read the text and complete it. Use the words from the boxes.*

When Rico first (1) to the US from Mexico, he felt like (2). He couldn't speak very much (3) and his clothes were different from the (4) which the other kids wore to school. His parents didn't have (5) money so they couldn't spend (6) of dollars on smart clothes for their son. Some of the kids laughed at him. But Rico was (7), more intelligent than many of the other kids in his school. He was really good at (8) and he often helped other kids who didn't know how to do the (9) in class. Then he entered a (10) competition and he won first prize. He had to design and make an alien. The (11) at NASA invited Rico and his class to Florida. They spent a day in a 'space' school there. It was great fun! After they got home again, Rico was one of the most popular (12) in the school. He never felt like an alien again.

immigrated | kids | experiments | an alien | Science | ones | English | a lot of | intelligent | hundreds | 'space' | scientists

b) *Rewrite the text about Rico. Use different words for the numbers.*
Start like this: When Rico first **came** to the US from Mexico, he felt like **a stranger**.
He couldn't … .

NOW YOU CAN

✓ talk about inventions.	→	*Describe an important invention. What can you do with it?*
✓ talk about high-tech equipment.	→	*Name 3 things that are done by high-tech in your home.*
✓ understand instructions.	→	*Tell a partner how to use a digital camera.*
✓ tell a story about an alien.	→	*Talk about your favourite alien.*
✓ work in a group.	→	*Write 3 polite phrases which you can use in the group.*

1 Collecting information

a) *You can use the Internet to find information for a project. Here are some tips to help you.*

INTERNET SKILLS

Surfing

1. Surf the first three or four German sites[1] in your search engine[2] first. → You can go to Wikipedia, where you can find a lot of useful information.
2. Choose one topic and find out more about it. → Save the information which you find.
3. Change the language on your search engine to English. → Find English sites on your topic and save the information.
4. Look at any official sites. They usually give true facts. → Check the information here against the information from other sites.
5. Click on Images[3] to find visuals[4] for your project. → Save some photos and cartoons.

b) *Use the skills box in part a) and find out about the American city, Detroit. Answer the questions.*

1. Which state is Detroit in?
2. How many people live in the city?
3. What is Detroit famous for?
4. Here are three flags of American cities. Which one is Detroit's flag?

1

2

3

5. Which sport do the Detroit Redwings play?
6. Here are photos of three American cities. Which one is Detroit?

1

2

3

c) *Choose one topic about Detroit from the list below and collect information about it.*

1. The pros of city life: hospitals and transport[5], shops
2. The cons of city life: too many people, pollution, crime
3. Things to do in the city: sports, parks, music, museums

d) *Make a list of important new words. Use them in a text about your topic.*

[1]site [saɪt] – *Seite*, [2]search engine ['sɜːtʃˌendʒɪn] – *Suchmaschine*, [3]image ['ɪmɪdʒ] – *Bilder*, [4]visuals ['vɪʒuəlz] – *Bildmaterial*, [5]transport ['træntspɔːt] – *öffentliche Verkehrsmittel*

2 Preparing a computer presentation

a) *Before you switch on your computer, you should prepare your presentation on paper. Use the skills box and prepare a presentation on one of the topics from exercise 1 c).*

PRESENTATION SKILLS

Planning

1. Decide on a topic. → Write down main headings.
2. Decide how long you want to speak. → Don't prepare too much or talk for too long.
3. Plan your presentation. → Make a list or a mind map.
4. Think about pictures. → Add grids, cartoons, photos etc.
5. Try to make your audience laugh. → A joke can keep them happy.

b) *You can now make slides[1] for your presentation. Use the skills box and make five or six slides about your topic. Remember to click on the HELP button if you need more help.*

PRESENTATION SKILLS

Making slides

1. Keep the slides simple. → Use short phrases, single[2] words or pictures.
2. Use large letters. → They should be 24pt or larger.
3. Prepare a text about each slide. → Don't put the text on a slide.
4. Use animation[3]. → Don't use it on every slide.
5. Use video or sound clips[4]. → A change of voice or speed[5] is good for your audience.

c) *Copy your list of important new words from exercise 1 d) to give to your audience.*

d) *Make a handout[6]. Use the texts which you have prepared on each slide. Add Internet links and pictures.*

3 The presentation (→ p. 40/ex. 1)

a) *Use the skills box and present your topic on Detroit to the class.*

PRESENTATION SKILLS

Talking to an audience

1. Don't hide! Stand near your audience.
2. Don't stand in front of the screen.
3. Use the remote control.
4. Look at people in your audience and be friendly.
5. Speak slowly. Don't try to finish as fast as you can.
6. Don't turn your back on the audience.

b) *What mistakes is this speaker making?*

[1]slide [slaɪd] – *hier: Folie*, [2]single ['sɪŋgl] – *einzeln*, [3]animation [ænɪ'meɪʃn] – *Animation*, [4]clip [klɪp] – *Clip*, [5]speed [spi:d] – *Geschwindigkeit*, [6]handout ['hændaʊt] – *Handout*

Nature and technology

Hi, kids! I'm Joss Baxter. I'm a national park ranger so, as you can imagine, I'm interested in nature. I am also worried, not about our national parks but about the climate. The US is one of the most modern countries in the world. We have all the newest technologies: Cars, planes, refrigerators and air-conditioning are just a few of them. They make life easier for us. But they produce gases which are changing the world's climate. The Earth is getting warmer. Some of you think, "That's great! We'll have longer summers and even greater beach parties!"
And that's true! But it means disaster not only for animals like the polar bear, whose home is disappearing. In the US, for example, we have always had tornados. But higher temperatures mean more storms and bigger storms. The tornado which hit New Orleans in August 2005 was more than 100 miles across. Tornados bring strong winds, rain and floods but higher temperatures also bring drought[1] to many countries, which have no rain for years.
So what can we do? We can't just stop using the things which technology has given us and we can't yet use technology to stop tornados or make it rain! But we can all change the way we live. For a start we can use less electricity, drive smaller cars and use public transport[2]. So before you switch on the air-conditioning or jump in the car to drive to the shopping mall for an ice-cream, think! Maybe you can get cool under a tree with a large glass of lemonade!

[1]drought [draʊt] – *Dürre(zeit),* [2]public transport ['træntspɔːt] – *öffentliche Verkehrsmittel*

A Reading

1 Skills

Read the article and find the English words for these German words.

a. Klima b. Klimaanlage c. Ranger d. Gase
e. Eisbär f. Stürme g. Tornado

2 Understanding

Read the article again and complete the sentences.

a. Joss Baxter is a	1 teacher.	2 park ranger.	3 farmer.
b. She is worried about	1 nature.	2 the national parks.	3 the climate.
c. Technology makes life	1 warmer.	2 easier.	3 longer.
d. They have always had	1 tornados.	2 polar bears.	3 beach parties.
e. Tornados bring	1 rain and floods.	2 drought and rain.	3 winds and gases.
f. We can all	1 make it rain.	2 change how we live.	3 drive bigger cars.
g. You could get cool	1 in a refrigerator.	2 in the sea.	3 under a tree.

B Language

Write these sentences. Add the word 'the' if you think that you need it.

a. Joss Baxter is interested in … nature.
b. She is worried about … climate.
c. She lives in one of … most modern countries in … world.
d. … technology makes … life easier.
e. Higher temperatures also bring … drought to many of … countries.

C Mediation and communication

You and your cousin are talking to an American kid about the weather. What can you say?

Cousin: Wie ist das Wetter, wo du herkommst?
You: …
American: I come from Florida. We get terrible tornados there.
You: …
Cousin: Habt ihr auch Überschwemmungen?
You: …
American: Yes! But other states have had worse floods.
You: …
Cousin: Machen sich viele Amerikaner Sorgen wegen dieser Stürme?
You: …
American: Oh, yes! Many have started to change the way they live.
You: …

11 ## D Listening

a. A visitor asks Joss three questions. What is she looking for?

1 the bathroom 2 a restaurant 3 information

b. What is Joss's answer to her last question?

1 She doesn't know. 2 It is closed today. 3 It opens again after lunch.

E Writing

1 Your opinion

"We need new technologies."
What do you think? Write 2–3 sentences.

2 A letter

Write a letter to your local newspaper. Suggest some things which the people in your town could do to stop the Earth getting warmer. Write 5–6 sentences.

Unit 4 Home and away

1 The Skywalk: A platform on the Hualapai Reservation in the Grand Canyon, Arizona

1 High over the canyon

a) *What do you know about places in the American Southwest?*

b) *How do you think the people feel in picture 1?*
What do you think they're saying to each other?

c) *What do you think of or feel when you look at the picture?*

d) *Arizona is a state in the Southwest of the US. Find the other states in the southwest on the map at the back of your book. Do the exercises there.*

WORDS

scenery ['si:nri] – *Landschaft*
dizzy ['dɪzi] – *schwindelig*
overwhelming [ˌəʊvə'welmɪŋ] – *überwältigend*
gorge [gɔ:dʒ] – *Schlucht*
sacred ['seɪkrɪd] – *heilig*
tribe [traɪb] – *(Volks-) Stamm*
national park [ˌnæʃnl 'pɑ:k] – *Nationalpark*

2

2 Modern cowboys on a ranch

3 Trucks on a highway in the Southwest

4 Las Vegas lights

3

4

DID YOU KNOW?

You have to travel great distances to see the famous sights in the US because it's a huge country.

- The US Interstate Highway system has over 46 thousand miles of roads (Germany has over 12,000 km). Route 66 from Chicago to LA is maybe the most famous.
- Truckers with their huge trucks (some are over 60 tons) use the highway to transport goods over vast distances across the US. They often eat in roadside diners. Some sleep in their trucks, others stay at motels.
- You can still find cowboys in the Southwest. But many only ride horses at rodeos. On the ranch they often use motorbikes.
- Tourists from all over the world come to Las Vegas to win (or lose!) money in its casinos.
- With 4.5 million visitors per year Grand Canyon is the most popular National Park.

2 Let's talk: More about the photos (→ p. 43/ex. 1)

Read the fact box, look at all the photos and find the places on your map. Which of the places in the Southwest do you find interesting and why? Talk to a partner.

3 For my folder: The Southwest (→ p. 43/ex. 2)

a) *Choose a state in the Southwest in your group and find out more about it from books, brochures or the Internet. Include information such as population, cities, sights, jobs, history, state flag etc. Use the skills box.*

b) *Make a poster with all your information and present it in class.*

INTERNET SKILLS

1. Use a search engine.
2. Put in the country, the place and a topic, e.g. US, Las Vegas, casinos.
3. Always check the first 4–5 articles first.
4. You can also search under Images.

▶ You use an if-clause with **simple present** to present a certain situation:
If you're 14–16 …, then **you'll** love … .

You use **future** to give the result:
If you …, **you won't** want to … .

→ G7

If you're 14 – 16 years old and you like adventure, then you'll love

BILLABONG WAVES SUMMER CAMP

And you won't want to leave us! Of course, you'll meet lots of young people. But if you don't want to surf every day, we'll take you out in boats and you'll learn all about life in the ocean. And if you're on our photography course, then you'll use our modern underwater cameras. Don't worry: You won't miss out on discos and parties. No way! If you stay at Billabong, you'll help to organize your own events, right here on the beach! We're *the* camp in California for surfing and ocean science! You'll sleep in tents in small groups of kids.
Cost/week: $200 – $350 all inclusive, minimum two weeks

Forest Springs Summer Camp, near the Grand Canyon, Arizona

For fun and adventure! From just $650 per week!
Our campers are 7–16 years of age.
You'll live in cabins in the woods.

We offer over 80 different activities. You'll
- visit our fabulous Grand Canyon.
- go whitewater rafting.
- enjoy campfire events (games, rapping/singing).
- make campfires and cook on them.
- learn to identify tracks, birds and plants.
- make a bow and arrow and use it.
- act and produce a play in the forest.
- help to make a movie about nature.

1 Brochures for a summer camp (→ p. 44/ex. 3)

a) *Which brochure is better? Why? Think about headings, pictures and layout.*

b) *What will/won't kids do if they go to the first camp?*
Example: **If they go** to …, **they'll meet** … .

c) *Abby is 14. Read what she likes and hates.*
What will/won't she do at the two camps?

d) *Which camp do you think is better for her? Why?*

acting • rapping • parties • taking photos • meeting people

cooking • sports • nature • camping • making things

2 Role play: A talk with parents (→ p. 44/ex. 4, 5)

Abby doesn't want to go to a camp. What could Abby say to her parents? Act out the dialogue.

3 News from Forest Springs

Uy

Read Abby's e-mail and find four things that she doesn't like about the camp.

Hi Lynn,

Makeup ale & ste

My parents thought I'd have a great time if I went to summer camp near Grand Canyon. But it's boring here. If I was at home in LA, I would be at a disco or a party every night. Or we would go to a movie. All I can do here is sit round a stupid campfire and sing songs. In the afternoons we would go shopping or meet friends in the café. Here we go for long walks and look at plants and try to find animals. If you were with me, you wouldn't like it here at all. What would happen if I left the camp and went home? If I hid behind some trees during our walk tomorrow, the leaders wouldn't see me. Would they notice if I didn't come back with the others? If I told the other kids in my tent, they wouldn't say anything. The counselors would look for me if I didn't come back for supper. If they didn't find me, they would phone the rescue services. If the helicopter pilot didn't have any luck, the camp leaders would phone my parents. If they phoned my parents, they would be very worried. If I arrived home in the middle of the night, my mum would be really mad at me. I think I'll stay here. There is nothing worse than my mum when she's mad at me. I'll mail you again soon. It would be great if you came to visit me.

Love, Abby

4 Detective work: Find the rule (→ p. 45/ex. 6)

▶ Find all the if-sentences in the e-mail and make a grammar rule.
Check if your rule is right. → G8

5 If Lynn visited Abby (→ p. 45/ex. 7; p. 46/ex. 8, 9)

What would/wouldn't happen if Lynn visited Abby? First match the parts and then write sentences.

Example: 1. If Lynn **visited** Abby, she **wouldn't like** the camp.

1. Lynn (*to visit*) Abby
2. Abby and Lynn (*to hide*) behind a tree
3. the girls (*not to come*) back from a walk
4. they (*to tell*) the other kids
5. they (*not to come back*) for supper
6. they (*to arrive*) at Abby's house

- the leaders (not to see) them
- she (not to like) the camp
- her mum (not to be) very happy
- the leaders (to look for) them
- the others (not to notice)
- they (not to say) anything

6 Let's talk: Life in the city or life in the country (→ p. 46/ex. 10)

a) *Make a grid. Use the brochures and Abby's e-mail. Add more pros and cons.*

b) *Check the classroom phrases at the back of your book and discuss.*

	pros	cons
city	discos shopping …	expensive traffic …
country	…	…

Home for Thanksgiving

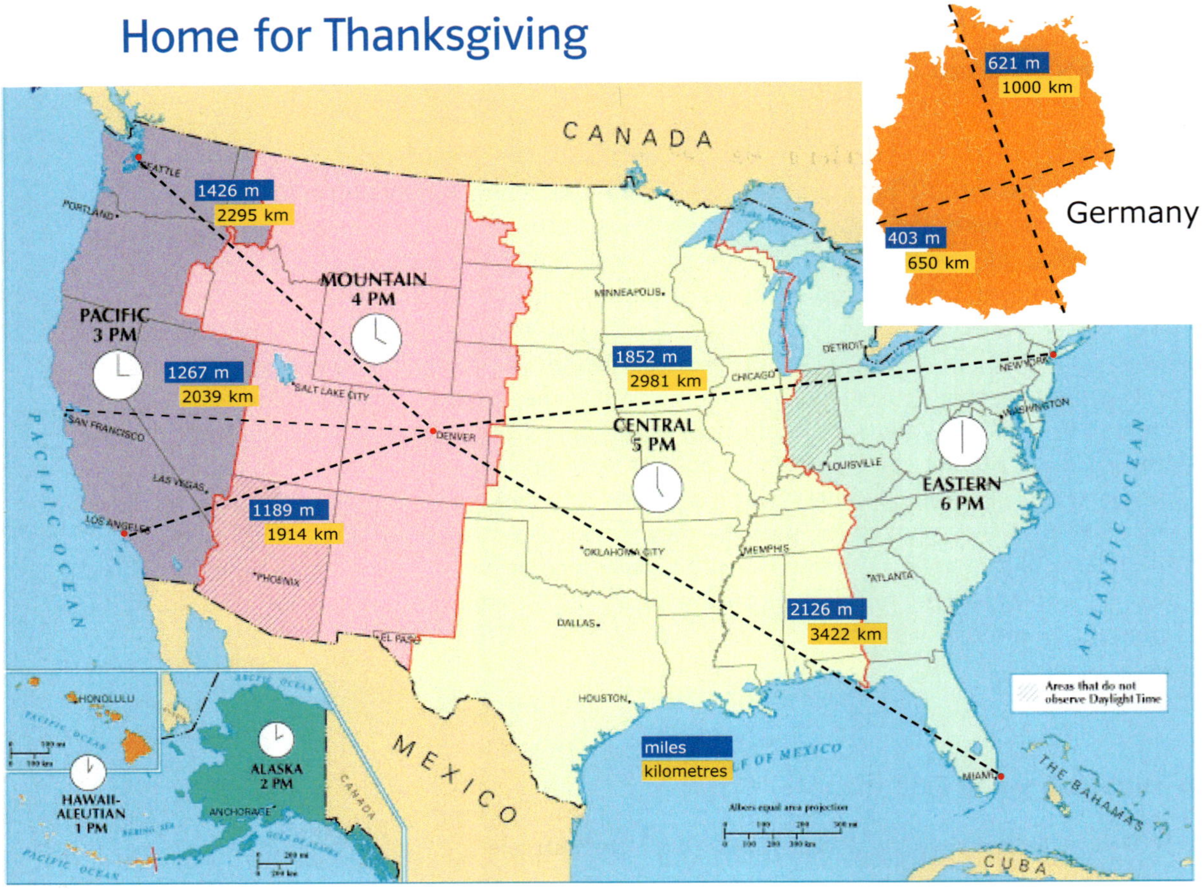

1 Let's talk: Times and distances (→ p. 47/ex. 11)

The US is huge. So a lot of people travel long distances to visit friends and family, for example, for the most important holiday in the US – Thanksgiving. Find out more on page 101.

a) *Look at the map above. How far is it from Seattle to Miami? And from LA to NYC? Ask your partner more questions like these about distances.*

b) *Look at the time zones on the map. If it's 9:30 a.m. in NYC, what is the time in Chicago and LA? Ask your partner more questions about the difference in time between cities in the US.*

c) *Look at the map and the info in the grid. Talk about how you can travel from Denver to other cities. Use the phrases below.*

▶ How far is it from Denver to …?
It's about/more than/less than …miles/km.
How long does it take by plane/by car?
It takes about/more than/less than … .
It takes … hours/almost a day.
I think we should go by … because … .

Denver to …	by car*	by plane*
Seattle	28:30	2:50
San Francisco	25:20	2:40
Los Angeles	23:50	2:30
Chicago	20:20	2:20
Miami	42:30	3:35
New York City	37:00	3:40
Honolulu	—	9:00
Anchorage	90:00	7:00

*in hours and minutes

2 Role play: Thanksgiving troubles

a) *Read the texts. Which text tells you:*

1. that lots of Americans never cook?
2. that different states have different weather?
3. about what Americans eat?
4. what motorways in the US are called?
5. about problems at airports?
6. about a phone number you can call?

A

I hope this address is still OK. I just saw the weather report on TV. Do you really have snow up there in Colorado? It's over 80 degrees here in New Mexico. They showed pictures of the chaos on the Interstates. And lots of flights are delayed. By the way, you'll be one of 56 million Americans who are traveling home for Thanksgiving tomorrow! So don't get lost!

B

HOTLINE! HOTLINE! HOTLINE! HOTLINE!

It's Thanksgiving! Your mom just came back from the mall with the turkey for Thanksgiving – it's in the trunk of her car. But like many Americans she never cooks so what should she do with a 20lb frozen bird?
Tell her not to panic! She can phone the 'Turkey hotline'. They'll tell her how to thaw, cook and serve it.

C

DINER

If you are stranded or have a breakdown, don't spend Thanksgiving at a rest area on the Interstate 40.
Our new motel/diner is just past Exit 140.
OK, it isn't home and you won't get a turkey dinner. But our pancakes with bacon and eggs (over easy or sunny side up) are real tasty and our rooms are comfortable!

b) *You have a problem with your flight, your turkey or your car. Who can you call? What can you say?*

Hello/Hi! Is that the airport/the turkey .../the ...?
I have a problem. I just saw .../bought .../had a ... on the ... .
Can you please tell me when .../how .../where ...?

2-14

3 Let's listen: On time?

a) *Listen: Where do you think these people are?*

b) *Listen again. What are the people in the dialogues doing?*

the trucker • the trucker's son • Cindy and her dad • Maxi and her brother, Kit

4 For my folder: Tourist info

a) *Choose one aspect of life in Germany (special holidays, weather, travel, food, ...) and collect ideas in a mind map.*

b) *Make an info sheet for American tourists (or for an American friend). Think about what could be interesting to them. Where would they like to go? What would they like to see? You can add pictures and more infos from the Internet.*

WRITING

SKILLS

Writing a factual text

- You write factual texts to give information or statistics without feelings or opinions.
- When you write a factual text, you should keep it short. You should write your text in three parts:
  1. a short introduction (to catch the reader's interest)
  2. the 'main part' (a few paragraphs with your main points/information)
  3. an ending (to round off the text)
- Remember to connect your sentences. Use 'but', 'and', 'if', 'so that', 'because', etc.
- Don't repeat words too often. For example, for 'students', you can use 'the class', 'they', etc.

Topic of survey: Free time and holidays **Survey group:** 7–8th Grade, high school, California **Number:** 200				
What's your favorite kind of vacation?	summer camp 14.5%	beach 72%	city trip 9%	other 4.5%
What's your favorite place (in US)?	California 45%	Hawaii 26 %	Las Vegas 2%	other 27%
What's your favorite place (outside US)?	Mexico 55%	Canada 19%	Europe 7%	other 19%

These statistics were from a survey of 200 7th and 8th Grade students at a Californian high school. The topic was 'Free time and holidays'. The first questions were about kinds of vacations and favorite places.

First of all, if you look at the results, you'll see that less than a sixth of the young people chose summer camp as their favorite type of vacation and only nine per cent wanted to visit a city. But almost three quarters of the class said a beach holiday was best. Less than five per cent wanted a different type of vacation.

Secondly, California was more popular than Hawaii or Las Vegas in the US. But outside the US Mexico was the most popular country. In fact, over half the class chose it. Canada was the second most popular foreign country. And very few students, less than one tenth, chose a holiday in Europe.

So the results show that a beach holiday was the most popular type of holiday in this survey group and that Mexico was the most popular place.

1 From numbers to words (→ p. 48/ex. 12)

Look at the statistics and the report on how some students would like to spend their holidays.

1. What is the students' favourite kind of holiday?
2. What are the most popular and second most popular places in the US?
3. Which country do they like better – Canada or Mexico?

2 Your survey (→ p. 48/ex. 13, 14)

a) *Do a holiday survey in your class and collect statistics.*

favourite kind of holiday	skiing … %	beach … %	…
favourite place (in Germany)	… … %	… … %	…
favourite country (in Europe)	… … %	… … %	…

b) *Write a short text on the topic. The tips and the phrases can help you.*

▶ First of all / Secondly … . — more popular than
The results show that … . — very few/less than a third/quarter
the most/second most popular — … per cent of … /over half

c) *Find another topic. Do a survey and write a text on it.*

2, 15 1 Let's Listen: Red chip on a red carpet (→ p. 49/ex. 15)

a) *Before you listen: What do you know about Las Vegas? (Where is it? What is it famous for?)*

b) *While you are listening, answer these questions:*

1. Where is Pablo's job?
2. What does he do there?
3. Who is Mr Gusman?
4. What does Pablo find?

c) *What do you think happened next? You can use the pictures for ideas.*

d) *Discuss your endings. Which did you like best and why?*

2, 16 2 Sounds: Spot the American! (→ p. 49/ex. 16, 17)

a) *Write down these words from the book:*
transport, brochure, Thanksgiving, address, adult.

b) *You will hear them first in BE and then in AE.*
Where is the stress in BE? And in AE?

c) *Find more words in your book which have a different stress in AE and BE.*

> ▶ Remember:
> In AE and BE they often put the stress in a different place.
> *Example:* café (BE), café (AE)

2, 17 3 A song: Las Vegas

(Johan K. Fransson/Niklas R. Johnsson/Tim M. Larsson/Tobias L. Lundgren
© Warner-Chappell Music Scand AB/Neue Welt Musikverlag GmbH & Co. KG)

I've got a room here at the Mandalay Bay
I take a shower then I'm on my way
I bring a friend if someone picks a fight[1]
Here in Las Vegas tonight

It's close to midnight when I hit the strip[2]
The maiden[3] voyage on my Vegas trip
The night is young, and everything's alright
Here in Las Vegas tonight

Dancing girls and cabarets[4]
You can spend your money in a million ways
Let's have a ball[5], The winner takes it all

In Las Vegas in the neon lights
You'll be a star, if you do it right
In Las Vegas, you'd better hold on tight[6]

In Las Vegas can't believe your eyes
Your luck can turn in a throw[7] of a dice[8]
In Las Vegas, you'd better hold on tight
Here in Las Vegas tonight

Answer the questions.

1. What does the singer do before he goes out for the night?
2. Has he been here before? How do you know?
3. What can he do in Las Vegas?
4. What could happen and how?

[1]to pick a fight [ˌpɪk‿ə 'faɪt] – *Streit anfangen,* [2]strip [strɪp] – *hier: Amüsiermeile,* [3]maiden ['meɪdn] – *jungfräulich,* [4]cabaret ['kæbəreɪ] – *Tanzrevue,* [5]to have a ball [bɔːl] – *richtig Spaß haben,* [6]to hold on tight [taɪt] – *sich gut festhalten,* [7]throw [θrəʊ] – *Wurf,* [8]dice [daɪs] – *Würfel*

L2, 18–24 Going places

A *Marita was tired. She had crossed the border into Mexico four hours ago and now she needed a drink. She stopped when she saw the first bar sign, went in and ordered a drink. The barman was friendly, like most Mexican barmen, but he looked a bit lonely so she started chatting with him. She soon discovered that he wasn't Mexican. His name was Rick and he came from New York. Marita was surprised.*
"So how did you end up in a bar in a place like this, Rick?" she asked him.
"It's a long story, Señorita, and you'll never believe it, but every word of it is true …"

1

B Since I was a small boy, I've wanted to have my own car – not just any old car, but a cool, green Cadillac. Well, when I got my driver's license, I worked hard, saved my money and bought an old model for $300. Then my friend Donny, who is a mechanic, helped me to repair it. It was a real adventure. I'll never forget the day that we sprayed it grass green. Wow, what a feeling! Soon after that Donny said, "So now what?" That's when our action plan began. I mean, with a car like that you really need to go places … We decided to leave the East Coast and go west. Going to California was Donny's big dream – you know, surfing and all that stuff. Again we worked long hours in different jobs till we thought we had enough money for the trip. Then we set off. We had planned carefully but we knew that the money might not last. We had some great times. And some parts of the States are awesome. I mean, Geography at school cannot begin to describe places like the Grand Canyon or Apache Lake.

C Anyway, our money didn't last so we worked here and there. And it wasn't all good. We had some pretty awful experiences: Once we met these girls, Sandy and Denise, in a diner on Route 66 – really nice girls, or so we thought. Well, Denise went to the restroom and we chatted on with Sandy. Then she said, "Hey, you guys, I'll just go and see if Denise is OK, she's been away so long." Luckily, I had to go to the restroom, too. On the way I passed the entrance to the café. I just looked out and saw those girls in the parking lot. Denise was fiddling with the door of our Cadillac! I ran across to Sandy, grabbed her arm and stuck my finger against her back. "Move away from the car! Now! Or your friend here's gonna get it!" I roared. Donny and some other people heard me shouting so I soon had help. That was a close one, I can tell you.

D Well, we got across the border into California all right, but we were having money problems again. Then we got lucky: Donny got a job as a mechanic – and I became a fruit picker. Boy, was that hard work! Most of the pickers were Mexicans. I made friends and was happy that I could speak Spanish, like at home. You know, I'm part Hispanic. And, well, I was starting to feel homesick.

E One morning something terrible happened. It was still dark outside. Suddenly the sound of barking woke us up. It was a police raid! The cops grabbed all the pickers without papers – me, too. You see, Donny had the Cadillac and my papers were in it. But the police didn't believe me. It was really awful! They drove us into Mexico and just left us in the middle of nowhere. We pickers shared what little we had and somehow we made it to a village. I felt helpless but the people there were very friendly. Then a trucker gave me a ride to this place. I had no money and I was as hungry as a bear. The owner said I could work here. I slept in their back room and ate with the family.

F Finally, I could call Donny. Of course, he was very worried when he drove out to see me on the day of the raid – and I was gone! And he got no information from the police. Well, he sent me my papers and he wants to drive over here soon. But, you know, I've decided to stay here. The bar looks really good now. And we have live music on some nights. That attracts tourists to make a break on their way down to Mexico City. And as you know, this is the only place for miles with Internet access …

G *"Wow, what a story!" said Marita. "Well, look, I must move on now. If I have time, I'll stop here on my way back. Tell me, what was your e-mail address again?"*

1 Before you read: The pictures

Look at the pictures. What do you think is happening?

2 Places in the story (→ p. 50/ex. 19, 20)

a) *Read the story. Where are the people in the pictures? Were you right about the pictures (in exercise 1)?*

b) *What info is in one of the pictures that isn't in the text?*

c) *Copy the map of the US at the back of your book. Mark the places from the story on your map and make notes about what happened there.*

3 Rick's experiences

a) *Make a graph about Rick's good and bad experiences (+ or –) on his journey west.*

b) *Compare your graphs.*

c) *Write about your results.*

4 For my folder: Going places (→ p. 50/ex. 21)

Imagine you are going on an adventure trip. Write a short text about it. These questions can help you:

- Where would you go? Why?
- Would you take anyone with you?
- What would you need for your trip?
- How would you travel?
- What problems could you have?

1 Transport and nature

a) *Collect words and phrases in mind maps for 'transport' and 'nature'.*

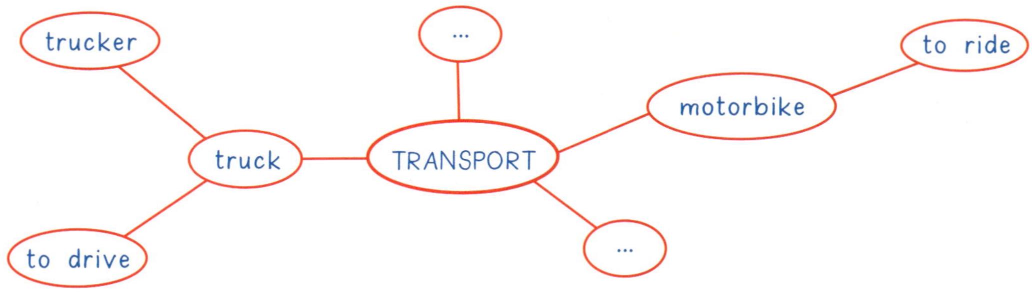

b) *Write four sentences each about transport and about nature in the US Southwest.*

2 Let's look: At summer camp (→ p. 51/ex. 22)

What can visitors do at the Crazy Horse Summer Camp?

3 Definitions: What is it? (→ p. 51/ex. 23)

a) *What are the things in the pictures?*

b) *Match the definitions with the things from a).*

1. People want to win money there.
2. They're very big roads in the US.
3. They're big and transport goods.
4. You wear them on a ranch.
5. It travels on roads and only has two wheels.
6. Kids sit around it and sing songs.

c) *Choose six words from the unit and write definitions as a quiz for your partner.*

4 Tourists' talk

a) *This is what some tourists in the US said. Complete with a word from the box.*

1. If you want to … a lot of money, then go to Las Vegas.
2. The view from the top of the Grand Canyon was … .
3. We got our tickets at the … to the rodeo.
4. The flight from New York City to Denver lasts … three hours.
5. British motorways are not … as American highways.
6 I don't like my eggs cooked on both sides. I like them … .

awesome • entrance • sunny side up • win • more than • the same

b) *Find the opposite of the words in the box.*

c) *Make new sentences with your words from b).*

5 Word building (→ p. 51/ex. 24)

a) *Find nouns for the verbs.*
Examples: to ride → ride, to define → definition, to sleep → sleep

to transport | to cook | to organize | to visit | to travel | to choose | to drive | to exercise | to invent | to live

b) *Continue to collect verbs with which you can make nouns.*

1 Family promises and warnings ('if'-clauses + future → G7) (→ p. 52/ex. 25)

a) *When Abby wants something, she often tries to promise her parents something. What does she promise?*
Example: **If you let me go to the disco, I'll** wash the car.

let/go/disco	→	wash/car
drive/station	→	cook/dinner
wash/sports clothes	→	do/shopping
lend/digital camera	→	clean/windows
buy/new computer	→	make/family website

b) *Sometimes her parents have to use threats on Abby. What do they say?*
Example: 1. If you **don't finish your homework**, we **won't** let you go to the disco.
2. If you …, we **won't** drive … .

2 Warnings ('if'-clauses + future → G7)

At the summer camp the leaders often warn the kids. What do they say? Make short dialogues.

Example: 1. A: What will happen if I/we **try to carry too much wood**?
B: If you …, you'll drop it.

3 Vacations ('if'-clauses + would → G8) (→ p. 52/ex. 26)

Write full sentences. What would you do on vacation in these situations?

1. If it rained on vacation, I'd visit a … .
2. If I lost my cell phone, … .
3. If someone stole my bags, … .
4. If I got lost, … .
5. If I felt bored, … .
6. If I missed my flight home, … .

4 Imagine (′if′-clauses + would → G8) (→ p. 52/ex. 27, 28)

a) *What do you think these people would do in these situations? Use the verbs to help you.*
Example: 1. If a trucker **saw** …, I think he **would** call … and **would** follow … .

1 call + follow

2 wait + talk to

3 pick up + tell

4 turn round + run away

5 stop + put

6 look at + take

b) *What about you? What would you do in the situations in part a)?*
Start like this: If I **saw …, I'd** take some photos/phone …/tell …/… .

5 Cloze text: Abby's friend (→ p. 53/ex. 1)

Abby's English friend, Max, sends her this e-mail. Use the words in the boxes and complete it.

Dear Abby, first I'd like to answer the (1) which you asked in your last e-mail. If I (2) in the US, I would live in LA. It's a huge (3) so there must be lots to do there. I'm sure I (4) never be (5) there. And it isn't (6) from the coast. I wouldn't like to be in a place like Utah, hundreds of (7) from the nearest beach. If I (8) rich, I would have an apartment in New York and a (9) in the mountains, too. Of course, they (10) be smart homes with cameras everywhere. If you (11) interested, (12) send you some photos of my home. We live in a (13) home. It's in the (14), near Manchester.

far | question | lived | would | cabin | city | was | miles | I'll | would | bored | country | smart | are

NOW YOU CAN

- ✔ talk about the Southwest of the US. → *Say four things about the Southwest of the US.*
- ✔ give promises and warnings. → *Give a partner a promise and a warning.*
- ✔ imagine what you would do if … . → *What would you do if you won a million dollars?*
- ✔ compare city life and country life. → *Name three things which are better in each.*
- ✔ talk about the geography of the US. → *Talk about how you can travel from New York to LA.*
- ✔ write a factual text. → *Write a short text about hobbies in your class.*

A letter to a magazine

Dear Newtech,
Your article on the Skywalk last month describes the new platform as 'a great piece of tribal[1] technology'.
I'm one of the oldest members[2] of the Hualapai tribe and I'm worried. I see the Skywalk as a big problem: Our land is for everyone, for us, for our ancestors[3], for our children and our children's children. We must look after it. We get all our food from it and water from the rivers and lakes. So we must respect[4] it.
The Skywalk will bring too many tourists to our land. They'll take our rocks[5] as souvenirs and damage the land. And they'll leave all their garbage[6].
And they'll use our water. We already don't have enough water – they'll come and use it all up with their toilets and showers!
Some land is very sacred to the Hualapai people. This means we mustn't build anything on it. But our tribal council[7] has let others do this on sacred Hualapai ground!
The Skywalk is like a monster which shows no respect for our ancestors. It could stop people on their way to better lands after they die.
I'm sure that one day the people from our tribe who said 'yes' to this monster will be sorry. But by then it'll be too late!
Yours,
Rory Quasala, *Peach Springs*

[1]tribal ['traɪbl] – *Stammes-*, [2]member ['membə] – *Mitglied*, [3]ancestors ['ænsestəz] – *Vorfahren/Ahnen*, [4]to respect [rɪ'spekt] – *respektieren*, [5]rock [rɒk] – *Stein*, [6]garbage ['gɑːbɪdʒ] – *Müll*, [7]council ['kaʊnsl] – *Rat*

A Reading

1 Understanding

Read the text and find the best answer.

a. The letter is about …
   1 a technology park. 2 a new platform. 3 a monster film.
b. Rory Quasala is …
   1 a tourist. 2 a member of a tribe. 3 an ancestor.
c. He thinks the Skywalk will …
   1 bring too many children. 2 be good for the land. 3 be bad for his tribe.
d. The tourists will use …
   1 too many rocks. 2 the tribe's water. 3 a lot of garbage.
e. The Skywalk is built on land which is …
   1 full of souvenirs. 2 better for tribes. 3 sacred to the Hualapai.

2 Skills

Read the text again. Collect reasons why Rory is against the Skywalk. Put them in a mind map.

B Language

Find the words in the text with the same or a similar meaning.

a. report b. take care of c. visitors d. stones e. rubbish f. land

26
C Listening

1 Part a)

Right or wrong? Listen to the radio chat show.

a. Today's guest is called Louisa Quasala.
b. She works at the Skywalk.
c. She lives on the reservation.
d. Some older members are against the Skywalk.
e. Rory Quasala is her grandad.
f. Louisa is very angry.

2 Part b)

Listen to more of the chat show and answer the questions.

a. Is Louisa for or against the Skywalk?

b. Which of these reasons does she give for her opinion?
1 The Hualapai need money. 2 There are other platforms. 3 It's beautiful.
4 It gives work to her people. 5 Visitors can learn about her tribe. 6 It's not very big.

c. What is the number of the highway which goes through Peach Springs?

D Speaking

1 Skills

Make two lists of pros and cons from A Reading and C Listening.

2 Role play

One of you is Rory, the other is Louisa. Discuss the Skywalk with each other.

E Writing

1 Your opinion

Do you think a platform like the Skywalk is a good idea? Why or why not?
Write 2–3 sentences.

2 A letter to a magazine

Write a letter to the Newtech magazine. Say if you agree with Rory or not. Say why.
Write 45–50 words.

Unit 5 Stars in your eyes?

1 Nicole Kidman: Actress

2 Jennifer Hudson: Actress

3 Zandra Rhodes: Fashion designer

1 Is it the 'Dress awards'?

Describe the women in photos 1–3. What are they wearing? What do you think of their clothes?

2 The big night (→ p. 54/ex. 1)

a) *Read the fact box and look at all the photos. Try to match each with an award.*

b) *Which award do you think is the most exciting and why?*

WORDS

evening dress ['iːvnɪŋ 'dres] – *Abendkleid*
low-cut [ləʊ'kʌt] – *tief ausgeschnitten*
backless ['bækləs] – *rückenfrei*
glamorous ['glæmrəs] – *glamourös*
outrageous [ˌaʊt'reɪdʒəs] – *ausgefallen*
to hold [həʊld] – *halten*

4 Green Day

5 Nelly Furtado

6 Sean Paul

DID YOU KNOW?

- The center of the film industry in the US is in Hollywood, Los Angeles, where it all started. Music production is big there, too.
- The Academy Awards are the most important US movie awards. No one knows why they are called 'Oscars'. Some say the trophy looked like an Academy member's Uncle Oscar!
- In 1984 MTV gave the first video music awards – a statue of an astronaut. There are now other MTV awards, for example for movies and music.
- Grammy Awards are given for the best record, album or song. There are over a hundred categories, which include rap, R&B, Latino, folk, country, rock, pop, dancehall, reggae and soul.
- Before each ceremony stars and guests pose on the red carpet for TV cameras and press photographers. The women's dresses often get more attention than the stars themselves.

3 Let's listen: Some of the stars

a) *What are the people in pictures 4–6 famous for? What sort of music do they make?*

b) *What is happening in each picture?*

c) *Listen. Which awards was the reporter at? Which star did he see there? Who did he miss?*

4 For my folder: Info from the Internet (→ p. 54/ex. 2)

Find out more on the Internet and then answer the questions. You can use 'film awards', 'music awards' and 'video awards' as search words.

1. Which film won the first Oscar for the best picture?
2. What is the nickname for winners of MTV awards?
3. When did they present the first Grammys?
4. What does the Grammy award look like?
5. What film, music or video awards are given in Germany?

FILMS FIRST

It took about 100 years from the first still (still picture) to the first talkie (movie with sound). Since then movies (motion pictures) have got better and better and have become more and more complex.

1877

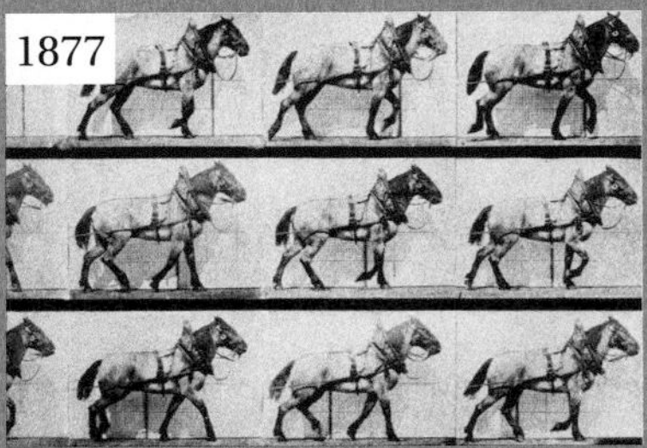

The first series of stills which showed motion was produced. But the pictures weren't taken by a photographer. They were taken by a horse. Cameras were set up by **Eadweard Muybridge**. A string was attached to the shutter of each camera. As the horse ran, it broke the strings. The shutters were opened, one after the other. Light fell on the film and a photo was produced.

1894

Some people say that the Kinetoscope wasn't invented by **Thomas Edison**, but by one of his team. It was a cabinet with a film, a light bulb and a window in the top. The film was a series of stills. But when it was moved quickly across the lamp, viewers saw it as a 'movie'. These 'movies' were seen for the first time in New York.

1903

The first science fiction (sci-fi) movie, was made in France by **Georges Méliès**. The director used trick photography to make us believe that a rocket was moving farther away from the Earth. The first public movie wasn't seen in the US until a year later when **Edwin Porter** made the first western 'The Great Train Robbery'.

1911

The first film studio was built in Hollywood by two brothers from New Jersey. At this time the actors were paid for their work but their names weren't published by the studios. But this soon changed and the rise of movie stars began. **Charlie Chaplin** was one of the first.

1927

The first 'talkie', 'The Jazz Singer', made film history. Two years later the first Oscars were given for Best Film. Later awards were given not only for films but also for music scores and songs in the movies.

1 Movie words

Read the texts and explain these words.
Example: A movie is another word for a motion picture.

movie • talkie • camera • the Kinetoscope • Oscars • science fiction • movie stars •

2 Detective work: Find the rule (→ p. 55/ex. 3)

a) ▶ Collect passive forms from the text and make a grammar rule.
Check if your rule is right.
→ G9

b) *Complete with 'was'/ 'were' or 'wasn't'/ 'weren't' and the right form of the verb.*

1. In 1877 the first photos of motion … (*to produce*).
2. As the horse ran, each string … (*to break*) and each shutter … (*to open*).
3. The first science-fiction movie … (*to film*) in the US. It … (*to make*) in France.
4. The first studio … (*to build*) in New York. It … (*to set up*) in Hollywood.
5. Actors' names … (*to publish*) at first. But the actors … (*to pay*) for their work.

3 People in the movie business (→ p. 55/ex. 4, 5; p. 56/ex. 6)

▶ by a photographer
by Thomas Edison
→ G9

Read the text again and make sentences.

1. The first pictures of motion	weren't published by	Eadweard Muybridge.
2. The cameras	wasn't invented by	the studios.
3. The first sci-fi movie	were taken by	Thomas Edison.
4. The first movie studios	were built by	a horse.
5. Actors' names	were set up by	George Méliès.
6. Some say the Kinetoscope	was made by	two brothers from New Jersey.

4 Academy Awards for music (→ p. 56/ex. 7; p. 57/ex. 8)

Complete the text. Use the passive form of the verb in brackets. Add 'by' where it is needed.
Start like this: The first award for a music score **was won by** a musical. It … .

The first award for a music score … (*to win/a musical*). It … (*to call*) 'One night of love'. In the 1930s musicals … (*to make/a lot of studios*). Later the awards for best song and best score .. (*to win/other types of film*). In 1970, for example, the Beatles … (*to give*) a special award for their film 'Let it be!' But the music score award … (*to receive/serious movies like Titanic*), too. In 2003 the awards for best song and for best score … (*to present*) to 'Lord of the Rings'.

5 A quiz: Who was it sung by? (→ p. 57/ex. 9)

▶ Who was … sung **by**?
Who were the … films produced **by**?
→ G9

a) *Find the answers to the quiz questions.*

1. Who was 'We are the Champions' sung by?
2. Who was 'Star Wars III' produced by?
3. Who was Harry Potter played by in 'The Philosopher's Stone'?

b) *Write more quiz questions for your partner.*

Music matters

1 Let's talk: My music

a) *What sort of music do you like/not like? Make two lists and add the names of singers/rappers/groups that make this sort of music.*

b) *Talk to partner about the music and the people in your lists in part a). Why do/don't you like them?*

So you like /don't like … . Why?
Because … is a great/rubbish/ … guitar player/singer/… .
Because the music/song/… makes me feel happy/sick /… .

2 Messages in a music chat room

a) *Use slang words or short forms only in chat rooms or cell-phone messages. Read these messages and make two lists.*

slang/short form	normal/long form
Peace!	Hello!
ur	you are (you're)
boyz	…

Welcome to **Teentalk's message boards.**

You have to register before you can post a message. Just click on register. To view a message, just click on the forum that you want to visit.

Strictly for gangstas
Peace! If ur Atlanta (home of OutKast and Lil Jon) boyz or girlies (14–16) and hip hop muzik and bling bling are ur style then cum to the Harland Club Teen Center next Saturday at 6 pm and learn to rap with uz. If u have written a rap then bring it with u. We'll teach u how to freestyle and diss other rappers. So chill out! Peace and c ya soon. Tuzie and Blugirl

Rock is our thing
Hi! We're 14 and 15 and we're from Atlanta! My homie and I like indie and rock music – Green Day, Led Zeppelin, etc. but we don't wanna diss any1. We can only listen 2 good music on old CDs. Does any1 know of a disco where we can listen 2 'our' music? Just post us a message. CU. Carly + Jo

Any musicians (rock, metal, punk) in/around Austin?
Hi. If you're from Austin and you want to make music then read this! My friends and I live in Round Rock, a suburb of Austin. We aren't gangsters and we don't wear jewelry. We're trying to form a band and we're looking for a drummer, a bass player and a singer. We're 3 guys: 2 guitar players and a singer. We're into almost everything (rock, pop, funk, Latino, EXCEPT HIP HOP (no disrespect!). We're both 15 and are at high school. So if you're around our age and are interested, e-mail us or check us out at myspace.com. We hope to hear from ya! CU Rick, Sally an' Sam

b) *Which music is most popular with these kids? Where do they play it or listen to it?*

c) *Use the words from part a) and write your own chat room message. Choose an idea:*

1. You and your homies are hip hop fans. You are angry that people think you are all gangsters.
2. You are a rock fan and want to start a teen's disco. Tell Carly and Jo about it.
3. Tell the group from Austin what you can play and what sort of music you like.

3 Messages in an Internet forum (→ p. 58/ex. 10)

PRIVATE OFFERS

DRUMS

nearly new, only used twice, $50. And two rock guitars with 12 strings. White and blue. Only $80 each. Contact Jojo as soon as possible.

TICKETS TICKETS TICKETS TICKETS TICKETS TICKETS TICKETS

Has any 1 got 2 tickets that they don't want for the hip hop concert on Saturday? Will pay $15 per ticket. Phone Paul on 0945213 after 4 pm.

New music shop! JAMAICA JAM

JAMAICA JAM opens on 16th at 9am. Everything from rap to reggae. Free CD and cup of coffee for the first 20 customers.

WANTED! 2ND HAND DRUMS

Do you have a 2nd hand drum set that you don't need? Then please give me your e-mail address. I lost everything in the floods last week and I can't live without my drums.

BREAK DANCE

Are you fit and healthy? Are you 13 to 16 years old? Do you wanna learn to break-dance? Then give it a go. We meet in the Teen Center on Saturdays at 7. CU there!

WANTED! HIP HOP FREESTYLE

Is hip hop yur style? Do ya wanna battle?
Do you wanna be gangstas with bling bling?
If you can freestyle, then join the Raprace 2nite in The HIP Bar.

a) *What are the messages about? Which do you think is the most interesting and why?*

b) *Write an answer to one of the messages.*

4 Let's talk: Volunteers needed! (→ p. 58/ex. 11)

a) *Read the text of a message on the Internet and answer the questions.*

Hi, all ya rappers, gangstas, girlies and boyz!
Have you had enough hip hop battles? Do u wanna do something different at weekends? Then come and entertain the kids in the City Hospital on Sunday afternoons. We are three rappers but we need more volunteers. The idea is that we should do a show for the sick kids in the hospital. We want to teach them all about rapping and do some break dancing for them. If you think that you can help, phone and leave a message and we'll get back to you.

1. Who is the notice for?
2. What can they do to help?

b) *Write a phone message for someone and practise it with your partner.*

c) *The person calls you back. Write a dialogue and act it with your partner.*

LISTENING S K I L L S

Understanding a song in English

Many songs are like stories. Some are about young people's lives or problems or have a special 'message'. But without the lyrics, it can be difficult to understand them. Here are some helpful tips:

1. Look at the title/photo on the CD. → These often give you a clue about the song itself.
2. Listen to the song. → Write down any words which you know.
3. Listen again. → Listen to the sentences which have got your words in them.
4. A new word? Don't panic. → If you hear a strange word, try to think what it could mean. Does it sound like a German word? Is it like any other English words which you know? Listen to the sentence which has got the new word in it. Can you now guess the meaning? Check in your dictionary.
5. Now listen to the refrain. → The refrain often contains the song's main idea or problem. What is the problem/idea?
6. Listen to each verse. → The verses usually tell the 'story'. Write notes.
7. Listen to the song again. → Sit back and enjoy it!

L2, 28 ◎ **1 A song: Boulevard of Broken Dreams** (→ p. 59/ex. 12) (Green Day)

a) *Follow the steps in the skills box as you listen to the song. Answer the questions.*

1. a) What is a 'boulevard'? The photo can help you.
   b) The dreams in the song are 'broken': What does that suggest to you about the feelings in the song?
2. Which of these words are in the song?

   local • lonely • road • street • city • country • sleeps • leaves • shed • shadow • half • heart • eating • beating • border • bored • mind • mile • lines • lives • end • edge

3. What could 'vital signs' mean? When you listen again, stop when you hear this phrase. Listen to the sentence it is in. Does it sound like any German word or any other English word which you know?
4. What other words or phrases can you get from their context? Look them up to see if you were right.
5. What does the refrain tell you about the person in the song? (Where is he? Is it day/night? How does he feel? …)
6. Choose the best 'idea' for each of the three verses:

   I've lost my way to the city. • I don't know where I'm going in life. • I've reached the border of a different country. • I'm on the edge and have to decide what to do. • What was good/bad in my life? Am I still alive? • I have to read all about life.

b) *Listen to another song. Use the tips in the skills box to help you understand it.*

1 Before you listen: Musicians

a) *Describe the three people in the pictures. What are they wearing?*

b) *What impression do you get of the musicians: friendly/unfriendly, …? Why?*

c) *Which musician would you like to meet? Why? What would you ask him or say to him?*

29–32 ## 2 Let's listen: Their music (→ p. 60/ex. 13, 14)

a) *Listen to three interviews. Match each interview with a picture from exercise 1 a). Why do you think this?*
Example: I think picture … is of the guy in the first interview.
He looks like … who is a famous … singer/musician/ … star.

b) *Now listen to some music. Match the music style with a picture from exercise 1 a).*

c) *Choose a music style. Find out more about it (history, famous singers/bands, fashion) from the Internet. Write six sentences, and present your report in class. You can play a short example if you have a CD with a song in that style.*

3 A cartoon: A cowboy rapper

a) *Look at the cartoon and describe it. Who can you see and what is he doing with his hands?*

b) *What sort of music do you expect from the man? Why?*

c) *Think of a different title for the cartoon.*

© Mike Baldwin/Cornered

GLAMOROUS*

Fergie

Ludacris

If you ain't got no money take yo'broke ass home
You say: If you ain't got no money take yo'broke ass home
G-L-A-M-O-R-O-U-S, yeah G-L-A-M-O-R-O-U-S
[Fergie/B Section:] We flyin' first class
Up in the sky, poppin' champagne
Livin' my life in the fast lane
And I won't change
By the Glamorous, oh the flossy flossy
[Chorus:] The glamorous, the glamorous, glamorous
By the Glamorous, oh the flossy flossy ...
[Fergie:] Wear them gold and diamonds rings
All them things don't mean a thing
Chaperons and limousines
Shopping for expensive things
I be on the movie screens
Magazines and boogie scenes
I'm not clean, I'm not pristine
I'm no queen, I'm no machine
I still go to Taco Bell
Drive through, raw as hell
I don't care, I'm still real
No matter how many records I sell
After the show or after the Grammies
I like to go cool out with the family
Sippin', reminiscing on days when I had a Mustang
Fergie/B section; chorus (2x)
[Ludacris:] I'm talking Champagne wishes, caviar dreams
You deserve nothing but all the finer things
Now this whole world has no clue what to do with us
I've got enough money in the bank for the two of us
Brother gotta keep enough lettuce to support your shoe fetish
Lifestyles so rich and famous, Robin Leach will get jealous
Half a million for the stones, taking trips from here to Rome
So if you ain't got no money, take yo'broke ass home
G-L-A-M-O-R-O-U-S, yeah G-L-A-M-O-R-O-U-S
Fergie/B section; chorus (2x)
[Fergie:] I got problems up to here I've got people in my ear
Telling me these crazy things that I don't want to know
I've got money in the bank and I'd really like to thank
All the fans, I'd like to thank - thank you really though
Cause I remember yesterday when I dreamt about the days
When I'd rock on MTV, that be really dope
Damn, It's been a long road and the industry is cold
I'm glad my daddy tell me, so he let his daughter know ...

*W. Adams/Chr. Br. Bridges/St. Ferguson/Jam. F. Jones/Elv. Will. Jr.

1 Before you read: The title

Look at the title of the song.
What do you think the song is about?

2 The lyrics (→ p. 61/ex. 15)

Read the lyrics and look at the collage.
Make a list of the things in the collage which are in the lyrics.
Which things aren't in the lyrics?

3 A glamorous or a normal life? (→ p. 61/ex. 16)

a) *What is glamorous in the song?*
What belongs to the singer's normal life?

b) *What does the singer say about the music industry, her fans and about her life as a music star?*

c) *Why does she feel like this?*
What do you think?

4 For my folder: A song project (→ p. 61/ex. 17)

a) *Choose a song which you want to present in class.*

b) *Use the skills box on page 82 as you read and/or listen to the lyrics. Write notes.*
Don't forget to say why you chose the song (style of music, singer's voice, story/message in the lyrics, …).

c) *Make a collage for your song.*
You can draw pictures or use some from magazines.

d) *Present your song to the class.*
Use your collage.

e) *Surf the Internet to find out more about the singer and the song.*
Why did he or she write it?
Was there a special reason?

1 Media awards

a) *Sort the words and phrases below into lists under the headings 'film' and 'music'.*

Academy Awards • concert • Grammy Awards • CDs • talkies • rock • trick photography • rap • science fiction • Kinetoscope • movie stars • lyrics • Oscars • motion • score • song

b) *Add as many words as you can to your lists. Compare with your partner. Add those words from your partner's list that are missing on your list. Check each other's spelling.*

2 Let's look: Old science fiction movies

These things were used in some old science fiction movies.
Which ten pieces of everyday equipment did they use?

Example: 1. **An old chair** was used to make **a robot**.
2. **Boxes** were used to … .

3 Movie opposites (→ p. 62/ex. 18)

Find the opposite of each highlighted word in the box. Correct the sentences.

1. At the award ceremonies the women's dresses often get less attention than the stars.
2. In 1984 MTV gave the last video awards.
3. The Oscars are the least important movie awards.
4. Since the first talkies movies have got worse and worse.
5. They have also become less and less complex.
6. People believed that the rocket was moving nearer to the Earth.
7. The first public movie was seen in the US a year earlier.
8. There is little money in movies today.

more and more | a lot of | better and better | first | more | most | farther away from | later

4 Three musicians (→ p. 62/ex. 19)

a) *What words can you use to describe the pictures? Make a mind map for each one.*

1 A rapper

2 A rock guitar player

3 A Latino singer

b) *Look at each picture again for five seconds. Then close your book and answer the questions.*

1. Which musician isn't wearing a hat?
2. Who has a tattoo?
3. Who is wearing jewellery?
4. What is one of the musicians playing?

5 Synonyms (→ p. 62/ex. 20)

a) *Find the word with the same meaning.*
Examples: movie → film

A: movie • trophy • homie • still • produce • type • alien

B: make • style • strange • award • photo • film • friend

b) *Use the words in box B to explain the words in box A.*
Examples: 'Movie' is a synonym for 'film'. (It's American English (AE).)

1 What happened when? (the simple past form of the passive → G9) (→ p. 63/ex. 21)

Look back at page 78, correct the year and make sentences about the pictures.

Example: 1. The first series of stills **wasn't produced** in … . It **was produced** in … .

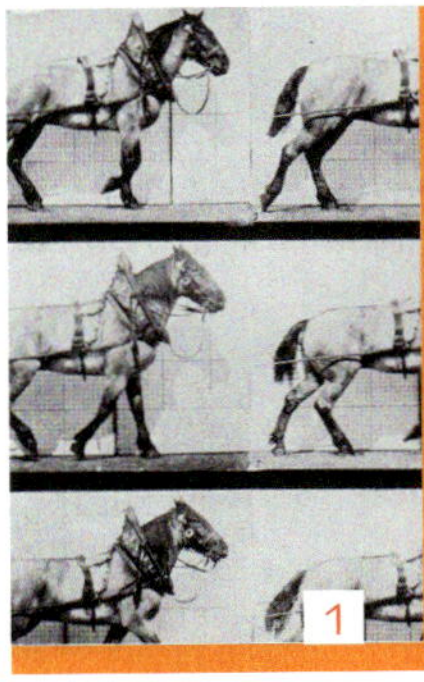
1

1911
produced/first series of stills

2

1877
saw/first movie/ in New York

3

1927
make/first western movie

4

1894
build/first film studio/in Hollywood

5

1903
show/first talkie

2 More 'firsts' (the simple past form of the passive → G9) (→ p. 63/ex. 22)

Choose the correct fact about the things in the pictures.

Example: 1. The first westerns **weren't shown** in … . They **were shown** in … .

1

Europe/the US • show

2

1970s/1870s • use

3

Hollywood/London • produce

4

19th/20th century • build

5

Shakespeare/Gutenberg • print

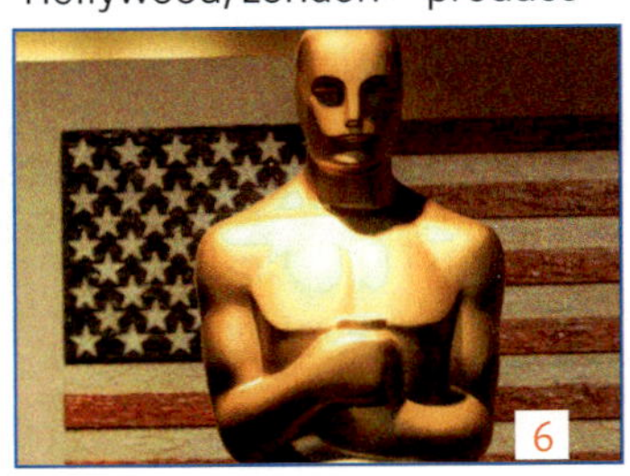
6

videos/movies • produce

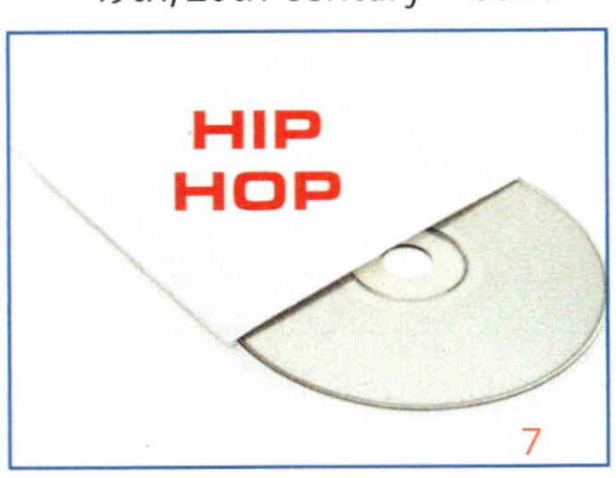

7

pop groups/DJs • make

8

New York/Mannheim • drive

9

1890s/1990s • give

3 The history of break dancing (the simple past form of the passive → G9)

Use the correct form of the verb in brackets and complete the sentences.

1. Some people say that break dancing … *(to invent)* in the late 1970s by DJs from NYC.
2. They noticed that people danced better in the 'breaks' when only music … *(to play)*.
3. These breaks … *(to put)* together by the DJs to make dance music for discos and parties.
4. Others say that this type of dancing … *(to start)* by a different group of young people.
5. People who break-danced … *(not/to see)* on the streets of NYC until the early 1980's.
6. It … *(not/to call)* break dancing then.
7. 'Breaking' or 'b-boying' were the names which … *(to give)* to it by dancers.
8. The dances … *(not/to perform)* at discos or parties.
9. They … *(to use)* instead of fights, if two gangs had an argument.
10. The battle … *(to win)* by the gang with the best dancers.

4 Cloze text: A dangerous job (→ p. 64/ex. 1)

Read the magazine article and complete the sentences.

When I was a kid at school, I (1) want to be in the fire brigade or the (2) like my homies. Jobs like that were too (3) for me. I decided to make movies. I was (4) my first camera when I was ten and I (5) pictures of everything: my school, my family, my dog, (6) moon and the stars. But they weren't movies, they (7) all stills.
When I was twelve, Dad lent me (8) movie camera. It was summer. We were all on (9) in California. I made movies about everyone in my (10), even about my older sister and her boyfriend. She (11) furious. One sunny day we were all on the (12). I had my dad's new movie camera. My sister was (13) beach volleyball with some friends and I was (14) them. I was standing near the water. Suddenly someone (15) the ball. The wind caught it and it was (16) towards the sea. I turned too quickly and was (17) by a wave. I fell on my back into the (18). I got wet but I saved the movie (19). I held it above my head until I was (20) by my dad. After that I decided it was (21) dangerous to be a director than to be a (22) so I became a detective.

his | more | took | policeman | were | police | rescued | was | hit | threw | playing | given | water | beach | vacation | filming | camera | didn't | the | dangerous | blown | family

NOW YOU CAN

- ✓ talk about media awards. → *Tell a partner about one media award.*
- ✓ use the passive form for past actions. → *Talk about 3 things which were done to you by s.o. else.*
- ✓ tell the history of movies. → *Talk about three events in the history of movies.*
- ✓ understand chat room messages. → *Explain three chat room words.*
- ✓ talk about a song. → *Tell the class about a song which you like.*
- ✓ describe people. → *Think of a(n) (un)friendly person and describe him or her.*

HOLLYWOOD – more than films

Many people think that the history of Hollywood began at the beginning of the 20th century when the first film studios were opened. But Hollywood was born many years before that.

The area which is now known as Hollywood was first discovered by Spanish explorers[2] in the 17th century. At that time several[3] tribes of Native Americans were living in the area. The land was divided[4] into two huge ranches and the farmers grew[5] grain[6], pineapples[7] and bananas.

These ranches were divided again in the 1880s into smaller ranches. In 1886 a man called Harvery Henderson Wilcox (1832 to 1891) from Kansas bought one of these smaller ranches. Some say that it was named 'Hollywood' by his wife. Others say that it was called this because there was a lot of holly[8] on the land. Wilcox was not a farmer, he sold real estate[9]. Soon he had made a new community[10] out of the ranch. He paved[11] the street which is known today as Hollywood Boulevard and sold land to rich Americans from the Midwest who wanted to spend their winters in California. Mrs Wilcox was busy, too. She collected money to build churches, schools and a library[12]. By 1900 they had a population of 500, a post office, a newspaper and two markets. They had everything, in fact, that a town needed – except water. So they turned to[13] their larger neighbor, Los Angeles, for help. In 1910 they became a part of this city, which then gave them all the water they needed. After the first film studio was opened in 1911 by the Nestor Company, Hollywood started to grow. And since then the name has stood for one of the largest film industries in the world. But the real Hollywood is older than the films.

TEXT SKILLS

A factual text has these parts:
- The title – a summary of the text
- The introduction – the topic of the text
- Paragraphs – other points or facts
- The conclusion[1] – the final point
- Pictures – sometimes help the reader

1

2

3

4

5

[1]conclusion [kən'klu:ʒn] – *Schluss,* [2]explorer [ɪk'splɔ:rə] – *Forscher/in,* [3]several ['sevrəl] – *einige,* [4]divided [dɪ'vaɪdɪd] – *aufgeteilt,* [5]to grow [grəʊ] – *anbauen, wachsen,* [6]grain [greɪn] – *Getreide,* [7]pineapple ['paɪnˌæpl] – *Ananas,* [8]holly ['hɒli] – *Stechpalme,* [9]real estate ['rɪəl‿ɪˌsteɪt] – *Immobilien,* [10]community [kəm'ju:nəti] – *Gemeinde,* [11]to pave [peɪv] – *pflastern,* [12]library ['laɪbrəri] – *Bücherei,* [13]to turn to ['tɜ:n tə] – *sich wenden an*

1 A factual text

a) *Read the text on the opposite page and use the skills box to answer the questions.*

1. What information do you get from the title?
2. What is the topic of the text?
3. What points or facts do you learn about in each paragraph?
4. What is the final point?

b) *Match the pictures with sentences from the text.*

2 More about Hollywood (→ p. 65/ex. 1)

a) *Read the sentences below. They give a lot of information. Use the skills box and make a better factual text. Write the parts that aren't here.*

In 1903 Hollywood became a city. But it wasn't free for very long.

In 1910 it became a part of Los Angeles because it needed water.

Many people say that Wilcox named the area 'Hollywoodland'.

In 1923 two men, Woodruff and Shoults, who worked in real estate, decided to build houses in Beachwood Canyon above Hollywood.

They called it 'Hollywoodland' and described it as a 'superb[1] environment … on the Hollywood side of the hills[2]'.

One year later they paid the Crescent Sign Company to put up a huge sign which said 'Hollywoodland' on the side of the hill.

The owner of the sign company, Thomas Fisk Goff (1890–1984), designed the sign in letters which were 50 feet high and needed 4,000 light bulbs.

The light bulbs burned out[3] or were stolen a year or two later.

They were never replaced.

In 1949 the end of the sign was cut off so that the word 'land' was not a part of it.

In 1978, the sign was rebuilt. It is painted and repaired every few years. The sign is now a national monument[4].

b) *Find one or two photos and use them to help the reader.*

c) *Use your text and photos to make a poster about your text.*

[1]superb [suːˈpɜːb] – *großartig,* [2]hill [hɪl] – *Hügel,* [3]to burn out [bɜːnˌˈaʊt] – *durchbrennen,*
[4]monument [ˈmɒnjəmənt] – *Denkmal*

READING AND WRITING

SKILLS

Keeping[1] a reader's diary

1. A reader's diary is more than just a report. You will need a new exercise book, a folder or a real diary for it. You can write about any[2] texts which you have read, for example about a science fiction story, a magazine article or even about a whole book. A reader's diary can help you to remember the important parts of a text.
   You can note/record
   - the title,
   - the names of the characters[3] in the text,
   - adjectives which describe the characters in the text,
   - a summary of each chapter[4],
   - a timeline,
   - … .
2. You can also write about what you liked or didn't like in the text.
3. You can use lists, grids, mind maps, clusters, pictures, maps, diagrams, or you can write articles, a different ending for the text, dialogues, reports or poems in your diary. You can also draw a comic strip.

Step 1: Before you start

Here are some pages from a pupil's diary about a reader[5] called 'Lost in the USA'.

a) *Think about the title. What could the text be about?*

b) *What other texts do you know about lost things or lost people?*

Step 2: More information

Now have a look at parts from the first page of a reader's diary on the story 'Lost in the USA'. What can you find out about the story? Discuss with your partner and write 4–6 sentences in your diary.

[1]to keep [ki:p] – *hier: führen,* [2]any ['eni] – *hier: jeden/alle,* [3]character ['kærəktə] – *Figur/Person/Charakter,* [4]chapter ['tʃæptə] – *Kapitel,* [5]reader ['ri:də] – *hier: Lektüre,* [6]Easter ['i:stə] – *Oster-,* [7]cattle ['kætl] – *Vieh*

Step 3: The second page

Read the summary of the first five chapters and put the pictures below in the right order.

A summary - chapters 1-5

Frank, a German boy, flies to the US to spend his Easter holidays with his aunt. He wants to improve his English. At the airport in New York he gets into a van. He thinks it is a shuttle bus[1] to the place where his aunt lives. But the van goes to Manhattan. The three men in the front[2] are not bus drivers - they are gangsters called Smitty, Pancho and Fats. They kidnap[3] Frank, take his passport and lock[4] him in a hotel room. Fats, who brings Frank food and drinks, feels a bit sorry for him. Later the three men take Frank by private plane to a lonely place. Frank grabs a pouch[5] before he leaves the plane. He knows his passport is in it but he doesn't know that there are diamonds in the pouch, too.
The gangsters fly off. Frank finds a road and ends up[6] in a gas station[7]. The gangsters can't find the diamonds and realize[8] that Frank must have them. They go back to look for him and almost find him at the gas station. He escapes in a cattle truck and meets Linda, who has run away from home. When the truck slows down[9], they jump off and hide.

Step 4: A mind map

Draw a mind map of the characters in the story. Who belongs to whom? Work with a partner.

Step 5: Your own pages

Use this diary and add to it when you read the following extract[10] from 'Lost in the USA'.

[1]shuttle bus ['ʃʌtl ˌbʌs] – *Zubringerbus,* [2]in the front [ˌɪn ðə 'frʌnt] – *auf dem Vordersitz,* [3]to kidnap ['kɪdnæp]– *kidnappen,* [4]to lock [lɒk] – *einsperren,* [5]pouch [paʊtʃ] – *Brustbeutel,* [6]to end up [end‿'ʌp] – *landen,* [7]gas station ['gæs ˌsteɪʃn] – *Tankstelle,* [8]to realize ['rɪəlaɪz] – *bemerken,* [9]to slow down [sləʊ 'daʊn] – *langsamer werden,* [10]extract ['ekstrækt] – *Auszug*

'Lost in the USA' by Rolf W. Roth

a) *Read what happens in chapters 6 and 7.*

The train was very long. It just went on and on[1], and the children waited until they saw an open boxcar[2]. Then they ran, faster and faster, and finally jumped and were on the train.

In the boxcar Frank and Linda sat on the floor and watched the prairie[3] fly by[4] through the open door.

"In Winslow you have to go to the police right away," Linda said. "They can help you."

"Come with me, Linda."

"No! They will take me back home."

They were quiet then.

"Why are those men after you[5]? You must have something they want."

"But I don't. The only thing I have is this pouch here," Frank said and took it from around his neck[6]. "And I don't want that. I don't want anything from them." He took his passport and the ticket out, put them in his jeans pocket and threw the pouch out through the open door.

b) *Why does he do this?*

They were quiet again after that – until Frank said, "I want to go home. You should go home, too. Come to the police with me."

Linda shook her head and looked out of the door. "Was there anything in that pouch? I mean besides[7] your passport and ticket?" she asked.

Now Frank shook his head. "No, just some paper at the bottom. That's all."

"What kind of paper?"

"I don't know. Just paper. Bags often have paper in them to keep their – er –"

"Their shape[8]," Linda helped him with the word. "Yes, I know, but maybe there was something important on the paper."

Frank looked at her. "Maybe, but I don't think so. And it's gone now."

"Yes," Linda said and got up. She walked to the door and looked out – then pulled her head in again fast. "Hey, Frank, come here!"

Frank went to the door and looked out with her. The pouch was hanging on[9] a piece of metal and flapping[10] in the wind.

"Quick, let's get it back," Linda said and leaned out. "Hold onto[11] me."

"No, Linda, it's too dangerous," Frank told her, but she was already hanging out of the door, and Frank held onto her quickly.

The wind was strong as Linda stretched[12] and tried to get the pouch – and just as it was about to[13] fly off, she grabbed it, and Frank pulled her back in.

"Boy, that was close[14]," she said.

"You'll see, it's only paper," Frank said to her – and then they sat down again and opened the pouch.

c) *Find three mistakes in the picture above. Draw the correct picture in your reader's diary.*

Pancho, Fats and Smitty were waiting for the train in Winslow.

[1]on and on ['ɒn‿ənd‿ɒn] – *weiter und weiter*, [2]boxcar ['bɒkskɑː] – *Güterwaggon*, [3]prairie ['præri] – *Prärie*, [4]to fly by [flaɪ 'baɪ] – *vorbeifliegen*, [5]to be after sb. [bɪ 'ɑːftə] – *jmd. verfolgen*, [6]neck [nek] – *Hals*, [7]besides [bɪ'saɪdz] – *außer*, [8]shape [ʃeɪp] – *Form*, [9]to hang on ['hæŋ‿ɒn] – *hängen an*, [10]to flap [flæp] – *flattern*, [11]to hold onto [həʊld 'ɒntə] – *festhalten*, [12]to stretch [stretʃ] – *sich strecken*, [13]to be about to [bɪ ə'baʊt] – *gerade im Begriff sein etw. zu tun*, [14]close [kləʊs] – *knapp*

"I'm sure he's on that train," Pancho said.

"He has to be!" Smitty said, "Or you two will be in real trouble."

"He has to be," Fats said. "We found tracks."

"What if he doesn't get off here?" Pancho asked.

"Then we'll get on the train and find him," Smitty said.

d) *What do the three men want from Frank? Who is the boss? Which line tells you this?*

e) *What do you think the men look like? Find pictures in a magazine that match the characters and put them in your diary.*

For a long moment the friends just sat there and looked at the stones on the floor.

"Well," Linda finally said, "everything's clear now. I'm sure they're diamonds, and they want them back."

"How much are they, Linda?"

"You mean, how much are they *worth*[1]?"

"Yes, worth."

"I don't know, but you have to take them to the police now. Those men will not stop hunting[2] you as long as you have them. And you will be OK here. They don't know you're on the train."

"Yes, I will go, in Winslow," Frank said and looked at her.

"No," Linda said. "I won't come with you."

When the train stopped in Winslow, Frank looked out and when he didn't see anyone, he got off quickly. Linda came to the door, waved to him and then went back into the boxcar.

Frank looked around. There wasn't even a station here – just a place for the train to stop and a little town on the other side of the tracks. Frank crossed them and walked towards the houses.

f) *What is Frank thinking? Write down his thoughts in your diary.*

Behind a wooden building near him, Pancho, Fats and Smitty were waiting.

"Let's get him now," Pancho said and started to run out.

"No, you idiot," Smitty said and held him back. "Somebody might see us."

"Yeah, but we have to get him before he can go to the police."

"Just wait."

Frank was on Main Street now. It looked just like the ones he had seen in films: it was very wide[3], cars were parked[4] on both sides and there were shops in low buildings on both sides, too. There were only a few people on the sidewalks. The town was peaceful[5].

A young woman with a little girl came by[6] then, and Frank spoke to her. "Can you tell me the way to the police station, please?" he asked her.

The woman smiled. "Sure, honey[7]. It's –"

"Mum, I know that boy," her little girl said then. "I saw his picture on TV."

"Sure you did[8], Peggy," her mother laughed. "She watches too much TV," she said to Frank. "Now, young man, you go down this street and then –"

"But, Mum, I really did –"

"Now you hush[9], Peggy, when I'm talking

[1]worth [wɜːθ] – *wert,* [2]to hunt [hʌnt] – *jagen, verfolgen,* [3]wide [waɪd] – *breit,* [4]to park [pɑːk] – *parken,* [5]peaceful ['piːsfl] – *ruhig, friedlich,* [6]to come by [kʌm 'baɪ] – *vorbeikommen,* [7]honey ['hʌni] – *Liebling,* [8]Sure you did! ['ʃɔː jʊ dɪd] – *Ja, natürlich (ironisch),* [9]to hush [hʌʃ] – *ruhig sein*

to somebody! OK, young man, down this street and then you turn north at the second traffic light[1]. It'll be the low red building on the west side. Did you understand?"

Frank said 'yes' and thanked her and left fast before Peggy could start again.

g) *How could the girl know him from TV?*

"We have to move now," Pancho said. "I'm sure he asked her about the police station. That's where he's going. It's down that way. I saw it when we drove in."

"OK, OK, just wait until he's off the main street. Let's get to the car."

"It'll be too late. The police station's just around the corner[2]."

"Let's hurry[3] then," Smitty said.

Frank walked down the street fast. Now what had she said? The second traffic light – and turn north. Which way was that? Frank tried to remember what he had learned about the sun. It was almost noon[4]. Frank looked up at the big blue sky. The sun should be right in the south now. Yes, there it was to his left. So north was to the right. He walked on, got to the second traffic light and went around the corner.

It all happened very fast after that: Frank came around the corner, a car door opened suddenly, someone pulled him in and put a hand over his mouth, the door closed and the car raced[5] away.

"Hey, that was close," Frank heard Fats say next to him, and on his other side Smitty said, "OK, where are the diamonds?"

"Thought we were gone, didn't you?" Pancho laughed.

"Shut up[6] and drive!" Smitty shouted.

"Look what I've got here, Frank," Fats said and gave him his baseball hat. "We found it."

Frank took it and put it on. "Thanks," he said to Fats.

"Hey, what is this?" Smitty was angry. "A reunion[7]? Where are the diamonds?"

"I don't know what you mean," Frank said.

"Where's the pouch?" Smitty shouted and grabbed Frank.

"The what?" Frank tried to look puzzled[8].

"The little bag you took, you idiot!"

"Oh that. I threw it away."

"Threw it away?" Smitty said in a funny way. "Well, you had it when you were on the road. We know that. And your passport was in it. You didn't throw that away?"

"No, I've got that right here," Frank started to take it out of his pocket, but Smitty grabbed his hand and took it out for him. "But I threw the pouch out of the train," Frank added.

"Sure you did, but you took your passport out first," the thin[9] man held it up, "and that means you've got the rest, too. Stop the car somewhere, Pancho. We will search him," Smitty ordered[10].

h) *The three men are different. Find words or sentences in the text that tell you about their characters. Write down in your diary what you have found out.*

When Pancho had found a good place to stop, the men searched Frank. He fought

[1]traffic light ['træfık ˌlaıt] – *Ampel*, [2]corner ['kɔ:nə] – *Ecke*, [3]to hurry ['hʌri] – *sich beeilen*, [4]noon [nu:n] – *Mittag*, [5]to race [reıs] – *rasen*, [6]Shut up! ['ʃʌt‿ʌp] – *Halt den Mund!*, [7]reunion [ri:'ju:nıən] – *Wiedersehenstreffen*, [8]puzzled ['pʌzld] – *verwirrt*, [9]thin [θın] – *dünn*, [10]to order ['ɔ:də] – *befehlen*

them, but they held him down[1] and Fats found the diamonds in his back pocket.

"All right, then," Smitty smiled for the first time. "We've got them. We're back in business. Let's get to the plane, Pancho. Fast."

"Right, boss. We'll leave this car in the bushes and then we'll be off to Mexico."

"Shut up, you idiot! Don't tell him where we're going," Fats said.

"Doesn't matter," Smitty answered. "This time we'll do the job right. He won't be able to[2] talk to anybody."

Pancho raced down the road another mile, then turned off onto a dirt road[3] with small trees on both sides. He drove on until they came to an open place. The plane was there.

"Just leave the car over there and let's go. Everything will be OK," Smitty was happy.

"Yeah," Pancho laughed and showed all his big teeth.

"For us, but not for him," he said as they pulled Frank over[4] to the plane.

i) *What does Frank feel in this situation? What do you think?*

Inside the plane, Smitty went to the cockpit[5] right away while his partners took Frank to the back. Smitty tried to start the plane, but the engine wouldn't turn over[6]. He tried again. "Damn!" he said. "There's a problem!"

"There's a problem back here, too," a strange voice said behind him. Smitty turned round fast – and saw a policeman with a gun.

Outside the plane, the police handcuffed[7] Smitty and his men, and took them over to some police cars, which were now there.

"Great," an older police officer said to Frank. "We found you, and you're OK! And we got these guys with all their diamonds. You know there's a big reward[8] for this."

"Reward?" Frank asked.

"Money for catching them," somebody said behind him. Frank turned round.

"Linda!" Frank shouted, and hugged[9] her.

"She saved you," the officer said.

"It's good to see you, Frank," she laughed. "But you were on that train."

"Yes, but as it was leaving, I saw those three guys. So I jumped out and went to the police as fast as I could."

j) *What did Linda tell the police? Write the dialogue in your diary.*

"But now, Linda, the police will take you –" Frank started but didn't go on.

k) *Here's the summary of a possible ending. Do you like it? Say why/why not.*

At his aunt's house in Oklahoma Frank meets his parents who flew to the US when they heard that Frank had disappeared. Linda also gets back home. Her parents are very angry with her and she has to go to a boarding school.[10]
Frank is worried about Linda. But he can't help her. Linda's parents think she ran away because of[11] Frank. So they don't want her to keep in touch[12] with him. They have to send e-mails secretly. Later Linda has a boyfriend and forgets Frank. They never meet again.

l) *Write a different ending in your diary.*

m) *Did you like the story? Write in your diary what you liked/didn't like about it.*

n) *Interested? Read the whole reader by Rolf W. Roth (Klett reader) and find out what really happened.*

[1]to hold down [həʊld 'daʊn] – *festhalten,* [2]to be able to ['eɪbl tə] – *fähig sein etw. zu tun,* [3]dirt road ['dɜːt rəʊd] – *Schotterweg, Waldweg,* [4]over ['əʊvə] – *hinüber,* [5]cockpit ['kɒkpɪt] – *Cockpit,* [6]to turn over [tɜːn‿'əʊvə] – *anspringen,* [7]to handcuff ['hænkʌf] – *Handschellen anlegen,* [8]reward [rɪ'wɔːd] – *Belohnung,* [9]to hug [hʌg] – *umarmen,* [10]boarding school ['bɔːdiŋ ˌskuːl] – *Internat,* [11]because of [bɪ'kɔːs‿əv] – *wegen,* [12]to keep in touch [ˌkiːp‿ɪn 'tʌtʃ] – *in Kontakt bleiben*

Berry Middle School

1 At first sight

a) *Have a look at the website and find out the full name of the school and the town in the US. Now find the town in an atlas[2].*

b) *What does the picture tell you about the climate[3]?*

c) *Look at the different buttons. What do you think is behind them? Talk to a partner.*

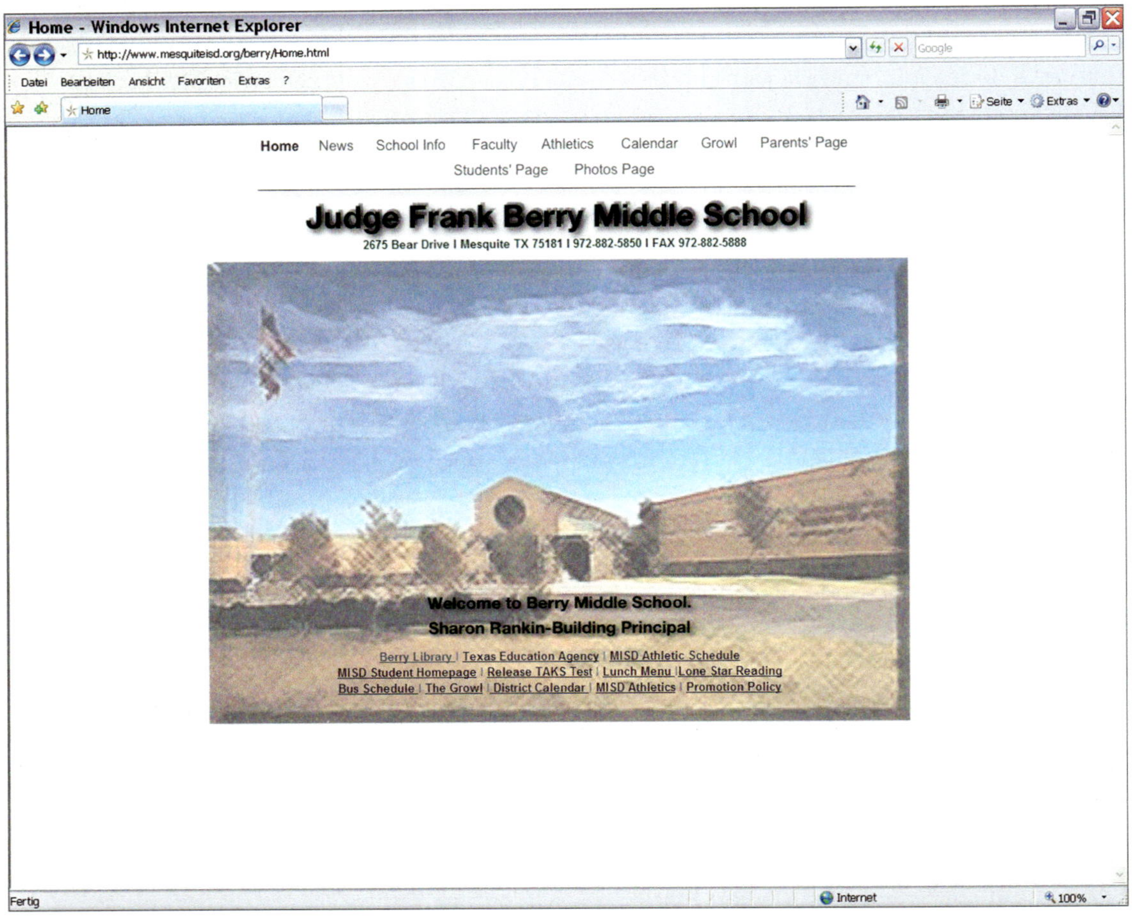

2 The layout

Do you like the layout of the website? Say why/why not. Talk about the size/choice/ … of the picture/the colours … .

[1]homepage ['həʊmpeɪdʒ] – *Homepage*, [2]atlas ['ætləs] – *Atlas*, [3]climate ['klaɪmət] – *Klima*

3 A web[1] quiz

Visit the high school's homepage (use a search engine) and answer the questions below. You will find the answers on the website. Who is fastest?

1. Find the names of the principal[2] and the assistant principals.
2. Find the class schedule[3]. When does the first period start?
3. Find the school motto.
4. Find five sports at Berry Middle School.
5. What is the 'Growl'?
6. Find the name of the nurse at Berry Middle School.
7. Who or what are the 'Bears'?

4 A closer look

a) *Now have a look at the homepage again. Do you get enough information about the topics? Which topic would you like to know more about?*

b) *Compare Berry Middle School with your school. What is the same, what is different? Talk to a partner.*

5 Your own homepage

Use the skills box and make a homepage for your class.

COMPUTER SKILLS

Before you switch on your computer	→ Collect ideas for topics: students, teachers, your last class trip …
Find a provider[4]	→ A provider is a company which offers space on the Internet for websites for example.
Think of a structure[5]	→ Plan it on paper first.
Work in groups	→ Each group chooses a topic. The group skills on page 48 can help you.
Decide on tasks	→ What do you have to do (take pictures, write texts …)? Make a list.
Decide on people	→ Who should do what and when? Make a plan.
Fill in your homepage	→ Put in all the information, pictures, etc. you have collected. Ask your teacher if you need help.

[1]web [web] – *das Netz,* [2]principal ['prɪnsəpl] – *Direktor/Direktorin,* [3]schedule ['ʃedju:l] – *Stundenplan,* [4]provider [prə'vaɪdə] – *Anbieter,* [5]structure ['strʌktʃə] – *Struktur, Aufbau*

Special days in the US

1

2

3

4

A

Remember the American soldiers[1]

Memorial Day is the last Monday in May. It's the day when Americans remember their soldiers who have died and are still dying for their country in war.

B

Stars and Stripes[4] and more

On July 4th Americans celebrate[5] the day in 1776 when they got their independence[6] from Britain. On **Independence Day** they have big parties, fireworks and parades. Many put on red, white and blue clothes (the colors of the American flag) and paint their faces in these colors.

C

"I have a dream …"

… is one of the most famous phrases in American history. Martin Luther King said it when he was fighting to get the same rights[2] for black and white Americans. On **Martin Luther King Day** (the third Monday in January) Americans remember this great leader[3].

D

Green rivers, green hair

No, this is not a special day for Greenpeace, but it looks like it. On **St. Patrick's Day** (March 17th) everything in the US is green! Irish people (and almost everybody else!) dye their hair green, wear green clothes, and in Chicago they even dye the river green for the day! And they don't like people who don't wear green clothes, so be careful!!

1 Different or the same? (see Presentation skills on page 57)

a) *Look at the texts and pictures and match them.*

b) *Which of these days are special days in Germany, too?*

c) *Do you know any other special days, for example in other countries? What is different? Talk about them in your group and present one special day to your class.*

[1]soldier ['səʊldʒə] – *Soldat/Soldatin*, [2]right [raɪt] – *Recht*, [3]leader ['li:də] – *Anführer/Anführerin*, [4]stripes [straɪps] – *Streifen (auf amerikanischer Flagge)*, [5]to celebrate ['seləbreɪt] – *feiern*, [6]independence [ɪndɪ'pendəns] – *Unabhängigkeit*

E

"Ich bin ein Berliner"

On the third Monday in February many Americans (but not all!) do not have to work. On this day they remember all American presidents. Some states celebrate Lincoln's birthday (February 12th) and/or Washington's birthday (February 22nd). No state has a holiday on all three **Presidents' Days**. Here's a funny little story about one president: In 1963 President Kennedy wanted to tell the people of Berlin that he was one of them. But he said, "Ich bin ein Berliner!" (I am a jelly doughnut[1])! The word 'ein' was one word too many.

F

Eat sausages and stay happy

It's never fun when summer holidays are over and school starts again. That's why **Labor[2] Day** is so great. This is the day on which America remembers its workers, and that's a good thing. But the best thing is that Labor Day is always on the first Monday in September. That means that it gives everyone a three-day weekend at the end of summer for parties and trips!

G

Turkey time

The US is a land of immigrants, and they are glad when people in their new country help them. The early English settlers[3] were glad, too, when the native Americans helped them during their first years in New England in the 17th century. They had their first **Thanksgiving** to say 'thank you'. Today Americans still get together on this day. It is always the fourth Thursday in November and many people travel from one end of the country to the other just to be with their family on this special day. They eat turkey and the famous pumpkin pie[4].

H

Vampire[5] meets old witch[6]

Have you already got plans for October 31st? I want to be a ghost this year. Last year I was a vampire and I met a real witch – she didn't even need to put on black clothes. We knocked on her door and when she opened it, we said, "Trick or treat[7]!" But she didn't give us any sweets. She told us that a long time ago **Halloween** was the night when people tried to frighten bad spirits[8] away. And we agreed with her. We decided to play a trick on her. We went back two hours later and made scary noises outside her house.

[1]jelly doughnut [ˌdʒeli ˈdəʊnʌt] – *Berliner,* [2]labor [ˈleɪbə] – *Arbeit,* [3]settler [ˈsetlə] – *Siedler/Siedlerin,* [4]pumpkin pie [ˌpʌmpkɪn ˈpaɪ]– *Kürbiskuchen,* [5]vampire [ˈvæmpaɪə] – *Vampir,* [6]witch [wɪtʃ] – *Hexe,* [7]treat [triːt] – *Süßigkeit,* [8]spirit [ˈspɪrɪt] – *Geist, Seele*

Scenes from American history

40,000 BC 1400 1450 1500 1550 1600 1650

Christopher Columbus was not the first person who landed in North America. People had lived there for many years before he arrived. About 40,000 BC the first settlers[1] came from Russia. At first they killed and ate mammoths[2]. Later they built homes and became farmers.
In 1492 Christopher Columbus sailed across the Atlantic Ocean and discovered America. He called the people who lived there 'Indians'[3] because he thought that he had reached India.
After that Europeans travelled to America to start a new life there. They came from countries like Spain, England and Ireland. They left Europe for many reasons, for example because they were hungry or had no jobs.

Christopher Columbus

Later slaves[4] were brought to the 'New World' which was a British colony[5]. There they had to work for white farmers.
Britain had lost a lot of money in wars. So they decided to put a tax[6] on paper, tea, etc. to get money again. In 1773 the people of Boston threw tea from ships into the water to say 'no' to the tax on tea. This event is called 'The Boston Tea Party'.
The American Revolution[7] began in 1775 and ended in 1783. The Americans fought against Britain because they wanted to become independent.
With the Declaration of Independence[8] in 1776 the colonies became the United States of America. George Washington became the first president.

A project: An information stand[9] (see Group skills on page 48)

Plan a stand about American history for your next school project week and tell the visitors about different topics: first settlers, Declaration of Independence …

[1]settler ['setlə] – *Siedler/Siedlerin,* [2]mammoth ['mæməθ] – *Mammut,* [3]Indian ['ɪndiən] – *Indianer/Indianerin,* [4]slave [sleɪv] – *Sklave/Sklavin,* [5]colony ['kɒləni] – *Kolonie,* [6]tax [tæks] – *Steuer,* [7]revolution [revl'u:ʃn] – *Revolution,* [8]Declaration of Independence [deklə'reɪʃn‿əv‿ɪndɪˌpendəns] – *Unabhängigkeitserklärung,* [9]stand [stænd] – *Stand*

George Washington

The war between the North and the South of America was from 1861–1865. One important reason for the war was the slavery[1] in the South. More than 600,000 people were hurt or killed during this war.
Martin Luther King was against revolution but he was also against the discrimination[2] of Blacks. They couldn't vote and they couldn't get good jobs. In the 1950s and 60s he tried to change this. King was killed in 1968.

Martin Luther King

1700 1750 1800 1850 1900 1950 2000 today

Step 1: Before you start

Make groups of four or five and decide which group should do which topic(s).

Step 2: Organize your work

In your group talk about what you have to do (for example find information, draw posters, etc.). Decide who does what and when. Make a plan. Look at the group skills on page 48 for help.

Step 3: Plan your stand

After you have finished your group projects, plan the information stand with your teacher.

[1]slavery ['sleɪvri] – *Sklaverei,* [2]discrimination [dɪˌskrɪmɪ'neɪʃn] – *Diskriminierung*

The wild 'Wild West'

1 History in pictures

a) *What do you think of when you hear the phrase 'Wild West'? Start a mind map.*

b) *Look at the pictures and read the captions to find out more. Add to your mind map.*

1 Before Europeans[1] arrived, there were lots of different tribes of natives[2] in the country.

2 In the middle of the 19th century European settlers[3] took land from the Native Americans, who they called 'Indians'[4]. The Indians fought back.

3 But they couldn't stop the settlers and had to move farther West. Many of them died on the way.

4 Many settlers were farmers with huge farms. The men who helped them were called 'cowboys'.

5 In 1840 they built the first railroad[5] so that people could travel faster from East to West. So even more land was taken away from the Native Americans, who called the train the 'Iron[6] Horse'.

6 Thousands of people went West when gold was found in 1848. Some of them were outlaws[7]. They robbed banks and trains.

c) *Why do you think it was called The 'Wild West'?*

[1]European [jʊərə'pi:ən] – *Europäer/Europäerin,* [2]native ['neɪtɪv] – *Eingeborener/Eingeborene,* [4]settler ['setlə] – *Siedler/Siedlerin,* [5]Indian ['ɪndiən] – *Indianer/Indianerin,* [6]railroad ['reɪlrəʊd] – *Eisenbahn,* [7]iron ['aɪən] – *eisern,* [8]outlaw ['aʊtlɔ:] *Gesetzloser/Gesetzlose, Bandit/Banditin*

2 A quiz on tribes (see Internet skills on page 56)

a) *Choose a Native American tribe (Cherokee, Navajo ...) for your group.*

b) *Find out about their history, traditions and where they live now. Use books or the Internet.*

c) *Write ten questions about your topic. Swap questions and answer them. Which group is fastest?*

3 Native Americans today

Use the diagram and the map and answer the questions.

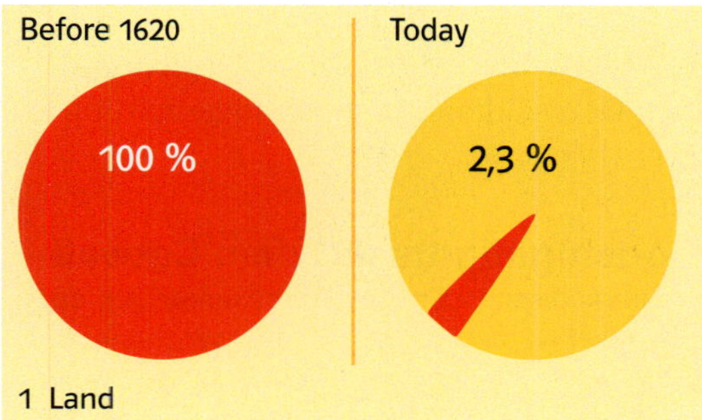

1 Land

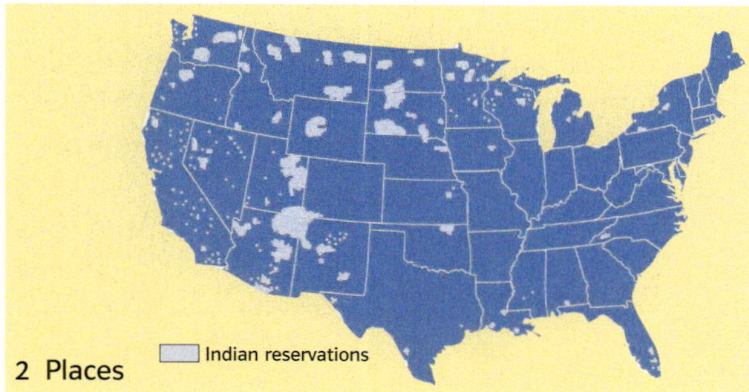

2 Places

1. What percentage[1] of land do the Native Americans now have?
2. Where are the reservations? Which is the biggest one? Where is it?

2, 33 4 A rap: Does Hawk[2] know why?

Kai Desheny ('Willow Tree')

Dear Rocks – millions of years old
New steel[3] – new, hard and cold
Hear! Wounded[4] Mountain lets out a cry
And Hawk up high wonders[5] why,
Flies round and round – over the ground
Do the Diné not hear his loud, warning sound?
No, they're too busy betraying[6] Mother Earth
Nowhere do we care – for what she is worth[7]!

Dear Father – so good, wise[8] and old
Yes, it is steel – and maybe it's cold
But hear! Wounded Diné – hear how we cry
Now, I wonder, does Hawk know why?
From o'er the reservation he looks down on the ground,
Where some drunk[9], jobless[10] Diné are just hanging around.
That's history – no mystery – of us Diné on Earth
So it's time, too, to care – for what WE are worth!

Listen to the rap about the 'Diné' (which means 'The People' in the Navajo language) and answer the questions.

1. Who is speaking to whom? What do you think?
2. What is the first speaker unhappy about?
3. Which lines tell you that people destroy the Earth?
4. What has happened to the Diné (second verse)? How can they change that?
5. Which speaker do you agree with? Why?

[1]percentage [pə'sentɪdʒ] – *Prozentsatz*, [2]hawk [hɔ:k] – *Falke*, [3]steel [sti:l] – *Stahl*, [4]wounded ['wu:ndɪd] – *verwundet*, [5]to wonder ['wʌndə] – *sich fragen*, [6]to betray [bɪ'treɪ] – *betrügen, verraten*, [7]worth [wɜ:θ] – *wert*, [8]wise [waɪz] – *klug*, [9]drunk [drʌŋk] – *betrunken*, [10]jobless ['dʒɒbləs] – *arbeitslos*

Mediation and communication

Unit 1

COMMUNICATION S K I L L S

In den letzten Jahrzehnten sind in einigen Themenbereichen viele neue Wörter entstanden, die so oder so ähnlich auch in andere Sprachen übernommen wurden, z. B. im Bereich „Kleidung und Mode". Beim Übertragen von Informationen in eine andere Sprache sind sie wichtige Schlüsselwörter, die die Verständigung erleichtern. Aber Vorsicht! Es gibt auch die so genannten *false friends*, die eine ganz andere Bedeutung haben. Diese musst du dir gut einprägen.

Situation: Dein/e Brieffreund/in aus der Modestadt New York ist bei dir zu Besuch und interessiert sich auch besonders für Modetrends in Deutschland. In eurer Tageszeitung findet ihr folgende Fotos mit Kommentar.

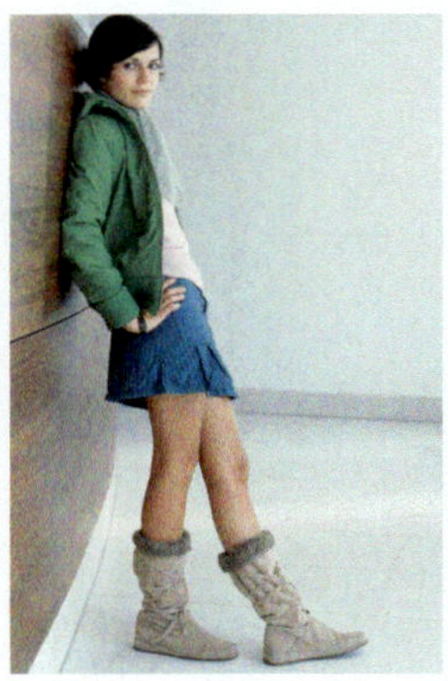

Modehighlights auf dem Catwalk
Diese modischen Ensembles bekamen auf der Modenschau im Cityhotel am Wochenende besonders viel Applaus. Zur weißen Hose trägt der Herr ein braunes Jackett, eine Art Freizeitlook für vielerlei Gelegenheiten. Die Dame präsentiert einen blauen Rock und einen multi-funktionalen Anorak, der besonders bei schlechtem Wetter nützlich sein kann. Passend zum Outfit gab es zusätzlich ein großes Angebot an Make-up und Aftershave-Präparaten sowie passende Handytaschen.

a) Ihr schaut euch gemeinsam Fotos und Text an. Übertrage die wichtigsten Informationen für deine/n Freund/in ins Englische.
- Welches Ereignis findet wo statt?
- Was gibt es dort zu sehen?
- Welche zusätzlichen Angebote werden gemacht?

b) Dein/e Freund/in hatte auch eine Menge verstanden. Welche gleichen/ähnlichen Wörter haben euch beim Übertragen besonders geholfen? Kennst du noch weitere?

c) Mit einigen Wörtern, die im Englischen unterschiedliche Bedeutung haben, hat dein/e Freund/in Probleme. Hilf ihm/ihr und erkläre die Begriffe.

1. Friend: I don't understand 'Modehighlight' and 'Modenschau'. 'Mode' means 'the kind' or 'the way'. Are they talking here about the way the models are presenting the clothes or what does it mean?
   You: 'Mode' is the German word for … .
2. Friend: In the US 'hose' means socks. But I can't see any in the photos. What does it mean here?
   You: The German word 'Hose' means … .
   Friend: In the US we call them 'pants'.
3. Friend: What is 'Handytaschen'? Something that's useful is called 'handy'. But I cannot imagine what 'taschen' could be. What do they want to say?
   You: …

Unit 2

COMMUNICATION SKILLS

Wenn du historische Texte liest, musst du daran denken, dass sich manche Wörter im Laufe der geschichtlichen Entwicklung verändert haben können und dass auch grammatische Regeln möglicherweise früher anders waren. Trotzdem kannst du mit deinen Kenntnissen das Wichtigste daraus ableiten. Suche die Schlüsselwörter und kombiniere logisch.

Situation: Bei einem Schulprojekt findet ihr beim Recherchieren im Internet auch diesen Text mit historischen Auszügen. Für euer Projekt sind folgende Fragen wichtig:

1. Wer war George Washington?
2. Worüber waren seine Regeln?
3. Hat er sie selbst geschrieben?
4. Was war seine 95. Regel?
5. Was machen die Amerikaner heute?
6. Was machen die Engländer?
7. Welchen Inhalt haben sinngemäß seine 94. und 98. Regel?
8. Gelten sie heute noch bei uns?

George Washington's Rules *of* Civility *&* Decent Behavior

Americans use a knife and fork differently from Europeans – and this goes back to George Washington (1732–1799), who was the first US president.
As a young boy he wrote his famous 110 rules on how to behave correctly.
He got his ideas from an old English book from the 17th century.

George Washington's 95th rule was
"Put not your meat to your mouth with your knife in your hand."

And that's just what we Americans still do today: We cut up our food, put down our knife, take our fork in our right hand and then eat with it. But most people in England today use knives and forks together. This habit came from France in the 18th century but it didn't reach America!

Some other rules say:
94th "If you soak bread in the sauce, let it be no more than what you put in your mouth at a time."
98th "Drink not nor talk with your mouth full neither gaze about you while you are drinking."

Unit 3

COMMUNICATION SKILLS

Bei technischen Geräten werden heute Gebrauchsanweisungen häufig in englischer Sprache mitgeliefert. Viele der verwendeten Wörter wurden inzwischen auch in den deutschen Sprachgebrauch übernommen. Es ist nützlich, wenn du dir diese gut einprägst.

Situation: Du besuchst mit deiner Familie Freunde in den USA. Zur Familie dort gehört auch ein zwölfjähriger Junge, für den du als Geschenk ein ferngesteuertes Spielzeugauto mitgebracht hast. Leider ist die Gebrauchsanweisung diesmal auf Deutsch geschrieben, und so musst du dem Jungen die wichtigsten Informationen übermitteln.

Dieses schnelle Auto ist außerordentlich schön. Es fegt durch die Straßen und garantiert Groß und Klein viel Spaß.
9,6 V Fahrakku, Fernsteuerung und Batteriebox gehören mit zur Ausrüstung. Türen und Dach öffnen automatisch.

Technische Daten: Länge: ca. 540 mm, Breite: ca. 280 mm, Höhe: 220 mm, Gewicht: ca. 1,6 kg

Funktionen: vorwärts, rückwärts, links, rechts

Für den Fahrakku benötigen Sie ein extra Ladegerät. Bei anderen Voltangaben muss ein Adapter benutzt werden.

1. Sage ihm, für wen das Auto gedacht ist.
2. Welche Ausrüstung gehört dazu?
3. Was sind die technischen Daten?
4. Welche Funktionen hat das Auto?
5. Die Voltangaben in den USA sind anders. Was braucht er?

Unit 4

COMMUNICATION SKILLS

Auf Flughäfen hört man häufig Ansagen für Fluggäste, die nicht immer leicht zu verstehen sind. Konzentriere dich deshalb auf Schlüsselwörter wie Namen, Zeit- und Ortsangaben sowie Zahlen. Beachte außerdem, dass die Hauptinformation meistens, wenn auch häufig mit anderen Worten, wiederholt wird. Höre deshalb konzentriert bis zum Schluss zu und versuche so, die fehlende Information zu erschließen.

L2, 34 **Situation:** Du bist mit deiner Familie in den USA und ihr wollt gerade den Rückflug nach Frankfurt antreten. Aus irgendwelchen Gründen verzögert sich das Einchecken noch. Ihr hört verschiedene Durchsagen und deine Mutter ist schon sehr nervös aus Angst, dass ihr etwas Wichtiges überhört haben könntet. Wie beruhigst du sie in diesen Situationen?

1. This is the final call for passengers on Flight 485 to Los Angeles. Please go to Gate 26 now. Any passengers for Flight 485 are asked to go to Gate 26 now. This is the final call for this flight.
   Sie denkt bei Ansage 1: Ihr müsst jetzt an Gate 26 einchecken.
2. This is a passenger announcement for Mr John Jones who is booked on the 11:20 flight to Denver. Please go to the information desk in the departure hall where a message is waiting for you. There is a message for Mr John Jones at the information desk in the departure hall. Please go there now.
   Sie denkt bei Ansage 2: Ihr sollt euch in der Abfertigungshalle melden.
3. This is an announcement for all passengers. Please do not leave your luggage anywhere. All passengers are asked to keep their things with them at all times. Any bags that are found without an owner will be taken away and destroyed.
   Sie denkt bei Ansage 3: Etwas mit eurem Gepäck ist nicht in Ordnung.

Unit 5

COMMUNICATION SKILLS

Wenn du dich mit jemandem unterhältst, musst du gleichzeitig das Wichtigste verstehen und sofort darauf sprachlich reagieren. Halte dich deshalb nie an einzelnen Wörtern auf, die du nicht kennst und nicht übersetzen kannst. Gib immer den Sinn dessen wieder, was gesagt werden soll, und finde dafür eine passende Ausdrucksmöglichkeit.

Situation: Du bist mit einem Freund auf der Berlinale. Ihr hofft, ein Interview für eure Schülerzeitung zu ergattern. Dein Freund ist für die Fragen zuständig. Deine Aufgabe ist es, die Fragen und Antworten jeweils aus dem bzw. ins Englische zu übertragen.

Friend: Wie viele Oscars haben Sie?
You: …
Film star: I've got three Oscars.
You: …
Friend: Wann wurde Ihnen der erste Oscar verliehen?
You: …
Film star: I was given my first Oscar in 1960 for 'Butterfield 8'.
You: …
Friend: Wurde er auch in deutschen Kinos gezeigt?
You: …
Film star: Yes, it was shown here but it wasn't very successful.
You: …
Friend: Warum sind Sie jetzt hier in Deutschland?
You: …
Film star: Well, I was invited by the organizers of the Berlinale.
You: …
Friend: Bekommen Sie dann eine Auszeichnung?
You: …
Film star: Perhaps. I don't know yet.
You: … – Well, good luck! Thanks for the interview.

Hallo! Hier beginnen die Grammatikseiten deines Schülerbuches. Erinnerst du dich? Wir sind Jack und Jane und helfen dir auch in diesem Jahr durch das Dickicht des Grammatikdschungels. Wir zeigen dir wieder Wege und auch Tricks, wie du gut durch den Dschungel hindurch kommst. So kannst du Grammatik begreifen und lernen, die Regeln im englischen Sprachgebrauch zu nutzen. Unser Freund Nutty ist auch wieder dabei und hilft dir, besonders schwierige Nüsse zu knacken. So bringen wir dich sicher ans Ziel und versprechen dir, dass wir auch eine Menge Spaß zusammen haben werden.

Erinnerst du dich? So arbeitest du mit dem Grammatikanhang:

GRAMMAR **SKILLS**

- Jeden Grammatikpunkt kannst du am besten verstehen, indem du ihn mit deinen eigenen Worten erklärst.

1. Lege dir dazu in deinem *folder* ein Kapitel *My grammar* an oder arbeite weiter mit deinen *grammar cards*. Notiere darauf die Überschrift des Grammatikpunkts und schreibe einige Beispiele mit Übersetzung. Formuliere nun die Regel.
2. Überprüfe alle Teile der Regel an Beispielen. Arbeite dabei mit verschiedenen Farben, Unterstreichungen usw.
3. Du kannst oft eine kurze Bildungsformel entwickeln, z. B. ***be + ing*** für das *present progressive*. Zusammenhänge und Regeln lassen sich auch grafisch darstellen. Hierfür kannst du deine eigenen Symbole entwickeln oder diese verwenden:

- - - - -➤	Dauer einer Handlung
X	Zeitpunkt
└────↑	Wort/Satzglied wird an eine andere Stelle gesetzt
- - - - -➤|	Ende einer Handlung

Du hast sicher selbst noch viele Einfälle.

- Reime und Eselsbrücken helfen beim Einprägen. Du kannst natürlich auch selber reimen!
- Zum Schluss kannst du an einer kleinen Aufgabe in *Test yourself* überprüfen, ob du alles verstanden hast.

G1 Die einfache Vergangenheit *The simple past*

Du benutzt das *simple past*, um zu beschreiben, was in der Vergangenheit geschehen ist. Dies signalisieren dir Wörter wie ***ago, yesterday, last*** … oder **Jahresangaben für historische Daten**.
Die regelmäßigen Verben bilden das *simple past* durch Anhängen der Endung ***-ed***.
Die Formen der unregelmäßigen Verben (**2. Stammform**) musst du auswendig lernen (vgl. Liste der unregelmäßigen Verben S. 207).
Bei Verneinungen verwendest du ***didn't*** vor der **Grundform des Verbs.**
Fragen beginnen mit ***Did*** bzw. mit **Fragewort** und ***did.*** Auch hier steht das Verb in der Grundform.
Achtung! In der deutschen Übersetzung verwenden wir oft dafür eine andere Zeitform, das Perfekt.

Yesterday, ago und *last* … stehen stets mit *simple past!*

Aussagen

More than 400 years <u>ago</u> immigrants start**ed** to go across the Atlantic.	*Vor mehr als 400 Jahren begannen/(haben) Einwanderer (begonnen), den Atlantik zu überqueren.*
In the <u>18th and 19th centuries</u> immigration **became** more and more popular.	*Im 18. und 19. Jahrhundert wurde Einwanderung immer populärer.*

Verneinung

They **didn't have** any food.	*Sie hatten kein Essen/nichts zu essen.*

Fragen

Did most of the immigrants **come** from Europe?	*Kamen die meisten Einwanderer aus Europa?*
Why did so many immigrants **come** to the US?	*Warum kamen/(sind) so viele Einwanderer in die USA (gekommen)?*

Das *simple past* von *am/is/are* heißt ***was/were***. Hier brauchst du bei Fragen und Verneinungen kein *did*.

Simple present – am/is/are, simple past – was/were. Na klar!

In 1845 there **was** famine in Ireland. We **were** all more dead than alive. The journeys on ships **weren't** easy. **Why were** the people more dead than alive?

My grammar
Schreibe die Beispielsätze zum *simple past* oben in dein Heft und erläutere deinem/r Nachbarn/in, worauf man bei jedem Satz achten muss. Nutze dazu die Regeln.

On their trip around the world Jack and Jane wanted to see the jungle.

Test yourself
Complete these sentences and answer the questions.
1. Jack and Jane … in the jungle[1] some time ago. (*to arrive*)
2. Why … they … their country? (*leave*)
3. What … they … at home? (*not have*)

[1]jungle ['dʒʌŋgl] – *Dschungel*

G 2 Die vollendete Vergangenheit — *The past perfect*

Mit dem ***past perfect*** kannst du ausdrücken, dass eine **Handlung in der Vergangenheit vor einer anderen** stattgefunden hat. Bei den regelmäßigen Verben bildest du diese Zeitform mit ***had*** und der **Grundform** des Verbs mit der Endung ***-ed***. Bei den unregelmäßigen Verben mit ***had*** und der **3. Stammform**. Da ***had*** ein Hilfsverb ist, brauchst du bei Verneinungen und Fragen kein *did*, sondern kannst mit ***hadn't*** verneinen und Fragen direkt mit ***Had*/Fragewort + *had*** beginnen.

Aussagen	
<u>After</u> they **had** landed, they went to the immigration station.	*Nachdem sie gelandet waren, gingen sie ins Aufnahmelager/sind sie … gegangen.*
Verneinung	
They **hadn't eaten** for days.	*Sie hatten seit Tagen nichts gegessen.*
Fragen	
Had they **eaten** anything before they arrived?	*Hatten sie etwas gegessen, ehe sie ankamen/angekommen waren?*
What had they **eaten** before they arrived?	*Was hatten sie gegessen, ehe sie ankamen/angekommen waren?*

G 3 Die Zeiten der Vergangenheit — *The past tenses*

The simple past

Handlungen, die in **der Vergangenheit stattgefunden haben**, werden mit dem *simple past* ausgedrückt.
Du verwendest es auch, wenn du in einer Erzählung oder einem Bericht **mehrere Ereignisse der Reihe nach** erwähnen möchtest.
Achtung: In der deutschen Übersetzung verwenden wir für die Vergangenheit manchmal das Perfekt.

The past perfect

Wenn du betonen möchtest, dass ein Ereignis **weiter in der Vergangenheit zurückliegt** als ein anderes, so drückst du das mit dem *past perfect* aus. Die nachfolgende Handlung steht im *simple past*. Dies zeigen dir Signalwörter wie ***when, before*** und ***after*** an.

<u>After</u> Dutch immigrants **had founded** New Amsterdam, the English **named** it New York in 1644.
Nachdem holländische Einwanderer 1613 New Amsterdam gegründet hatten, nannten es die Engländer 1644 New York.

My grammar

1. Suche aus der Zeittabelle S.10 noch weitere Sätze heraus, in denen betont wird, dass eine Handlung weiter in der Vergangenheit zurückliegt. Stelle die Handlungen grafisch dar. Markiere die frühere Handlung grün und die nachfolgende rot.
2. Erkläre dann deinem/r Partner/in die Regeln für die Verwendung der Zeiten. Schreibe eine Bildungsformel.

Test yourself

Translate this sentence and write it down.
Nachdem in Irland eine Hungersnot ausgebrochen war, gingen viele Menschen nach Amerika.

G 4 Das Perfekt

The present perfect

Du benutzt das *present perfect*, wenn du über eine **vergangene Handlung** sprichst, die du **mit der Gegenwart verbindest** bzw. von der ein **Ergebnis** vorliegt.
Dies signalisieren dir Wörter wie ***already, just, never*** und ***yet***. Du benutzt das Perfekt auch in Fragen mit ***ever***. Bei unregelmäßigen Verben wird das *present perfect* mit ***have/has*** und der **3. Stammform** gebildet. Bei regelmäßigen Verben folgt nach ***have/has*** das Verb mit der **Endung *-ed***.

Aussagen

I'm sure some of you **have** already **been** to the US. — *Ich bin sicher, einige von euch waren schon in den USA.*

Verneinung

You probably **haven't heard** about yearbooks. — *Ihr habt wahrscheinlich noch nichts von Jahrbüchern gehört.*

Fragen

Have you ever **visited** a high school in the US? — *Habt ihr schon jemals eine High School in den USA besucht?*

What has already **happened** during the year? — *Was ist schon im Lauf des Jahres passiert?*

Sollen *already, never* und *just* richtig passen, musst du sie zwischen den Verbteilen lassen.

Achtung! Im Deutschen steht das Objekt zwischen den beiden Teilen des Prädikats, im Englischen steht es immer dahinter.

My grammar

1. Schreibe zwei weitere Beispielsätze (S. 26) in dein Heft und übersetze sie ins Deutsche.
2. Unterstreiche die Signalwörter und markiere die Bildung der Zeitform. Wenn ein Objekt vorhanden ist, kringele die Position nach den Verbformen ein.
3. Erkläre nun deinem/r Nachbarn/in, welche Verbindung der Handlung zur Gegenwart besteht.

Test yourself

Jack and Jane are organizing a jungle party.
What have they done? What haven't they done yet?

G 5 Die modalen Hilfsverben

The modal verbs 'should', 'may', 'must'/'mustn't'

Mit den modalen Hilfsverben *should, may, mustn't,* kannst du ausdrücken, was jemand **tun sollte *(should)*, tun darf *(may)*, nicht tun darf *(must not/mustn't)*.** Du kannst damit also **Regeln, Empfehlungen** und **Verbote** ausdrücken. Sie sind für alle Personen gleich und können **nur im *simple present*** verwendet werden. Das **Vollverb** dahinter steht immer in der **Grundform**. Bei Fragen setzt du (wie im Deutschen auch) **das modale Hilfsverb einfach an den Anfang** der Frage bzw. hinter das Fragewort.

Aussagen und Verneinung

Absent students **should** make sure that the school gets an absence slip.	*Fehlende Schüler sollten sicherstellen, dass die Schule eine schriftliche Entschuldigung erhält.*
Students **must not** sign the slip.	*Die Schüler dürfen diese nicht unterschreiben.*
Only a parent or adult **may** do this.	*Nur ein Elternteil oder Erwachsener darf das tun.*

Fragen

What must students **not** do?	*Was dürfen Schüler nicht (tun)?*
May students with a problem contact their teachers?	*Dürfen Schüler, die ein Problem haben, sich an ihre Lehrer wenden?*

Beachte: Die Verneinung von *may* und *should* wird einfach durch Anhängen von *not* gebildet – *may not, should not (shouldn't).*
Jedoch: ***must not (mustn't)*** heißt **‚nicht dürfen'**. Die Verneinung von *must* ist *need not (needn't)* – ‚nicht müssen'.

My grammar

1. Mit welchen Modalverben drückst du eine Erlaubnis, eine Empfehlung oder ein Verbot aus?
2. Worin unterscheiden sich Modalverben und Vollverben? Nenne drei Unterschiede.

Test yourself

a) *Read the notices on the tree. Now write the jungle rules. Use 'must' or 'mustn't'.*

b) *Your friend has got some problems. What should your friend do?*

1. Your friend hurts his/her foot. (*go to the doctor*)
2. Your friend has taken a DVD from a shop. (*take back*)
3. Your friend has found a lot of money. (*go to the police*)

G 6 Das Passiv im *simple present* — *The passive voice: 'simple present'*

Erinnere dich: Für die Wortstellung im englischen Satz hast du bisher gelernt S – V – O. Ein Ding oder eine Person führt eine Handlung aus: *The program switches the lights on and off a few times.*
Das Programm knipst das Licht mehrfach an und aus.
Diese Betrachtungsweise nennt man Aktiv. (Das Programm/der Handelnde ist aktiv.) Es ist aber auch möglich, dass die Handlung selber (das, was mit einer Sache geschieht) wichtig ist, z. B.:
The lights are switched off and on a few times.
Das Licht wird mehrfach an- und ausgeschaltet.
(Hier ist nicht der Handelnde, sondern **das, was passiert, wichtig**.) Diese Betrachtungsweise nennt man **Passiv**. Solche Sätze werden häufig in **Zeitungsberichten, Protokollen oder technischen Beschreibungen** verwendet. Die Handelnden sind hier nicht bekannt oder für die Mitteilung nicht wichtig.

Aussagen

Everything **is done** by remote control.	*Alles wird mit der Fernbedienung gemacht.*
Any burglars **are frightened** away.	*Einbrecher werden abgeschreckt.*

Verneinung

The lights **aren't switched** on and off.	*Das Licht wird nicht an- und ausgeschaltet.*
The water **isn't turned** off.	*Das Wasser wird nicht abgestellt.*

Fragen

What is turned off?	*Was wird abgeschaltet?*
Are the lights **switched** on?	*Wird das Licht angeschaltet?*

Du bildest das Passiv im *simple present* mit ***am/is/are*** und der **3. Stammform des Verbs**.
Bei Verneinungen hängst du ***not*** an ***am/is/are*** an. Fragen beginnen mit ***Am/Is/Are*** bzw. **Fragewort** + ***am/is/are***. Soll der/die Handelnde(n) doch einmal im Passivsatz genannt werden, kann/können er/sie am Ende mit dem Wort ***by*** angefügt werden.

My grammar

1. Lies den Text auf S. 44 und schreibe drei weitere Beispielsätze heraus. Finde gute Übersetzungen.
2. Markiere die Verbformen und finde eine kurze Bildungsformel.
3. Erkläre deinem/r Nachbarn/in das Passiv. Gib Tipps.

Test yourself

a) *Look at the picture. What is done by the animals?*

b) *Today the animals are on vacation. What happens? Complete these sentences.*

1. The shopping … (*not do*).
2. The clothes … (*not wash*).
3. The sandwiches … (*not make*).
4. The floor … (*not clean*).

G 7 Bedingungssätze (Typ I) — *Conditional clauses (Type I)*

Bedingungssätze bestehen aus zwei Teilen: dem Nebensatz mit *if* und dem Hauptsatz.
Mit dem *if*-Satz drückst du eine Bedingung aus, mit dem Hauptsatz, was passiert, wenn diese Bedingung (nicht) erfüllt wird. Bei den Bedingungssätzen vom Typ I wird immer eine **erfüllbare Bedingung** ausgedrückt. *If you like adventure, you'll love this summer camp.* – Wenn du das Abenteuer liebst, wird dir dieses *summer camp* gefallen. (Das ist sicher.)
Der ***if*-Satz** steht dabei im ***simple present*** und im **Hauptsatz** wird meist das ***'will'-future*** verwendet. Der *if*-Satz kann am Anfang oder am Ende des Satzes stehen. Steht er am Anfang, wird er durch Komma abgetrennt.
Bei der **Verneinung** wird *will/'ll* im Hauptsatz zu ***won't***. Im *if*-Satz steht vor der **Grundform des Verbs *don't/doesn't***.
Achtung! In der deutschen Übersetzung wird manchmal anstelle des Futurs im Hauptsatz die Gegenwart verwendet.

Aussagen

***If*-Satz**	**Hauptsatz**
If you **like** photography,	then you'**ll love** this camp.
Wenn du gern fotografierst,	*wirst du dieses Ferienlager lieben.*

Verneinung

***If*-Satz**	**Hauptsatz**
If you **don't go** to this camp,	you **won't see** the ocean.
Wenn du nicht in dieses Ferienlager gehst,	*wirst du das Meer nicht sehen.*

If you let me out, I'll give you all my food.

My grammar

1. Schreibe einen weiteren Beispielsatz aus dem Text S. 62 in dein Heft. Markiere die erfüllbare Bedingung grün und das, was dann passiert, rot.
2. Warum ist die Bedingung erfüllbar?
3. Erkläre deinem/r Nachbarn/in, auf welche Fehlerquellen man bei Bedingungssätzen besonders achten muss.

Test yourself

Complete these sentences. Write them in your exercise book.
If it rains this afternoon, … .
If the weather is nice tomorrow, … .
If I go to the shops on Saturday, … .

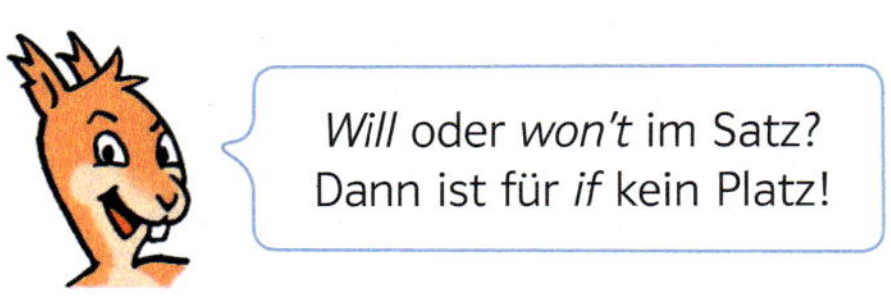

G 8 Bedingungssätze (Typ II) — *Conditional clauses (Type II)*

Bedingungssätze vom Typ II drücken eine **offene Bedingung** aus. Sie beschreiben zum einen Bedingungen, die zwar **prinzipiell noch möglich, aber relativ unwahrscheinlich** sind. (*If you went by plane, you would get there earlier.* – Wenn du mit dem Flugzeug flögest, wärst du eher dort.)
Zum anderen beschreiben sie aber auch Umstände, die nicht mehr anders eintreten können. (*If I was American, I would live in New York.* – Wenn ich Amerikaner/in wäre, würde ich in New York leben.)
Der *if*-Satz steht hier im ***simple past***. Er hat aber keine Beziehungen zur Vergangenheit, sondern drückt eine **gedachte Möglichkeit** aus. Im Hauptsatz steht ***would/'d*** vor dem Vollverb.
Der *if*-Satz kann wieder am Anfang oder Ende stehen. Steht er am Anfang, wird er durch Komma abgetrennt. Bei Verneinungen wird *would* zu ***wouldn't***. Im *if*-Satz steht ***didn't*** vor dem Vollverb.
Bei Fragen wandert ***would*** bzw. **Fragewort** und ***would*** an den Satzanfang.

Aussagen

My parents thought **I'd have** a great time if I **went** to a summer camp.
Meine Eltern dachten, ich würde eine tolle Zeit verbringen, wenn ich ins summer camp *führe/fahren würde.*
If I **was** at home, I **would go** to a disco.
Wenn ich zu Hause wäre, würde ich in die Disco gehen.

Verneinung

If you **were** with me, you **wouldn't like** it here at all.
Wenn du mit hier wärst, würde es dir überhaupt nicht gefallen.
If they **didn't find** me, they **would** phone the rescue services.
Wenn sie mich nicht fänden, würden sie den Rettungsdienst anrufen.

Fragen

What would they do if I **hid** behind the tree?
Was würden sie tun, wenn ich mich hinter einem Baum versteckte?
Would they **notice** if I **didn't come** back?
Würden sie es merken, wenn ich nicht zurückkäme?

Hier sind noch einmal die *simple past*-Formen von *be*.
Beachte: In *if*-Sätzen, besonders in der formalen Sprache, findest du manchmal auch *were* anstelle von *was* nach *I, he, she, it.*

simple past* von *be

I was	*we were*
you were	*you were*
he/she/it was	*they were*

My grammar
Gehe mit deinem/r Nachbarn/in noch einmal die Regel durch und finde für jeden Regelteil in den Beispielen einen Beleg.

Test yourself
Complete these sentences.
1. If I had lots of money, I'd … .
2. If I had holidays now, … .
3. If I worked on the moon, … .
4. If I didn't live in Germany, … .

If we lived in New York, we'd buy an umbrella.

G 9 Das Passiv im *simple past* — *The passive voice: 'simple past'*

Das Passiv im *simple present* hast du bereits gelernt (G 6). Wiederhole noch einmal die Bedeutung und die Bildung.
In **Zeitungsberichten, Protokollen oder technischen Beschreibungen** wird auch sehr häufig über Geschehnisse in der Vergangenheit berichtet. Dazu musst du das Passiv im *simple past* verwenden.
Du setzt *am/is/are* in das *simple past* und erhältst ***was/were***. Es folgt wieder das **Verb mit der Endung *-ed*** bei regelmäßigen Verben bzw. die **3. Stammform des Verbs** bei unregelmäßigen Verben.
Bei Verneinungen hängst du ***not*** einfach an ***was/were*** an. Dann folgt wieder das **Verb** mit ***-ed*** bzw. die **3. Stammform**. Fragen beginnen mit ***Was/Were*** bzw. **Fragewort + *was/were***.

Aussagen

The first series of stills which showed motion **was produced** in 1877. — *Die erste Serie von Standfotos, die Bewegung zeigten, wurde 1877 produziert.*

The first pictures **were taken** by a horse. — *Die ersten Bilder wurden von einem Pferd gemacht.*

Verneinung

The pictures **weren't taken** by a photographer. — *Die Bilder wurden nicht von einem Fotografen gemacht.*

Fragen

Was a photo **produced** when light fell on the film? — *Wurde ein Foto gemacht, als Licht auf den Film fiel?*

What was attached to each camera? — *Was wurde an jeder Kamera befestigt?*

My grammar

1. Überlege dir eine Bildungsformel für das Passiv im *simple past*.
2. Schreibe noch jeweils zwei Aussagen und zwei verneinte Sätze aus dem Text S. 78 in dein Heft und markiere die Formen, die für die Bildung wichtig sind.
3. Erkläre deinem/r Nachbarn/in anhand deiner Beispiele mit deiner Bildungsformel, was man zum Passiv im *simple past* wissen muss.

Test yourself

Look at the sentences that you wrote in G6. Imagine that Jack tells a friend later about what happened.

a) *Put the sentences into the simple past.*

1. The shopping was done by Nutty. 2. …

b) *What happened when the animals were on vacation?*

1. The shopping wasn't done … . 2. …

Grammatical terms

(Lateinisch) / Deutsch	Englisch	Englisches Beispiel
Adjektiv / Eigenschaftswort	adjective	quick, small, nice, old
Adverb / Umstandswort	adverb	always, often, quickly, loudly
Adverbialbestimmung des Ortes	adverbial phrase of place	to Stonehenge
Adverbialbestimmung der Zeit	adverbial phrase of time	last week, around 600 years later
Aktiv **G6**	active voice	The program switches the lights off.
Bedingungssätze **G7, 8**	conditional clauses	If it's sunny, we'll go swimming.
Demonstrativpronomen/hinweisendes Fürwort	demonstrative pronoun	this, that, these, those
Futur / Zukunft **G7**	'will'-future	It will be sunny at the weekend.
Häufigkeitsadverb	adverb of frequency	always, often, sometimes, never
Hauptsatz **G7, 8**	main clause	She will buy a key.
Hilfsverb **G5**	auxiliary	be, have got, do
Infinitiv / Grundform des Verbs **G1, 2, 5, 7**	infinitive	to do, to go, to see
Mengenangaben	expressions of quantity	some, any, a lot of, much, many
modales Hilfsverb / Modalverb **G5**	modal verb	must/n't, need/n't, should/n't
Nebensatz **G7, 8**	sub-clause	If she arrives late, ...
Objektpronomen	object pronoun	me, you, him, her, it, us, them
Passiv **G6, 9**	passive voice	Everything is done by remote control.
Perfekt **G4**	present perfect	Tom has painted the walls.
Personalpronomen / persönliches Fürwort	personal pronoun	I, you, she, he, it, we, you, they
Plural / Mehrzahl	plural	girls, children, babies
Plusquamperfekt / vollendete Vergangenheit **G2, 3**	past perfect	After they had explained their idea, the reporters wrote articles.
Possessivbegleiter / besitzanzeigendes Fürwort	possessive pronoun	my, your, his, her, its, our, their
Präposition	preposition	in, on, at, about, over
Präsens / einfache Gegenwart **G6, 7**	simple present	I live in Greenwich.
Präteritum / einfache Vergangenheit **G1, 3, 8, 9**	simple past	I watched TV yesterday.
Reflexivpronomen / rückbezügliches Fürwort	reflexive pronoun	myself, ourselves
Relativpronomen	relative pronoun	Sam is the boy who I like.
Relativsatz	relative clause	Everyone who lives here can speak English.
Signalwort **G3, 4**	signal word	last, ago, yesterday, ever, yet
Steigerung von Adjektiven	comparison of adjectives	old – older – the oldest, good – better – the best
Stützwort *one/ones*	prop word 'one/ones'	Which one do you like best?
Substantiv / Hauptwort	noun	book, dog, sandwich
Verb / Tätigkeitswort	verb	to be, to go, to do, to write
Verlaufsform der Gegenwart	present progressive	We are having a party.
Verlaufsform der Vergangenheit	past progressive	I was walking my dog in the park.
Vollverb	verb	to go, to do, to write
Wortstellung im Aussagesatz **G6**	word order in a sentence	S – V – O: The people rebuilt the stone circle.
Zusammensetzungen mit *some* und *any*	compounds of 'some' and 'any'	somebody, anybody, someone, anyone, something, anything, somewhere, anywhere

VOCABULARY

SKILLS

Diese Checkliste kann dir helfen, Fehler zu vermeiden und deine Rechtschreibung zu verbessern. Prüfe alle deine Texte damit.

- Schreibung:
  - ☐ ‚gh' wird meist nicht gesprochen. Vergiss es beim Schreiben nicht.
  - ☐ ‚k' kommt vor ‚t' so gut wie nie vor, z.B. action – Aktion, October – Oktober
- Gleiche Aussprache, unterschiedliche Schreibung:
  - ☐ [i:] z.B. **teacher**, **meeting**, **media**, **magazine**, **people**, **field**
  - ☐ [u:] z.B. **food**, **route**, **to do**, **swimsuit**, **supermarket**, **true**, **crew**
- Gleiche Aussprache, unterschiedliche Schreibung und Bedeutung:
  - ☐ [i:] z.B. **see** – sehen, **sea** – Meer; **meet** – treffen, **meat** – Fleisch
  - ☐ [u:] z.B. **two** – zwei, **too** – auch
- Verdoppelung der Endkonsonanten:
  - ☐ to stop – stopping, stopped
  - ☐ to plan – planning, planned
- ‚y' wird zu ‚ie':
  - ☐ in der 3. Person Singular: z.B. to carry – he carries; to cry – she cries; **aber**: to buy – she buys
  - ☐ im Plural: z.B. city – cities, party – parties; **aber**: boy – boys
  - ☐ bei der Steigerung von Adjektiven: z.B. happy – happier – (the) happiest; easy – easier – (the) easiest
- Ähnlich und doch anders:
  - ☐ Wortendung ‚le': z.B. *engl.* **simple** – *dt.* simpel; *engl.* **title** – *dt.* Titel; *engl.* **middle** – *dt.* Mittel
  - ☐ ‚ph' statt ‚f': z.B. *engl.* **phone** – *dt.* Telefon; *engl.* **photo** – *dt.* Foto
- Großschreibung:
  - ☐ Monatsnamen: z.B. January, July, December
  - ☐ Wochentage: z.B. Monday, Wednesday, Saturday
  - ☐ Eigennamen: z.B. Tom, Lisa, the Brooks, the London Eye, the Thames
  - ☐ geografische Namen: Bristol, Greenwich, Germany, Italy
- Plural:
  - ☐ Der Plural bekommt normalerweise ein -s: z.B. friend – friends, chair – chairs, film – films
  - ☐ Endet ein Wort auf s oder x, wird -es angehängt: z.B. bus – buses, box – boxes
  - ☐ Manche Wörter haben einen unregelmäßigen Plural: z.B. man – men, child – children, shelf – shelves, mouse – mice
- Apostroph:
  - ☐ bei Kurzformen: z.B. she is → she's; they are → they're
  - ☐ beim Genitiv-s: z.B. Sam's bike, Emma's family, the Jacksons' house, the children's games
- Wörterbuch:
  - ☐ Prüfe die Schreibung aller Wörter, bei denen du dir nicht ganz sicher bist, indem du sie im Wörterbuch nachschlägst.

Vocabulary

Auf den folgenden Seiten findest du alle neuen englischen Wörter und Ausdrücke. Sie stehen in der Reihenfolge, wie sie im Buch vorkommen. Diese Wortliste ist in drei Spalten aufgeteilt:

- Links stehen die englischen Wörter und Sätze.
- In der Mitte werden sie übersetzt.
- Rechts findest du Beispiele, Erklärungen und Tipps, die dir beim Lernen helfen.

Die fett gedruckten Wörter musst du lernen. Normal gedruckte Wörter solltest du wiedererkennen, wenn du sie hörst oder liest.
Gleich nach jedem neuen englischen Wort steht die Lautschrift in eckigen Klammern. Sie zeigt dir, wie das neue Wort ausgesprochen wird. Wie du diese Lautzeichen liest, siehst du unten.

Englische Laute

Mitlaute

[b]	bed	[p]	picture
[d]	day	[r]	red
[ð]	the	[s]	six
[f]	family	[ʃ]	she
[g]	go	[t]	ten
[ŋ]	morning	[tʃ]	lunch
[h]	house	[v]	video
[j]	you	[w]	we, one
[k]	can, milk	[z]	easy
[l]	letter	[ʒ]	revision
[m]	man	[dʒ]	page
[n]	no	[θ]	thank you

Selbstlaute

[ɑ:]	car
[æ]	apple
[e]	pen
[ə]	again
[ɜ:]	girl
[ʌ]	but
[ɪ]	it
[i]	happy
[i:]	teacher
[ɒ]	dog
[ɔ:]	ball
[ʊ]	book
[u]	January
[u:]	too, two

Doppellaute

[aɪ]	I, my
[aʊ]	now, mouse
[eɪ]	name, they
[eə]	there, pair
[ɪə]	here, idea
[əʊ]	hello
[ɔɪ]	boy
[ʊə]	sure

[:] der vorangehende Laut ist lang, z. B. *you* [ju:]

[ˈ] die folgende Silbe wird betont, z. B. *hello* [həˈləʊ]

In jeder *Unit* findest du Tipps zum Vokabellernen sowie einen Kasten mit *Useful phrases*, die dir helfen, dich auf Englisch zu verständigen.

Außerdem gibt es zu jeder *Unit* einen Kasten, in dem du Interessantes zur Landeskunde erfährst.

Am Ende der *Units* kannst du wieder nützliche Ausdrücke für deinen *Folder* sammeln.

Auf das *Vocabulary* folgt das *Dictionary*, eine alphabetische Wortliste aller englischen Wörter im Buch. Wenn du ein Wort nicht verstehst, kannst du es hier nachschlagen

Abkürzungen und Zeichen

pl	Plural, Mehrzahl	!	Achtung!
sing	Singular, Einzahl	↔	ist das Gegenteil von
10	Auf dieser Seite kommen die Wörter vor.	→	ist verwandt mit
		=	entspricht

! *Homework* hat keine Mehrzahl.
old ↔ new
teach → teacher
Dear Sam = Lieber Sam

Unit 1 I love New York

Erinnerst du dich an die Tipps vom letzten Schuljahr?

In den ersten drei Bänden hast du schon viele nützliche Tipps kennen gelernt, die dir das Vokabellernen erleichtern. Hier nochmals eine kleine Zusammenfassung zur Erinnerung:

- Lerne möglichst immer am gleichen Arbeitsplatz.
- Führe deine Vokabeldatei fort.
- Nimm dir mehrmals am Tag kleine Lernportionen vor, die du dann jeweils für eine kurze Zeit (10 Minuten) bearbeitest.
- Stelle für jedes neue Wort so viele Zusammenhänge wie möglich her.
- Gestalte das Lernen spannender, indem du mit anderen lernst oder Vokabellernspiele spielst.

Check-in

8	**background** ['bækgraʊnd]	Hintergrund	
	as [æz; əz]	*hier:* während	
9	**foreground** ['fɔ:graʊnd]	Vordergrund →	*foreground* ↔ background
	jogger ['dʒɒgə]	Jogger/Joggerin →	to jog → *a jogger*
	kickboard ['kɪkbɔ:d]	Kickboard, Roller	
	step [step]	Stufe, Schritt	
	neon ['ni:ɒn]	neonfarben →	There are lots of *neon* lights on Times Square.
	theater *(AE)* ['θɪətə]	Theater; Kino →	*theater (AE) – theatre (BE)*
	borough ['bʌrə]	Bezirk, Stadtteil →	Queens is one of New York's five *boroughs*.
	neighborhood *(AE)* ['neɪbəhʊd]	Viertel; Nachbarschaft →	*neighborhood (AE) – neighbourhood (BE)*
	hub [hʌb]	Mittelpunkt, Zentrum →	Times Square is the *hub* of Manhattan.
	native American [ˌneɪtɪv‿ə'merɪkən]	Ureinwohner/Ureinwohnerin Amerikas, Indianer/Indianerin →	The Mohawks are *native Americans*.
	native ['neɪtɪv]	eingeboren, einheimisch, gebürtig	
	skyscraper ['skaɪˌskreɪpə]	Wolkenkratzer →	A *skyscraper* is a very high building.
	harbor *(AE)* ['hɑ:bə]	Hafen →	*harbor (AE) – harbour (BE)*
	symbol ['sɪmbl]	Symbol, Sinnbild, Zeichen	
	freedom ['fri:dəm]	Freiheit →	free → *freedom*
	immigrant ['ɪmɪgrənt]	Immigrant/Immigrantin, Einwanderer/Einwanderin →	somebody who has left their home country and come to live in another one
	public ['pʌblɪk]	öffentlich →	private ↔ *public*

Language

10 past [pɑ:st]	vergangen; frühere/ früherer/früheres	
immigration [ˌɪmɪ'greɪʃn]	Immigration, Einwanderung →	immigrant → *immigration*

Interessantes über New York

In Manhattan verlaufen die Straßen in einem Raster wie mit dem Lineal gezeichnet. Die Straßen haben Nummern statt Namen und verlaufen entweder von Norden nach Süden (*Avenues* genannt) oder von Westen nach Osten (*Streets*). Viele Straßen in New York sind Einbahnstraßen. Hier gilt die Regel: Der Verkehr verläuft in Straßen mit geraden Nummern nach Osten, in Straßen mit ungeraden Nummern nach Westen. In New York leben etwa 5000 obdachlose Menschen in stillgelegten U-Bahntunneln. Diese Menschen werden *mole people* (Maulwurfmenschen) genannt. Sie leben meist in größeren Gruppen zusammen und haben sogar ihre eigene Kultur.

Etwa 35000 Läufer nehmen jedes Jahr am New-York-City-Marathon teil. Sie laufen am ersten Sonntag im November durch die verschiedenen Stadtteile und werden dabei von 12 000 Helfern betreut.

New Yorks größtes Kaufhaus „Macy's" hat eine Verkaufsfläche von 198 500 m^2 und verkauft über 50 0000 verschiedene Produkte. Ausländer erhalten bei der Anmeldung Gutschein für eine Reduzierung auf alle Produkte. So erhalten z. B. Deutsche in allen Geschäften der Kette 19 % Rabatt.

Würdest du gern in einer Großstadt wie New York leben? Was sind deiner Meinung nach die Vor- und Nachteile einer solchen Stadt im Vergleich zu deiner Heimatstadt?

to **emigrate** ['emɪgreɪt]	emigrieren, auswandern →	If you *emigrate*, you leave your own country to live in another one.
famine ['fæmɪn]	Hungersnot →	In a *famine*, people don't have enough to eat.
poverty ['pɒvəti]	Armut →	poor → *poverty*
war [wɔ:]	Krieg →	Countries at *war* are fighting against each other.
oppression [ə'preʃn]	Unterdrückung	
Dutch [dʌtʃ]	niederländisch; Niederländer/ Niederländerinnen	
to **found** [faʊnd]	gründen	
English ['ɪŋglɪʃ]	Engländer/Engländerinnen	
to **name** [neɪm]	(be)nennen →	If you *name* something, you give it a name.
Irish ['aɪrɪʃ]	Iren/Irinnen →	The *Irish* come from Ireland.
seasick ['si:sɪk]	seekrank →	If you feel bad on a boat or a ship, you are *seasick*.
ball [bɔ:l]	*hier:* Knäuel	
yarn [jɑ:n]	Garn, Faden	
farther and farther ['fɑ:ðə]	immer weiter	

farther ['fɑ:ðə]	weiter	
to **unwind**, **unwound**, **unwound** [ʌn'waɪnd, ʌn'waʊnd, ʌn'waʊnd]	sich abwickeln →	The balls of yarn *unwound*.
to **run out** [ˌrʌn‿'aʊt]	ausgehen *(Zeit)*, ablaufen *(Zeit)*; hinausrennen →	Time is *running out.* = There isn't much time left.
thread [θred]	Zwirn, Garn, Faden	
quota ['kwəʊtə]	Quote →	There were *quotas* for immigrants.
Belgian ['beldʒən]	belgisch; Belgier/Belgierin	
official [ə'fɪʃl]	Beamter/Beamtin	
little ['lɪtl]	wenig	
hope [həʊp]	Hoffnung →	to hope → *hope*
11 pros and cons [ˌprəʊz‿ənd 'kɒnz]	Für und Wider, Pro und Kontra, Vor- und Nachteile	
opinion [ə'pɪnjən]	Meinung	
research [rɪ'sɜ:tʃ]	Recherche, Forschung, Untersuchung	

Useful phrases: At the deli

Die folgenden *phrases* helfen dir im Restaurant oder im Deli.

Hi! I'd like a … and a …, please.	Guten Tag! Ich hätte gerne … und … .
Would you like it with or without … ?	Hätten Sie es gerne mit … oder ohne … ?
Can I also have some … ?	Kann ich auch … bekommen?
Would you like to have anything to drink?	Möchten Sie gerne etwas zu trinken?
OK. That's … dollars and … cents, please.	O.k. Das macht … Dollar und … Cent.
Here's … . Give me … and you can keep the change.	Hier sind … . Bitte geben Sie mir … und behalten Sie den Rest.
I hope you enjoy it!	Guten Appetit!

Everyday English

12 **deli** *(AE)* ['deli]	Imbissstube, Deli	
coffee ['kɒfi:]	Kaffee →	A lot of people drink tea or *coffee* in the morning.
to go [tə‿'gəʊ]	zum Mitnehmen	
Danish ['deɪnɪʃ]	dänisch; *hier:* Plundergebäck →	"I'd like a *Danish* and a coffee to go, please."
cupcake ['kʌpkeɪk]	rundes Küchlein →	A *cupcake* is a small cake.
pancake ['pænkeɪk]	Pfannkuchen	
maple ['meɪpl]	Ahorn	
syrup ['sɪrəp]	Sirup →	I love pancakes with maple *syrup*!
bacon ['beɪkn]	Schinkenspeck →	*Bacon* comes from pigs.
bagel ['beɪgl]	Bagel	
toast [təʊst]	Toast →	A lot of people eat *toast* for breakfast.
cream cheese [ˌkri:m 'tʃi:z]	Frischkäse	

	cream [kri:m]	Creme, Sahne	
	slice [slaɪs]	Scheibe →	a *slice* of bread
	pastrami [pəs'trɑ:mi]	Pastrami →	*Pastrami* is a kind of meat.
	turkey ['tɜ:ki]	Truthahn, Pute	
	French fries *(AE)* ['frentʃ ˌfraɪz]	Pommes frites →	*French fries (AE)* – chips *(BE)*
	milkshake ['mɪlkʃeɪk]	Milchshake →	milk + shake = *milkshake*
	strawberry ['strɔ:bri]	Erdbeere	
	cherry ['tʃeri]	Kirsche →	A *cherry* is a kind of fruit.
	monster ['mɒnstə]	Monster	
	vacation *(AE)* [və'keɪʃn]	Ferien, Urlaub →	*vacation (AE)* – holiday *(BE)*
	special ['speʃl]	Spezialität →	special → *a special*
	to **put in** [pʊt‿'ɪn]	hinzufügen	
	dollar ['dɒlə]	Dollar *(Währung)* →	"How much did you pay for the food?" – "Six *dollars* per person."
	free [fri:]	kostenlos, umsonst →	It's *free!* You needn't pay for it.
	tip [tɪp]	Trinkgeld →	Before you leave a café or restaurant, it's normal to leave a *tip*.
13	snack bar ['snæk bɑ:]	Café, Imbissstube	
	to highlight ['haɪlaɪt]	hervorheben, markieren	
	cent [sent]	Cent *(Währung)* →	There are a hundred *cents* in a dollar.
	dime [daɪm]	Zehncentstück *(Währung)* →	10 cents are a *dime*.
	nickel ['nɪkl]	Nickel *(Währung)* →	5 cents are a *nickel*.
	quarter ['kwɔ:tə]	Vierteldollar *(Währung)* →	25 cents are a *quarter*.

Get fit!

14	factual ['fæktʃʊəl]	Sach-, sachlich	
	unknown [ʌn'nəʊn]	unbekannt →	to know → *unknown*
	to note [nəʊt]	notieren	
	festival ['festɪvl]	Festival, Fest	
	either … or … ['aɪðə; 'i:ðə … ɔ:]	entweder … oder …	
	candy *(AE)* ['kændi]	Süßigkeiten →	*candy (AE)* = sweets *(BE)*
	lower ['ləʊə]	untere/unterer/unteres	
	low [ləʊ]	niedrig, tief →	high ↔ *low*
	population [ˌpɒpjə'leɪʃn]	Bevölkerung →	The people who live in a town or country are its *population*.
	mostly ['məʊstli]	überwiegend, hauptsächlich, größtenteils →	most → *mostly*
	such as ['sʌtʃ‿æz]	wie	
	Puerto Rican [ˌpwɜ:tə‿'ri:kən]	Puertorikaner/Puertorikanerin	
	paper ['peɪpə]	Papier; Zeitung; Dokument →	You use a pen and *paper* to write a letter.
	decoration [ˌdek'reɪʃn]	Dekoration →	People put up *decorations* for parties or festivals.
	firework ['faɪəwɜ:k]	Feuerwerkskörper; *Plural:* Feuerwerk	
	to **go on** [gəʊ‿'ɒn]	andauern; weitermachen →	The festival *goes on* for five days.

parade [pə'reɪd]	Parade, Umzug	
dragon ['drægn]	Drache →	In the Chinese tradition *dragons* bring good luck.
friendly ['frendli]	freundlich, nett	
business ['bɪznɪs]	Geschäft, Branche	
activity [æk'tɪvəti]	Aktivität →	to act → *activity*

Overheard

15	sidewalk *(AE)* ['saɪdwɔ:k]	Gehweg
	mansion ['mænʃn]	Villa
	house-sitter ['haʊsˌsɪtə]	Haussitter/Haussitterin
	steelworker ['sti:lˌwɜ:kə]	Stahlarbeiter/Stahlarbeiterin
	painter ['peɪntə]	Maler/Malerin

American English – British English I

Obwohl in den USA auch Englisch gesprochen wird, gibt es einige Unterschiede zu dem Englisch, das man in Großbritannien spricht. Wir unterscheiden daher *Britisch English* (BE) und *American English* (AE). Unterschiede gibt es bei der Schreibung und Aussprache, oder es wird im amerikanischen Englisch ein komplett anderes Wort verwendet.

American English (AE)	***British English (BE)***	***German***
apartment	*flat*	Wohnung
cab	*taxi*	Taxi
café	*cafeteria*	Cafeteria
*col**or***	*col**our***	Farbe
cop (slang)	*policeman*	Polizist
*fav**o**rite*	*fav**ou**rite*	Lieblings-
French fries	*chips*	Pommes frites
*harb**or***	*harb**our***	Hafen
***in** school*	***at** school*	in der Schule
*neighb**or***	*neighb**our***	Nachbar
*neighb**or**hood*	*neighb**our**hood*	Nachbarschaft
vacation	*holidays*	Ferien
yeah (slang)	*yes*	ja

Facts and fiction

16	**tour** [tʊə]	Tour, Fahrt, Reise →	a trip from one place to another
	pilot ['paɪlət]	Pilot/Pilotin →	A *pilot* flies a plane or a helicopter.
	cool [ku:l]	kühl	
	to **sit back** [ˌsɪt 'bæk]	sich zurücklehnen →	*Sit back* and enjoy the trip!
	to **relax** [rɪ'læks]	sich entspannen, sich ausruhen →	Are you worried? Just *relax*, everything is OK.
	to **roar** [rɔ:]	dröhnen →	The engine *roared*.

to **take off** [ˌteɪk‿ˈɒf]	abheben, starten, abfliegen	
very [ˈveri]	aller-	
yeah *(slang)* [jeə]	ja →	= yes
folks *(Anrede)* [fəʊks]	Leute *(Anrede)*	
loads of [ˈləʊdz‿əv]	viele →	There are *loads of* shops in Manhattan.
to **be into** [biː‿ˈɪntə]	interessiert sein an	
sort [sɔːt]	Art, Sorte →	all *sorts* of things
flat [flæt]	flach, platt →	Skyscrapers often have *flat* roofs.
to **point (to)** [pɔɪnt]	zeigen (auf), deuten (auf)	
apartment *(AE)* [əˈpɑːtmənt]	Wohnung, Apartment →	*apartment (AE)* – flat *(BE)*
snapshot [ˈsnæpʃɒt]	Schnappschuss →	If you take a *snapshot*, you take a quick photo.
to **flash** [flæʃ]	blitzen, blinken	
Fahrenheit (F) [ˈfærnhaɪt]	Fahrenheit →	100° *Fahrenheit* is 37.8 °Celsius.
dizzy [ˈdɪzi]	schwindelig →	Some people feel *dizzy* when they look down from a high building.
to **lean, leant, leant** [liːn, lent, lent]	(sich) lehnen	
forward [ˈfɔːwəd]	nach vorne, vorwärts →	to lean *forward*
17 **cop** *(AE)* [kɒp]	Polizist/Polizistin →	*cop (AE)* – policeman *(BE)*
round [raʊnd]	(um …) herum	
to **switch off** [ˌswɪtʃ‿ˈɒf]	ausschalten	
mister [ˈmɪstə]	*hier:* Sie *(Anrede)*	
to **faint** [feɪnt]	ohnmächtig werden →	Kim *fainted* when she hit her head.
heat [hiːt]	Hitze →	hot → *heat*
quite [kwaɪt]	ziemlich; ganz, völlig →	Andreas only started to learn English last year. He already speaks *quite* well. I'm *quite* sure. = I'm 100 % sure.
workman, workmen *(pl)* [ˈwɜːkmən; ˈwɜːkmen]	Handwerker →	to work → a *workman*
to **repair** [rɪˈpeə]	reparieren →	If something is broken, you can try to *repair* it.
electric [ɪˈlektrɪk]	elektrisch	
drill [drɪl]	Bohrer, Bohrmaschine	
so far [ˈsəʊ fɑː]	bis jetzt	
instruction [ɪnˈstrʌkʃn]	Instruktion, Anweisung	

Wordwise

18 opposite [ˈɒpəzɪt]	Gegenteil	

For my folder: New York

In dieser Unit hast du einiges über New York erfahren. Was würdest du unternehmen, wenn du einen Tag in New York verbringen könntest? Suche Fotos und mache ein Poster mit den verschiedenen Dingen, die du unternehmen würdest. Schreibe zu jedem einen Satz auf English.

Unit 2 A new school year

Lerntipp: Sprich verschiedene Sinne an

Das Gehirn merkt sich neue Informationen am besten, wenn so viele Sinnesorgane wie möglich mit der neuen Information beschäftigt werden:

- Lies dir die neuen Vokabeln erst leise durch.
- Lies die neuen Vokabeln nun laut vor.
- Schreibe die neuen Vokabeln ab. Am besten immer nur fünf auf einmal.
- Lasse dir die Vokabeln von jemand anderem vorlesen.
- Wiederhole nun das Schema so lange, bis du dir alle Vokabeln merken kannst.

Dieses Prinzip kannst du mit kleinen Änderungen auch für andere Fächer anwenden. Statt wie hier die Vokabeln abzuschreiben, kannst du die zu lernenden Infos zum Beispiel zu einem Text zusammenfassen, mit dem du genauso vorgehst.

Check-in

24 **curriculum** [kə'rɪkjələm]	Lehrplan, Stundenplan	
student ['stju:dnt]	Student/Studentin, Schüler/Schülerin →	*student (AE)* – pupil *(BE)*
high school ['haɪ ˌsku:l]	High School *(weiterführende Schule in den USA, Oberstufe)* →	A *high school* is a school in the USA for people between the ages of 14/15 and 18.
yearbook ['jɪəbʊk]	Jahrbuch →	a book which comes out every year, with information about events and students at the school
homecoming ['həʊmkʌmɪŋ]	Homecoming *(Schulfest an amerikanischen High Schools)*	
cheerleader ['tʃɪəˌli:də]	Cheerleader *(Mädchen, das in einer Gruppe eine Sportmannschaft anfeuert)* →	There are often *cheerleaders* at football games.
tryout ['traɪaʊt]	Auswahlverfahren →	to try → *tryout*
rally ['ræli]	Jugendtreffen, Versammlung; Rallye	
breaking news [ˌbreɪkɪŋ 'nju:z]	neueste Nachrichten	
difference ['dɪfrnts]	Unterschied →	different → *difference*
grade *(AE)* [greɪd]	Klasse; Note →	*grade (AE)* – year *(BE)*
prize [praɪz]	Preis →	something valuable which you get if you win a competition or do very good work
theme park ['θi:m ˌpɑ:k]	Freizeitpark	
guess [ges]	Vermutung	

25 to **pledge** [pledʒ]	geloben	
allegiance [ə'li:dʒns]	Treue →	to pledge *allegiance* to the flag
brand [brænd]	brand- →	I've just bought this dress. It's *brand* new.
homecoming queen [ˌhəʊmkʌmɪŋ 'kwi:n]	Ballkönigin	
captain ['kæptɪn]	Kapitän →	*captain* of a sports team
everybody ['evribɒdi]	jeder; alle →	*everybody* ↔ nobody
formal ['fɔ:ml]	formal, formell, förmlich	
dress [dres]	Kleid, Kleidung →	Everybody wears formal *dress* at the dance.
jeans *(pl)* [dʒi:nz]	Jeans →	I like blue *jeans*.
ballroom dancing [ˌbɔ:lrʊm 'dɑ:ntsɪŋ]	Gesellschaftstanz →	a formal kind of dancing
ballroom ['bɔ:lrʊm]	Ballsaal	
dancing ['dɑ:ntsɪŋ]	Tanzen →	to dance → *dancing*
supporter [sə'pɔ:tə]	Anhänger/Anhängerin →	A *supporter* agrees with you and helps you.
to **chant** [tʃɑ:nt]	rhythmisch rufen; singen	
pompom ['pɒmpɒm]	Pompon *(bunte Quaste der Cheerleader)* →	Cheerleaders wave *pompoms*.
cluster ['klʌstə]	Cluster	

Cheerleading

Das Wort *cheerleading* besteht aus den Begriffen *to cheer* (Beifall) und *to lead* (führen). Cheerleading bedeutet also sinngemäß „das Publikum zum Beifall führen". Mittlerweile trainieren die meisten Cheerleader-Mannschaften jedoch, um möglichst gut bei den Cheerleader-Meisterschaften auf nationaler und sogar internationaler Ebene abzuschneiden. Die ersten Cheerleader-Teams gab es 1898 in den USA, an der University of Minnesota. Dort war Cheerleading am Anfang ein reiner Männersport. Erst im Laufe der Zeit wurden auch Frauen zugelassen. Typische Sportarten, bei denen Cheerleader auftreten, sind American Football und Basketball, aber auch im Eishockey, Fußball und Handball wächst die Zahl der Cheerleader-Gruppen, die man auch Squads nennt.

Gibt es bei dir in der Nähe auch einen Cheerleader-Verein? Würde dir Cheerleading als Sportart Spaß machen? Denkst du es macht einen Unterschied, ob eine Sportmannschaft eine eigene Cheerleading-Gruppe zu Unterstützung hat oder nicht?

Language

26 to link [lɪŋk]	verbinden	
to **date** [deɪt]	sich verabreden →	If you *date* someone, you go out with them.
luckily ['lʌkɪli]	glücklicherweise →	lucky → *luckily*
to **have a look (at)** [ˌhæv‿ə 'lʊk]	anschauen, einen Blick werfen (auf) →	to look → *to have a look*
material [mə'tɪəriəl]	Material; Stoff →	things (for example ideas, information, etc.) which help you to make or write something
to **edit** ['edɪt]	bearbeiten →	You can *edit* a photo or a text.

	report [rɪ'pɔːt]	Bericht, Meldung; Zeugnis	
	advert ['ædvɜːt]	Anzeige, Werbespot →	This is a good *advert* for milk.
	to **think up** [θɪŋk‿'ʌp]	(sich) ausdenken	
	caption ['kæpʃn]	Untertitel, Bildunterschrift →	a short text, under a picture or cartoon, for example
27	**absent** ['æbsnt]	abwesend →	If you are *absent*, you are away.
	absence ['æbsns]	Abwesenheit →	absent → *absence*
	slip [slɪp]	Beleg, Schein →	If you are absent from school, you must bring an absence *slip*.
	parent ['peərnt]	Elternteil →	*parent* = mother or father
	adult ['ædʌlt]	Erwachsener/Erwachsene →	child ↔ *adult*
	may [meɪ]	*hier:* dürfen	
	alcohol ['ælkəhɒl]	Alkohol	
	drug [drʌg]	Droge; Medikament *(im Amerikanischen)* →	You mustn't bring alcohol or *drugs* to school.
	tobacco [tə'bækəʊ]	Tabak →	*Tobacco* smoke is very unhealthy.
	to **belong (to)** [bɪ'lɒŋ]	gehören (zu) →	Who does this bag *belong to?* = Whose bag is this?
	gang [gæŋ]	Gang, Bande	
	zone [zəʊn]	Zone	
	recess *(AE)* ['rɪses]	Pause →	A *recess* is a break.
	permission [pə'mɪʃn]	Erlaubnis	
	straight [streɪt]	gerade, direkt →	Let's go *straight* to our lesson.
	to **contact** ['kɒntækt]	kontaktieren, sich in Verbindung setzen mit →	If you want to *contact* someone, you can call them or write an e-mail.
	period *(AE)* ['pɪəriəd]	Unterrichtsstunde; Periode, Zeitabschnitt →	*period (AE)* – lesson *(BE)*

Useful phrases: Dating

Wenn du mit einem Mädchen oder einem Jungen ausgehen möchtest, kannst du die folgenden *phrases* verwenden.

Hi, there! Would you like to go to the movies with me?	Hallo! Hast du Lust, mit mir ins Kino gehen?
Do you want to go to the dance with me?	Möchtest du mit mir zur Tanzparty gehen?
Oh yes, that would be great!	Oh ja, das wäre toll!
Yes, I'd love to go with you!	Ja, ich würde gern mit dir hingehen!
Thank you, but I've already got other plans for the weekend.	Danke, aber ich habe schon andere Pläne fürs Wochenende.
Oh, I'm so sorry! I'm already going out with … .	Es tut mir leid, aber ich gehe schon mit … aus.
Shall we meet at … ?	Sollen wir uns am … treffen?
I'll pick you up at eight o'clock.	Ich hole dich um acht Uhr ab.
You're looking cute.	Du siehst hübsch aus.
Well, I'll see you around.	Man sieht sich.

Everyday English

28	**date** [deɪt]	Verabredung →	If you want to go out with someone, you have to ask for a *date*.
	movies *(AE)* ['mu:viz]	Kino →	to go to the *movies (AE)* = to go to the cinema *(BE)*
	movie *(AE)* ['mu:vi]	Film →	A *movie* is a film.
	Hi, there! ['haɪ ðeə]	Hallo!	
	awesome ['ɔ:səm]	toll →	Wow, you look *awesome*!
	to **overdo, overdid, overdone** [ˌəʊvə'du:, ˌəʊvə'dɪd, ˌəʊvə'dʌn]	übertreiben →	If you *overdo* something, you do or say too much.
	attractive [ə'træktɪv]	attraktiv →	This girl is very *attractive*.
	thoughtful ['θɔ:tfl]	aufmerksam, fürsorglich →	to think → *thoughtful*
	jerk *(slang)* [dʒɜ:k]	Trottel →	Don't call anyone a *jerk*! It will make them very angry.
	kiss [kɪs]	Kuss	
	hot [hɒt]	toll; scharf →	My date wasn't so *hot*.
	still [stɪl]	*hier:* dennoch	
	to **end** [end]	beenden, abschließen →	*End* your date politely!
	See you around! [ˌsi: jə ə'raʊnd]	Bis dann! Bis … . →	Bye. *See you* then! *See you* later!
29	**move** [mu:v]	Schritt, Bewegung	
	hurtful ['hɜ:tfl]	verletzend →	to hurt → hurt → *hurtful*
	to **graduate** ['grædjueɪt]	den Schulabschluss machen →	If you *graduate*, you leave school *(AE)* or university *(BE)* after your final exams.
	mini ['mɪni]	Mini-	

Wortbildung I

Im Englischen kannst du durch das Anfügen der Endung *-ing* aus vielen Verben ein Nomen machen.

to begin	→	*the beginning*	der Anfang
to build	→	*a building*	ein Gebäude
to date	→	*dating*	Verabreden
to feel	→	*a feeling*	ein Gefühl
to mean	→	*the meaning*	die Bedeutung
to meet	→	*a meeting*	ein Treffen
to paint	→	*a painting*	ein Gemälde

Get fit!

30	to avoid [ə'vɔɪd]	(ver)meiden	
	to improve [ɪm'pru:v]	(sich) verbessern	
	to **pass** [pɑ:s]	bestehen →	to *pass* an exam or a test
	upper ['ʌpə]	oberer/obere/oberes	
	elementary school *(AE)* [elɪ'mentri ˌsku:l]	Grundschule →	the first school where American children go

	middle school *(AE)* ['mɪdl ˌskuːl]	Mittelschule *(weiterführende Schule in den USA, Mittelstufe)* →	Children at *middle school* in the US are usually 11 to 14 years old.
	public school [ˌpʌblɪk 'skuːl]	staatliche Schule (USA), Privatschule (GB)	
	correction [kə'rekʃn]	Korrektur	

Overheard

31	Attention! [ə'tentʃn]	Achtung!	
	any day ['enɪ deɪ]	jeden Tag	
	robotics [rə'bɒtɪks]	Robotertechnik	
	soccer *(AE)* ['sɒkə]	Fußball →	*soccer (AE)* – football *(BE)*
	chant [tʃɑːnt]	Sprechgesang →	to chant → a *chant*
	less [les]	weniger →	more ↔ *less*
	to **dare** [deə]	wagen, riskieren →	Nobody *dares* to go. = Everyone is too frightened to go.
	to **take care** [teɪk 'keə]	aufpassen, sich kümmern	

Facts and fiction

32	**(shopping) mall** [mɔːl]	Einkaufszentrum, Einkaufspassage →	Young people in the US often meet in a *mall* after school.
	right [raɪt]	genau, direkt →	She is *right* in front of me.
	latte ['lɑːteɪ]	Café latte →	a coffee drink with milk
	You're kidding. [jə 'kɪdɪŋ]	Du machst Witze. →	I don't believe you! *You're kidding!*
	embarrassed [ɪm'bærəst]	verlegen →	When you're *embarrassed*, you feel stupid and don't know what to say.
	to **cheer up** [tʃɪer‿'ʌp]	wieder guten Mutes sein →	*Cheer up!* = Kopf hoch!
	bro [brəʊ]	Bruderherz	
	Yuk! [jʌk]	Igitt! →	*Yuk*! That tastes horrible!
	to **start up** [stɑːt‿'ʌp]	eröffnen →	We must *start up* the dance.
	definitely ['defɪnətli]	definitiv, bestimmt	
	to **vote (for)** [vəʊt]	abstimmen, wählen, stimmen (für) →	The students *vote for* the homecoming queen.
	to **pose** [pəʊz]	(sich) darstellen, posieren	
	cheerleading ['tʃɪəˌliːdɪŋ]	Cheerleading	
	kind [kaɪnd]	freundlich, nett →	to be friendly and good to others
	to **hang around** *(AE)* [ˌhæŋ‿ə'raʊnd]	rumhängen, herumlungern	
	to **train** [treɪn]	trainieren →	Miles *trains* for football every day.
	guy [gaɪ]	Typ, Kerl; *pl.:* Leute	
	to **waste** [weɪst]	verschwenden →	Don't *waste* my time!
	to **gossip** ['gɒsɪp]	tratschen, klatschen, schwatzen	
	gossip ['gɒsɪp]	Tratsch, Klatsch	
	to **warm up** [wɔːm‿'ʌp]	(sich) aufwärmen	
	(not ...) at all [ˌnɒt ... ət‿'ɔːl]	überhaupt (nicht) →	If you hate something, you don't like it *at all*.

juice [dʒuːs]	Saft	
bar [bɑː]	Bar, Kneipe	
awful ['ɔːfl]	schrecklich, furchtbar →	another word for 'terrible'
to **pay for** [peɪ]	bezahlen	
honest ['ɒnɪst]	ehrlich →	That's not true! Be *honest!*
rival ['raɪvl]	Rivale/Rivalin, Konkurrent/Konkurrentin	
33 to **fill** [fɪl]	füllen →	full → *to fill*
arm [ɑːm]	*hier:* Ärmel →	A T-shirt has short *arms*.
suit [suːt]	Anzug	
band [bænd]	Band, Kapelle →	Peter plays in a *band*.
dance floor ['dɑːnts flɔː]	Tanzfläche	
to **step** [step]	treten, steigen, gehen →	step → *to step*
Hey, clumsy! ['klʌmzi]	He, du Tollpatsch!	
clumsy ['klʌmzi]	ungeschickt, tollpatschig →	She is really *clumsy*.
to **miss** [mɪs]	verfehlen	
front [frʌnt]	Vorderseite →	Some houses have a small garden at the *front*.
shoulder ['ʃəʊldə]	Schulter →	I can't use my left arm. My *shoulder* hurts.
to **fix** [fɪks]	*hier:* manipulieren →	She tried to *fix* the vote.
vote [vəʊt]	Abstimmung; Stimme →	to vote → a *vote*
to **lie** [laɪ]	lügen →	That's not true! You're *lying*!
mean [miːn]	gemein →	She was really *mean* to me. = She hurt my feelings.
couple ['kʌpl]	Paar	
character ['kærəktə]	Charakter; Figur	

For my folder: Schools

In dieser Unit hast du einiges über die amerikanische High School erfahren. Vergleiche die Paradise Valley Junior High School mit deiner Schule. Gibt es bei euch auch verschiedene Clubs oder AGs? Gibt es etwas Ähnliches wie einen „Homecoming-Ball"? Sammle Gemeinsamkeiten und Unterschiede und mache eine Tabelle.

my school	PVHS
football club	football club
…	baseball club
…	…

Unit 3 Our smart world

Lerntipp: Vokabeln nebenbei wiederholen

Lerne deine Vokabeln. Wenn du damit fertig bist, schreibe die Vokabeln, die dir Schwierigkeiten bereitet haben (beim Lernen oder bei der Aussprache), auf kleine farbige Kärtchen. Verwende pro Vokabel ein Kärtchen. Hänge diese nun an verschiedenen, gut sichtbaren Stellen bei dir zu Hause auf. Wähle Orte, an die du während des Nachmittags noch öfters kommen wirst (z. B. Kühlschranktür, Haustür, Telefon, Toilettenspiegel …). Jedes Mal, wenn du ein Kärtchen siehst, sprich die Vokabel dreimal laut.

Du wirst sehen: Bald kannst du dir diese schwierigen Vokabeln mindestens genauso gut merken wie die einfacheren.

Check-in

42	**smart** [smɑːt]	schlau, klug	
	space station ['speɪs ˌsteɪʃn]	Weltraumstation	
	space [speɪs]	Raum, Platz; Weltraum →	There is a lot of *space* in a castle, but there isn't a lot in a shed.
	outer space [ˌaʊtə 'speɪs]	Weltraum, Weltall	
	astronaut ['æstrənɔːt]	Astronaut/Astronautin →	An *astronaut* works in space.
	earth [ɜːθ]	Erde →	= our world
	to **control** [kən'trəʊl]	leiten, führen; überwachen, kontrollieren	
	scientific [ˌsaɪən'tɪfɪk]	wissenschaftlich →	a scientist → *scientific*
	equipment [ɪ'kwɪpmənt]	Ausrüstung, Ausstattung	
43	**tractor** ['træktə]	Traktor →	Farmers use *tractors*.
	to **plough** [plaʊ]	pflügen →	A farmer *ploughs* rows with a tractor.
	to **monitor** ['mɒnɪtə]	überwachen →	to watch something/someone carefully
	pacemaker ['peɪsˌmeɪkə]	Herzschrittmacher	
	virtual ['vɜːtʃuəl]	virtuell →	In a computer game, everything you do is *virtual*, not real.
	reality [ri'æləti]	Realität, Wirklichkeit →	real → *reality*
	robot ['rəʊbɒt]	Roboter	
	invention [ɪn'ventʃn]	Erfindung →	to invent → *invention*
	spin-off ['spɪn‿ɒf]	Nebenprodukt	
	research [rɪ'sɜːtʃ]	Forschung, Recherche, Untersuchung	
	agency ['eɪdʒnsi]	Agentur, Behörde →	NASA is the US space *agency*.
	to **operate** ['ɒpəreɪt]	bedienen; operieren →	If you *operate* a machine, you make it do its work.
	remote control [rɪˌməʊt kən'trəʊl]	Fernbedienung, Fernsteuerung →	You need a *remote control* for your TV.
	control [kən'trəʊl]	Kontrolle	
	to **explore** [ɪk'splɔː]	erkunden, erforschen →	If you *explore* a place, you travel around in it to find out what it is like.
	planet ['plænɪt]	Planet →	The Earth is a *planet*.

human ['hju:mən]	Mensch; menschlich →	*human* ↔ alien
to **defuse** [ˌdi:'fju:z]	entschärfen	
bomb [bɒm]	Bombe →	People use robots to defuse *bombs*.
spaceship ['speɪsʃɪp]	Raumschiff →	Astronauts travel in *spaceships*.
to **exist** [ɪg'zɪst]	existieren →	to live or to be there
to **launch** [lɔ:nʃ]	starten, abschießen	
shuttle ['ʃʌtl]	Raumfähre →	You can't launch a *shuttle* in bad weather.
satellite ['sætlaɪt]	Satellit →	Achtung Aussprache!
to **forecast, forecast, forecast** ['fɔ:kɑ:st; 'fɔ:kɑ:st; 'fɔ:kɑ:st]	vorhersagen *(Wetter)* →	forecast → *to forecast*
modern ['mɒdn]	modern	

Die NASA

Die **N**ational **A**eronautics and **S**pace **A**dministration (NASA) wurde 1958 gegründet. Sie ist die zivile US-Bundesbehörde für Luft- und Raumfahrt.
Zur Zeit ist die NASA mit anderen Ländern gemeinsam am Bau der Internationalen Raumstation (ISS) beteiligt. Ein weiteres aktuelles Projekt ist das Constellation-Programm. Es sieht vor, dass Menschen zum Mond und später auch zum Mars fliegen. Für solche bemannten Missionen wird das Space Shuttle eingesetzt. Das Space Shuttle ist außen mit hitzebeständigen Kacheln verkleidet, so dass es beim Wiedereintritt in die Erdatmosphäre nicht zu stark beschädigt wird und für weitere Missionen verwendet werden kann.
Viele Projekte der NASA werden aber unbemannt durchgeführt, indem Sonden und Roboter zur Erforschung losgeschickt werden. Hierfür verwendet man Raumkapseln, die nur einmal eingesetzt werden können, da sie beim Wiedereintritt in die Erdatmosphäre stark beschädigt werden. Auf unbemannten Missionen erforscht die NASA z. B. den Mond, unser Sonnensystem und vorbeifliegende Kometen.

Gibt es in Deutschland eine ähnliche Einrichtung wie die NASA? Wie viele deutsche Astronauten waren schon im All? Würdest du gern einmal zum Mond oder zum Mars fliegen?

Language

44	**intelligent** [ɪn'telɪdʒnt]	intelligent, klug, vernünftig →	An *intelligent* person learns quickly.
	high-tech [ˌhaɪ'tek]	high-tech →	*High-tech* homes are called 'smart' homes.
	by [baɪ]	von	
	to **switch on** [ˌswɪtʃ‿'ɒn]	einschalten, anmachen →	*to switch on* ↔ to switch off
	refrigerator [rɪ'frɪdʒreɪtə]	Kühlschrank →	A *refrigerator* keeps food fresh.
	to **cook** [kʊk]	kochen →	Have you ever *cooked* an Indian curry?
	sink [sɪŋk]	Waschbecken *(im Amerikanischen)*, Spülbecken	
	to **leak** [li:k]	auslaufen, lecken →	The bathroom sink is *leaking*.
	plug [plʌg]	Stecker, Stöpsel →	I left the *plug* in the sink.
	faucet *(AE)* ['fɔ:sɪt]	Wasserhahn	
	to **remove** [rɪ'mu:v]	entfernen →	to take away something
	to **run away** [ˌrʌn‿ə'weɪ]	ablaufen *(Wasser)*	

	to **dry** [draɪ]	trocknen	
	to **flood** [flʌd]	überfluten, überschwemmen →	The faucet is leaking and the bathroom is *flooded*.
	electrical [ɪ'lektrɪkl]	elektrisch	
	washing machine ['wɒʃɪŋ məˌʃi:n]	Waschmaschine →	I don't wash the clothes myself. I've got a *washing machine*.
	tumble drier ['tʌmbl ˌdraɪə]	Wäschetrockner	
	electricity [ˌelɪk'trɪsəti]	Elektrizität, Strom →	electrical → *electricity*
	to **cut, cut, cut (off)** [kʌt‿'ɒf, kʌt, kʌt]	(ab)schneiden	
	blackout *(AE)* ['blækaʊt]	Stromausfall →	If there is a *blackout*, there is no electricity.
	cell phone *(AE)* ['sel fəʊn]	Mobiltelefon, Handy →	*cell phone (AE)* – mobile *(BE)*

Everyday English

46	motel [məʊ'tel]	Motel	
	object ['ɒbdʒɪkt]	Objekt, Gegenstand	
	switch [swɪtʃ]	Schalter →	to switch on/off → a *switch*
	socket ['sɒkɪt]	Steckdose →	Put the plug in the *socket*.
	lamp [læmp]	Lampe, Leuchte	
	curtain ['kɜ:tn]	Vorhang →	Most people close the *curtains* when it gets dark outside.
	microwave ['maɪkrəʊweɪv]	Mikrowelle	
	hairdryer ['heəˌdraɪə]	Fön →	to dry → a *hairdryer*
	light bulb ['laɪt bʌlb]	Glühbirne →	light → *light bulb*
	adaptor [ə'dæptə]	Adapter	
	cord *(AE)* [kɔ:d]	Kabel; Schnur →	Mobiles don't have a *cord*.
	to **turn on** [ˌtɜ:n‿'ɒn]	einschalten, anmachen	
	to **keep** [ki:p]	*hier:* aufbewahren →	*Keep* the milk in the refrigerator.
47	to **drip** [drɪp]	tropfen (lassen), tröpfeln →	The faucet is *dripping*.
	dead [ded]	*hier:* leer →	The battery is *dead*.
	I'm afraid … [ˌaɪm‿ə'freɪd]	leider, Ich fürchte …	
	closed [kləʊzd]	zu, geschlossen	
	useful ['ju:sfl]	nützlich →	You can often use that phrase. So it's a *useful* phrase.

Useful phrases: Something's wrong

Die folgenden *phrases* helfen dir, wenn etwas kaputt ist oder nicht richtig funktioniert.

The light bulb is broken.	Die Glühbirne ist kaputt.
The bathroom sink is leaking.	Das Waschbecken im Bad läuft aus.
The faucet is dripping.	Der Wasserhahn tropft.
The TV isn't working.	Der Fernseher funktioniert nicht.
The battery is dead.	Die Batterie ist leer.
The plug is missing.	Der Stecker fehlt.
The cord is damaged.	Das Kabel ist beschädigt.

Get fit!

48 to lead, led, led [li:d, led, led]	führen	
layout ['leɪaʊt]	Layout, Anordnung	
result [rɪ'zʌlt]	Ergebnis, Resultat	
chance [tʃɑ:nts]	Chance, Möglichkeit, Gelegenheit	
task [tɑ:sk]	Aufgabe, Auftrag	
sleep [sli:p]	Schlaf →	to sleep → some *sleep*
stress [stres]	Stress; Betonung	
on time [ɒn 'taɪm]	pünktlich	
textbook ['teksbʊk]	Schulbuch →	A *textbook* is a school book.
order ['ɔ:də]	Reihenfolge, Ordnung	
code [kəʊd]	Verschlüsselung, Code	
fridge [frɪdʒ]	Kühlschrank →	*Fridge* is a short form for 'refrigerator'.
length [leŋkθ]	Länge →	long → *length*
warning ['wɔ:nɪŋ]	Warn-; Warnung →	a *warning* sound
plus [plʌs]	plus, zuzüglich →	There are twenty-three in our class *plus* our teacher.
recording [rɪ'kɔ:dɪŋ]	Aufnahme, Aufzeichnung →	to record → *recording*
to **brush** [brʌʃ]	putzen, bürsten	
to search [sɜ:tʃ]	(durch)suchen	

Die unregelmäßigen Verbformen

Auch wenn Verben unregelmäßige Formen haben, gibt es einige Hilfen, mit denen du sie dir besser merken kannst.

Bei einigen Verben sind die 2. und die 3. Stammform gleich:

to bring	***brought***	***brought***	bringen
to find	***found***	***found***	finden
to have	***had***	***had***	haben
to hear	***heard***	***heard***	hören
to leave	***left***	***left***	verlassen
to meet	***met***	***met***	treffen
to read	***read***	***read***	lesen
to teach	***taught***	***taught***	lehren
to win	***won***	***won***	gewinnen

Bei anderen Verben sind die 1. und 3. Stammform sehr ähnlich, wie z. B.

*to **be***	*was*	***be**en*	sein
*to **do***	*did*	***do**ne*	machen, tun
*to **give***	*gave*	***give**n*	geben
*to **hide***	*hid*	***hid**den*	verstecken
*to **ride***	*rode*	***rid**den*	fahren, reiten
*to **see***	*saw*	***see**n*	sehen
*to **write***	*wrote*	***writ**ten*	schreiben

Overheard

49	doll [dɒl]	Puppe	
	mechanic [məˈkænɪk]	Mechaniker/Mechanikerin →	Somebody who repairs cars, etc.
	advantage [ədˈvɑːntɪdʒ]	Vorteil	
	disadvantage [ˌdɪsədˈvɑːntɪdʒ]	Nachteil →	advantage ↔ *disadvantage*

Facts and fiction

50	**alien** [ˈeɪliən]	fremd, ausländisch	
	to **discover** [dɪˈskʌvə]	entdecken →	to find out
	secret [ˈsiːkrət]	geheim, heimlich →	These are *secret* papers!
	agent [ˈeɪdʒnt]	Agent/Agentin, Vertreter/ Vertreterin →	agency → *agent*
	to **...** **on** [ɒn]	weiter-	
	glasses *(pl)* [ˈglɑːsɪz]	*hier:* Brille	
	undercover [ˌʌndəˈkʌvə]	geheim, verdeckt →	an *undercover* agent
	actually [ˈæktʃuəli]	eigentlich, tatsächlich →	! *Actually* heißt nicht ‚aktuell'!
	Zap! [zæp]	Zapp!	
	memory [ˈmemri]	Erinnerung; Gedächtnis →	If you can remember things easily, you have a good *memory*.
	to **erase** [ɪˈreɪz]	löschen, ausradieren →	to remove something
	bug [bʌg]	Käfer, Wanze; Bazillus →	Most people don't like *bugs*.
	suspense [səˈspens]	Spannung →	An exciting story has a lot of *suspense*.
	mountain [ˈmaʊntɪn]	Berg	
	visa, visas *(pl)* [ˈviːzə]	Visum *(pl. Visa)*, Einreisebewilligung →	If you want to go to the US, you need a *visa*.
	factory [ˈfæktri]	Fabrik, Werk →	a large building or group of buildings where things are made
	worker [ˈwɜːkə]	Arbeiter/Arbeiterin, Angestellter/Angestellte	
	hell [hel]	Hölle	
	toothache [ˈtuːθeɪk]	Zahnschmerzen →	tooth → *toothache*
	dentist [ˈdentɪst]	Zahnarzt/Zahnärztin →	If you've got a toothache, you should go to a *dentist*.
	social security number [ˌsəʊʃl sɪˈkjʊərəti ˌnʌmbə]	Sozialversicherungs-nummer →	In the US, everyone needs a *social security number*.
	social [ˈsəʊʃl]	sozial, gesellschaftlich	
	security [sɪˈkjʊərəti]	Sicherheit	
	risk [rɪsk]	Risiko	
	illegal [ɪˈliːgl]	illegal, unrechtmäßig, rechtswidrig	
	thought [θɔːt]	Gedanke →	to think → a *thought*
	political [pəˈlɪtɪkl]	politisch →	*Political* trouble can make people's lives very difficult.
	band [bænd]	Bande	
	robber [ˈrɒbə]	Räuber/Räuberin →	to rob → a *robber*

	pain [peɪn]	Schmerz →	The feeling you have when something hurts a lot.
	couple ['kʌpl]	Paar →	A girl and her boyfriend are a *couple.*
	legal ['li:gl]	legal, rechtlich, Rechts- →	*legal* ↔ illegal
51	to **describe** [dɪ'skraɪb]	beschreiben →	*to describe* → a description
	V-shaped ['vi:ˌʃeɪpt]	V-förmig →	something which looks like the letter 'V'
	object ['ɒbdʒɪkt]	Objekt, Gegenstand	
	across [ə'krɒs]	*hier:* breit, im Durchmesser	
	air traffic controller [ˌeə træfɪk kən'trəʊlə]	Fluglotse/Fluglotsin	
	crew [kru:]	Crew, Besatzung, Mannschaft →	the people who work on a ship or a plane
	to **report** [rɪ'pɔ:t]	berichten; (sich) melden →	a report → *to report*
	investigator [ɪn'vestɪgeɪtə]	Ermittler/Ermittlerin	
	flare [fleə]	Leuchtfeuer; Lichtschein	
	whole [həʊl]	ganz	
	distance ['dɪstnts]	Distanz, Entfernung, Abstand →	Things that are in the *distance* are things that you can see that are far away (such as mountains).
	simple ['sɪmpl]	einfach; simpel	
	on board [ɒn 'bɔ:d]	an Bord →	*on board* a ship
	to form [fɔ:m]	formen, bilden	
	expert ['ekspɜ:t]	Experte/Expertin	

Check-out

54	passive ['pæsɪv]	passiv; Passiv	

For my folder: Technology

Nun kennst du schon viele Begriffe zum Thema „Technik“. Schreibe sie in deinen *folder* und lege für die Begriffe Wortfelder an.

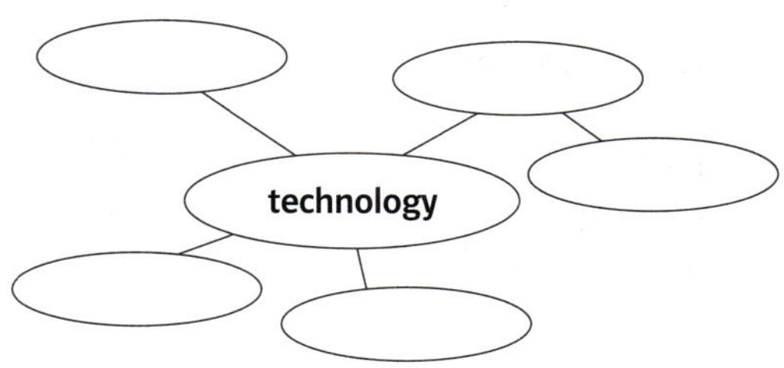

Unit 4 Home and away

11th june + 1,60-170 18 Sätze

Lerntipp: Lerne die schwierigen Vokabeln wie die Gedächtnisweltmeister

Kaum zu glauben, aber es gibt wirklich Weltmeisterschaften im Begriffemerken. Weltmeister wird derjenige, der sich in einer bestimmten Zeit die meisten vorgegebenen Begriffe in der richtigen Reihenfolge merken kann.

Besonders gut kann man sich schwere Vokabeln merken, wenn man sie mit etwas Bekanntem verbindet. Das bedeutet, wenn deine neue Vokabel zum Beispiel *to glow* (leuchten) ist, überlege dir einen deutschen Begriff dazu, mit dem du das Wort „leuchten" verbindest. Das funktioniert auch mit einem Beispielsatz, am besten mit einen ganz außergewöhnlichen:

- ***glow*** → leuchten → **Gl**ühwürmchen leuchten.
- *expressive* → ausdrucks**stark** → Espresso (klingt ähnlich wie *expressive*) ist ein **starker** Kaffee.

Probiere die Weltmeister-Methode aus und du wirst sehen, dass du dir schwierige Vokabeln viel leichter merken kannst.

Check-in

60	**reservation** [ˌrezəˈveɪʃn]	Reservat; Reservierung	
	canyon [ˈkænjən]	Schlucht, Canyon	
	scenery [ˈsiːnri]	Landschaft →	what you see around you when you're out in the country
	overwhelming [ˌəʊvəˈwelmɪŋ]	überwältigend →	The scenery is *overwhelming*!
	gorge [gɔːdʒ]	Schlucht, Klamm →	This *gorge* is very deep.
	sacred [ˈseɪkrɪd]	heilig	
	tribe [traɪb]	(Volks-)Stamm	
	national park [ˌnæʃnl ˈpɑːk]	Nationalpark	
61	**cowboy** [ˈkaʊbɔɪ]	Rinderhirte, Cowboy	
	ranch [ræntʃ]	Ranch →	Cowboys work on *ranches*.
	truck *(AE)* [trʌk]	Lastwagen, Truck	
	highway *(AE)* [ˈhaɪweɪ]	Bundesstraße, Highway	
	fabulous [ˈfæbjələs]	fabelhaft, fantastisch	
	sight [saɪt]	Sehenswürdigkeit; Sicht, Anblick →	what you can see or an interesting thing to see
	Interstate *(AE)* [ˌɪntəˈsteɪt]	Autobahn →	*interstate (AE)* – motorway *(BE)*
	trucker *(AE)* [ˈtrʌkə]	Lastwagenfahrer/ Lastwagenfahrerin, Trucker →	a truck → a *trucker*
	to **transport** [trænˈspɔːt]	transportieren →	to take from one place to another
	goods *(pl)* [gʊdz]	Güter, Waren →	things which you sell or buy
	vast [vɑːst]	riesig, ausgedehnt →	a *vast* country = a huge country
	roadside [ˈrəʊdsaɪd]	Straßenrand	
	diner *(AE)* [ˈdaɪnə]	Imbissstube	
	rodeo [rəʊˈdeɪəʊ; ˈrəʊdiəʊ]	Rodeo →	You can see lots of horses at a *rodeo*.
	motorbike [ˈməʊtəbaɪk]	Motorrad	
	casino [kəˈsiːnəʊ]	Casino →	a place where you can play games for money

brochure ['brəʊʃə]	Broschüre, Prospekt	
to include [ɪn'klu:d]	einschließen, beinhalten, aufnehmen	
search engine ['sɜ:tʃ ˌendʒɪn]	Suchmaschine	
search [sɜ:tʃ]	Suche	
image ['ɪmɪdʒ]	Bild, Image, Abbild, Vorstellung	

Las Vegas

Las Vegas ist wohl die berühmteste Spielerstadt der Welt. Sie wurde 1905 gegründet und liegt mitten in der Wüste von Nevada. Neben den unzähligen Spielautomaten, an denen man sieben Tage die Woche 24 Stunden lang spielen kann, ist die Stadt vor allem für ihre riesigen Hotels bekannt. Diese bieten neben großen Hallen mit Spielautomaten und Spielcasinos auch Touristenattraktionen, so dass viele Menschen extra nach Las Vegas kommen, um diese Hotels zu besichtigen.
Vor dem *Hotel Mirage* steht ein großer Vulkan tagsüber friedlich in der Lagune zwischen Palmen und Wasserfällen. Nach Einbruch der Dämmerung kündigt er seinen Ausbruch mit einem dumpfen Grollen an und speit dann Feuer und Lava bis zu 40 Meter hoch in die Luft.
Auf dem *Stratosphere Tower* des Hotels *Stratosphere Las Vegas* befindet sich in 350 m Höhe der höchstgelegene Vergnügungspark der Welt. Dort kann man sich noch einmal 48 Meter nach oben schießen lassen und für einige Sekunden die Schwerelosigkeit genießen, bevor man abgebremst wird. Das futuristische Kettenkarussell „Insanity" dreht sich außerhalb der Aussichtsplattform und ist nichts für schwache Nerven.
Im Hotel *Mandalay Bay* kann man im Shark-Reef-Aquarium gefährliche und ungewöhnliche Wassertiere aus aller Welt bewundern, wie z. B. 13 unterschiedliche Haifischarten, Krokodile, Meer- und Süßwasserfische und Seeschildkröten.
Im *Bellagio Hotel* spielen die vermögendsten Pokerspieler um die höchsten Einsätze. Um Eintritt zu erhalten, muss man bereit sein, um mindestens 80 000 Dollar zu spielen.

Würdest du gern nach Las Vegas fahren, wenn du volljährig bist? Warum/warum nicht? Gibt es auch Nachteile einer solchen „Spielerstadt"?

Language

62	if-clause ['ɪfklɔ:z]	if-Satz	
	simple present [ˌsɪmpl 'preznt]	Gegenwart, Präsens	
	camp [kæmp]	Camp, Lager →	a group of buildings or tents
	photography [fə'tɒgrəfi]	Fotografie →	a photo → *photography*
	course [kɔ:s]	Kurs	
	underwater [ˌʌndə'wɔ:tə]	Unterwasser- →	an *underwater* camera
	to **miss out (on)** [mɪss‿'aʊt]	verpassen, versäumen, zu kurz kommen (bei) →	You won't *miss out on* parties.
	No way! [ˌnəʊ‿'weɪ]	Auf keinen Fall!	
	cost [kɒst]	Preis, Kosten	
	all inclusive [ˌɔ:l‿ɪŋ'klu:sɪv]	alles inklusive	
	minimum ['mɪnɪməm]	Minimum	

	forest ['fɒrɪst]	Wald	
	camper ['kæmpə]	Camper/Camperin →	a camp → a *camper*
	cabin ['kæbɪn]	Hütte →	a small wooden house
	wood [wʊd]	*hier:* Wald →	in the *woods* = in the forest
	to **offer** ['ɒfə]	anbieten	
	whitewater ['waɪtwɔ:tə]	Wildwasser	
	rafting ['rɑ:ftɪŋ]	Rafting →	Whitewater *rafting* is a very exciting sport.
	campfire ['kæmpfaɪə]	Lagerfeuer	
	to **identify** [aɪ'dentɪfaɪ]	erkennen, identifizieren	
	track [træk]	Spur; Gleis →	Some animals leave *tracks* in the forest.
	bow [bəʊ]	Bogen	
	arrow ['ærəʊ]	Pfeil	
	to **produce** [prə'dju:s]	herstellen, produzieren, inszenieren *(Theaterstück)*	
	nature ['neɪtʃə]	Natur	
63	**counselor** ['kaʊnsələ]	Berater/Beraterin, Betreuer/Betreuerin →	*counselor (AE) – counsellor (BE)*
	to **mail** [meɪl]	mailen, per E-Mail schicken →	to send by e-mail
	pros and cons [ˌprəʊz‿ənd 'kɒnz]	Für und Wider, Pro und Kontra, Vor- und Nachteile	

Useful phrases: Problems

Die folgenden *phrases* können dir weiterhelfen, wenn du ein Problem hast.

Hi! Is that the airport?	Hallo! Ist da der Flughafen?
Hello! Is that the Turkey Hotline?	Hallo! Spreche ich mit der Truthahn-Hotline?
I have a problem.	Ich habe ein Problem.
I've had a breakdown.	Ich habe eine Panne.
I just saw/bought … .	Ich habe gerade … gesehen/gekauft.
Can you please tell me when there is a flight to … ?	Können Sie mir sagen, wann ein Flug nach … geht?
Can you please tell me how to cook the turkey?	Können Sie mir sagen, wie ich den Truthahn zubereiten muss?
Can you please tell me where I can find a rest area?	Können Sie mir sagen, wo ich einen Warteraum finde?

Everyday English

64	**holiday** ['hɒlədeɪ]	Feiertag →	There's no school today, it's a public *holiday*.
65	**motorway** ['məʊtəweɪ]	Autobahn	
	chaos ['keɪɒs]	Chaos, Durcheinander →	When everything goes wrong at the same time, there's *chaos*.
	delayed [dɪ'leɪd]	verspätet, verzögert →	If there's bad weather, flights are often *delayed*.
	by the way [ˌbaɪ ðə 'weɪ]	übrigens	
	hotline ['hɒtlaɪn]	Hotline	
	mom *(AE)* [mɒm]	Mama, Mutti →	*mom (AE)* – mum *(BE)*
	trunk *(AE)* [trʌŋk]	Kofferraum	

frozen ['frəʊzn]	gefroren	
to **thaw** [θɔ:]	auftauen →	You must *thaw* a frozen bird before you can cook it.
to **serve** [sɜ:v]	servieren; (be)dienen →	service → *to serve*
stranded ['strændɪd]	gestrandet	
breakdown ['breɪkdaʊn]	Autopanne; Zusammenbruch	
rest area ['rest ˌeəriə]	Rastplatz →	If you need a break during your trip, you can go to a *rest area*.
exit ['eksɪt]	Ausgang, Abgang, Ausfahrt	
dinner ['dɪnə]	Abendessen, Mittagessen	
over easy [ˌəʊvər‿'i:zi]	beidseitig gebraten *(Ei)*	
sunny side up [ˌsʌni saɪd‿'ʌp]	Spiegelei →	You can have your eggs over easy or *sunny side up*.
comfortable ['kʌmpftəbl]	komfortabel, bequem →	If your shoes are *comfortable*, they don't hurt your feet when you walk.
aspect ['æspekt]	Aspekt, Gesichtspunkt, Seite	
sheet [ʃi:t]	Blatt; Bettlaken	

Get fit!

66	statistics *(pl)* [stə'tɪstɪks]	Statistik	
	interest ['ɪntrəst]	Interesse	
	paragraph ['pærəgrɑ:f]	Paragraf, Absatz	
	to round off [raʊnd‿'ɒf]	abrunden	
	to connect [kə'nekt]	verbinden, anschließen	
	to repeat [rɪ'pi:t]	wiederholen	
	first of all [ˌfɜ:st‿ɒf‿'ɔ:l]	zuerst, zuallererst, zunächst	
	result [rɪ'zʌlt]	Ergebnis, Resultat →	What was the *result* of the survey?
	type [taɪp]	Typ, Art, Sorte →	a *type* of holiday = a kind of holiday
	per cent (%) [pə 'sent]	Prozent →	60 *per cent* of 10 students = 6 students
	secondly ['sekndli]	zweitens	
	skiing ['ski:ɪŋ]	Skifahren →	You can go *skiing* in Canada, too.

American English – British English II

Zwischen *British English* und *American English* gibt es einige Unterschiede in der Aussprache.

	American English (AE)	British English (BE)
after	['æftə]	['ɑ:ftə]
ask	[æsk]	[ɑ:sk]
car	[kɑ:r]	[kɑ:]
work	[wɜ:rk]	[wɜ:k]
better	['bedə]	['betə]
water	['wɔ:də]	['wɔ:tə]

Overheard

67 chip *(AE)* [tʃɪp]	Chip	
carpet ['kɑ:pɪt]	Teppichboden	
cleaner ['kli:nə]	Raumpfleger/ Raumpflegerin, Putzkraft →	to clean → a *cleaner*
staff [stɑ:f]	Personal; Kollegium →	the people who work for a company, school, etc.
to **be allowed to** (do sth) [bi:‿ə'laʊd]	dürfen →	Children *aren't allowed to* drive cars.
to spot [spɒt]	entdecken, erkennen	

Facts and fiction

68 to **go places** [ˌgəʊ 'pleɪsɪz]	herumreisen	
to **cross** [krɒs]	überqueren, kreuzen →	across → to *cross*
border ['bɔ:də]	Grenze →	the line between one country or state and another
barman, barmen *(pl)* ['bɑ:mən, 'bɑ:men]	Barmann, Barkeeper	
Mexican ['meksɪkən]	mexikanisch; Mexikaner/ Mexikanerin	
to **end up** [ˌend‿'ʌp]	enden, landen →	I don't want to *end up* with a job which I don't enjoy.
driver's license *(AE)* ['draɪvəz ˌlaɪsnts]	Führerschein	
to **spray** [spreɪ]	(be)sprühen, lackieren →	We *sprayed* the car blue.
stuff [stʌf]	Zeug, Sachen →	= things
till [tɪl]	bis →	another word for 'until'
to **set off** [set‿'ɒf]	aufbrechen, sich auf den Weg machen →	to start a journey
might [maɪt]	könnte/könnten →	Maybe he'll play well in the match. He *might* even win it!
to **last** [lɑ:st]	dauern, anhalten →	Hot weather doesn't usually *last* very long.
anyway ['eniweɪ]	jedenfalls, sowieso	
pretty ['prɪti]	ganz schön →	Something that is *pretty* good is really quite good.
experience [ɪk'spɪəriənts]	Erfahrung, Erlebnis	
restroom *(AE)* ['restrʊm]	Toilette →	*restroom (AE)* – toilet(s) *(BE)*
entrance ['entrənts]	Eingang; Eintritt →	The place – often a gate or door – where you go in.
parking lot *(AE)* ['pɑ:kɪŋ ˌlɒt]	Parkplatz	
to **fiddle (with)** ['fɪdl]	herumfummeln (an)	
to **stick, stuck, stuck** [stɪk, stʌk, stʌk]	kleben; stecken	
gonna (= going to) ['gɒnə]	werden	
to **get it** ['get‿ɪt]	*hier:* bestraft werden	
That was a close one. [ˌðæt wəz‿ə 'kləʊz‿wʌn]	Das war knapp.	

	all right [ɔːl 'raɪt]	gut; in Ordnung, alles klar →	= OK
	to **get lucky** *(AE)*	Glück haben	
	picker ['pɪkə]	Pflücker/Pflückerin →	to pick → a *picker*
	to **make friends (with)** [ˌmeɪk 'frendz]	Freundschaft schließen (mit) →	to meet a person who becomes a friend
	Spanish ['spænɪʃ]	spanisch, Spanisch	
	Hispanic [hɪ'spænɪk]	hispanisch, lateinamerikanisch; Hispano-Amerikaner/-Amerikanerin	
	to **feel homesick** [ˌfiːl 'həʊmsɪk]	Heimweh haben →	If you *feel homesick*, you are sad because you miss your home.
69	**raid** [reɪd]	Razzia; Angriff →	There was a police *raid*.
	somehow ['sʌmhaʊ]	irgendwie	
	ride [raɪd]	*hier:* Mitfahrgelegenheit	
	bear [beə]	Bär/Bärin	
	to **attract** [ə'trækt]	anziehen	
	for miles [fəˌ'maɪlz]	meilenweit	
	access ['ækses]	Zugang →	If you have *access* to something, it is possible for you to use it or see it.
	graph [grɑːf]	Diagramm, Graph, Schaubild	

Check-out

72	to **warn** [wɔːn]	warnen; ermahnen	

Wortbildung II

Es gibt verschiedene Möglichkeiten, um aus einem Verb ein Nomen abzuleiten.

1. Du kannst die Endung *-ing* anhängen:

   to build → a building
   to meet → a meeting

2. Manche Nomen werden mit der Endung *-er* oder *-or* gebildet. Solche Nomen bezeichnen meistens eine Person:

   to ride → a rider
   to visit → a visitor

3. Es gibt auch die Endung *-ion*:

   to define → a definition
   to invent → an invention

4. Sehr oft haben auch Verb und Nomen dieselbe Form:

   to call → a call
   to dream → a dream
   to forecast → a forecast

For my folder: The USA

In dieser Unit hast du etwas über die verschiedenen Bundesstaaten und Regionen der USA gelernt. Zeichne oder kopiere dir den Umriss der USA. Trage die Bundesstaaten ein und schreibe jeweils zu jedem Bundesstaat dazu, was du bis jetzt darüber gelernt hast.

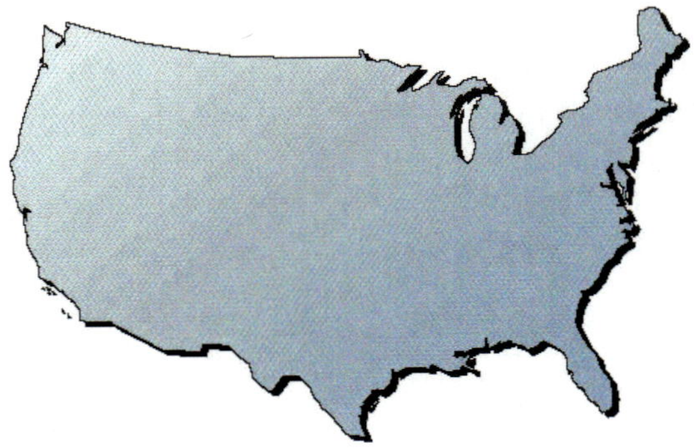

Unit 5 Stars in your eyes?

Slang words

In Internetforen oder SMS werden oft Slangausdrücke oder Abkürzungen verwendet.

2	*to*	*homie*	*friend*
2nite	*tonight*	*lil*	*little*
an'	*and*	*muzik*	*music*
any1	*anyone*	*peace*	*hi, hello*
bling bling	*jewellery*	*u*	*you*
boyz	*boys*	*ur*	*you're*
cu	*see you*	*uz*	*us*
cum	*come*	*wanna*	*want to*
c ya	*see you*	*ya*	*you*

Check-in

76	**designer** [dɪ'zaɪnə]	Designer/Designerin →	to design → a *designer*
	award [ə'wɔːd]	Auszeichnung, Preis →	There are movie *awards* in a lot of countries.
	evening dress ['iːvnɪŋ ˌdres]	Abendkleid	
	low-cut ['ləʊkʌt]	tief ausgeschnitten	
	backless ['bækləs]	rückenfrei →	a *backless* evening dress
	glamorous ['glæmrəs]	glamourös →	The women wear *glamorous* dresses at the Oscars.
	outrageous [aʊt'reɪdʒəs]	ausgefallen, gewagt; empörend →	This hairstyle is *outrageous*!
	to **hold**, **held**, **held** [həʊld, held, held]	halten, festhalten	
77	**production** [prə'dʌkʃn]	Herstellung, Produktion	
	trophy ['trəʊfi]	Trophäe, Preis →	The Academy Award is a *trophy*.

member ['membə]	Mitglied →	If you belong to a club, you are a *member* of it.
statue ['stætʃu:]	Statue, Standbild →	Oh look, that's not a *statue*, it's a man!
record ['rekɔ:d]	Schallplatte →	to record → a *record*
album ['ælbəm]	Album →	If there are more than two songs on a CD, it's an *album*.
category ['kætəgri]	Kategorie →	There are over a hundred *categories* of awards.
to **include** [ɪn'klu:d]	einschließen, beinhalten, aufnehmen	
R&B [ˌɑ:r‿n'bi:]	R&B	
Latino [lə'ti:nəʊ]	Latinomusik; Latino	
folk [fəʊk]	Volksmusik	
country ['kʌntri]	Countrymusik	
rock [rɒk]	Rockmusik; Stein, Felsen	
pop [pɒp]	Popmusik	
dancehall ['dɑ:nshɔ:l]	Dancehall *(Musikrichtung)*	
reggae ['regeɪ]	Reggae	
soul [səʊl]	Soulmusik; Seele	
ceremony ['serɪməni]	Zeremonie →	The actors get the awards at a *ceremony*.
carpet ['kɑ:pɪt]	Teppichboden	
press [pres]	Presse →	newspapers, magazines etc.
photographer [fə'tɒgrəfə]	Fotograf/Fotografin →	a photo → a *photographer*
attention [ə'tentʃn]	Aufmerksamkeit, Achtung	
picture ['pɪktʃə]	*hier:* Film	
nickname ['nɪkneɪm]	Spitzname	
to **present** [prɪ'zent]	präsentieren; verleihen	

Hollywood

Hollywood ist für viele der Inbegriff der Filmindustrie. Eigentlich ist Hollywood ein Stadtteil von Los Angeles und heißt übersetzt „Stechpalmenwald". 1911 wurde dort das erste Filmstudio gegründet und im selben Jahr siedelten sich noch zehn weitere Filmstudios dort an. Das sonnige Kalifornien war ideal zum Filme drehen, da es zu dieser Zeit noch kein geeignetes Kunstlicht gab.
Heute sind die wichtigsten Hollywoodstudios die *Universal Studios* (*Miami Vice, The Fast and the Furious, Bridget Jones*) und die *Warner Brothers* (*Herr der Ringe, Matrix, Harry Potter*). Wer nach Hollywood kommt, erwartet natürlich, überall Stars zu sehen. Auch wenn die Wahrscheinlichkeit relativ hoch ist, einen Prominenten zu sehen, wohnen die meisten von ihnen nicht direkt in Hollywood, sondern eher im nahe gelegenen Beverly Hills, in Malibu oder in anderen Teilen von Los Angeles.

Welche deutschen Filmproduktionen kennst du? Ist Hollywood für dich eine reine Glamourwelt oder siehst du auch Nachteile darin?

Language

78	**still (picture)** ['stɪl ˌpɪktʃə]	Standfoto →	A *still or still picture* is a photo.
	talkie ['tɔːki]	Tonfilm →	A *talkie* is a film with sound.
	motion ['məʊʃn]	Bewegung →	to move → *motion*
	complex ['kɒmpleks]	kompliziert, komplex →	Movies have become more and more *complex*.
	to **set up** [set‿'ʌp]	einrichten, aufbauen, gründen	
	string [strɪŋ]	Schnur, Kordel, Bindfaden	
	to **attach** [ə'tætʃ]	anbringen, anfügen, anhängen →	They *attached* strings to the cameras.
	shutter ['ʃʌtə]	Verschluss, Klappe, Blende	
	Kinetoscope [kɪ'netəskəʊp]	Kinetoskop	
	cabinet ['kæbɪnət]	Kasten, Schrank; Kabinett →	A *cabinet* is a box.
	rocket ['rɒkɪt]	Rakete →	NASA uses *rockets* to fly to the moon.
	western ['westən]	Western →	A *western* is a film with cowboys.
	to **publish** ['pʌblɪʃ]	veröffentlichen, publizieren, verlegen	
	rise [raɪz]	Aufstieg, Anstieg →	to rise → a *rise*
	(music) score [skɔː]	Partitur	
79	bracket ['brækɪt]	Klammer	
	to **receive** [rɪ'siːv]	empfangen, erhalten →	= to get
	serious ['sɪəriəs]	ernst, ernsthaft →	If something terrible happens, the situation is *serious*.

Music styles

alternative	Alternative	*Latino*	Latinomusik
country	Countrymusik	*pop*	Pop
dancehall	Dancehall	*punk*	Punk
folk	Volksmusik	*R&B*	R&B
funk	Funk	*rap*	Rap
heavy metal	Heavy Metal	*reggae*	Reggae
hip hop	Hip Hop	*rock*	Rock
independent (indie)	Independent (Indie)	*soul*	Soul
metal	Metal		

Everyday English

80	**matter** ['mætə]	Angelegenheit, Frage	
	to **matter** ['mætə]	von Bedeutung sein, ausmachen →	It doesn't *matter* how rich you are. It's what you do with your life that really *matters*.
	rapper ['ræpə]	Rapper/Rapperin →	to rap → a *rapper*
	guitar [gɪ'tɑː]	Gitarre →	play the *guitar*/play a *guitar* → David can play the *guitar*.

chat room ['tʃæt rʊm]	Chatroom *(Internetforum, wo man sich online unterhalten kann)*	
slang [slæŋ]	Slang	
to **register** ['redʒɪstə]	(sich) registrieren, (sich) anmelden	
to **post** [pəʊst]	aufgeben *(einen Brief)*, abschicken, posten *(im Internetforum)* →	You can *post* a message in a chatroom.
to **view** [vjuː]	anschauen, betrachten →	a view → to *view*
forum ['fɔːrəm]	Forum →	an Internet *forum*
gangster ['gæŋkstə]	Gangster/Gangsterin, Verbrecher/Verbrecherin →	'Gangsta' is a slang word for *gangster*.
bling bling *(slang)* [ˌblɪŋ 'blɪŋ]	Klunker →	*Bling bling* is a slang word for 'jewellery'.
to **freestyle** *(slang)* ['friːstaɪl]	improvisieren	
to **diss** *(slang)* [dɪs]	beleidigen; schneiden →	If you *diss* someone, you say something which makes them angry.
to **chill out** [tʃɪl‿'aʊt]	sich entspannen, chillen	
homie *(slang)* ['həʊmi]	Kumpel →	*Homie* is a slang word for 'friend'.
indie ['ɪndi]	Indie *(Musikrichtung)*	
musician [mjuː'zɪʃn]	Musiker/Musikerin →	music → musical → *musician*
metal ['metl]	Metal *(Musikrichtung)*; Metall	
suburb ['sʌbɜːb]	Vorort	
to **form** [fɔːm]	formen, bilden	
drummer ['drʌmə]	Schlagzeuger/Schlagzeugerin →	A *drummer* is a person who plays the drums.
bass [beɪs]	Bass →	! Achtung Aussprache: *'bass'* reimt sich auf 'face'.
funk [fʌŋk]	Funk *(Musikrichtung)*	
except [ɪk'sept]	außer →	Everybody's here, *except* Jenny.
disrespect [ˌdɪsrɪ'spekt]	Respektlosigkeit, Verachtung	
to **e-mail** ['iːmeɪl]	E-Mail schreiben →	! Statt *to e-mail* heißt es oft nur *to mail*.
to **check out** [tʃek‿'aʊt]	auschecken; *hier:* sich etwas ansehen	
81 **offer** ['ɒfə]	Angebot	
jam [dʒæm]	*hier:* Jamsession	
set [set]	Satz, Gerät	
to **give it a go** [ˌgɪv‿ɪt‿ə 'gəʊ]	es versuchen	
to **battle** ['bætl]	kämpfen →	= to fight
to **join** [dʒɔɪn]	beitreten, sich anschließen, verbinden →	Scott is new in the club – he *joined* last week.
volunteer [ˌvɒlən'tɪə]	Freiwilliger/Freiwillige	
battle ['bætl]	Schlacht, Kampf →	to battle → a *battle*
to **entertain** [ˌentə'teɪn]	unterhalten	
to **get back to** [get 'bæk tə]	zurückkommen (zu/nach); *hier:* sich melden (bei)	

Useful phrases: An Internet forum

Die folgenden *phrases* kannst du im Internetforum benutzen.

Do you have … ?	Haben Sie … ?
Do you sell … ?	Verkaufen Sie … ?
Has anyone got … ?	Hat irgendjemand … ?
Is … your style?	Gefällt Ihnen … ?
Are you interested in … ?	Interessieren Sie sich für … ?
Then please give me your e-mail address.	Bitte geben Sie mir Ihre E-Mail-Adresse.
Contact … as soon as possible.	Bitte nehmen Sie so schnell wie möglich Kontakt mit … auf.
If you like it, then give it a go.	Wenn es Ihnen gefällt, probieren Sie es doch.
Please contact … .	Bitte wenden Sie sich an … .

Get fit!

82 lyrics ['lɪrɪks]	Liedtext	
refrain [rɪ'freɪn]	Refrain	
to contain [kən'teɪn]	enthalten	
verse [vɜːs]	Vers, Strophe	
boulevard ['buːləvɑːd]	Boulevard, Prachtstraße	
shadow ['ʃædəʊ]	Schatten →	In the evening sun, *shadows* are longer than they are in the middle of the day.
heart [hɑːt]	Herz	
to **beat, beat, beaten** [biːt, biːt, biːtn]	besiegen, schlagen →	We're winning, come on, we can *beat* the other team!
edge [edʒ]	Rand, Kante	
vital signs *(pl)* [ˌvaɪtl 'saɪnz]	Lebenszeichen	
vital ['vaɪtl]	lebenswichtig, unerlässlich; Lebens-	
phrase [freɪz]	Redewendung, Ausdruck	
context ['kɒntekst]	Kontext, Zusammenhang →	Words can have different meanings in different *contexts*.

Overheard

83 **unfriendly** [ʌn'frendli]	unfreundlich	

Facts and fiction

84 **broke** [brəʊk]	pleite, abgebrannt →	If you are *broke*, you haven't got any money.
ass *(AE)* [æs]	Hintern, Arsch	
to **pop** [pɒp]	knallen (lassen) →	To *pop* means to open a bottle.
champagne [ʃæm'peɪn]	Champagner →	*Champagne* is very expensive.
lane [leɪn]	Fahrspur, Gasse	
flossy *(slang)* ['flɒsi]	aufgemotzt	
chorus ['kɔːrəs]	Refrain →	the part of a song that you sing again and again (between the different verses)

	chaperon ['ʃæprəʊn]	Begleitperson, Anstandswauwau	
	limousine [ˌlɪmə'zi:n]	Limousine →	A *limousine* is a big and expensive car.
	boogie ['bu:gi]	Boogie *(Tanzstil)*	
	pristine ['prɪsti:n]	makellos, rein →	= very clean
	raw [rɔ:]	grob, roh	
	no matter [nəʊ 'mætə]	egal	
	to **sip** [sɪp]	schlürfen, schluckweise trinken	
	to **reminisce** [ˌremɪ'nɪs]	zurückdenken, in Erinnerungen schwelgen →	= to think back, to remember
	caviar ['kæviɑ:]	Kaviar	
	to **deserve** [dɪ'zɜ:v]	verdienen →	Take it. You *deserve* it.
	but [bʌt]	*hier:* außer	
	to **have no clue** [ˌhæv nəʊ 'klu:]	keine Ahnung haben	
	bank [bæŋk]	Bank →	Take your money to the *bank*.
	lettuce *(slang)* ['letɪs]	*hier:* Geld	
	to **support** [sə'pɔ:t]	unterstützen, stützen →	If you *support* people, you agree with them and help them.
	fetish ['fetɪʃ]	Fetisch	
	lifestyle ['laɪfstaɪl]	Lebensart →	life → *lifestyle*
	though [ðəʊ]	trotzdem, dennoch	
	to **rock** [rɒk]	rocken; schaukeln →	rock → to *rock*
	dope *(slang)* [dəʊp]	*hier:* toll	
	damn [dæm]	verdammt →	People often say this when they are angry.
	daughter ['dɔ:tə]	Tochter	
85	collage [kɒl'ɑ:ʒ]	Collage	

Wordwise

86	everyday ['evrideɪ]	alltäglich	
87	least [li:st]	am wenigsten	
	synonym ['sɪnənɪm]	Synonym	

For my folder: Oscars

Finde die Namen der Gewinner der letzten Oscarverleihung heraus.
Wer hat den Oscar in diesen Kategorien gewonnen:

- bester Film
- bester Dokumentarfilm
- Regie
- beste Hauptdarstellerin
- bester Hauptdarsteller
- bester fremdsprachiger Film?

Dictionary

In dieser alphabetischen Liste ist das Vokabular von *Orange Line 1* bis *4* enthalten. Namen werden in einer gesonderten Liste am Ende des Vokabulars aufgelistet.
Das Zeichen ° bei einem Eintrag weist darauf hin, dass das Wort zum rezeptiven Wortschatz zählt.
Die mit * gekennzeichneten Verben sind unregelmäßig.
Wendungen, die aus mehreren Wörtern bestehen, werden meist unter mehreren Stichwörtern aufgeführt.
So ist z. B. *at home* unter *at* und *home* zu finden.
Die Fundstellen verweisen auf das erstmalige Vorkommen der Wörter, z. B.
absent ['æbsnt] abwesend **IV U2,** 27 kommt zum ersten Mal vor in Band IV, Unit 2, Seite 27.
colour ['kʌlə] Farbe **I LUA,** 24 kommt zum ersten Mal vor in Band I, Link-up A, Seite 24.
U = Unit, LU = Link-up, FA = Fakultativer Anhang (nur Namen)

A

a, an [ə; ən] ein/eine **I U1,** 10
a bit [ə 'bɪt] ein bisschen **I U2,** 35
a few [ə 'fjuː] einige, ein paar **II U4,** 52
a lot [ə 'lɒt] viel **II U1,** 15
a lot of [ə 'lɒt‿əv] viel/viele, eine Menge **I U2,** 30
a week [ə 'wiːk] pro Woche, in der Woche **II U4,** 52
about [ə'baʊt] über **I U3,** 40; ungefähr, circa, etwa **III U1,** 11
out and about ['aʊt‿nd‿ə'baʊt] unterwegs °**I U4,** 54
to jump about [ˌdʒʌmp‿ə'baʊt] herumspringen **III U4,** 68
What about … ? [wɒt‿ə'baʊt] Was ist mit …?; Wie wäre es mit …? **I U2,** 30
What's the film about? [wɒts ðə 'fɪlm‿əˌbaʊt] Wovon handelt der Film? °**II U3,** 43
above [ə'bʌv] oben, über, oberhalb **II U5,** 70
abroad [ə'brɔːd] im/ins Ausland **III U4,** 67
absence ['æbsns] Abwesenheit **IV U2,** 27
absent ['æbsnt] abwesend **IV U2,** 27
absolutely [ˌæbsə'luːtli] absolut, völlig **III U5,** 88
accent ['æksnt] Akzent **II U3,** 36
access ['ækses] Zugang **IV U4,** 69
accident ['æksɪdnt] Unfall **II U3,** 41
across [ə'krɒs] waagerecht *(im Kreuzworträtsel)* °**II U3,** 42; über, hinüber, quer durch/darüber **III U1,** 10; breit, im Durchmesser **IV U3,** 51
to **act** [ækt] spielen *(Theater)* **I U7,** 90
action ['ækʃn] Handlung, Aktion **III U1,** 9
active ['æktɪv] aktiv **III U1,** 12
activity [æk'tɪvəti] Aktivität **IV U1,** 14
actor ['æktə] Schauspieler **I U7,** 96
actress ['æktrəs] Schauspielerin **III U2,** 29
actually ['æktʃuəli] eigentlich, tatsächlich **IV U3,** 50
adaptor [ə'dæptə] Adapter **IV U3,** 46
to **add** [æd] hinzufügen, addieren **III U2,** 30
address [ə'dres] Adresse **I U5,** 70
adjective ['ædʒəktɪv] Adjektiv, Eigenschaftswort °**I U1,** 22
adult ['ædʌlt] Erwachsener/ Erwachsene **IV U2,** 27
advanced [əd'vɑːnst] fortgeschritten **III U4,** 67
advantage [əd'vɑːntɪdʒ] Vorteil °**IV U3,** 49
adventure [əd'ventʃə] Abenteuer **II U6,** 80
adverb ['ædvɜːb] Adverb °**II U7,** 90
adverb of manner [ˌædvɜːb‿əv 'mænə] Adverb der Art und Weise °**II U7,** 90
advert ['ædvɜːt] Anzeige, Werbespot **IV U2,** 26
advice [əd'vaɪs] Rat, Ratschlag °**II U4,** 52
to **advise** [əd'vaɪz] raten **III U4,** 69
I'm **afraid …** [ˌaɪm‿ə'freɪd] leider, Ich fürchte … °**IV U3,** 47
after ['ɑːftə] nach **I LUB,** 39; nachdem **III U2,** 30
afternoon [ˌɑːftə'nuːn] Nachmittag **I U2,** 34
afternoon tea [ˌɑːftənuːn 'tiː] Nachmittagstee **I U7,** 94
in the afternoon [ˌɪn ðiː ˌɑːftə'nuːn] nachmittags, am Nachmittag **I U3,** 47
aftershave ['ɑːftəʃeɪv] Aftershave, Rasierwasser **III U3,** 52
again [ə'gen] wieder **I U3,** 48
against [ə'genst] gegen **III U1,** 9
age [eɪdʒ] Alter, Zeitalter **III U3,** 46
of age [əv‿'eɪdʒ] im Alter von **III U4,** 67
agency ['eɪdʒnsi] Agentur, Behörde **IV U3,** 43
agent ['eɪdʒnt] Agent/Agentin, Vertreter/Vertreterin **IV U3,** 50
ago [ə'gəʊ] vor *(zeitlich)* **II U2,** 26
to **agree** [ə'griː] zustimmen, einer Meinung sein **III U5,** 88
air [eə] Luft **II U4,** 55
air traffic controller [ˌeə træfɪk kən'trəʊlə] Fluglotse/Fluglotsin **IV U3,** 51
on the air [ˌɒn ði‿'eə] auf Sendung **II U4,** 55
airport ['eəpɔːt] Flughafen **II U7,** 89
alarm [ə'lɑːm] Alarm **II U7,** 90
alarm clock [ə'lɑːm ˌklɒk] Wecker **I U5,** 75
album ['ælbəm] Album **IV U5,** 77
alcohol ['ælkəhɒl] Alkohol **IV U2,** 27
A-levels *(pl)* ['eɪlevlz] brit. Abitur **III U4,** 67
alien ['eɪliən] Fremder/Fremde, Außerirdischer/Außerirdische **III U5,** 82; fremd, ausländisch **IV U3,** 50
alive [ə'laɪv] lebendig **III U4,** 70
all [ɔːl] alle/alles; ganz **I U3,** 50
all inclusive [ˌɔːl‿ɪŋ'kluːsɪv] alles inklusive **IV U4,** 62

all over [ˌɔːlˈəʊvə] überall **III U3,** 49
all right [ɔːl ˈraɪt] gut; in Ordnung, alles klar **IV U4,** 68
(not ...) at all [ˌnɒt ... ətˈɔːl] überhaupt (nicht) **IV U2,** 32
in all [ɪnˈɔːl] insgesamt, im Ganzen **III U4,** 63
allegiance [əˈliːdʒns] Treue **IV U2,** 25
*to be **allowed** to (do sth) [biːəˈlaʊd] dürfen **IV U4,** 67
almost [ˈɔːlməʊst] fast, beinahe **III U3,** 45
alone [əˈləʊn] alleine **III U3,** 47
along [əˈlɒŋ] entlang **I U7,** 91
alphabet [ˈælfəbet] Alphabet, Abc **I U1,** 15
alphabetical [ˌælfəˈbetɪkl] alphabetisch **I U6,** 88
already [ɔːlˈredi] schon **I U2,** 34
also [ˈɔːlsəʊ] auch **I U5,** 68
although [ɔːlˈðəʊ] obwohl **III U3,** 52
always [ˈɔːlweɪz] immer, ständig **I U1,** 16
a.m. [ˌeɪˈem] vormittags (*Uhrzeit*) **III U3,** 49
ambulance [ˈæmbjələnts] Krankenwagen **II U4,** 55
American [əˈmerɪkən] amerikanisch; Amerikaner/Amerikanerin **II U4,** 50
American football [əˌmerɪkən ˈfʊtbɔːl] Football **III U1,** 8
native American [ˌneɪtɪvəˈmerɪkən] Ureinwohner/Ureinwohnerin Amerikas, Indianer/Indianerin **IV U1,** 9
ancient [ˈeɪnʃnt] alt **III U1,** 16
and [ænd] und **I U1,** 11
angry [ˈæŋgri] verärgert, böse **II U1,** 18
to be angry with [biː ˈæŋgri wɪð] böse sein auf **II U2,** 26
animal [ˈænɪml] Tier **I U6,** 82
announcement [əˈnaʊntsmənt] Ankündigung, Durchsage **III U3,** 52
anorak [ˈænəræk] Anorak **II U6,** 82
another [əˈnʌðə] noch ein/eine, ein anderer/eine andere/ein anderes **II U3,** 44
answer [ˈɑːnsə] Antwort **I U4,** 58
to **answer** [ˈɑːnsə] antworten, beantworten °**I LUA,** 24
answerphone [ˈɑːnsəfəʊn] Anrufbeantworter **III U4,** 69
any [ˈeni] einige; etwas **II U4,** 54
any day [ˈeni deɪ] jeden Tag **IV U2,** 31
anybody [ˈeniˌbɒdi] irgendjemand, jeder (beliebige) **III U5,** 83
anyone [ˈeniwʌn] irgendjemand, jeder (beliebige) **III U5,** 83
anything [ˈeniθɪŋ] etwas, irgendetwas **I U5,** 66
anyway [ˈeniweɪ] jedenfalls, sowieso **IV U4,** 68
anywhere [ˈeniweə] überall, irgendwo **III U3,** 45
apartment (*AE*) [əˈpɑːtmənt] Wohnung, Apartment **IV U1,** 16
apple [ˈæpl] Apfel **I U1,** 14
April [ˈeɪprl] April **I U5,** 70
architect [ˈɑːkɪtekt] Architekt/Architektin **III U2,** 30
area [ˈeəriə] Gebiet; Fläche **II U7,** 94
rest area [ˈrest ˌeəriə] Rastplatz **IV U4,** 65
arena [əˈriːnə] Arena, Stadion **II U2,** 22
to **argue** [ˈɑːgjuː] streiten, argumentieren **III U2,** 34
argument [ˈɑːgjəmənt] Streit; Argument **III U4,** 62
to have an argument [ˌhævənˈɑːgjəmənt] sich streiten **III U4,** 62
arm [ɑːm] Arm **II U3,** 40; *hier:* Ärmel **IV U2,** 33
around [əˈraʊnd] um ... herum, umher **II U6,** 78; ungefähr, zirka, etwa **III U3,** 49
See you around! [ˌsiː jə əˈraʊnd] Bis dann! Bis .... **IV U2,** 28
to hang around [ˌhæŋəˈraʊnd] rumhängen, herumlungern **IV U2,** 32
to **arrest** [əˈrest] festnehmen, verhaften **III U5,** 90
to **arrive** [əˈraɪv] ankommen **I U6,** 86
arrow [ˈærəʊ] Pfeil **IV U4,** 62
Art [ɑːt] Kunst **II U1,** 10
article [ˈɑːtɪkl] Artikel **III U2,** 30
as [æz; əz] als, wie **II U4,** 52; während °**IV U1,** 8
as ... as [æz ... æz; əz ... əz] so ... wie ... **II U4,** 52
as long as [əz ˈlɒŋəz] solange **I U7,** 94
as soon as [əz ˈsuːnəz] sobald **III U4,** 66
as well as [əz ˈweləz] sowohl ... als auch **III U4,** 67
to **ask** [ɑːsk] fragen **I U3,** 44
to ask (for) [ˈɑːsk fə] fragen (nach), bitten (um) **I U4,** 60
*to be **asleep** [ˌbiːəˈsliːp] schlafen **II U7,** 94
aspect [ˈæspekt] Aspekt, Gesichtspunkt, Seite °**IV U4,** 65
ass (*AE*) [æs] Hintern, Arsch **IV U5,** 84
assembly [əˈsembli] Versammlung, Morgenappell **II U1,** 10
assistant [əˈsɪstnt] Assistent/Assistentin **III U5,** 87
shop assistant [ˈʃɒpəˌsɪstnt] Verkäufer/Verkäuferin **II U5,** 67
astronaut [ˈæstrənɔːt] Astronaut/Astronautin **IV U3,** 42
at [æt; ət] auf **I U1,** 10
at first [ət ˈfɜːst] zuerst, zunächst **II U6,** 80
at home [ət ˈhəʊm] zu Hause **I U2,** 26
at least [ət ˈliːst] wenigstens, mindestens **I U6,** 87
at night [ət ˈnaɪt] nachts **II U3,** 47
at once [ət ˈwʌnts] sofort, plötzlich **II U7,** 94
at the back [ət ðə ˈbæk] im hinteren Teil, hinten **III U1,** 8
at the bottom [ət ðə ˈbɒtəm] unten, im unteren Teil **III U1,** 14
at the front [ət ðə ˈfrʌnt] im vorderen Teil, vorne **III U1,** 8
at the moment [æt ðə ˈməʊmənt] im Augenblick, momentan **I U7,** 90
at the top [ət ðə ˈtɒp] oben, im oberen Teil **III U1,** 14
to **attach** [əˈtætʃ] anbringen, anfügen, anhängen **IV U5,** 78
to **attack** [əˈtæk] angreifen **III U5,** 84
attention [əˈtentʃn] Aufmerksamkeit **IV U5,** 77
Attention! [əˈtentʃn] Achtung! °**IV U2,** 31
to **attract** [əˈtrækt] anziehen **IV U4,** 69
attraction [əˈtrækʃn] Attraktion, Sehenswürdigkeit **III U3,** 49
attractive [əˈtræktɪv] attraktiv **IV U2,** 28
audience [ˈɔːdiəns] Publikum **III U4,** 63
audition [ɔːˈdɪʃn] Vorsprechen, Vorsingen, Vortanzen **II U5,** 64
August [ˈɔːgəst] August **I U5,** 70
aunt [ɑːnt] Tante **I U2,** 28
Australian [ɒsˈtreɪliən] australisch; Australier/Australierin **II U4,** 50
autograph [ˈɔːtəgrɑːf] Autogramm **I U7,** 96
autumn [ˈɔːtəm] Herbst **I U6,** 79
average [ˈævrɪdʒ] durchschnittlich **III U5,** 80
to **avoid** [əˈvɔɪd] (ver)meiden °**IV U2,** 30
award [əˈwɔːd] Auszeichnung, Preis **IV U5,** 76
away [əˈweɪ] weg **I U3,** 48

C

cabin ['kæbɪn] Hütte **IV U4,** 62
cabinet ['kæbɪnət] Kasten, Schrank; Kabinett **IV U5,** 78
café ['kæfeɪ] Café **I U3,** 48
cafeteria [ˌkæfə'tɪəriə] Cafeteria **I U1,** 20
cake [keɪk] Kuchen **I U5,** 68
calendar ['kæləndə] Kalender **I U5,** 71
call [kɔːl] Anruf °**I U6,** 83
phone call ['fəʊn ˌkɔːl] (Telefon-)Anruf °**II U4,** 57
to **call** [kɔːl] rufen, anrufen, nennen **I U3,** 48
That's what I call .... [ˌðæts wɒt‿'aɪ ˌkɔːl] Das nenne ich .... **II U1,** 14
called [kɔːld] genannt **III U5,** 86
caller ['kɔːlə] Anrufer/Anruferin °**III U4,** 69
calm [kɑːm] ruhig **II U6,** 80
camera ['kæmrə] Kamera, Fotoapparat **II U5,** 62
camp [kæmp] Camp, Lager **IV U4,** 62
camper ['kæmpə] Camper/Camperin **IV U4,** 62
campfire ['kæmpfaɪə] Lagerfeuer **IV U4,** 62
camping ['kæmpɪŋ] Camping, Zelten **I U6,** 84
*__can__ [kæn] können, dürfen **I U1,** 19
candy *(AE)* ['kændi] Süßigkeiten **IV U1,** 14
to **canoe** [kə'nuː] Kanu fahren **III U3,** 46
canyon ['kænjən] Schlucht, Canyon **IV U4,** 60
cap [kæp] Kappe, Mütze **I U5,** 66
capital letter [ˌkæpɪtl 'letə] Großbuchstabe °**II U3,** 37
capsule ['kæpsjuːl] Kapsel **III U2,** 26
captain ['kæptɪn] Kapitän **IV U2,** 25
caption ['kæpʃn] Untertitel; Bildunterschrift **IV U2,** 26
car [kɑː] Auto **I U3,** 49
card [kɑːd] Karte **I LUB,** 38
*to take **care** [teɪk 'keə] aufpassen, sich kümmern **IV U2,** 31
to **care** [keə] sich kümmern, sich interessieren, wichtig nehmen **III U4,** 70
I don't care. [aɪ dəʊnt 'keə] Es ist mir egal. **II U4,** 58
careful ['keəfl] vorsichtig; sorgfältig **II U6,** 80
caretaker ['keəˌteɪkə] Hausmeister/Hausmeisterin **I U1,** 12
carpet ['kɑːpɪt] Teppichboden **IV U5,** 77
carrot ['kærət] Karotte, Mohrrübe **II U1,** 15
to **carry** ['kæri] tragen **I U6,** 80; befördern **III U2,** 34
cartoon [kɑː'tuːn] Cartoon, Zeichentrickfilm **III U5,** 80
pencil **case** ['pensl ˌkeɪs] Mäppchen **I U1,** 14
casino [kə'siːnəʊ] Casino **IV U4,** 61
castle ['kɑːsl] Schloss, Burg **II U7,** 88
cat [kæt] Katze **I U2,** 26
*to **catch** [kætʃ] fangen, erreichen **III U1,** 8
catcher ['kætʃə] Fänger/Fängerin **III U1,** 14
catchy ['kætʃi] eingängig **III U5,** 80
category ['kætəgri] Kategorie **IV U5,** 77
cathedral [kə'θiːdrl] Kathedrale, Dom **III U2,** 28
caviar ['kæviɑː] Kaviar **IV U5,** 84
CD [ˌsiː'diː] CD **I U5,** 69
CD player [ˌsiː'diː ˌpleɪə] CD-Player **II U4,** 56
cell phone *(AE)* ['sel fəʊn] Mobiltelefon, Handy **IV U3,** 44
Celsius (C) ['selsiəs] Celsius **II U6,** 78
cent [sent] Cent *(Währung)* **IV U1,** 13
centimetre ['sentɪˌmiːtə] Zentimeter **III U3,** 48
centre ['sentə] Zentrum, Mittelpunkt **I LUC,** 52
information centre [ɪnfə'meɪʃn ˌsentə] Informationszentrum **I LUC,** 52
century ['sentʃri] Jahrhundert **III U1,** 8
ceremony ['serɪməni] Zeremonie **IV U5,** 77
chain [tʃeɪn] Kette **II U3,** 40
chair [tʃeə] Stuhl **I U1,** 18
champagne [ʃæm'peɪn] Champagner **IV U5,** 84
chance [tʃɑːnts] Chance, Möglichkeit, Gelegenheit °**IV U3,** 48
to take your chance [ˌteɪk jɔː 'tʃɑːns] etwas wagen, etwas riskieren **III U3,** 53
change [tʃeɪndʒ] Wechselgeld; Änderung **II U4,** 55
change of place [ˌtʃeɪndʒ‿əv 'pleɪs] Ortswechsel °**III U4,** 65
to **change** [tʃeɪndʒ] (ver)ändern, tauschen, wechseln **II U3,** 42; umsteigen **III U2,** 28
to change your mind [ˌtʃeɪndʒ jə 'maɪnd] deine Meinung ändern **III U1,** 17
channel ['tʃænl] Kanal; Programm **III U3,** 45
chant [tʃɑːnt] Sprechgesang **IV U2,** 31
to **chant** [tʃɑːnt] rhythmisch rufen; singen **IV U2,** 25
chaos ['keɪɒs] Chaos, Durcheinander **IV U4,** 65
chaperon ['ʃæprəʊn] Begleitperson, Anstandswauwau **IV U5,** 84
character ['kærəktə] Charakter; Figur °**IV U2,** 33
charity ['tʃærɪti] Wohltätigkeit, Wohltätigkeitsverein **I U7,** 90
chart [tʃɑːt] Schaubild, Diagramm °**II U4,** 51
charts *(pl)* [tʃɑːts] Charts, Hitparade **III U5,** 82
chat [tʃæt] Geplauder, Unterhaltung **I U2,** 33
chat room ['tʃæt rʊm] Chatroom *(Internetforum, wo man sich online unterhalten kann)* **IV U5,** 80
to **chat** [tʃæt] sich unterhalten **I U2,** 33
cheap [tʃiːp] billig **I U5,** 68
to **check** [tʃek] überprüfen **I U6,** 82; untersuchen; kontrollieren **II U3,** 40
to check out [tʃek‿'aʊt] sich etwas ansehen; auschecken **IV U5,** 80
to **cheer up** [tʃɪer‿'ʌp] wieder guten Mutes sein **IV U2,** 32
cheerleader ['tʃɪəˌliːdə] Cheerleader *(Mädchen, das in einer Gruppe eine Sportmannschaft anfeuert)* **IV U2,** 24
cheerleading ['tʃɪəˌliːdɪŋ] Cheerleading **IV U2,** 32
cheese [tʃiːz] Käse **I U5,** 68
cream cheese [ˌkriːm 'tʃiːz] Frischkäse **IV U1,** 12
cherry ['tʃeri] Kirsche **IV U1,** 12
chicken ['tʃɪkɪn] Huhn, Hähnchen **II U4,** 49
child, children *(pl)* [tʃaɪld; 'tʃɪldrɪn] Kind **I U2,** 26
only child ['əʊnli ˌtʃaɪld] Einzelkind **I U2,** 26
to **chill out** [tʃɪl‿'aʊt] sich entspannen, chillen **IV U5,** 80
Chinese [tʃaɪ'niːz] chinesisch **II U4,** 49
chip (AE) [tʃɪp] Chip °**IV U4,** 67
chips *(pl)* [tʃɪps] Pommes frites **II U1,** 14
chocolate ['tʃɒklət] Schokolade **I U1,** 18
choice [tʃɔɪs] Auswahl, Wahl **III U4,** 70
to **choke** [tʃəʊk] ersticken **III U4,** 70
*to **choose** [tʃuːz] wählen, auswählen **I U4,** 54

chorus ['kɔ:rəs] Refrain **IV U5,** 84
church [tʃɜ:tʃ] Kirche **I LUC,** 52
cigarette [ˌsɪgr'et] Zigarette °**III U3,** 51
cinema ['sɪnəmə] Kino **II U1,** 18
circle ['sɜ:kl] Kreis **III U3,** 45
city ['sɪti] Stadt, Großstadt **II U7,** 89
to **clap** [klæp] klatschen **I U1,** 15
class [klɑ:s] Schulklasse, Klasse **I U1,** 16; Kurs, Unterricht **II U1,** 18
classroom ['klɑ:srʊm] Klassenzimmer **I U1,** 16
if-**clause** ['ɪfklɔ:z] if-Satz °**IV U4,** 62
to **clean** [kli:n] säubern, reinigen **II U3,** 40
clean [kli:n] sauber **III U3,** 46
cleaner ['kli:nə] Raumpfleger/Raumpflegerin, Putzkraft **IV U4,** 67
clear [klɪə] klar **II U7,** 90
to **click** [klɪk] klicken **II U5,** 64
cliff [klɪf] Klippe **II U7,** 93
to **climb** ['klaɪm] klettern, steigen, besteigen **II U2,** 30
clock [klɒk] Uhr **I U4,** 54
alarm clock [ə'lɑ:m ˌklɒk] Wecker **I U5,** 75
o'clock [ə'klɒk] Uhr *(Zeitangabe)* **I U3,** 40
to **close** [kləʊz] schließen, zumachen **I LUC,** 53
close [kləʊs] nahe **III U5,** 90
That was a close one. [ˌðæt wəz‿ə 'kləʊz‿wʌn] Das war knapp. **IV U4,** 68
closed [kləʊzd] zu, geschlossen **IV U3,** 47
clothes *(pl)* [kləʊθs] Kleider, Kleidung **II U2,** 23
cloud [klaʊd] Wolke **II U7,** 94
cloudy ['klaʊdi] wolkig **II U6,** 78
club [klʌb] Klub, Verein, Arbeitsgemeinschaft **I LUB,** 39
clue [klu:] Hinweis **II U1,** 13
to have no clue [ˌhæv nəʊ 'klu:] keine Ahnung haben **IV U5,** 84
clumsy ['klʌmzi] ungeschickt, tollpatschig **IV U2,** 33
Hey, clumsy! ['klʌmzi] He, du Tollpatsch! **IV U2,** 33
cluster ['klʌstə] Cluster °**IV U2,** 25
coast [kəʊst] Küste **II U7,** 88
coastline ['kəʊstlaɪn] Küstenlinie **III U3,** 44
coat [kəʊt] Mantel **II U7,** 90
code [kəʊd] Verschlüsselung, Code **IV U3,** 48
coffee ['kɒfi:] Kaffee **IV U1,** 12
coke [kəʊk] Cola **II U4,** 49

cold [kəʊld] kalt **I U4,** 62
to be cold [bi: 'kəʊld] frieren **II U2,** 24
collage [kɒl'ɑ:ʒ] Collage °**IV U5,** 85
to **collect** [kə'lekt] sammeln **I LUB,** 38; abholen **II U5,** 71
college ['kɒlɪdʒ] College; Institut **III U4,** 67
colour ['kʌlə] Farbe **I LUA,** 24
colourful ['kʌləfl] bunt, farbig **III U5,** 80
*to **come** [kʌm] kommen **I U2,** 33
Come on. [kʌm‿'ɒn] Komm./Kommt. **I U2,** 35
to come down [kʌm 'daʊn] herunterkommen, sich legen **III U1,** 16
to come in [kʌm‿'ɪn] hereinkommen **I U3,** 48
to come over [kʌm‿'əʊvə] herüberkommen **I U2,** 27
to come true [kʌm 'tru:] wahr werden **III U2,** 30
comedy ['kɒmədi] Komödie **III U5,** 80
comfortable ['kʌmpftəbl] komfortabel, bequem **IV U4,** 65
comic ['kɒmɪk] Comic, Comicheft **I LUB,** 38
company ['kʌmpəni] Gesellschaft, Firma; Kompanie **III U2,** 34
comparative [kəm'pærətɪv] Komparativ **II U4,** 50
to **compare** [kəm'peə] vergleichen **III U4,** 67
competition [ˌkɒmpə'tɪʃn] Wettbewerb, Turnier **III U1,** 9
to **complete** [kəm'pli:t] vervollständigen **III U2,** 30
complex ['kɒmpleks] kompliziert, komplex **IV U5,** 78
comprehensive school [kɒmprɪ'hensɪv ˌsku:l] Gesamtschule **III U4,** 66
compulsory [kəm'pʌlsri] obligatorisch, zwingend **III U4,** 67
computer [ˌkəm'pju:tə] Computer **I LUA,** 25
concert ['kɒnsət] Konzert **II U2,** 23
to **connect** [kə'nekt] verbinden, anschließen °**IV U4,** 66
conqueror ['kɒŋkrə] Eroberer °**III U2,** 31
to **construct** [kən'strʌkt] bauen, konstruieren **III U2,** 30
to **contact** ['kɒntækt] kontaktieren, sich in Verbindung setzen mit **IV U2,** 27
to **contain** [kən'teɪn] enthalten °**IV U5,** 82
content ['kɒntent] Inhalt **III U4,** 63
context ['kɒntekst] Kontext, Zusammenhang **IV U5,** 82

to **continue** [kən'tɪnju:] weitergehen, weitermachen °**II U2,** 27
contrast ['kɒntrɑ:st] Kontrast, Gegensatz **III U5,** 80
in contrast to [ɪn 'kɒntrɑ:st tə] im Gegensatz zu **III U5,** 80
control [kən'trəʊl] Kontrolle **IV U3,** 43
remote control [rɪˌməʊt kən'trəʊl] Fernbedienung, Fernsteuerung **IV U3,** 43
to **control** [kən'trəʊl] leiten, führen; überwachen, kontrollieren **IV U3,** 42
air traffic **controller** [ˌeə træfɪk kən'trəʊlə] Fluglotse/Fluglotsin **IV U3,** 51
conversation [ˌkɒnvə'seɪʃn] Unterhaltung °**III U3,** 51
to **convince** [kən'vɪnts] überzeugen °**III U5,** 81
cook [kʊk] Koch/Köchin **III U5,** 82
to **cook** [kʊk] kochen **IV U3,** 44
cooking ['kʊkɪŋ] Kochen, Koch- **I U3,** 40
cool [ku:l] cool, prima **I U1,** 20; kühl **IV U1,** 16
cop *(AE)* [kɒp] Polizist/Polizistin **IV U1,** 17
copy ['kɒpi] Kopie °**III U5,** 86
to **copy** ['kɒpi] abschreiben, kopieren **II U5,** 63
cord *(AE)* [kɔ:d] Kabel, Kordel; Schnur **IV U3,** 46
cornflakes ['kɔ:nfleɪks] Cornflakes **I U5,** 68
Cornish ['kɔ:nɪʃ] kornisch; aus Cornwall **III U3,** 48
to **correct** [kə'rekt] korrigieren, verbessern °**I LUB,** 38
correct [kə'rekt] richtig, korrekt **II U1,** 10
correction [kə'rekʃn] Korrektur °**IV U2,** 30
corridor ['kɒrɪdɔ:] Gang, Flur, Korridor **I U7,** 96
cost [kɒst] Preis, Kosten **IV U4,** 62
cottage ['kɒtɪdʒ] kleines Landhaus, Ferienhaus **III U4,** 64
couch [kaʊtʃ] Couch, Sofa **III U1,** 12
couch potato ['kaʊtʃ pəˌteɪtəʊ] Stubenhocker **III U1,** 12
***could** [kʊd] konnte/konnten **II U4,** 52; könnte/könnten **III U1,** 12
counselor ['kaʊnsələ] Berater/Beraterin, Betreuer/Betreuerin **IV U4,** 63
countdown ['kaʊntdaʊn] Countdown **III U5,** 82
country ['kʌntri] Countrymusik **IV U5,** 77

country, countries *(pl)* ['kʌntri; 'kʌntriz] Land **I U2,** 29
in the country [ˌɪn ðə 'kʌntri] auf dem Land **I U6,** 78
to the country [tʊ ðə 'kʌntri] aufs Land **III U2,** 32
couple ['kʌpl] Paar **IV U3,** 50
courier ['kʊriə] Kurier **III U2,** 34
course [kɔ:s] Gang *(Menü)* **II U4,** 49; Kurs **IV U4,** 62
of course [əv 'kɔ:s] natürlich, selbstverständlich **I U1,** 19
court [kɔ:t] Spielfeld **III U1,** 10
cousin ['kʌzn] Cousin/Cousine **I U2,** 28
cover ['kʌvə] Einband, Titelseite **II U5,** 64
cow [kaʊ] Kuh **I U6,** 82
cowboy ['kaʊbɔɪ] Rinderhirte, Cowboy **IV U4,** 61
at the **crack of dawn** [ˌkræk‿əv 'dɔ:n] im Morgengrauen **III U2,** 34
Crash! [kræʃ] Bumm!, Krach! **III U3,** 53
to **crawl** [krɔ:l] kriechen, krabbeln, schleichen **III U3,** 53
crazy ['kreɪzi] verrückt **I U7,** 96
to drive crazy [draɪv 'kreɪzi] verrückt machen **II U5,** 71
to **creak** [kri:k] knarren, quietschen **II U7,** 94
cream [kri:m] Creme, Sahne **IV U1,** 12
cream cheese [ˌkri:m 'tʃi:z] Frischkäse **IV U1,** 12
ice-cream [aɪs'kri:m] Eis, Eiscreme **I U7,** 92
crew [kru:] Besatzung, Mannschaft, Crew **IV U3,** 51
cricket ['krɪkɪt] Kricket **I U7,** 92
crime [kraɪm] Verbrechen; Kriminalität **III U5,** 84
crisp [krɪsp] Kartoffelchip **I U1,** 18
to **cross** [krɒs] überqueren, kreuzen **IV U4,** 68
crossword (puzzle) ['krɒswɜ:d 'pʌzl] Kreuzworträtsel °**I U5,** 71
crowd [kraʊd] Menschenmenge **III U1,** 17
crown [kraʊn] Krone **III U2,** 26
cruise [kru:z] Kreuzfahrt **III U3,** 45
cry [kraɪ] Schrei **III U5,** 86
to **cry** [kraɪ] weinen; schreien, rufen **II U3,** 36
cup [kʌp] Tasse, Kelch; Pokal **III U1,** 15
cupboard ['kʌbəd] Küchenschrank, Schrank **I U1,** 18
cupcake ['kʌpkeɪk] rundes Küchlein **IV U1,** 12
curriculum [kə'rɪkjələm] Lehrplan, Stundenplan **IV U2,** 24
curry ['kʌri] Curry *(Gewürz oder Gericht)* **II U4,** 49
curtain ['kɜ:tn] Vorhang **IV U3,** 46
curve [kɜ:v] Kurve **III U4,** 70
customer ['kʌstəmə] Kunde/Kundin **III U2,** 34
customs *(pl)* ['kʌstəmz] Zoll **II U7,** 90
*to **cut (off)** [kʌt‿'ɒf] (ab)schneiden **IV U3,** 44
to **cycle** ['saɪkl] Rad fahren **III U1,** 12

D

dad [dæd] Papa, Vati **I LUA,** 25
daily ['deɪli] täglich **III U5,** 80
dairy ['deəri] Molkerei **III U2,** 34
to **damage** ['dæmɪdʒ] beschädigen **III U2,** 32
damn [dæm] verdammt **IV U5,** 84
dance [dɑ:nts] Tanz **III U1,** 13
dance floor ['dɑ:nts flɔ:] Tanzfläche **IV 2,** 33
to **dance** [dɑ:nts] tanzen **I U3,** 40
dancehall ['dɑ:ntshɔ:l] Dancehall *(Musikrichtung)* **IV U5,** 77
dancing ['dɑ:ntsɪŋ] Tanzen **IV U2,** 25
ballroom dancing [ˌbɔ:lrʊm 'dɑ:ntsɪŋ] Gesellschaftstanz **IV U2,** 25
dangerous ['deɪndʒrəs] gefährlich **II U4,** 56
Danish ['deɪnɪʃ] dänisch; *hier:* Plundergebäck **IV U1,** 12
to **dare** [deə] wagen, riskieren **IV U2,** 31
dark [dɑ:k] Dunkelheit **III U5,** 88
dark [dɑ:k] dunkel **I U2,** 34
date [deɪt] Datum **I U5,** 70; Verabredung **IV U2,** 28
to **date** [deɪt] sich verabreden **IV U2,** 26
daughter ['dɔ:tə] Tochter **IV U5,** 84
at the crack of **dawn** [ˌkræk‿əv 'dɔ:n] im Morgengrauen **III U2,** 34
day [deɪ] Tag **I LUB,** 39
Have a nice day. [ˌhæv‿ə naɪs 'deɪ] Einen schönen Tag (noch). **II U4,** 55
any day ['enɪ deɪ] jeden Tag **IV U2,** 31
one day [wʌn 'deɪ] eines Tages **II U3,** 36
sports day ['spɔ:ts deɪ] Sportfest **I U7,** 90
dead [ded] tot **III U5,** 86; *hier:* leer **IV U3,** 47
dear [dɪə] lieb **I U3,** 44; Schatz *(Anrede)* **III U4,** 70
Dear [dɪə] Lieber ..., Liebe ... *(Anrede in Briefen)* **II U3,** 36
December [dɪ'sembə] Dezember **I U5,** 70
to **decide** [dɪ'saɪd] entscheiden **II U5,** 64
decoration [ˌdek'reɪʃn] Dekoration **IV U1,** 14
deep [di:p] tief °**III U5,** 86
to **define** [dɪ'faɪn] definieren °**III U3,** 48
definitely ['defɪnətli] definitiv, bestimmt **IV U2,** 32
definition [ˌdefɪ'nɪʃn] Definition **II U1,** 20
to **defuse** [ˌdi:'fju:z] entschärfen **IV U3,** 43
degree (°) [dɪ'gri:] Grad **II U6,** 78
delayed [dɪ'leɪd] verspätet, verzögert **IV U4,** 65
to **delete** [dɪ'li:t] löschen *(Text)* **II U5,** 63
deli *(AE)* ['deli] Imbissstube, Deli **IV U1,** 12
to **deliver** [dɪ'lɪvə] liefern **III U2,** 34
dentist ['dentɪst] Zahnarzt/Zahnärztin **IV U3,** 50
department store [dɪ'pɑ:tmənt stɔ:] Kaufhaus **I LUC,** 52
departure [dɪ'pɑ:tʃə] Abflug, Abreise **II U7,** 90
to **describe** [dɪ'skraɪb] beschreiben **IV U3,** 51
description [dɪ'skrɪpʃn] Beschreibung °**III U1,** 15
to **deserve** [dɪ'zɜ:v] verdienen **IV U5,** 84
to **design** [dɪ'zaɪn] entwerfen; zeichnen **III U2,** 30
designer [dɪ'zaɪnə] Designer/ Designerin **IV U5,** 76
desk [desk] Schreibtisch **I U1,** 18; Schalter **II U7,** 90
dessert [dɪ'zɜ:t] Dessert, Nachtisch **II U4,** 49
to **destroy** [dɪ'strɔɪ] zerstören **III U2,** 32
detective [dɪ'tektɪv] Detektiv/Detektivin **II U2,** 30
detective story [dɪ'tektɪv ˌstɔ:ri] Krimi **III U5,** 80
store detective ['stɔ: dɪˌtektɪv] Kaufhausdetektiv/Kaufhausdetektivin **II U2,** 30
diagram ['daɪəgræm] Diagramm °**III U1,** 14
dialogue ['daɪəlɒg] Dialog, Gespräch **III U2,** 33
diamond ['daɪəmənd] Diamant **III U5,** 82
diary ['daɪəri] Tagebuch; Terminkalender **III U4,** 64

dictionary ['dɪkʃnri] Wörterbuch °**II U3,** 46
to **die** [daɪ] sterben **III U2,** 31
diet [daɪət] Diät **II U4,** 52
to go on a diet [ˌgəʊ‿ɒn‿ə 'daɪət] eine Diät machen **II U4,** 52
difference ['dɪfrnts] Unterschied **IV U2,** 24
different ['dɪfrnt] anders, verschieden **I U6,** 78
difficult ['dɪfɪklt] schwierig **II U1,** 13
*to **dig up** [dɪg‿'ʌp] ausgraben **III U1,** 16
digital ['dɪdʒɪtl] digital **II U5,** 62
dime [daɪm] Zehncentstück *(Währung)* **IV U1,** 13
diner *(AE)* ['daɪnə] Imbissstube **IV U4,** 61
dining room ['daɪnɪŋ rʊm] Esszimmer, Speisesaal **I LUA,** 24
dinner ['dɪnə] Abendessen, Mittagessen **IV U4,** 65
direct [dɪ'rekt] direkt **III U4,** 63
director [dɪ'rektə] Direktor/Direktorin, Regisseur/Regisseurin **III U5,** 87
dirty ['dɜ:ti] schmutzig **II U1,** 10
disadvantage [ˌdɪsəd'vɑ:ntɪdʒ] Nachteil °**IV U3,** 49
to **disappear** [ˌdɪsə'pɪə] verschwinden **II U6,** 83
disappointed [ˌdɪsə'pɔɪntɪd] enttäuscht **III U4,** 62
disaster [dɪ'zɑ:stə] Desaster, Katastrophe **III U4,** 64
disco ['dɪskəʊ] Disko **I U5,** 74
to **discover** [dɪ'skʌvə] entdecken **IV U3,** 50
to **discuss** [dɪ'skʌs] diskutieren °**III U1,** 14
disrespect [ˌdɪsrɪ'spekt] Respektlosigkeit, Verachtung **IV U5,** 80
to **diss** *(slang)* [dɪs] beleidigen; schneiden **IV U5,** 80
distance ['dɪstnts] Distanz, Entfernung, Abstand **IV U3,** 51
to **dive** [daɪv] tauchen **III U3,** 47
divorced from [dɪ'vɔ:st frəm] geschieden von **I U2,** 28
dizzy ['dɪzi] schwindelig **IV U1,** 16
DJ [ˌdi:'dʒeɪ] DJ **I U2,** 33
*to **do** [du:] machen, tun **I U1,** 15
to do sports [du: 'spɔ:ts] Sport treiben **I U7,** 92
doctor ['dɒktə] Arzt/Ärztin **II U3,** 40
to see a doctor [si: ə 'dɒktə] zum Arzt gehen **II U4,** 52
docu soap ['dɒkju ˌsəʊp] Dokusoap **III U5,** 80
documentary [ˌdɒkjə'mentri] Dokumentarfilm **III U5,** 80
dog [dɒg] Hund **I U2,** 27
dog-tired [ˌdɒg'taɪəd] hundemüde **I U3,** 49
to walk the dog [wɔ:k ðə 'dɒg] mit dem Hund spazieren gehen **I U3,** 42
doll [dɒl] Puppe °**IV U3,** 49
dollar ['dɒlə] Dollar *(Währung)* **IV U1,** 12
domino ['dɒmɪnəʊ] Dominospiel °**II U2,** 26
door [dɔ:] Tür **I U1,** 18
next door [ˌnekst 'dɔ:] nebenan **III U1,** 16
doorbell ['dɔ:bel] Türklingel **II U5,** 66
doorstep ['dɔ:step] Türstufe **III U1,** 16
dope *(slang)* [dəʊp] *hier:* toll °**IV U5,** 84
double ['dʌbl] Doppelgänger, das Doppelte **I U7,** 97
down [daʊn] (nach) unten, herunter, hinunter, nieder **II U2,** 30; senkrecht *(im Kreuzworträtsel)* °**II U3,** 42
Go down .... ['gəʊ daʊn] Geh ... entlang. **I LUC,** 53
down under [daʊn‿'ʌndə] in Australien °**II U1,** 17
to come down [kʌm 'daʊn] herunterkommen, sich legen **III U1,** 16
to go down [gəʊ 'daʊn] hinuntergehen, entlanggehen **II U2,** 30
to lie down [laɪ 'daʊn] (sich) hinlegen, niederlegen **III U3,** 52
to sit down [sɪt 'daʊn] sich setzen, sich hinsetzen **I U1,** 19
to **download** [ˌdaʊn'ləʊd] herunterladen **II U5,** 63
downstairs [ˌdaʊn'steəz] unten, im unteren Stock **I U2,** 27; (die Treppe) hinunter/herunter **III U5,** 85
dragon ['drægn] Drache **IV U1,** 14
drama ['drɑ:mə] Theater, Drama **I U3,** 40
dramatic [drə'mætɪk] dramatisch **III U5,** 80
It's a **draw.** [ˌɪts‿ə 'drɔ:] Es steht unentschieden. **III U1,** 12
*to **draw** [drɔ:] zeichnen **I LUB,** 38
dream [dri:m] Traum **I LUA,** 25
dress [dres] Kleid, Kleidung **IV U2,** 25
evening dress ['i:vnɪŋ ˌdres] Abendkleid **IV U5,** 76
to **dress** [dres] sich anziehen **I U3,** 44
drill [drɪl] Bohrer, Bohrmaschine **IV U1,** 17
drink [drɪŋk] Getränk **I U7,** 95
*to **drink** [drɪŋk] trinken **I U5,** 75
to **drip** [drɪp] tropfen (lassen), tröpfeln **IV U3,** 47
*to **drive** [draɪv] fahren **I U6,** 86
to drive crazy [draɪv 'kreɪzi] verrückt machen **II U5,** 71
driver ['draɪvə] Fahrer/Fahrerin **I U4,** 54
driver's license *(AE)* ['draɪvəz ˌlaɪsnts] Führerschein **IV U4,** 68
to **drop** [drɒp] fallen, fallen lassen **II U1,** 18
drug [drʌg] Droge; Medikament *(im Amerikanischen)* **IV U2,** 27
drummer ['drʌmə] Schlagzeuger/Schlagzeugerin **IV U5,** 80
drums *(pl)* [drʌmz] Schlagzeug **I U2,** 26
to **dry** [draɪ] trocknen **IV U3,** 44
dump [dʌmp] Dreckloch, Müllkippe **II U7,** 88
during *(+ noun)* ['djʊərɪŋ] während *(+ Nomen)* **III U1,** 8
Dutch [dʌtʃ] niederländisch; Niederländer/Niederländerinnen **IV U1,** 10
DVD [di:vi:'di:] DVD **II U5,** 62
DVD player [ˌdi:vi:'di: 'pleɪə] DVD-Player **II U5,** 62
to **dye** [daɪ] färben **II U2,** 28

E

each [i:tʃ] jede/jeder/jedes **III U1,** 8; je, jeweils **III U4,** 63
each other [ˌi:tʃ‿'ʌðə] sich gegenseitig **II U1,** 19
ear [ɪə] Ohr **II U3,** 40
early ['ɜ:li] früh **I U3,** 46
earth [ɜ:θ] Erde **IV U3,** 42
east [i:st] Osten **I U4,** 54
easy ['i:zi] einfach, leicht **I U1,** 20
*to **eat** [i:t] essen, fressen **I U3,** 44
to **echo** ['ekəʊ] widerhallen **III U5,** 90
edge [edʒ] Rand, Kante **IV U5,** 82
to **edit** ['edɪt] bearbeiten **IV U2,** 26
education [edʒʊ'keɪʃn] Erziehung, Bildung **II U1,** 10
Physical Education (PE) [ˌfɪzɪkl‿edʒʊ'keɪʃn] Sport *(Schulfach)* **II U1,** 10
Religious Education (RE) [rɪˌlɪdʒəs‿edʒʊ'keɪʃn] Religionsunterricht **II U1,** 12
egg [eg] Ei **I U5,** 68
not ... **either** [ˌnɒt ... 'aɪðə] auch nicht **III U1,** 17

either ... or ... ['aɪðə; 'i:ðə ... ɔ:] entweder ... oder ... °**IV U1,** 14
elbow ['elbəʊ] Ellbogen **II U3,** 41
electric [ɪ'lektrɪk] elektrisch **IV U1,** 17
electrical [ɪ'lektrɪkl] elektrisch **IV U3,** 44
electricity [ˌelɪk'trɪsəti] Elektrizität, Strom **IV U3,** 44
elementary school *(AE)* [elɪ'mentri ˌsku:l] Grundschule **IV U2,** 30
elephant ['elɪfənt] Elefant **I U7,** 96
else [els] sonst, noch **I U5,** 66
someone else [ˌsʌmwʌn‿'els] jemand anderes °**III U1,** 13
e-mail ['i:meɪl] E-Mail **I U3,** 44
to **e-mail** ['i:meɪl] E-Mail schreiben **IV U5,** 80
embarrassed [ɪm'bærəst] verlegen **IV U2,** 32
embarrassing [ɪm'bærəsɪŋ] peinlich **II U2,** 26
emergency [ɪ'mɜ:dʒnsi] Notfall, Notlage **III U5,** 82
to **emigrate** ['emɪgreɪt] emigrieren, auswandern **IV U1,** 10
empty ['empti] leer **II U1,** 18
end [end] Ende, Schluss **II U6,** 84
in the end [ɪn ðiː‿'end] schließlich, zum Schluss **II U6,** 80
to **end** [end] enden **I U5,** 76; beenden, abschließen **IV U2,** 28
to end in ['end‿ɪn] enden auf °**II U7,** 90
to end up [ˌend‿'ʌp] enden, landen **IV U4,** 68
ending ['endɪŋ] Ende, Schluss *(einer Geschichte)* °**II U1,** 19
enemy ['enəmi] Feind/Feindin **II U3,** 43
engine ['endʒɪn] Maschine, Motor **III U3,** 56
search engine ['sɜ:tʃ ˌendʒɪn] Suchmaschine °**IV U4,** 61
English ['ɪŋglɪʃ] englisch **I U1,** 11; Engländer/Engländerinnen **IV U1,** 10
to **enjoy** [ɪn'dʒɔɪ] sich erfreuen, genießen **II U6,** 80
enormous [ɪ'nɔ:məs] enorm, riesig **III U5,** 90
enough [ɪ'nʌf] genug, genügend **III U1,** 12
to **enter** ['entə] sich beteiligen an; eintreten, betreten **III U2,** 30
to **entertain** [ˌentə'teɪn] unterhalten **IV U5,** 81
entrance ['entrənts] Eingang; Eintritt **IV U4,** 68
entry ['entri] Eintrag °**III U2,** 35
envelope ['envələʊp] Briefumschlag, Umschlag **II U7,** 90
environment [ɪn'vaɪərnmənt] Umwelt, Umgebung **II U6,** 74
equipment [ɪ'kwɪpmənt] Ausrüstung, Ausstattung **IV U3,** 42
er [ɜ:] äh °**I U1,** 12
to **erase** [ɪ'reɪz] löschen, ausradieren **IV U3,** 50
erm [ɜ:m] äh °**II U3,** 38
to **escape (from)** [ɪ'skeɪp] flüchten (vor), entkommen **II U6,** 78
etc. [ɪt'setrə] usw., et cetera **II U1,** 10
euro ['jʊərəʊ] Euro *(Währung)* **I U5,** 73
European [ˌjʊərə'pi:ən] europäisch **III U3,** 55
even ['i:vn] selbst, sogar **I U7,** 90
not even [nɒt‿'i:vn] nicht einmal **III U4,** 64
evening ['i:vnɪŋ] Abend **I U3,** 47
evening dress ['i:vnɪŋ ˌdres] Abendkleid **IV U5,** 76
in the evening [ˌɪn ðiː 'i:vnɪŋ] abends, am Abend **I U3,** 47
that evening [ˌdæt‿'i:vnɪŋ] an diesem Abend **II U1,** 19
this evening [ðɪs 'i:vnɪŋ] heute Abend **III U3,** 52
event [ɪ'vent] Veranstaltung, Ereignis **I U7,** 90
ever ['evə] jemals **II U5,** 66
every ['evri] jede/jeder/jedes **I U3,** 40
everybody ['evribɒdi] jeder; alle **IV U2,** 25
everyday ['evrideɪ] alltäglich °**IV U5,** 86
everyone ['evriwʌn] jeder **III U3,** 48
everything ['evriθɪŋ] alles **II U4,** 50
everywhere ['evriweə] überall **II U5,** 71
evidence ['evɪdnts] Beweis °**II U6,** 83
exact [ɪg'zækt] genau **III U3,** 49
exam [ɪg'zæm] Examen, Prüfung **III U4,** 67
example [ɪg'zɑ:mpl] Beispiel °**I U1,** 13
for example [ˌfər‿ɪg'zɑ:mpl] zum Beispiel **III U3,** 48
except [ɪk'sept] außer **IV U5,** 80
exchange [ɪks'tʃeɪndʒ] Austausch, Tausch **I U7,** 94
excited [ɪk'saɪtɪd] aufgeregt **I U5,** 74
exciting [ɪk'saɪtɪŋ] spannend, aufregend **II U4,** 51
Excuse me! [ɪk'skju:z mi:] Entschuldigung! **I U3,** 42
exercise ['eksəsaɪz] Übung, Aufgabe **I U1,** 19
exercise book ['eksəsaɪz ˌbʊk] Heft, Übungsheft **I U1,** 14
to **exercise** ['eksəsaɪz] üben, Sport machen **II U4,** 52
exhibition [ˌeksɪ'bɪʃn] Ausstellung, Vorführung **III U2,** 31
to **exist** [ɪg'zɪst] existieren **IV U3,** 43
exit ['eksɪt] Ausgang, Abgang, Ausfahrt **IV U4,** 65
to **expect** [ɪk'spekt] erwarten **III U2,** 34
expensive [ɪk'spentsɪv] teuer **I U5,** 68
experience [ɪk'spɪəriənts] Erfahrung, Erlebnis **IV U4,** 68
experiment [ɪk'sperɪmənt] Experiment, Versuch **II U1,** 13
expert ['ekspɜ:t] Experte/Expertin °**IV U3,** 51
to **explain** [ɪk'spleɪn] erklären, erläutern **II U5,** 64
to **explore** [ɪk'splɔ:] erkunden, erforschen **IV U3,** 43
expressive [ɪk'spresɪv] ausdrucksstark °**III U5,** 86
extra ['ekstrə] zusätzlich; Zusatz **III U4,** 68
eye [aɪ] Auge **I U2,** 35
eyebrow ['aɪbraʊ] Augenbraue **III U4,** 62

F

fabulous ['fæbjələs] fabelhaft, fantastisch **IV U4,** 61
face [feɪs] Gesicht **I U3,** 48
fact [fækt] Fakt, Tatsache **II U2,** 32
fact-file on ['fækt,faɪl] Datei mit Informationen über °**II U2,** 32
in fact [ɪn 'fækt] in der Tat, genau genommen **II U7,** 94
factory ['fæktri] Fabrik, Werk **IV U3,** 50
factual ['fæktʃʊəl] Sach-, sachlich °**IV U1,** 14
Fahrenheit (F) ['færnhaɪt] Fahrenheit **IV U1,** 16
to **faint** [feɪnt] ohnmächtig werden **IV U1,** 17
fair [feə] Messe, Jahrmarkt **I U7,** 90
summer fair ['sʌmə ˌfeə] Sommerfest **I U7,** 90
fair [feə] gerecht, fair **III U1,** 16; blond, hell **III U5,** 80
*to **fall** [fɔ:l] fallen, herunterfallen, hinfallen **II U2,** 26
to fall off [fɔ:l‿'ɒf] herunterfallen **II U3,** 40
family ['fæmli] Familie **I LUA,** 25

family tree ['fæmli tri:] Familienstammbaum °**I U2**, 28
famine ['fæmɪn] Hungersnot **IV U1**, 10
famous ['feɪməs] berühmt **I U4**, 54
fan [fæn] Fan **II U5**, 66
fantastic [fæn'tæstɪk] fantastisch, großartig **I U7**, 94
far [fɑ:] weit **II U6**, 78
so far ['səʊ fɑ:] bis jetzt °**IV U1**, 17
to go far [gəʊ 'fɑ:] weit kommen, es weit bringen **III U2**, 26
farm [fɑ:m] Bauernhof, Farm **I U6**, 78
farmer ['fɑ:mə] Bauer/Bäuerin, Landwirt/Landwirtin **I U6**, 82
farmhouse ['fɑ:mhaʊs] Bauernhaus **II U7**, 88
farther ['fɑ:ðə] weiter **IV U1**, 10
farther and farther ['fɑ:ðə] immer weiter **IV U1**, 10
fashion ['fæʃn] Mode **II U6**, 82
fast [fɑ:st] schnell **II U4**, 50
fast food [ˌfɑ:st 'fu:d] Schnellimbiss °**II U4**, 50
father ['fɑ:ðə] Vater **III U3**, 52
faucet *(AE)* ['fɔ:sɪt] Wasserhahn **IV U3**, 44
favourite ['feɪvrɪt] Lieblings- **I U1**, 12
February ['februəri] Februar **I U5**, 70
*to **feed** [fi:d] füttern **I U6**, 80
to be fed up [bi: ˌfed‿'ʌp] die Nase voll haben **I U2**, 34
*to **feel** [fi:l] fühlen, sich fühlen **II U3**, 40
to feel for ['fi:l fə] tasten nach **III U3**, 52
to feel homesick [ˌfi:l 'həʊmsɪk] Heimweh haben **IV U4**, 68
to feel sick [fi:l 'sɪk] Übelkeit verspüren **II U3**, 46
to feel sorry for [fi:l 'sɒri] Mitleid haben mit, bedauern **III U1**, 16
feeling ['fi:lɪŋ] Gefühl **III U4**, 64
ferry ['feri] Fähre **III U3**, 45
festival ['festɪvl] Festival, Fest **IV U1**, 14
fetish ['fetɪʃ] Fetisch °**IV U5**, 84
few [fju:] wenige **II U5**, 71
a few [ə 'fju:] einige, ein paar **II U4**, 52
fiction ['fɪkʃn] Erfindung, Fiktion **III U5**, 80
science fiction [ˌsaɪəns 'fɪkʃn] Sciencefiction **III U5**, 80
to **fiddle (with)** ['fɪdl] herumfummeln (an) **IV U4**, 68
field [fi:ld] Feld, Acker **I U6**, 88
sports field ['spɔ:ts fi:ld] Sportplatz **I U7**, 92
fierce [fɪəs] bösartig **II U5**, 70
fifth [fɪfθ] Fünftel **III U2**, 32
fight [faɪt] Kampf **III U1**, 16
*to **fight** [faɪt] streiten, kämpfen **III U4**, 69
figure ['fɪgə] Figur, Gestalt **II U7**, 94; Zahl, Ziffer °**III U1**, 15
to **fill** [fɪl] füllen **IV U2**, 33
to fill in [fɪl‿'ɪn] ausfüllen, einsetzen **II U5**, 64
film [fɪlm] Film **II U3**, 43
to **film** [fɪlm] filmen **III U5**, 87
final ['faɪnl] letzte/letzter/letztes **III U5**, 82
finally ['faɪnli] endlich, schließlich **III U2**, 28
*to **find** [faɪnd] finden **I U3**, 48
to find out [faɪnd‿'aʊt] herausfinden **I U4**, 62
fine [faɪn] Geldbuße, Geldstrafe **III U2**, 28
fine [faɪn] gut, in Ordnung, fein, schön **I U7**, 94
finger ['fɪŋgə] Finger **II U3**, 41
to **finish** ['fɪnɪʃ] beenden, erledigen, aufhören **I U2**, 34
fire [faɪə] Feuer, Brand **I U7**, 96; Feuerstelle, Kaminfeuer **III U2**, 32
fire brigade ['faɪə brɪˌgeɪd] Feuerwehr **III U2**, 32
Where's the fire? [ˌweəz ðə 'faɪə] Wo brennt's denn? **I U7**, 96
fireplace ['faɪəpleɪs] Kamin **III U5**, 89
firework ['faɪəwɜ:k] Feuerwerkskörper; *Plural:* Feuerwerk **IV U1**, 14
firm [fɜ:m] Firma **III U1**, 12
first [fɜ:st] zuerst; erste/erster/erstes **I U4**, 54
first of all [ˌfɜ:st‿ɒf‿'ɔ:l] zuerst, zuallererst, zunächst **IV U4**, 66
at first [ət 'fɜ:st] zuerst, zunächst **II U6**, 80
fish, fish *(pl)* [fɪʃ] Fisch **I U6**, 78
to **fish** [fɪʃ] fischen, angeln **I U6**, 82
fishing ['fɪʃɪŋ] Angeln, Fischen **I U6**, 78
*to have a **fit** [ˌhæv‿ə 'fɪt] einen Anfall bekommen, Zustände kriegen **III U4**, 70
to **fit** [fɪt] passen **II U6**, 76
fit [fɪt] fit **II U4**, 52
to **fix (to)** [fɪks] befestigen, anbringen, reparieren **III U2**, 30
to fix [fɪks] *hier:* manipulieren **IV U2**, 33
flag [flæg] Flagge, Fahne **I U2**, 29
flame [fleɪm] Flamme **III U2**, 32
flare [fleə] Leuchtfeuer; Lichtschein **IV U3**, 51
flash [flæʃ] Aufblinken, Blitzen **II U7**, 95
flash flood ['flæʃ ˌflʌd] flutartige Überschwemmung, Sintflut **II U6**, 74
to **flash** [flæʃ] blitzen, blinken **IV U1**, 16
flat [flæt] Wohnung **I U2**, 26
flat [flæt] flach, platt **IV U1**, 16
flight [flaɪt] Flug **II U2**, 23
flood [flʌd] Überschwemmung, Hochwasser **II U6**, 74
flash flood ['flæʃ ˌflʌd] flutartige Überschwemmung, Sintflut **II U6**, 74
to **flood** [flʌd] überfluten, überschwemmen **IV U3**, 44
floor [flɔ:] Fußboden **II U5**, 71
flossy *(slang)* ['flɒsi] aufgemotzt °**IV U5**, 84
flower ['flaʊə] Blume **I U6**, 78
*to **fly** [flaɪ] fliegen **II U7**, 88; wehen **III U3**, 46
fog [fɒg] Nebel **II U6**, 78
foggy ['fɒgi] neblig **I U6**, 79
folder ['fəʊldə] Ordner, Mappe **I U4**, 60
folk [fəʊk] Volksmusik **IV U5**, 77
folks *(Anrede)* [fəʊks] Leute *(Anrede)* **IV U1**, 16
to **follow** ['fɒləʊ] hinterhergehen, folgen, befolgen **I U7**, 96
following ['fɒləʊɪŋ] folgend/folgender/folgende/folgendes **III U4**, 67
food [fu:d] Essen, Nahrung, Lebensmittel **I U7**, 95
fast food [ˌfɑ:st 'fu:d] Schnellimbiss °**II U4**, 50
foot, feet *(pl)* [fʊt; fi:t] Fuß **I U4**, 54; Fuß *(Längenmaß: 30,48 cm)* **III U1**, 11
on foot [ɒn 'fʊt] zu Fuß **I U4**, 57
football ['fʊtbɔ:l] Fußball **I U1**, 12
American football [əˌmerɪkən 'fʊtbɔ:l] Football **III U1**, 8
footstep ['fʊtstep] Schritt **III U3**, 52
for [fɔ:; fə] für **I U1**, 11; seit **II U5**, 69
for … [fɔ:; fə] … lang **III U2**, 32
for example [ˌfər‿ɪg'zɑ:mpl] zum Beispiel **III U3**, 48
for hours [fər‿'aʊəz] stundenlang **II U4**, 52
for miles [fə‿'maɪlz] meilenweit **IV U4**, 69
for supper [fə 'sʌpə] zum Abendessen **II U3**, 38
forecast ['fɔ:kɑ:st] Vorhersage *(Wetter)* **II U6**, 78
*to **forecast** ['fɔ:kɑ:st] vorhersagen *(Wetter)* **IV U3**, 43

English – German

foreground ['fɔ:graʊnd] Vordergrund **IV U1,** 9
foreign ['fɒrɪn] fremd, ausländisch **II U1,** 10
forest ['fɒrɪst] Wald **IV U4,** 62
*to **forget** [fə'get] vergessen **I U4,** 60
fork [fɔ:k] Gabel **II U4,** 50
form [fɔ:m] Form °**I U6,** 88; Formular, Form **II U5,** 64
long form ['lɒŋ fɔ:m] Langform °**I U1,** 16
to **form** [fɔ:m] formen, bilden **IV U5,** 80
formal ['fɔ:ml] formal, formell, förmlich **IV U2,** 25
fortress ['fɔ:trəs] Festung **III U2,** 31
forum ['fɔ:rəm] Forum **IV U5,** 80
forward ['fɔ:wəd] nach vorne, vorwärts **IV U1,** 16
to **found** [faʊnd] gründen **IV U1,** 10
free [fri:] frei **I U3,** 40; kostenlos, umsonst **IV U1,** 12
freedom ['fri:dəm] Freiheit **IV U1,** 9
to **freestyle** *(slang)* ['fri:staɪl] improvisieren **IV U5,** 80
French [frentʃ] französisch **II U1,** 18
French fries *(AE)* ['frentʃ ˌfraɪz] Pommes frites **IV U1,** 12
fresh [freʃ] frisch **II U4,** 54
Friday [fraɪdeɪ] Freitag **I LUB,** 39
fridge [frɪdʒ] Kühlschrank **IV U3,** 48
friend [frend] Freund/Freundin **I U1,** 16
to make friends (with) [ˌmeɪk 'frendz] Freundschaft schließen (mit) **IV U4,** 68
friendly ['frendli] freundlich, nett **IV U1,** 14
French **fries** *(AE)* ['frentʃ ˌfraɪz] Pommes frites **IV U1,** 12
to **frighten away** [ˌfraɪtn‿ə'weɪ] abschrecken **II U7,** 88
*to be **frightened (of)** [bi: 'fraɪtnd] Angst haben (vor) **II U6,** 83
frightening ['fraɪtnɪŋ] schrecklich, furchtbar, beängstigend **II U6,** 80
from [frɒm] aus, von **I U1,** 10
divorced from [dɪ'vɔ:st frəm] geschieden von **I U2,** 28
Where are you from? [ˌweər‿ə jə 'frɒm] Woher kommst du? **I U1,** 11
front [frʌnt] Vorderseite **IV U2,** 33
at the front [ət ðə 'frʌnt] im vorderen Teil, vorne **III U1,** 8
in front of [ɪn 'frʌnt‿əv] vor **I U3,** 49
frozen ['frəʊzn] gefroren **IV U4,** 65
fruit [fru:t] Obst, Frucht **II U1,** 15
frustrated [frʌs'treɪtɪd] frustriert **III U4,** 62
full (of) [fʊl] ganz, voll (von/mit) **III U1,** 11
fun [fʌn] Spaß **I U3,** 41
Have fun! [ˌhæv 'fʌn] Viel Spaß! **I U6,** 82
to be fun [bi: 'fʌn] Spaß machen **I U3,** 43
to have fun [ˌhæv 'fʌn] Spaß haben, sich amüsieren **I U6,** 82
funeral ['fju:nrəl] Beerdigung **II U6,** 76
funk [fʌŋk] Funk *(Musikrichtung)* **IV U5,** 80
funny ['fʌni] komisch, lustig **I LUA,** 25
furious ['fjʊəriəs] wütend **III U3,** 53
furniture ['fɜ:nɪtʃə] Möbel **I LUA,** 25
fuse-box ['fju:zbɒks] Sicherungskasten **III U3,** 53
fuss [fʌs] Aufregung, Wirbel **III U4,** 70
future ['fju:tʃə] Zukunft °**III U1,** 11

G

Gaelic ['geɪlɪk] gälisch **III U3,** 48
game [geɪm] Spiel **I U2,** 26
miming game ['maɪmɪŋ geɪm] Pantomime °**I U6,** 81
gang [gæŋ] Gang, Bande **IV U2,** 27
gangster ['gæŋkstə] Gangster/Gangsterin, Verbrecher/Verbrecherin **IV U5,** 80
garden ['gɑ:dn] Garten **I U2,** 26
gardener ['gɑ:dnə] Gärtner/Gärtnerin **III U2,** 34
gate [geɪt] Tor, Pforte; Gate **II U7,** 90
GCSE [ˌdʒi:si:es'i:] Prüfung zum Abschluss der Sekundarstufe **III U4,** 67
g'day [gə'deɪ] Tag, hallo *(australische Begrüßung)* °**II U1,** 14
ladies and **gentlemen** [ˌleɪdiz‿n 'dʒentlmən] meine Damen und Herren °**III U2,** 33
Geography [dʒi'ɒgrəfi] Geografie, Erdkunde **II U1,** 10
German ['dʒɜ:mən] deutsch; Deutscher/Deutsche **I U1,** 17
*to **get** [get] kommen, bekommen, besorgen **I U3,** 44; holen **II U2,** 26; werden **II U6,** 83
to get back (to) [get 'bæk tə] zurückkommen (zu/nach); *hier:* sich melden (bei) **IV U5,** 81
to get hungry [get 'hʌŋgri] Hunger bekommen **II U4,** 56
to get interested [get 'ɪntrəstɪd] sich interessieren **III U2,** 35
to get into [get‿'ɪntə] einsteigen in *(Auto)* **I U5,** 75
to get into such a state [get‿ˌɪntə 'sʌtʃ‿ə 'steɪt] durchdrehen, (sich) verrückt machen **III U4,** 70
to get it ['get‿ɪt] *hier:* bestraft werden **IV U4,** 68
to get lost [get 'lɒst] verloren gehen, sich verirren **I U3,** 48
to get lucky *(AE)* [get 'lʌki] Glück haben **IV U4,** 68
to get off [get‿'ɒf] aussteigen aus **I U4,** 59; wegräumen von, abräumen von **III U4,** 65
to get on [get‿'ɒn] aufsteigen, einsteigen *(in Zug, Bus …)* **III U5,** 86
to get onto [get‿'ɒntə] einsteigen *(Bus)* **II U1,** 19
to get out [get‿'aʊt] aussteigen **I U6,** 86; entkommen **III U3,** 53
to get out of bed [ˌget‿aʊt‿əv 'bed] aufstehen **II U7,** 94
to get ready [get 'redi] sich vorbereiten **II U5,** 68
to get … right/wrong [get … 'raɪt/'rɒŋ] richtig/falsch machen **II U3,** 44
to get up [get‿'ʌp] aufstehen **I U3,** 44
to get … wrong [get … 'rɒŋ] falsch verstehen °**II U3,** 47
ghost [gəʊst] Geist, Gespenst **I U2,** 34
girl [gɜ:l] Mädchen **I U1,** 16
girlfriend ['gɜ:lfrend] Freundin *(in einer Paarbeziehung)* **II U3,** 39
*to **give** [gɪv] geben, schenken **I U4,** 60
to give … a dirty look [ˌgɪv‿ə dɜ:ti 'lʊk] einen vernichtenden Blick zuwerfen **II U1,** 10
to give a talk [ˌgɪv‿ə 'tɔ:k] einen Vortrag/eine Rede halten °**III U1,** 14
to give it a go [ˌgɪv‿ɪt‿ə 'gəʊ] es versuchen **IV U5,** 81
to give up [gɪv‿'ʌp] aufgeben **III U2,** 30
glad [glæd] froh **III U4,** 68
glamorous ['glæmrəs] glamourös **IV U5,** 76
glare [gleə] blendender Glanz, grelles Licht **III U4,** 70
glass [glɑ:s] Glas **II U4,** 50
glasses *(pl)* ['glɑ:sɪz] *hier:* Brille **IV U3,** 50
glee [gli:] Entzücken **III U4,** 70
glove [glʌv] Handschuh **III U1,** 8
to **glow** [gləʊ] leuchten **III U5,** 88

*to **go** [gəʊ] gehen **I U1,** 19
Go down … . ['gəʊ daʊn] Geh … entlang. **I LUC,** 53
Go left. [gəʊ 'left] Biege nach links ab. **I LUC,** 52
Go right. [gəʊ 'raɪt] Biege nach rechts ab. **I LUC,** 52
*gonna (= going to) ['gɒnə] werden °**IV U4,** 68
to go [tə͜'gəʊ] zum Mitnehmen **IV U1,** 12
to go bananas [ˌgəʊ bə'nɑ:nəz] verrückt werden, durchdrehen **II U5,** 66
to go bump [gəʊ 'bʌmp] rumsen °**II U7,** 94
to go down [gəʊ 'daʊn] hinuntergehen, entlanggehen **II U2,** 30
to go far [gəʊ 'fɑ:] weit kommen, es weit bringen **III U2,** 26
to go for a walk [ˌgəʊ fər͜ə 'wɔ:k] spazieren gehen **III U5,** 88
to go in [gəʊ 'ɪn] hineingehen **II U2,** 26
to go + -ing [gəʊ] … gehen **II U4,** 52
to go off [gəʊ͜'ɒf] losgehen *(Alarm)* **II U7,** 95
to go on [gəʊ͜'ɒn] andauern; weitermachen **IV U1,** 14
to go on a diet [ˌgəʊ͜ɒn͜ə 'daɪət] eine Diät machen **II U4,** 52
to go out [gəʊ͜'aʊt] (hin)ausgehen, erlöschen **II U3,** 38
to go over [gəʊ͜'əʊvə] hinübergehen **II U3,** 38
to go places [ˌgəʊ 'pleɪsɪz] herumreisen **IV U4,** 68
to go red [gəʊ 'red] rot werden **II U1,** 11
to go up [gəʊ͜'ʌp] hinaufgehen °**I U4,** 61
to go weak [gəʊ 'wi:k] schwach werden **III U4,** 70
to go (together) with ['gəʊ wɪð] passen zu **III U5,** 81
to go without [ˌgəʊ wɪ'ðaʊt] ohne … auskommen **II U4,** 52
to go wrong [gəʊ 'rɒŋ] schief gehen **II U6,** 85
goal [gəʊl] Tor, Ziel **I U1,** 12
goal post ['gəʊl pəʊst] Torpfosten **III U1,** 15
winning goal ['wɪnɪŋ gəʊl] Siegtreffer **III U4,** 68
goalkeeper ['gəʊlˌki:pə] Torwart **III U1,** 10
goblin ['gɒblɪn] Kobold **II U7,** 90
My **God!** [maɪ 'gɒd] Mein Gott! **II U6,** 82
gold [gəʊld] Gold **II U7,** 90
good [gʊd] gut **I U1,** 16
Good grief! [gʊd 'gri:f] Du liebe Zeit! **II U2,** 28
Good luck! [ˌgʊd 'lʌk] Viel Glück! **I U4,** 63
Good morning! [ˌgʊd 'mɔ:nɪŋ] Guten Morgen! **I U1,** 16
I'm good at … [aɪm 'gʊd͜ət] ich bin gut in … **I U1,** 20
to be good with … [bi: 'gʊd wɪð] gut mit … umgehen können **I U2,** 34
to have a good time [ˌhæv͜ə gʊd 'taɪm] sich amüsieren **I U5,** 75
goodbye [gʊd'baɪ] auf Wiedersehen **I U1,** 19
goods *(pl)* [gʊdz] Güter, Waren **IV U4,** 61
gorge [gɔ:dʒ] Schlucht, Klamm **IV U4,** 60
gossip ['gɒsɪp] Tratsch, Klatsch **IV U2,** 32
to **gossip** ['gɒsɪp] tratschen, klatschen, schwatzen **IV U2,** 32
to **grab** [græb] greifen, schnappen **III U3,** 53
grade *(AE)* [greɪd] Klasse; Note **IV U2,** 24
to **graduate** ['grædjueɪt] den Schulabschluss machen **IV U2,** 29
grammar ['græmə] Grammatik °**II U1,** 16
grammar school ['græmə ˌsku:l] Gymnasium **III U4,** 67
gramme [græm] Gramm **III U1,** 11
grandad ['grændæd] Opa **I LUA,** 25
grandma ['grændmɑ:] Oma **I LUA,** 25
graph [grɑ:f] Diagramm, Graph, Schaubild °**IV U4,** 69
grass [grɑ:s] Gras **III U1,** 8
grave [greɪv] Grab **III U5,** 81
gravestone ['greɪvstəʊn] Grabstein **III U5,** 86
great [greɪt] großartig, toll **I U2,** 26; groß **III U2,** 26
Greek [gri:k] griechisch; Grieche/ Griechin **I U2,** 29
green [gri:n] grün **I LUA,** 24
greenhouse ['gri:nhaʊs] Gewächshaus **II U6,** 81
grey [greɪ] grau **III U5,** 89
grid [grɪd] Gitter, Tabelle **III U4,** 67
Good **grief!** [gʊd 'gri:f] Du liebe Zeit! **II U2,** 28
ground [graʊnd] Boden **II U2,** 26
group [gru:p] Gruppe **I U4,** 54
guard [gɑ:d] Wache; Wächter/ Wächerin **III U5,** 85
to **guard** [gɑ:d] bewachen **II U7,** 90
guess [ges] Vermutung °**IV U2,** 24
to **guess** [ges] raten, vermuten **III U4,** 66
guest [gest] Gast **III U5,** 85
guitar [gɪ'tɑ:] Gitarre **IV U5,** 80
gun [gʌn] Schusswaffe **III U5,** 90
gunshot ['gʌnʃɒt] Schuss **III U5,** 90
guy [gaɪ] Typ, Kerl; *pl.:* Leute **IV U2,** 32
gym [dʒɪm] Turnhalle **I U3,** 40

H

Ha! [hɑ:] Ha! °**III U4,** 68
hair [heə] Haar, Haare **II U2,** 28
hairdresser ['heəˌdresə] Friseur/ Friseurin **II U2,** 28
hairdryer ['heəˌdraɪə] Fön **IV U3,** 46
half [hɑ:f] halb **II U6,** 83; Hälfte **III U2,** 32
half an hour [ˌhɑ:f͜ən͜'aʊə] eine halbe Stunde **II U2,** 26
half past (two) ['hɑ:f pɑ:st] halb (drei) **I U3,** 40
half-price [ˌhɑ:f'praɪs] zum halben Preis **III U1,** 15
half-sister ['hɑ:fˌsɪstə] Halbschwester **I U2,** 26
half-time [ˌhɑ:f'taɪm] Halbzeit **III U1,** 12
hall [hɔ:l] Halle, Saal, Flur **I U3,** 40
ham [hæm] Schinken **II U4,** 49
hand [hænd] Hand **II U3,** 41
Hands off! [hændz͜'ɒf] Hände weg! **II U4,** 50
handbag ['hænbæg] Handtasche **III U2,** 28
*to **hang around** [ˌhæŋ͜ə'raʊnd] rumhängen, herumlungern **IV U2,** 32
to hang out [hæŋ͜'aʊt] sich herumtreiben **III U4,** 64
Hang on! ['hæŋ͜ɒn] Moment mal! Warte mal! **I U6,** 82
to **happen** ['hæpn] geschehen, passieren **I U6,** 86
happy ['hæpi] glücklich, froh **I U2,** 33
harbor *(AE)* ['hɑ:bə] Hafen **IV U1,** 9
hard [hɑ:d] hart, schwierig, stark **II U6,** 82
to try hard [traɪ͜'hɑ:d] sich stark bemühen **III U4,** 70
harm [hɑ:m] Schaden, Verletzung **III U4,** 70

English – German

hat [hæt] Hut **II U2,** 26
hate [heɪt] Hass **II U1,** 10
to **hate** [heɪt] hassen **II U1,** 10
*to **have** [hæv] haben **I U5,** 68
Have a nice day. [ˌhæv‿ə naɪs 'deɪ] Einen schönen Tag (noch). **II U4,** 55
Have fun! [ˌhæv 'fʌn] Viel Spaß! **I U6,** 82
to have a fit [ˌhæv‿ə 'fɪt] einen Anfall bekommen, Zustände kriegen **III U4,** 70
to have a good time [ˌhæv‿ə gʊd 'taɪm] sich amüsieren **I U5,** 75
to have a look (at) [ˌhæv‿ə 'lʊk] anschauen, einen Blick werfen (auf) **IV U2,** 26
to have an argument [ˌhæv‿ən‿'ɑ:gjəmənt] sich streiten **III U4,** 62
to have a party [ˌhæv‿ə 'pɑ:ti] eine Party feiern **I U5,** 68
to have fun [ˌhæv 'fʌn] Spaß haben, sich amüsieren **I U6,** 82
to have got [hæv 'gɒt] besitzen, haben **I U2,** 30
to have no clue [ˌhæv nəʊ 'klu:] keine Ahnung haben **IV U5,** 84
to have supper [hæv 'sʌpə] zu Abend essen **I U3,** 44
to have to ['hæv tə] müssen **II U5,** 64
he [hi:] er **I U1,** 12
head [hed] Kopf **II U3,** 36
heading ['hedɪŋ] Überschrift °**III U5,** 85
headphones *(pl)* ['hedfəʊnz] Kopfhörer **II U4,** 56
healthy ['helθi] gesund **II U4,** 50
*to **hear** [hɪə] hören **I U6,** 78
heart [hɑ:t] Herz **IV U5,** 82
heat [hi:t] Hitze **IV U1,** 17
heating ['hi:tɪŋ] Heizung **II U6,** 78
heavy ['hevi] schwer **II U4,** 51
height [haɪt] Höhe, Größe **III U1,** 11
helicopter ['helɪˌkɒptə] Helikopter, Hubschrauber **II U6,** 83
hell [hel] Hölle **IV U3,** 50
Hello! [he'ləʊ] Hallo! **I U1,** 10
helmet ['helmət] Helm **III U1,** 8
help [help] Hilfe **I U2,** 34
to **help** [help] helfen **I U2,** 34
helpful ['helpfəl] hilfreich **II U5,** 71
helpless ['helpləs] hilflos **III U3,** 52
helpline ['helplaɪn] telefonischer Beratungsdienst, Notruf °**III U4,** 69
her [hɜ:] ihr/ihre; sie **I U2,** 26
Her Majesty [hə 'mædʒəsti] Ihre Majestät °**III U5,** 90
here [hɪə] hier **I U1,** 12
Here you are! ['hɪə ju:‿ɑ:] Bitte schön! **I U1,** 20
hero, heroes *(pl)* ['hɪərəʊ; 'hɪərəʊz] Held **II U3,** 43
heroine ['herəʊɪn] Heldin **III U5,** 80
hey [heɪ] he °**I U1,** 16
Hi! [haɪ] Hi! **I U1,** 10
Hi, there! ['haɪ ðeə] Hallo! **IV U2,** 28
*to **hide** [haɪd] verstecken, sich verstecken **I U6,** 86
high [haɪ] hoch, groß **II U2,** 30
high-tech [ˌhaɪ'tek] high-tech **IV U3,** 44
high school ['haɪ ˌsku:l] High School *(weiterführende Schule in den USA, Oberstufe)* **IV U2,** 24
to **highlight** ['haɪlaɪt] hervorheben, markieren °**IV U1,** 13
highway *(AE)* ['haɪweɪ] Bundesstraße, Highway **IV U4,** 61
him [hɪm] ihn, ihm **I U4,** 60
himself [hɪm'self] sich (selbst) **III U1,** 17
hint [hɪnt] Hinweis, Spur, Anspielung °**III U3,** 53
hip hop ['hɪp hɒp] Hip-Hop °**III U4,** 63
his [hɪz] sein/seine **I LUA,** 25
Hispanic [hɪ'spænɪk] hispanisch, lateinamerikanisch; Hispano-Amerikaner/-Amerikanerin **IV U4,** 68
History ['hɪstəri] Geschichte **II U1,** 10
hit [hɪt] Hit **III U5,** 82
*to **hit** [hɪt] schlagen, treffen **II U3,** 36
hobby, hobbies *(pl)* ['hɒbi; 'hɒbiz] Hobby **I LUB,** 38
hockey ['hɒki] Hockey **II U1,** 16
ice hockey ['aɪs ˌhɒki] Eishockey **II U2,** 23
*to **hold** [həʊld] halten, festhalten **IV U5,** 76
holiday ['hɒlədeɪ] Feiertag **IV U4,** 64
holiday(s) ['hɒlədeɪ(z)] Urlaub, Ferien **II U7,** 88
home [həʊm] Zuhause, Heim; nach Hause **I U1,** 11; Heimat **III U1,** 8
at home [ət 'həʊm] zu Hause **I U2,** 26
home-made [ˌhəʊm'meɪd] selbst gemacht **III U1,** 16
home plate ['həʊm ˌpleɪt] Home Plate **III U1,** 14
to take home [ˌteɪk 'həʊm] nach Hause bringen **I U2,** 35
homecoming ['həʊmkʌmɪŋ] Homecoming *(Schulfest an amerikanischen High Schools)* **IV U2,** 24
homecoming queen [ˌhəʊmkʌmɪŋ 'kwi:n] Ballkönigin **IV U2,** 25
*to feel **homesick** [ˌfi:l 'həʊmsɪk] Heimweh haben **IV U4,** 68
homework ['həʊmwɜ:k] Hausaufgabe/Hausaufgaben **I U1,** 19
homie *(slang)* ['həʊmi] Kumpel **IV U5,** 80
honest ['ɒnɪst] ehrlich **IV U2,** 32
to **hoot** [hu:t] schreien, rufen *(Eule)* **II U7,** 94
hope [həʊp] Hoffnung **IV U1,** 10
to **hope** [həʊp] hoffen **I U5,** 72
horoscope ['hɒrəskəʊp] Horoskop **II U6,** 80
horrible ['hɒrəbl] schrecklich, furchtbar **II U2,** 24
horse [hɔ:s] Pferd **I LUB,** 38
hospital ['hɒspɪtl] Krankenhaus **II U3,** 36
host [həʊst] Gastgeber, Talkmaster **III U5,** 82
hot [hɒt] heiß **I U6,** 79; toll; scharf **IV U2,** 28
hotel [həʊ'tel] Hotel **III U5,** 84
hotline ['hɒtlaɪn] Hotline **IV U4,** 65
hound [haʊnd] Jagdhund **III U5,** 82
hour ['aʊə] Stunde **I U2,** 34
hours ['aʊəz] Öffnungszeiten **I U4,** 62
for hours [fər‿'aʊəz] stundenlang **II U4,** 52
half an hour [ˌhɑ:f‿ən‿'aʊə] eine halbe Stunde **II U2,** 26
house [haʊs] Haus **I LUA,** 25
house-sitter ['haʊsˌsɪtə] Haussitter/Haussitterin °**IV U1,** 15
how [haʊ] wie **I U1,** 11
How are you? [ˌhaʊ‿'ɑ: ju:] Wie geht es dir/Ihnen/euch? **I U6,** 83
how many [haʊ 'meni] wie viele **I U5,** 68
How much are … ? [ˌhaʊ 'mʌtʃ‿ɑ:] Wie viel kosten … ? **I U5,** 66
How much is … ? [ˌhaʊ 'mʌtʃ‿ɪz] Wie viel kostet … ? **I U5,** 66
How old are you? [haʊ‿'əʊld‿ɑ: ju:] Wie alt bist du? **I U1,** 11
how to … ['haʊ tə] wie man … °**II U3,** 37
hub [hʌb] Mittelpunkt, Zentrum **IV U1,** 9
huge [hju:dʒ] riesig, gewaltig **III U2,** 30
human ['hju:mən] Mensch; menschlich **IV U3,** 43
hundred ['hʌndrəd] hundert **II U2,** 23
hungry ['hʌŋgri] hungrig **II U1,** 14
to get hungry [get 'hʌŋgri] Hunger bekommen **II U4,** 56

hunting ['hʌntɪŋ] Jagen **III U5,** 86
*to be in a **hurry** [bi:‿ɪn‿ə 'hʌri] es eilig haben **I U2,** 30
Hurry up! [ˌhʌri‿'ʌp] Beeil dich! **I U2,** 30
*to **hurt** [hɜ:t] verletzen, weh tun **II U3,** 40
hurt [hɜ:t] verletzt **III U5,** 86
hurtful ['hɜ:tfl] verletzend **IV U2,** 29

I

I [aɪ] ich **I U1,** 10
I'd like to [ˌaɪd 'laɪk tə] ich würde gern **II U2,** 22
I don't care. [aɪ dəʊnt 'keə] Es ist mir egal. **II U4,** 58
I'd rather [aɪd 'rɑ:ðə] ich würde lieber **II U2,** 22
I'm afraid ... [ˌaɪm‿ə'freɪd] leider, Ich fürchte ... °**IV U3,** 47
I'm having .... [aɪm 'hævɪŋ] Ich nehme .... **II U1,** 14
I'm scared. [aɪm 'skeəd] Ich habe Angst. **II U3,** 44
I want my ... pierced. [aɪ 'wɒnt maɪ ... 'pɪəst] Ich möchte mein ... piercen lassen. **III U4,** 62
ice [aɪs] Eis **II U2,** 23
ice-cream [aɪs'kri:m] Eis, Eiscreme **I U7,** 92
ice hockey ['aɪs ˌhɒki] Eishockey **II U2,** 23
ice rink ['aɪs rɪŋk] Eis-/Schlittschuhbahn **II U2,** 23
icon ['aɪkɒn] Ikone **III U3,** 53
idea [aɪ'dɪə] Idee, Einfall **I LUB,** 38
no idea [ˌnəʊ‿aɪ'dɪə] keine Ahnung **III U3,** 52
to **identify** [aɪ'dentɪfaɪ] erkennen, identifizieren **IV U4,** 62
idiot ['ɪdɪət] Idiot, Dummkopf **I U1,** 21
if [ɪf] wenn, falls; ob **II U7,** 90
if-clause ['ɪfklɔ:z] if-Satz °**IV U4,** 62
illegal [ɪ'li:gl] illegal, unrechtmäßig, rechtswidrig **IV U3,** 50
image ['ɪmɪdʒ] Bild, Image, Abbild, Vorstellung °**IV U4,** 61
to **imagine** [ɪ'mædʒɪn] sich (etwas) vorstellen **III U1,** 12
immigrant ['ɪmɪgrənt] Immigrant/ Immigrantin, Einwanderer/ Einwanderin **IV U1,** 9
immigration [ˌɪmɪ'greɪʃn] Immigration, Einwanderung **IV U1,** 10
important [ɪm'pɔ:tnt] wichtig; einflussreich **II U6,** 74
impression [ɪm'preʃn] Eindruck °**II U4,** 57
to **improve** [ɪm'pru:v] (sich) verbessern °**IV U2,** 30
in [ɪn] in, herein **I U1,** 10
in all [ɪn‿'ɔ:l] insgesamt, im Ganzen **III U4,** 63
in fact [ɪn 'fækt] in der Tat, genau genommen **II U7,** 94
in front of [ɪn 'frʌnt‿əv] vor **I U3,** 49
in the end [ɪn ði:‿'end] schließlich, zum Schluss **II U6,** 80
inch [ɪnʃ] Zoll *(Längenmaß: 2,54 cm)* **III U1,** 11
to **include** [ɪn'klu:d] einschließen, beinhalten, aufnehmen **IV U5,** 77
all **inclusive** [ˌɔ:l‿ɪŋ'klu:sɪv] alles inklusive **IV U4,** 62
independent [ˌɪndɪ'pendənt] unabhängig **III U3,** 52
Indian ['ɪndiən] indisch **II U4,** 49
indie ['ɪndi] Indie *(Musikrichtung)* **IV U5,** 80
industry ['ɪndəstri] Industrie **III U5,** 80
info ['ɪnfəʊ] Info °**III U4,** 68
information [ˌɪnfə'meɪʃn] Information/ Informationen **I LUC,** 52
information centre [ɪnfə'meɪʃn ˌsentə] Informationszentrum **I LUC,** 52
inheritor [ɪn'herɪtə] Erbe/Erbin **III U5,** 88
inside [ɪn'saɪd] innen, drin, nach drinnen **I U5,** 75
inspector [ɪn'spektə] Inspektor **III U5,** 84
instead of [ɪn'sted‿əv] statt, anstatt **III U1,** 17
instruction [ɪn'strʌkʃn] Instruktion, Anweisung **IV U1,** 17
intelligent [ɪn'telɪdʒnt] intelligent, klug, vernünftig **IV U3,** 44
interest ['ɪntrəst] Interesse °**IV U4,** 66
interested ['ɪntrəstɪd] interessiert **II U1,** 18
to get interested [get 'ɪntrəstɪd] sich interessieren **III U2,** 35
interesting ['ɪntrəstɪŋ] interessant **II U4,** 51
international [ˌɪntə'næʃnl] international **III U3,** 45
Internet ['ɪntənet] Internet **II U1,** 14
to surf the Internet [ˌsɜ:f ði‿'ɪntənet] im Internet surfen **II U1,** 14
Interstate *(AE)* [ˌɪntə'steɪt] Autobahn **IV U4,** 61
interview ['ɪntəvju:] Interview **II U1,** 17
to **interview** ['ɪntəvju:] interviewen **II U1,** 17
into ['ɪntə] in; in ... hinein **I U3,** 44
to get into [get‿'ɪntə] einsteigen in *(Auto)* **I U5,** 75
to run into [rʌn‿'ɪntə] laufen gegen, stoßen gegen **III U1,** 17
intonation [ˌɪntə'neɪʃn] Satzmelodie °**III U5,** 86
introduction [ˌɪntrə'dʌkʃn] Einleitung °**II U4,** 55
to **invent** [ɪn'vent] erfinden **III U4,** 63
invention [ɪn'ventʃn] Erfindung **IV U3,** 43
investigator [ɪn'vestɪgeɪtə] Ermittler/ Ermittlerin **IV U3,** 51
invitation [ˌɪnvɪ'teɪʃn] Einladung **I U5,** 70
to **invite** [ɪn'vaɪt] einladen **I U5,** 68
Irish ['aɪrɪʃ] irisch **II U7,** 90; Iren/Irinnen **IV U1,** 10
to **iron** [aɪən] bügeln **II U7,** 90
irregular [ɪ'regjələ] unregelmäßig °**II U2,** 26
island ['aɪlənd] Insel **II U6,** 82
it [ɪt] es **I U1,** 12
It said .... [ɪt 'sed] Es lautete .... **II U2,** 30
Italian [ɪ'tæliən] italienisch; Italiener/ Italienerin **I U2,** 29
its [ɪts] sein/seine; ihr/ihre **III U1,** 8

J

jacket ['dʒækɪt] Jacke **I U6,** 86
jam [dʒæm] Marmelade **I U7,** 94; *hier:* Jamsession **IV U5,** 81
traffic jam ['træfɪk ˌdʒæm] Stau **III U2,** 26
January ['dʒænjuəri] Januar **I U5,** 70
jazz [dʒæz] Jazz **II U3,** 45
jealous (of) ['dʒeləs] eifersüchtig, neidisch (auf) **II U3,** 45
jeans *(pl)* [dʒi:nz] Jeans **IV U2,** 25
jerk *(slang)* [dʒɜ:k] Trottel **IV U2,** 28
jersey ['dʒɜ:zi] Trikot **III U1,** 12
jewel ['dʒu:əl] Juwel **III U2,** 26
jewellery ['dʒu:əlri] Schmuck **III U5,** 82
job [dʒɒb] Arbeitsstelle, Job **II U6,** 80
on the job [ˌɒn ðə 'dʒɒb] bei der Arbeit **III U5,** 82
to **jog** [dʒɒg] joggen **II U4,** 52
jogger ['dʒɒgə] Jogger/Joggerin **IV U1,** 9

English – German

to **join** [dʒɔɪn] beitreten, sich anschließen, verbinden **IV U5,** 81
joke [dʒəʊk] Witz **I U1,** 20
to **joke** [dʒəʊk] scherzen, Witze machen **I U6,** 82
journey ['dʒɜ:ni] Reise, Fahrt **II U7,** 90
judge [dʒʌdʒ] Richter, Kampfrichter **II U5,** 70
juice [dʒu:s] Saft **IV U2,** 32
July [dʒʊ'laɪ] Juli **I U5,** 70
long **jump** ['lɒŋ ˌdʒʌmp] Weitsprung **I U7,** 90
to **jump** [dʒʌmp] springen **II U2,** 30
to jump about [ˌdʒʌmp‿ə'baʊt] herumspringen **III U4,** 68
to jump up [dʒʌmp‿'ʌp] hochspringen, aufspringen **II U6,** 82
June [dʒu:n] Juni **I U5,** 70
just [dʒʌst] nur, gerade, einfach **I U2,** 30

K

kangaroo [ˌkæŋgər'u:] Känguru **°II U3,** 46
*to **keep** [ki:p] (be)halten **II U4,** 55; *hier:* aufbewahren **IV U3,** 46
Keep out! [ki:p‿'aʊt] Eintritt verboten! **I U2,** 26
key [ki:] Schlüssel **II U5,** 67
kick [kɪk] Kick **III U1,** 18
to **kick** [kɪk] treten **I U5,** 74
kickboard ['kɪkbɔ:d] Kickboard, Roller **IV U1,** 9
kid [kɪd] Kind **I U3,** 44
You're **kidding.** [jə 'kɪdɪŋ] Du machst Witze. **IV U2,** 32
to **kill** [kɪl] töten; *hier:* tot machen *(Volleyball)* **III U1,** 10
kilo (kg) ['kɪləʊ] Kilo(gramm) **II U4,** 54
kilometre ['kɪləʊˌmi:tə; kɪ'lɒmɪtə] Kilometer **III U3,** 45
kind [kaɪnd] Art, Sorte **III U2,** 34
kind [kaɪnd] freundlich, nett **IV U2,** 32
Kinetoscope [kɪ'netəskəʊp] Kinetoskop **°IV U5,** 78
king [kɪŋ] König **III U2,** 31
kiss [kɪs] Kuss **IV U2,** 28
to **kiss** [kɪs] küssen **III U5,** 80
PE **kit** [ˌpi:‿'i: kɪt] Sportzeug **II U1,** 10
kitchen ['kɪtʃɪn] Küche **I LUA,** 24
knee [ni:] Knie **II U3,** 41
knife, knives *(pl)* [naɪf; naɪvz] Messer **II U4,** 50
knight [naɪt] Ritter **II U2,** 22
knock [nɒk] Klopfen, Schlag **I U2,** 34
to **knock** [nɒk] klopfen; stoßen, schlagen **III U5,** 90
to knock out [nɒk‿'aʊt] k.o. schlagen, umhauen **III U1,** 17
*to **know** [nəʊ] wissen, kennen **I U4,** 58

L

lab(oratory) [læb; lə'bɒrətri] Labor **II U2,** 23
lad [læd] Junge **III U5,** 83
ladder ['lædə] Leiter **III U5,** 85
ladies and gentlemen [ˌleɪdiz‿n 'dʒentlmən] meine Damen und Herren **°III U2,** 33
lake [leɪk] See **III U3,** 57
lamb [læm] Lamm, Lammfleisch **II U4,** 49
lamp [læmp] Lampe, Leuchte **IV U3,** 46
land [lænd] Land **I LUB,** 38
to **land** [lænd] landen **III U3,** 45
landmark ['lændmɑ:k] Wahrzeichen, Markstein **III U2,** 30
lane [leɪn] Fahrspur, Gasse **IV U5,** 84
language ['læŋgwɪdʒ] Sprache **I U2,** 29
lantern ['læntən] Laterne **I U7,** 90
laptop ['læptɒp] Laptop **I U2,** 34
large [lɑ:dʒ] groß, riesig **I U5,** 66
lassi ['lasɪ] Lassi *(Jogurtgetränk)* **II U4,** 49
to **last** [lɑ:st] dauern, anhalten **IV U4,** 68
last [lɑ:st] letzte/letzter/letztes **I U7,** 90
last night [lɑ:st 'naɪt] gestern Abend/ Nacht **II U3,** 37
late [leɪt] spät, zu spät, verspätet **I U1,** 16
later ['leɪtə] später **I U2,** 30
Latino [lə'ti:nəʊ] Latinomusik; Latino **IV U5,** 77
latte ['lɑ:teɪ] Café latte **IV U2,** 32
to **laugh** [lɑ:f] lachen **I U5,** 74
to laugh at ['lɑ:f‿ət] auslachen, sich lustig machen über **II U3,** 36
to **launch** [lɔ:nʃ] starten, abschießen **IV U3,** 43
layout ['leɪaʊt] Layout, Anordnung **°IV U3,** 48
lead [led] Blei **III U4,** 70
*to **lead** [li:d] führen **°IV U3,** 48
leader ['li:də] Führer/Führerin, Anführer/Anführerin **II U6,** 80
leaf, leaves *(pl)* [li:f; li:vz] Blatt **III U4,** 70
leaflet ['li:flət] Flugblatt, Prospekt **III U4,** 66
to **leak** [li:k] auslaufen, lecken **IV U3,** 44
*to **lean** [li:n] (sich) lehnen **IV U1,** 16
to lean out [li:n‿'aʊt] (sich) hinauslehnen **II U7,** 94
*to **learn** [lɜ:n] lernen **I U3,** 40; erfahren **III U1,** 8
least [li:st] am wenigsten **°IV U5,** 87
at least [ət 'li:st] wenigstens, mindestens **I U6,** 87
*to **leave** [li:v] lassen, verlassen, abfahren **I U3,** 43; (weg)gehen **II U1,** 18
left [left] linke/linker/linkes; links **I U4,** 55
Go left. [gəʊ 'left] Biege nach links ab. **I LUC,** 52
on the left [ɒn ðə 'left] links **I U2,** 28
to turn left [tɜ:n 'left] links abbiegen **II U7,** 97
left [left] übrig **II U4,** 54
leg [leg] Bein **II U3,** 41
legal ['li:gl] legal, rechtlich, Rechts- **IV U3,** 50
lemonade [ˌlemə'neɪd] Limonade **I U5,** 68
*to **lend** [lend] leihen **II U7,** 90
length [leŋkθ] Länge **IV U3,** 48
leprechaun ['leprəkɔ:n] Gnom, Kobold **°II U7,** 90
less [les] weniger **IV U2,** 31
lesson ['lesn] Unterrichtsstunde **I U1,** 15
*to **let** [let] lassen **III U4,** 62
Let's .... [lets] Lasst uns .... **I U1,** 10
letter ['letə] Buchstabe, Brief **I U1,** 15
capital letter [ˌkæpɪtl 'letə] Großbuchstabe **°II U3,** 37
lettuce ['letɪs] Kopfsalat **II U4,** 54
lettuce *(slang)* ['letɪs] *hier:* Geld **°IV U5,** 84
level ['levl] Ebene, Niveau **III U4,** 67
driver's **license** *(AE)* ['draɪvəz ˌlaɪsnts] Führerschein **IV U4,** 68
to **lie** [laɪ] lügen **IV U2,** 33
*to **lie** [laɪ] liegen **III U3,** 52
to lie down [laɪ 'daʊn] (sich) hinlegen, niederlegen **III U3,** 52
life, lives *(pl)* [laɪf; laɪvz] Leben **II U3,** 42
lifeguard ['laɪfgɑ:d] Rettungsschwimmer/ Rettungsschwimmerin **III U3,** 46
lifestyle ['laɪfstaɪl] Lebensart **IV U5,** 84
to **lift** [lɪft] hochziehen, hochheben **III U2,** 30
light [laɪt] Licht **II U7,** 94
light bulb ['laɪt bʌlb] Glühbirne **IV U3,** 46

to **like** [laɪk] mögen, gern haben **I U3,** 44
I'd like to [ˌaɪd 'laɪk tə] ich würde gern **II U2,** 22
would like [wʊd 'laɪk] hätte gern, möchte gern **II U4,** 52
like [laɪk] wie *(Vergleich)* **I U6,** 86
limousine [ˌlɪmə'zi:n] Limousine **IV U5,** 84
line [laɪn] Zeile, Text, Linie **I U3,** 43
back line [ˌbæk 'laɪn] Grundlinie **III U1,** 10
ocean **liner** ['əʊʃn ˌlaɪnə] Ozeandampfer **III U3,** 45
link [lɪŋk] Verbindung, Bindeglied **III U5,** 82
to **link** [lɪŋk] verbinden °**IV U2,** 26
lion ['laɪən] Löwe **II U5,** 68
lip balm ['lɪp bɑ:m] Lippenpflegestift **II U6,** 82
list [lɪst] Liste **I U5,** 68
to **listen** ['lɪsn] zuhören, anhören **I U1,** 11
little ['lɪtl] klein **I U6,** 82; wenig **IV U1,** 10
to **live** [lɪv] wohnen, leben **I U3,** 45
live [laɪv] live **III U4,** 63
living room ['lɪvɪŋ rʊm] Wohnzimmer **I LUA,** 24
loads of ['ləʊdz‿əv] viele **IV U1,** 16
local ['ləʊkl] lokal, örtlich **III U2,** 28
loch [lɒx] See *(schottisch)* **III U3,** 57
to **lock** [lɒk] abschließen **III U3,** 53
locker ['lɒkə] Schließfach **II U1,** 10
lonely ['ləʊnli] einsam **III U1,** 16
long [lɒŋ] lang **I U3,** 44
long form ['lɒŋ fɔ:m] Langform °**I U1,** 16
long jump ['lɒŋ ˌdʒʌmp] Weitsprung **I U7,** 90
as long as [əz 'lɒŋ‿əz] solange **I U7,** 94
look [lʊk] Blick, Aussehen **II U1,** 10
to give … a dirty look [ˌgɪv‿ə dɜ:ti 'lʊk] einen vernichtenden Blick zuwerfen **II U1,** 10
to have a look (at) [ˌhæv‿ə 'lʊk] anschauen, einen Blick werfen (auf) **IV U2,** 26
to **look** [lʊk] sehen, schauen, aussehen **I U1,** 12
to look after [lʊk‿'ɑ:ftə] sich kümmern um, aufpassen auf **II U1,** 14
to look at ['lʊk‿ət] ansehen **I U6,** 82
to look for ['lʊk fə] suchen **I U6,** 81
to look out (for) [lʊk‿'aʊt] Ausschau halten (nach), suchen (nach) °**III U2,** 32
to look round [lʊk 'raʊnd] sich umsehen **II U1,** 18
to look up [lʊk‿'ʌp] (hin)aufschauen; nachschlagen **II U2,** 30
*to **lose** [lu:z] verlieren **II U4,** 52
to be lost [bi: 'lɒst] sich verirrt haben **III U3,** 46
to get lost [get 'lɒst] verloren gehen, sich verirren **I U3,** 48
a **lot** [ə 'lɒt] viel **II U1,** 15
a lot of [ə 'lɒt‿əv] viel/viele, eine Menge **I U2,** 30
parking lot *(AE)* ['pɑ:kɪŋ ˌlɒt] Parkplatz **IV U4,** 68
lots (of) ['lɒts‿əv] viel/viele **II U7,** 88
lots of love [ˌlɒts‿əv 'lʌv] viele Grüße *(am Briefende)* **III U4,** 68
loud [laʊd] laut **II U7,** 91
to say out loud [ˌseɪ‿aʊt 'laʊd] laut sagen °**III U4,** 67
love [lʌv] Herzliche Grüße *(am Briefende)*; Liebe **I U6,** 78
lots of love [ˌlɒts‿əv 'lʌv] viele Grüße *(am Briefende)* **III U4,** 68
to **love** [lʌv] gern mögen, lieben **I U3,** 44
low [ləʊ] niedrig, tief **IV U1,** 14
lower ['ləʊə] untere/unterer/unteres **IV U1,** 14
low-cut ['ləʊkʌt] tief ausgeschnitten **IV U5,** 76
luck [lʌk] Glück **I U4,** 63
Good luck! [ˌgʊd 'lʌk] Viel Glück! **I U4,** 63
bad luck [ˌbæd 'lʌk] Pech **I U4,** 63
lucky ['lʌki] glücklich **I U1,** 16
luckily ['lʌkɪli] glücklicherweise **IV U2,** 26
to get lucky *(AE)* [get 'lʌki] Glück haben **IV U4,** 68
you're lucky [jʊə 'lʌki] du hast Glück **I U1,** 16
luggage ['lʌgɪdʒ] Gepäck **II U7,** 90
lunch [lʌntʃ] Mittagessen **I U1,** 18
lunchtime ['lʌntʃtaɪm] Mittag, Mittagszeit **I U1,** 19
lyrics ['lɪrɪks] Liedtext °**IV U5,** 82

M

machine [mə'ʃi:n] Maschine, Apparat **III U4,** 66
vending machine ['vendɪŋ məˌʃi:n] Warenautomat **III U4,** 66
washing machine ['wɒʃɪŋ məˌʃi:n] Waschmaschine **IV U3,** 44
mad [mæd] verrückt; wütend **II U1,** 18
magazine [mægə'zi:n] Zeitschrift, Magazin **I U2,** 33
to **mail** [meɪl] mailen, per E-Mail schicken **IV U4,** 63
main [meɪn] Haupt- **II U4,** 49
Her **Majesty** [hə 'mædʒəsti] Ihre Majestät °**III U5,** 90
*to **make** [meɪk] machen, tun **I U1,** 11
to make friends (with) [ˌmeɪk 'frendz] Freundschaft schließen (mit) **IV U4,** 68
to make it ['meɪk‿ɪt] es schaffen **III U4,** 68
to make sure [meɪk 'ʃʊə] sichergehen **II U6,** 82
to make up [meɪk‿'ʌp] erfinden, sich ausdenken **I U4,** 62
make-up ['meɪkʌp] Make-up, Schminke **I U7,** 90
(shopping) mall [mɔ:l] Einkaufszentrum, Einkaufspassage **IV U2,** 32
man, men *(pl)* [mæn; men] Mann **I U4,** 62
manager ['mænɪdʒə] Manager/ Managerin **I U2,** 26
adverb of **manner** [ˌædvɜ:b‿əv 'mænə] Adverb der Art und Weise °**II U7,** 90
mansion ['mænʃn] Villa °**IV U1,** 15
many ['meni] viele, etliche **I U5,** 68
how many [haʊ 'meni] wie viele **I U5,** 68
map [mæp] Stadtplan, Landkarte **I LUC,** 52
mind map ['maɪnd mæp] Wörternetz *(eine Art Schaubild)* °**III U1,** 18
maple ['meɪpl] Ahorn **IV U1,** 12
March [mɑ:tʃ] März **I U5,** 70
mark [mɑ:k] Fleck **I U2,** 30; Note *(in der Schule)* **II U3,** 44
to **mark** [mɑ:k] markieren °**II U2,** 29
market ['mɑ:kɪt] Markt **II U2,** 22
married to ['mærid tə] verheiratet mit **I U2,** 28
to **marry** ['mæri] heiraten **III U2,** 31
match [mætʃ] Spiel, Wettkampf **II U2,** 24
to **match** [mætʃ] passen zu; zuordnen, zusammenfügen **III U3,** 50
to match up ['mætʃ‿ʌp] zusammenfügen °**II U4,** 52

material [mə'tɪəriəl] Material; Stoff **IV U2,** 26
Maths [mæθs] Mathematik **II U1,** 10
matter ['mætə] Angelegenheit, Frage **IV U5,** 80
What's the matter? [ˌwɒts ðə 'mætə] Was ist los? **III U5,** 88
no matter [nəʊ 'mætə] egal **IV U5,** 84
to **matter** ['mætə] von Bedeutung sein, ausmachen **IV U5,** 80
*__may__ [meɪ] kann/könnte(n) vielleicht **II U4,** 55; *hier:* dürfen **IV U2,** 27
May [meɪ] Mai **I U5,** 70
maybe ['meɪbi] vielleicht **I U7,** 96
me [mi:] mich, mir **I LUB,** 38
meal [mi:l] Mahlzeit **II U4,** 52
*to **mean** [mi:n] bedeuten, meinen **I U4,** 55
mean [mi:n] gemein **IV U2,** 33
meaning ['mi:nɪŋ] Bedeutung **III U2,** 33
measurement ['meʒəmənt] Maß, Maßeinheit °**III U3,** 55
meat [mi:t] Fleisch **III U3,** 50
mechanic [mə'kænɪk] Mechaniker/Mechanikerin **IV U3,** 49
media *(pl)* ['mi:diə] Medien °**II U5,** 62
medium ['mi:diəm] mittel **I U5,** 66
*to **meet** [mi:t] treffen, sich treffen **I U3,** 45
meeting ['mi:tɪŋ] Treffen, Besprechung **II U1,** 12
member ['membə] Mitglied **IV U5,** 77
memory ['memri] Erinnerung; Gedächtnis **IV U3,** 50
menagerie [mə'nædʒri] Menagerie **III U2,** 31
menu ['menju:] Speisekarte, Menü **II U1,** 14
Meow! [mi:'aʊ] Miau! °**I U2,** 35
mess [mes] Durcheinander **III U2,** 35
message ['mesɪdʒ] Nachricht **II U3,** 38
text message ['tekst ˌmesɪdʒ] SMS **I U6,** 80
metal ['metl] Metal *(Musikrichtung)*; Metall **IV U5,** 80
metre ['mi:tə] Meter **III U3,** 48
Mexican ['meksɪkən] mexikanisch; Mexikaner/Mexikanerin **IV U4,** 68
mice *(pl)* [maɪs] Mäuse **I U3,** 45
microphone ['maɪkrəfəʊn] Mikrofon **II U5,** 71
microwave ['maɪkrəʊweɪv] Mikrowelle **IV U3,** 46
middle ['mɪdl] Mitte; Mittel- **III U4,** 64
middle school *(AE)* ['mɪdl ˌsku:l] Mittelschule *(weiterführende Schule in den USA, Mittelstufe)* **IV U2,** 30
midnight ['mɪdnaɪt] Mitternacht **II U6,** 78
*__might__ [maɪt] könnte/könnten **IV U4,** 68
mile [maɪl] Meile *(brit. Längenmaß)* **II U6,** 74
for miles [fə‿'maɪlz] meilenweit **IV U4,** 69
milk [mɪlk] Milch **I U5,** 68
milkman, milkmen *(pl)* ['mɪlkmən; 'mɪlkmen] Milchmann **III U2,** 34
milkshake ['mɪlkʃeɪk] Milchshake **IV U1,** 12
millennium [mɪ'leniəm] Jahrtausend **III U2,** 30
million ['mɪlɪən] Million **II U2,** 23
to **mime** [maɪm] pantomimisch darstellen °**I U6,** 81
miming game ['maɪmɪŋ geɪm] Pantomime °**I U6,** 81
mind [maɪnd] Geist, Verstand **III U5,** 83
He had something on his mind. [maɪnd] Ihn beschäftigte etwas. **III U5,** 83
mind map ['maɪnd mæp] Wörternetz *(eine Art Schaubild)* °**III U1,** 18
to change your mind [ˌtʃeɪndʒ jə 'maɪnd] deine Meinung ändern **III U1,** 17
mineral ['mɪnərəl] Mineral- **II U4,** 49
mini ['mɪni] Mini- °**IV U2,** 29
minimum ['mɪnɪməm] Minimum **IV U4,** 62
minute ['mɪnɪt] Minute **I U4,** 64
mirror ['mɪrə] Spiegel **III U4,** 67
to **miss** [mɪs] vermissen, fehlen; verpassen **II U6,** 76; verfehlen **IV U2,** 33
to miss a turn [ˌmɪs‿ə 'tɜ:n] einmal aussetzen °**II U6,** 79
to miss out (on) [mɪss‿'aʊt] vermissen, zu kurz kommen (mit) **IV U4,** 62
Miss [mɪs] Frau *(Anrede)* **I U7,** 94
missing ['mɪsɪŋ] fehlend °**I U4,** 64
to be missing [bi: 'mɪsɪŋ] fehlen **III U1,** 14
mistake [mɪ'steɪk] Fehler **III U5,** 86
mister ['mɪstə] *hier:* Sie *(Anrede)* **IV U1,** 17
mixed bag ['mɪkst bæg] Vermischtes °**III U1,** 21
to **moan** [məʊn] (sich) (be)klagen **III U1,** 16
mobile ['məʊbaɪl] Handy, Mobiltelefon **I U1,** 11
modal auxiliary verb [ˌməʊdl‿ɔ:g'zɪljəri 'vɜ:b] modales Hilfsverb °**III U3,** 46
model ['mɒdl] Model, Modell **III U2,** 29
modern ['mɒdn] modern **IV U3,** 43
mom *(AE)* [mɒm] Mama, Mutti **IV U4,** 65
moment ['məʊmənt] Moment, Augenblick **I U7,** 90
at the moment [æt ðə 'məʊmənt] im Augenblick, momentan **I U7,** 90
monastery ['mɒnəstri] Kloster **III U2,** 31
Monday ['mʌndeɪ] Montag **I LUB,** 39
on Mondays [ɒn 'mʌndeɪz] montags **I LUB,** 39
money ['mʌni] Geld **I U5,** 67
pocket money ['pɒkɪt ˌmʌni] Taschengeld **II U2,** 22
to **monitor** ['mɒnɪtə] überwachen **IV U3,** 43
monster ['mɒnstə] Monster **IV U1,** 12
month [mʌnθ] Monat **I U5,** 70
moon [mu:n] Mond **II U7,** 94
moor [mɔ:] Hochmoor **II U6,** 74
more [mɔ:] mehr **I U2,** 29
morning ['mɔ:nɪŋ] Morgen, Vormittag **I U1,** 16
Good morning! [ˌgʊd 'mɔ:nɪŋ] Guten Morgen! **I U1,** 16
in the morning [ˌɪn ðə 'mɔ:nɪŋ] morgens, am Morgen, vormittags **I U3,** 47
the next morning [ðə ˌnekst 'mɔ:nɪŋ] am nächsten Morgen **II U1,** 18
most [məʊst] das meiste, die meisten **I U3,** 44
mostly ['məʊstli] überwiegend, hauptsächlich, größtenteils **IV U1,** 14
motel [məʊ'tel] Motel °**IV U3,** 46
mother ['mʌðə] Mutter **III U3,** 52
motion ['məʊʃn] Bewegung **IV U5,** 78
motorbike ['məʊtəbaɪk] Motorrad **IV U4,** 61
motorway ['məʊtəweɪ] Autobahn **IV U4,** 65
mountain ['maʊntɪn] Berg **IV U3,** 50
mouse [maʊs] Maus **I U1,** 10
mouth [maʊθ] Mund **II U3,** 41
move [mu:v] Schritt, Bewegung **IV U2,** 29
to **move** [mu:v] (sich) bewegen; umziehen **II U6,** 78
movie *(AE)* ['mu:vi] Film **IV U2,** 28
movies *(AE)* ['mu:viz] Kino **IV U2,** 28
MP3 [ˌempi:'θri:] MP3 **II U5,** 62

MP3 player [ˌempiːˈθriː ˌpleɪə] MP3-Player **II U5,** 62
Mr [ˈmɪstə] Herr *(Anrede)* **I U1,** 12
Mrs [ˈmɪsɪz] Frau *(Anrede)* **I U1,** 12
much [mʌtʃ] viel **I U5,** 66
How much are … ? [ˌhaʊ ˈmʌtʃ‿ɑː] Wie viel kosten … ? **I U5,** 66
How much is … ? [ˌhaʊ ˈmʌtʃ‿ɪz] Wie viel kostet … ? **I U5,** 66
mum [mʌm] Mama, Mutti **I LUA,** 25
to **murder** [ˈmɜːdə] ermorden **III U5,** 88
museum [mjuːˈziːəm] Museum **I LUC,** 52
music [ˈmjuːzɪk] Musik **I U2,** 34
musical [ˈmjuːzɪkl] Musical **III U5,** 80
musician [mjuːˈzɪʃn] Musiker/Musikerin **IV U5,** 80
*__must__ [mʌst] müssen **I U7,** 94
my [maɪ] mein/meine **I U1,** 10
My God! [maɪ ˈɡɒd] Mein Gott! **II U6,** 82
My name is … . [maɪ ˈneɪm‿ɪz] Ich heiße … . **I U1,** 10
mystery [ˈmɪstri] Geheimnis, Rätsel **III U3,** 49
myth [mɪθ] Mythos **III U5,** 81

N

name [neɪm] Name **I U1,** 10
My name is … . [maɪ ˈneɪm‿ɪz] Ich heiße … . **I U1,** 10
What's your name? [ˌwɒts jə ˈneɪm] Wie heißt du? **I U1,** 11
to **name** [neɪm] (be)nennen **IV U1,** 10
national [ˈnæʃnl] national **II U6,** 82; landesweit **III U1,** 10
national park [ˌnæʃnl ˈpɑːk] Nationalpark **IV U4,** 60
native [ˈneɪtɪv] eingeboren, einheimisch, gebürtig **IV U1,** 9
Native American [ˌneɪtɪv‿əˈmerɪkən] Ureinwohner/Ureinwohnerin Amerikas, Indianer/Indianerin **IV U1,** 9
nature [ˈneɪtʃə] Natur **IV U4,** 62
near [nɪə] in der Nähe von, nahe **I LUC,** 53
nearly [ˈnɪəli] fast, annähernd **III U1,** 16
to **need** [niːd] brauchen, benötigen, müssen **II U1,** 21
negative [ˈneɡətɪv] negativ, verneint °**III U5,** 82
negative statement [ˌneɡətɪv ˈsteɪtmənt] Verneinung °**III U5,** 82

neighborhood *(AE)* [ˈneɪbəhʊd] Viertel; Nachbarschaft **IV U1,** 9
neighbour [ˈneɪbə] Nachbar/Nachbarin **II U7,** 90
neon [ˈniːɒn] neonfarben **IV U1,** 9
nephew [ˈnefjuː] Neffe **III U5,** 88
nervous [ˈnɜːvəs] nervös, aufgeregt **II U5,** 71
net [net] Netz **III U1,** 10
never [ˈnevə] nie, niemals **I U3,** 44
new [njuː] neu **I U1,** 10
news *(sg.)* [njuːz] Nachricht(en), Neuigkeit(en) **III U3,** 48
breaking news [ˌbreɪkɪŋ ˈnjuːz] neueste Nachrichten **IV U2,** 24
newsagent [ˈnjuːsˌeɪdʒənt] Zeitschriftenhändler/Zeitschriftenhändlerin **I LUC,** 52
newspaper [ˈnjuːsˌpeɪpə] Zeitung **III U2,** 28
next [nekst] nächste/nächster/nächstes **I U5,** 69; als Nächstes °**II U1,** 19
next door [ˌnekst ˈdɔː] nebenan **III U1,** 16
next to [ˈnekst tə] neben **I U2,** 28
the next morning [ðə ˌnekst ˈmɔːnɪŋ] am nächsten Morgen **II U1,** 18
nice [naɪs] nett **I U1,** 12; schön **II U4,** 54
nickel [ˈnɪkl] Nickel *(Währung)* **IV U1,** 13
nickname [ˈnɪkneɪm] Spitzname **IV U5,** 77
night [naɪt] Nacht, Abend **I U3,** 44
night nurse [ˈnaɪt nɜːs] Nachtschwester **I U3,** 47
at night [ət ˈnaɪt] nachts **II U3,** 47
last night [lɑːst ˈnaɪt] gestern Abend/Nacht **II U3,** 37
no [nəʊ] nein, nicht; kein/keine **I U1,** 12
No way! [ˌnəʊ‿ˈweɪ] Auf keinen Fall! **IV U4,** 62
no idea [ˌnəʊ‿aɪˈdɪə] keine Ahnung **III U3,** 52
no one [ˈnəʊwʌn] niemand **II U2,** 30
nobody [ˈnəʊbədi] niemand **III U5,** 85
noise [nɔɪz] Geräusch, Lärm **I U2,** 35
none [nʌn] keiner/keine **II U7,** 88
normal [ˈnɔːml] normal **I U3,** 44
north [nɔːθ] Norden **I U4,** 55
nose [nəʊz] Nase **II U3,** 41
not [nɒt] nicht **I U1,** 16
not … yet [jet] noch nicht **II U5,** 66
(not …) at all [ˌnɒt … ət‿ˈɔːl] überhaupt (nicht) **IV U2,** 32
not … either [ˌnɒt … ˈaɪðə] auch nicht **III U1,** 17

not even [nɒt‿ˈiːvn] nicht einmal **III U4,** 64
note [nəʊt] Notiz, Anmerkung **II U1,** 11
sick note [ˈsɪk ˌnəʊt] Krankmeldung **II U2,** 28
to take notes [teɪk ˈnəʊts] sich Notizen machen °**II U4,** 55
to **note** [nəʊt] notieren °**IV U1,** 14
nothing [ˈnʌθɪŋ] nichts **II U4,** 50
notice [ˈnəʊtɪs] Anschlag, Notiz **III U4,** 66
notice board [ˈnəʊtɪs bɔːd] schwarzes Brett **III U4,** 66
to **notice** [ˈnəʊtɪs] bemerken **III U3,** 48
noun [naʊn] Nomen °**III U1,** 18
November [nəʊˈvembə] November **I U5,** 70
now [naʊ] jetzt, nun **I U1,** 20
right now [ˌraɪt ˈnaʊ] jetzt gleich, in diesem Augenblick **I U7,** 92
nowhere [ˈnəʊweə] nirgendwo, nirgendwohin **III U4,** 64
number [ˈnʌmbə] Nummer, Zahl **I U1,** 11
phone number [ˈfəʊn ˌnʌmbə] Telefonnummer **I U1,** 11
social security number [ˌsəʊʃl sɪˈkjʊərəti ˌnʌmbə] Sozialversicherungsnummer **IV U3,** 50
nurse [nɜːs] Krankenschwester, Krankenpfleger **I U3,** 47
night nurse [ˈnaɪt nɜːs] Nachtschwester **I U3,** 47
*to be **nuts about** [biː ˌnʌts‿əˈbaʊt] verrückt nach … sein **II U1,** 18

O

object [ˈɒbdʒɪkt] Objekt, Gegenstand **IV U3,** 51
observatory [əbˈzɜːvətri] Observatorium, Sternwarte **I U5,** 73
ocean [ˈəʊʃn] Ozean **III U3,** 45
ocean liner [ˈəʊʃn ˌlaɪnə] Ozeandampfer **III U3,** 45
October [ɒkˈtəʊbə] Oktober **I U5,** 70
odd one out [ɒd wʌn‿ˈaʊt] das nicht dazu passende (Wort) **II U5,** 72
of [ɒv; əv] von **I U2,** 26
of course [əv ˈkɔːs] natürlich, selbstverständlich **I U1,** 19
off [ɒf] herunter, ab, weg von **II U3,** 36
to get off [ɡet‿ˈɒf] aussteigen aus **I U4,** 59; wegräumen von, abräumen von **III U4,** 65
to send off [send‿ˈɒf] vom Platz verweisen **III U1,** 15

to take off [teɪk‿'ɒf] wegbringen, fortschaffen **III U1,** 17; ausziehen **III U3,** 52; abheben, starten, abfliegen **IV U1,** 16
offer ['ɒfə] Angebot **IV U5,** 81
to **offer** ['ɒfə] anbieten **IV U4,** 62
office ['ɒfɪs] Büro **II U2,** 31
post office ['pəʊst‿ɒfɪs] Postamt **III U2,** 35
officer ['ɒfɪsə] Beamter/Beamtin **III U3,** 45
official [ə'fɪʃl] Beamter/Beamtin **IV U1,** 10
official [ə'fɪʃl] offiziell **III U3,** 48
often ['ɒfn] oft **I U3,** 44
oh [əʊ] oh °**I U1,** 12
Oink-oink! [ɔɪŋk‿ɔɪŋk] Grunz! °**I U6,** 82
OK [əʊ'keɪ] o.k. **I U1,** 12
We're OK. [ˌwɪər‿əʊ'keɪ] Es geht uns gut. **I U6,** 83
is OK with us [ɪz‿əʊ'keɪ wɪð‿ʌs] ist uns recht **I U6,** 78
old [əʊld] alt **I U1,** 11
How old are you? [haʊ‿'əʊld‿ɑ: ju:] Wie alt bist du? **I U1,** 11
on [ɒn] auf, an **I U1,** 14
to … on [ɒn] weiter- **IV U3,** 50
on board [ɒn 'bɔ:d] an Bord **IV U3,** 51
on foot [ɒn 'fʊt] zu Fuß **I U4,** 57
on Mondays [ɒn 'mʌndeɪz] montags **I LUB,** 39
on record [ɒn 'rekɔ:d] verzeichnet, dokumentiert **III U3,** 46
on the air [ˌɒn ði‿'eə] auf Sendung **II U4,** 55
on the bus [ˌɒn ðə 'bʌs] im Bus **II U1,** 18
on the job [ˌɒn ðə 'dʒɒb] bei der Arbeit **III U5,** 82
on the left [ɒn ðə 'left] links **I U2,** 28
on the right [ɒn ðə 'raɪt] rechts **I U2,** 28
on time [ɒn 'taɪm] pünktlich **IV U3,** 48
to be on [bi:‿'ɒn] an der Reihe sein; im Gange sein, laufen **II U5,** 70; an sein, brennen *(Licht)* **II U7,** 94
once [wʌnts] einmal, einst **II U3,** 36
at once [ət 'wʌnts] sofort, plötzlich **II U7,** 94
one day [wʌn 'deɪ] eines Tages **II U3,** 36
one(s) [wʌn(z)] *(Platzhalter für ein Nomen)* **III U2,** 29
only ['əʊnli] nur, bloß, erst **I U2,** 26; einzige/einziger/einziges **III U5,** 88
only child ['əʊnli ˌtʃaɪld] Einzelkind **I U2,** 26
onto ['ɒntu:; 'ɒntə] (auf …) hinauf, auf **II U1,** 19
Oops! [u:ps] Hoppla! Huch! °**I U1,** 20
to **open** ['əʊpn] öffnen, aufmachen **I U1,** 19; sich öffnen, aufgehen **III U5,** 86
open ['əʊpn] offen; geöffnet **II U2,** 23
to **operate** ['ɒpəreɪt] bedienen; operieren **IV U3,** 43
opinion [ə'pɪnjən] Meinung **IV U1,** 11
opposite ['ɒpəzɪt] gegenüber °**II U4,** 49; Gegenteil °**IV U1,** 18
oppression [ə'preʃn] Unterdrückung **IV U1,** 10
or [ɔ:] oder **I U1,** 11
orange ['ɒrɪndʒ] Orange **II U4,** 54
order ['ɔ:də] Reihenfolge, Ordnung **IV U3,** 48
to **order** ['ɔ:də] bestellen **II U4,** 49
to **organize** ['ɔ:gənaɪz] organisieren **I U7,** 90
organizer ['ɔ:gənaɪzə] Organisator/Organisatorin, Veranstalter/Veranstalterin **III U4,** 63
other ['ʌðə] andere/anderer/anderes **I U7,** 91
each other [ˌi:tʃ‿'ʌðə] sich gegenseitig **II U1,** 19
our ['aʊə] unser/unsere **I U2,** 26
out [aʊt] heraus, hinaus; draußen, außerhalb **I U3,** 42
Keep out! [ki:p‿'aʊt] Eintritt verboten! **I U2,** 26
out and about ['aʊt‿nd‿ə'baʊt] unterwegs °**I U4,** 54
out of ['aʊt‿əv] aus … heraus **I U3,** 49
to get out [get‿'aʊt] aussteigen **I U6,** 86; entkommen **III U3,** 53
to hang out [hæŋ‿'aʊt] sich herumtreiben **III U4,** 64
to put out [pʊt‿'aʊt] hinausstellen **III U4,** 65
to sort out [sɔ:t‿'aʊt] klären, regeln *(ein Problem)* **I U2,** 30
to take out [teɪk‿'aʊt] herausnehmen **I U3,** 42
outrageous [aʊt'reɪdʒəs] ausgefallen, gewagt; empörend **IV U5,** 76
outside [aʊt'saɪd] außerhalb, draußen, nach draußen **I U2,** 30
oven ['ʌvn] Backofen **I U3,** 42
over ['əʊvə] vorbei, vorüber **II U5,** 70
over ['əʊvə] über **I U2,** 26
over easy [ˌəʊvər‿'i:zi] beidseitig gebraten *(Ei)* **IV U4,** 65
over there [ˌəʊvə 'ðeə] da drüben **I U5,** 66
all over [ˌɔ:l‿'əʊvə] überall **III U3,** 49
to come over [kʌm‿'əʊvə] herüberkommen **I U2,** 27
*to **overdo** [ˌəʊvə'du:] übertreiben **IV U2,** 28
overheard [ˌəʊvə'hɜ:d] zufällig mitgehört °**III U1,** 15
overwhelming [ˌəʊvə'welmɪŋ] überwältigend **IV U4,** 60
barn **owl** ['bɑ:n‿əʊl] Schleiereule **II U7,** 94
own [əʊn] eigener/eigene/eigenes **II U6,** 76
owner ['əʊnə] Besitzer/Besitzerin **II U5,** 71

P

pacemaker ['peɪsˌmeɪkə] Herzschrittmacher **IV U3,** 43
to **pack** [pæk] packen **I U6,** 80
packet ['pækɪt] Päckchen, Paket **I U5,** 68
page [peɪdʒ] Seite **I U1,** 19
pain [peɪn] Schmerz **IV U3,** 50
paint [peɪnt] Farbe **II U3,** 40
to **paint** [peɪnt] malen, anmalen, (an)streichen **I U7,** 90
painter ['peɪntə] Maler/Malerin °**IV U1,** 15
painting ['peɪntɪŋ] Gemälde **III U5,** 89
pair [peə] Paar °**I U1,** 22
palace ['pælɪs] Palast **III U2,** 26
pancake ['pænkeɪk] Pfannkuchen **IV U1,** 12
to **panic** ['pænɪk] sich aufregen **II U5,** 70
panther ['pænθə] Panter **II U2,** 25
paper ['peɪpə] Papier; Zeitung; Dokument **IV U1,** 14
parade [pə'reɪd] Parade, Umzug **IV U1,** 14
paradise ['pærəˌdaɪs] Paradies **III U3,** 46
paragraph ['pærəgrɑ:f] Paragraf, Absatz °**IV U4,** 66
parent ['peərnt] Elternteil **IV U2,** 27
parents ['peərənts] Eltern **I U2,** 26
park [pɑ:k] Park **I U3,** 40
national park [ˌnæʃnl 'pɑ:k] Nationalpark **IV U4,** 60
theme park ['θi:m ˌpɑ:k] Freizeitpark **IV U2,** 24
parking lot *(AE)* ['pɑ:kɪŋ ˌlɒt] Parkplatz **IV U4,** 68

part [pɑ:t] Teil **II U3,** 47; Rolle **II U5,** 70
to take part in [teɪk 'pɑ:t‿ɪn] teilnehmen an **III U4,** 63
partner ['pɑ:tnə] Partner/Partnerin **I U1,** 15
party ['pɑ:ti] Party, Feier **I U5,** 68
to have a party [ˌhæv‿ə 'pɑ:ti] eine Party feiern **I U5,** 68
to **pass** [pɑ:s] weitergeben, herüberreichen **II U1,** 18; vorbeigehen an **III U5,** 85; bestehen **IV U2,** 30
passenger ['pæsndʒə] Passagier/Passagierin, Beifahrer/Beifahrerin **III U3,** 45
passive ['pæsɪv] passiv; Passiv °**IV U3,** 54
passport ['pɑ:spɔ:t] Pass, Reisepass **III U3,** 50
passports *(pl)* ['pɑ:spɔ:ts] Passkontrolle **III U3,** 50
past [pɑ:st] Vergangenheit **II U1,** 13
past perfect [ˌpɑ:st 'pɜ:fɪkt] Plusquamperfekt °**III U2,** 31
simple past [ˌsɪmpl 'pɑ:st] einfache Vergangenheit °**III U2,** 28
past [pɑ:st] vorbei, vorüber **I U7,** 97; vergangen; frühere/früherer/früheres °**IV U1,** 10
past [pɑ:st] nach *(Uhrzeit)* **II U1,** 12
half past (two) ['hɑ:f pɑ:st] halb (drei) **I U3,** 40
pastrami [pəs'trɑ:mi] Pastrami **IV U1,** 12
path [pɑ:θ] Pfad, Weg **II U4,** 56
patient ['peɪʃnt] Patient/Patientin **III U5,** 82
pause [pɔ:z] Pause °**III U5,** 86
*to **pay** [peɪ] (be)zahlen **III U5,** 85
to pay for [peɪ] bezahlen **IV U2,** 32
PC [ˌpi:'si:] PC **II U5,** 63; Polizeibeamter/Polizeibeamtin °**III U5,** 83
pea [pi:] Erbse **II U4,** 54
peace [pi:s] Friede **II U7,** 88
pear [peə] Birne **II U4,** 54
pen [pen] Füller **I U1,** 14
pence *(pl)* [pents] Pence *(Währung)* **I U5,** 67
pencil ['pensl] Bleistift **I U1,** 14
pencil case ['pensl ˌkeɪs] Mäppchen **I U1,** 14
penknife, penknives *(pl)* ['pennaɪf; 'pennaɪvz] Taschenmesser **I U6,** 84
people ['pi:pl] Leute, Menschen **I U2,** 29

per [pɜ:] pro **III U5,** 80
per cent (%) [pə 'sent] Prozent **IV U4,** 66
past **perfect** [ˌpɑ:st 'pɜ:fɪkt] Plusquamperfekt °**III U2,** 31
to **perform** [pə'fɔ:m] aufführen, auftreten **III U4,** 63
performance [pə'fɔ:məns] Aufführung, Vorstellung **III U4,** 63
perhaps [pə'hæps] vielleicht **III U5,** 83
period *(AE)* ['pɪəriəd] Unterrichtsstunde; Periode, Zeitabschnitt **IV U2,** 27
permission [pə'mɪʃn] Erlaubnis **IV U2,** 27
person ['pɜ:sn] Person **II U3,** 42
personal ['pɜ:snl] persönlich °**III U1,** 11
pet [pet] Haustier, Liebling **III U5,** 82
phone [fəʊn] Telefon **I U1,** 11
phone box ['fəʊn ˌbɒks] Telefonzelle **III U3,** 50
phone call ['fəʊn ˌkɔ:l] (Telefon-)Anruf °**II U4,** 57
phone number ['fəʊn ˌnʌmbə] Telefonnummer **I U1,** 11
cell phone ['sel fəʊn] Mobiltelefon, Handy **IV U3,** 44
to **phone** [fəʊn] anrufen, telefonieren **I U2,** 33
phonetic [fə'netɪk] phonetisch °**III U5,** 86
photo ['fəʊtəʊ] Foto, Fotografie **II U5,** 64
photographer [fə'tɒgrəfə] Fotograf/Fotografin **IV U5,** 77
photography [fə'tɒgrəfi] Fotografie **IV U4,** 62
phrase [freɪz] Redewendung, Ausdruck **IV U5,** 82
physical ['fɪzɪkl] physisch, körperlich **II U1,** 10
Physical Education (PE) [ˌfɪzɪkl‿edʒʊ'keɪʃn] Sport *(Schulfach)* **II U1,** 10
to **pick** [pɪk] pflücken, auswählen **I U6,** 78
to pick up [pɪk‿'ʌp] aufheben, abholen **II U1,** 18
picker ['pɪkə] Pflücker/Pflückerin **IV U4,** 68
pickpocket ['pɪkˌpɒkɪt] Taschendieb/Taschendiebin **III U2,** 28
picture ['pɪktʃə] Bild **I U1,** 14; *hier:* Film **IV U5,** 77
to take pictures [teɪk 'pɪktʃəz] fotografieren, Fotos machen **II U5,** 62

piece [pi:s] Stück **III U2,** 30
I want my … **pierced.** [aɪ 'wɒnt maɪ … 'pɪəst] Ich möchte mein … piercen lassen. **III U4,** 62
pig [pɪg] Schwein **I U6,** 82
piggy bank ['pɪgi bæŋk] Sparschwein **II U2,** 23
pilot ['paɪlət] Pilot/Pilotin **IV U1,** 16
pink [pɪŋk] pink, rosa **I LUA,** 24
pipe [paɪp] Pfeife **III U5,** 84
pitch [pɪtʃ] Spielfeld **III U1,** 10
pitcher ['pɪtʃə] Werfer/Werferin **III U1,** 14
pizza ['pi:tsə] Pizza **I U5,** 68
place [pleɪs] Platz, Stelle, Ort **I U2,** 26
change of place [ˌtʃeɪndʒ‿əv 'pleɪs] Ortswechsel °**III U4,** 65
to go places [ˌgəʊ 'pleɪsɪz] herumreisen **IV U4,** 68
to take place [teɪk 'pleɪs] stattfinden **III U4,** 63
plan [plæn] Plan **II U5,** 66
to **plan** [plæn] planen **II U4,** 52
plane [pleɪn] Flugzeug **II U2,** 23
planet ['plænɪt] Planet **IV U3,** 43
plant [plɑ:nt] Pflanze **II U6,** 74
plate [pleɪt] Teller **II U4,** 50
home plate ['həʊm ˌpleɪt] Home Plate **III U1,** 14
platform ['plætfɔ:m] Plattform, Tribüne, Bahnsteig **III U2,** 30
play [pleɪ] Theaterstück, Spiel **I U7,** 90
to **play** [pleɪ] spielen **I U1,** 14
player ['pleɪə] Spieler/Spielerin, Mitspieler/Mitspielerin **III U1,** 8
CD player [ˌsi:'di: ˌpleɪə] CD-Player **II U4,** 56
DVD player [ˌdi:vi:'di: 'pleɪə] DVD-Player **II U5,** 62
playground ['pleɪgraʊnd] Schulhof, Spielplatz **I U1,** 18
please [pli:z] bitte **I U1,** 19
*to be **pleased** with [bi: 'pli:zd wɪð] zufrieden sein mit **I U6,** 87
to **pledge** [pledʒ] geloben **IV U2,** 25
to **plough** [plaʊ] pflügen **IV U3,** 43
plug [plʌg] Stecker, Stöpsel **IV U3,** 44
plural ['plʊrəl] Plural, Mehrzahl **I U6,** 88
plus [plʌs] plus, zuzüglich **IV U3,** 48
p.m. [ˌpi:'em] nachmittags *(Uhrzeit)* **III U3,** 47
pocket ['pɒkɪt] Hosen-/Jackentasche **II U2,** 22
pocket money ['pɒkɪt ˌmʌni] Taschengeld **II U2,** 22
poem ['pəʊɪm] Gedicht **III U4,** 63

English – German

poet ['pəʊɪt] Dichter/Dichterin, Poet/Poetin **III U4,** 63
poetry ['pəʊətri] Lyrik **III U4,** 63
poetry slam ['pəʊətri ˌslæm] Poetry Slam *(Gedichtwettbewerb)* **III U4,** 63
point [pɔɪnt] Punkt **II U4,** 53
to **point (to)** [pɔɪnt] zeigen (auf), deuten (auf) **IV U1,** 16
police [pə'li:s] Polizei **I U6,** 87
policeman, policemen *(pl)* [pə'li:smən; pə'li:smen] Polizist **II U2,** 31
Polish ['pəʊlɪʃ] polnisch **I U2,** 29
polite [pə'laɪt] höflich **II U3,** 39
political [pə'lɪtɪkl] politisch **IV U3,** 50
pollution [pə'lu:ʃn] (Umwelt-) Verschmutzung **III U2,** 34
pompom ['pɒmpɒm] Pompon *(bunte Quaste der Cheerleader)* **IV U2,** 25
pony ['pəʊni] Pony **II U6,** 74
pool [pu:l] Schwimmbecken **III U1,** 12
swimming pool ['swɪmɪŋ ˌpu:l] Schwimmbecken; Schwimmbad **III U1,** 12
poor [pɔ:; pʊə] arm **III U5,** 88
pop [pɒp] Popmusik **IV U5,** 77
to **pop** [pɒp] knallen (lassen) **IV U5,** 84
popular ['pɒpjələ] populär, beliebt **II U2,** 23
population [ˌpɒpjə'leɪʃn] Bevölkerung **IV U1,** 14
pork [pɔ:k] Schweinefleisch **II U4,** 49
port [pɔ:t] Hafen **III U3,** 45
to **pose** [pəʊz] (sich) darstellen, posieren **IV U2,** 32
position [pə'zɪʃn] Position **III U3,** 49
possible ['pɒsəbl] möglich **III U4,** 67
post [pəʊst] Pfosten, Mast **III U1,** 15
goal post ['gəʊl pəʊst] Torpfosten **III U1,** 15
post office ['pəʊst‿ɒfɪs] Postamt **III U2,** 35
to **post** [pəʊst] aufgeben *(einen Brief)*, abschicken, posten *(im Internetforum)* **IV U5,** 80
postcard ['pəʊstkɑ:d] Postkarte **I U6,** 78
poster ['pəʊstə] Poster, Plakat **I U1,** 11
pot [pɒt] Topf **II U7,** 90
potato, potatoes *(pl)* [pə'teɪtəʊ] Kartoffel **II U4,** 54
couch potato ['kaʊtʃ pəˌteɪtəʊ] Stubenhocker **III U1,** 12
pound (£) [paʊnd] Pfund *(Währung)* **I U5,** 66
pound (lb) [paʊnd] Pfund *(Gewicht)* **II U4,** 52
poverty ['pɒvəti] Armut **IV U1,** 10
powder ['paʊdə] Puder, Pulver **III U5,** 89
power ['paʊə] Kraft, Stärke, Macht **II U6,** 74
practice ['præktɪs] Training **III U1,** 16
to **practise** ['præktɪs] üben, proben, praktizieren **II U5,** 66
to **prepare** [prɪ'peə] vorbereiten, zubereiten °**III U1,** 14
preposition [ˌprepə'zɪʃn] Präposition °**III U1,** 19
present ['preznt] Geschenk **I U5,** 69; Gegenwart, Präsens °**II U2,** 26
present progressive [ˌpreznt prə'gresɪv] Verlaufsform des Präsens/der Gegenwart °**III U1,** 12
simple present [ˌsɪmpl 'preznt] Gegenwart, Präsens °**IV U4,** 62
to **present** [prɪ'zent] präsentieren; verleihen **IV U5,** 77
presentation [ˌprezn'teɪʃn] Präsentation °**III U1,** 14
president ['prezɪdnt] Präsident/Präsidentin °**II U3,** 42
press [pres] Presse **IV U5,** 77
to **press** [pres] drücken, pressen **II U7,** 95
to **pretend** [prɪ'tend] vorgeben, tun als ob °**III U1,** 13
pretty ['prɪti] ganz schön **IV U4,** 68
price [praɪs] Preis **I U7,** 95
half-price [ˌhɑ:f'praɪs] zum halben Preis **III U1,** 15
primary school ['praɪməri ˌsku:l] Grundschule **III U4,** 67
prince [prɪns] Prinz **III U2,** 29
to **print** [prɪnt] drucken **II U5,** 64
prison ['prɪzn] Gefängnis **III U2,** 31
pristine ['prɪsti:n] makellos, rein **IV U5,** 84
private ['praɪvɪt] privat **III U4,** 67
prize [praɪz] Preis **IV U2,** 24
pros and cons [ˌprəʊz‿ənd 'kɒnz] Für und Wider, Pro und Kontra, Vor- und Nachteile **IV U4,** 63
probably ['prɒbəbli] wahrscheinlich **II U7,** 88
problem ['prɒbləm] Problem, Schwierigkeit **I U1,** 20
to **produce** [prə'dju:s] herstellen, produzieren, inszenieren *(Theaterstück)* **IV U4,** 62
production [prə'dʌkʃn] Herstellung, Produktion **IV U5,** 77
profile ['prəʊfaɪl] Steckbrief; Profil, Porträt °**III U1,** 11
programme ['prəʊgræm] Programm, Sendung **III U5,** 80
project ['prɒdʒekt] Projekt **I U2,** 34
promise ['prɒmɪs] Versprechen °**II U6,** 77
to **promise** ['prɒmɪs] versprechen **II U6,** 77
pronoun ['prəʊnaʊn] Pronomen °**III U4,** 67
reflexive pronoun [rɪ'fleksɪv ˌprəʊnaʊn] Reflexivpronomen °**III U4,** 67
relative pronoun [ˌrelətɪv 'preʊnaʊn] Relativpronomen °**III U3,** 48
to **protect** [prə'tekt] (be)schützen °**III U2,** 32
proud of ['praʊd‿əv] stolz auf **III U4,** 68
public ['pʌblɪk] öffentlich **IV U1,** 9
public school [ˌpʌblɪk 'sku:l] staatliche Schule (USA), Privatschule (GB) **IV U2,** 30
to **publish** ['pʌblɪʃ] veröffentlichen, publizieren, verlegen **IV U5,** 78
pudding ['pʊdɪŋ] Pudding; Nachtisch **II U4,** 49
Puerto Rican [ˌpwɜ:tə‿'ri:kən] Puertorikaner/Puertorikanerin °**IV U1,** 14
to **pull** [pʊl] ziehen **II U4,** 57
punk [pʌŋk] Punk **III U2,** 35
pupil ['pju:pl] Schüler/Schülerin **I U1,** 10
purple ['pɜ:pl] lila, violett **I LUA,** 24
to **push** [pʊʃ] stoßen, schieben, drücken **II U3,** 36
*to **put** [pʊt] setzen, stellen, legen **I U3,** 42
to put down [pʊt 'daʊn] auflegen *(Telefon)*; hinlegen, hinstellen °**II U7,** 89
to put in [pʊt‿'ɪn] einsetzen **II U7,** 95; einschieben **III U4,** 68; hinzufügen **IV U1,** 12
to put on [pʊt‿'ɒn] anziehen, aufsetzen **I U6,** 81; auftragen *(Make-up)* **II U5,** 71
to put out [pʊt‿'aʊt] ausmachen; löschen **III U2,** 32; hinausstellen **III U4,** 65
to put up [pʊt‿'ʌp] aufstellen, aufbauen **I U6,** 84
puzzle ['pʌzl] Rätsel, Puzzle °**I U1,** 15
crossword (puzzle) ['krɒswɜ:d 'pʌzl] Kreuzworträtsel °**I U5,** 71

Q

quarter ['kwɔ:tə] Viertel **III U2,** 32; Vierteldollar *(Währung)* **IV U1,** 13
quarter past ['kwɔ:tə pɑ:st] Viertel nach **I U3,** 42
quarter to ['kwɔ:tə tə] Viertel vor **I U3,** 42
queen [kwi:n] Königin **II U5,** 62
homecoming queen [ˌhəʊmkʌmɪŋ 'kwi:n] Ballkönigin **IV U2,** 25
question ['kwestʃn] Frage **I U2,** 31
questionnaire [ˌkwestʃə'neə] Fragebogen °**II U4,** 53
queue [kju:] (Warte-)Schlange **III U2,** 26
quick [kwɪk] schnell **I U6,** 86
quiet ['kwaɪət] ruhig, still, leise **I U6,** 78; Ruhe, Stille **II U7,** 88
quite [kwaɪt] ziemlich; ganz, völlig **IV U1,** 17
quiz [kwɪz] Quiz, Rätsel °**I U1,** 13
quota ['kwəʊtə] Quote **IV U1,** 10

R

race [reɪs] Wettlauf, Rennen **I U7,** 92
to run a race [ˌrʌn‿ə 'reɪs] einen Wettlauf machen **I U7,** 92
racing ['reɪsɪŋ] Renn- **III U1,** 12
radio ['reɪdiəʊ] Radio **I U2,** 33
radio show ['reɪdiəʊ ˌʃəʊ] Radiosendung **I U2,** 33
rafting ['rɑ:ftɪŋ] Rafting **IV U4,** 62
raid [reɪd] Razzia; Angriff **IV U4,** 69
rain [reɪn] Regen **II U6,** 78
to **rain** [reɪn] regnen **I U4,** 62
rainy ['reɪni] regnerisch, verregnet **I U6,** 79
rally ['ræli] Jugendtreffen, Versammlung; Rallye **IV U2,** 24
ranch [ræntʃ] Ranch **IV U4,** 61
rap [ræp] Rap **I U1,** 15
to **rap** [ræp] rappen **I U3,** 40
rapper ['ræpə] Rapper/Rapperin **IV U5,** 80
I'd **rather** [aɪd 'rɑ:ðə] ich würde lieber **II U2,** 22
raw [rɔ:] grob, roh **IV U5,** 84
R&B [ˌɑ:r‿n'bi:] R&B **IV U5,** 77
to **reach** [ri:tʃ] erreichen **II U6,** 78
*to **read** [ri:d] lesen **I LUB,** 38
reader ['ri:də] Leser/Leserin °**III U5,** 91
reading ['ri:dɪŋ] Lesen °**III U5,** 86
ready ['redi] fertig, bereit **II U4,** 50
to get ready [get 'redi] sich vorbereiten **II U5,** 68
real [rɪəl] echt, richtig, wirklich **II U3,** 38
reality [ri'æləti] Realität, Wirklichkeit **IV U3,** 43
reality show [ri'æləti ˌʃəʊ] Realityshow **III U5,** 80
really ['rɪəli] wirklich **I U2,** 34
reason ['ri:zn] Grund °**III U4,** 62
*to **rebuild** [ˌri:'bɪld] wieder aufbauen; wiederherstellen **III U3,** 49
to **receive** [rɪ'si:v] empfangen, erhalten **IV U5,** 79
reception [rɪ'sepʃn] Rezeption, Empfang **III U5,** 84
receptionist [rɪ'sepʃnɪst] Empfangschef/Empfangschefin **III U5,** 85
recess *(AE)* ['rɪses] Pause **IV U2,** 27
recipe ['resɪpi:] Rezept **I U7,** 94
record ['rekɔ:d] Schallplatte **IV U5,** 77
on record [ɒn 'rekɔ:d] verzeichnet, dokumentiert **III U3,** 46
to **record** [rɪ'kɔ:d] aufnehmen, aufzeichnen **II U5,** 63
recording [rɪ'kɔ:dɪŋ] Aufnahme, Aufzeichnung **IV U3,** 48
red [red] rot **I LUA,** 24
to go red [gəʊ 'red] rot werden **II U1,** 11
referee [ˌrefr'i:] Schiedsrichter/ Schiedsrichterin **III U1,** 12
reflexive pronoun [rɪ'fleksɪv ˌprəʊnaʊn] Reflexivpronomen °**III U4,** 67
refrain [rɪ'freɪn] Refrain °**IV U5,** 82
refrigerator [rɪ'frɪdʒreɪtə] Kühlschrank **IV U3,** 44
reggae ['regeɪ] Reggae **IV U5,** 77
to **register** ['redʒɪstə] (sich) registrieren, (sich) anmelden **IV U5,** 80
registration [ˌredʒɪ'streɪʃn] Registrierung, Erfassung **II U1,** 10
regular ['regjələ] regelmäßig °**III U1,** 10; Stammkunde/Stammkundin **III U2,** 35
to **rehearse** [rɪ'hɜ:s] proben *(ein Theaterstück)* **I U7,** 90
relative pronoun [ˌrelətɪv 'preʊnaʊn] Relativpronomen °**III U3,** 48
to **relax** [rɪ'læks] sich entspannen, sich ausruhen **IV U1,** 16
religious [rɪ'lɪdʒəs] religiös **II U1,** 12
Religious Education (RE) [rɪˌlɪdʒəs‿edʒʊ'keɪʃn] Religionsunterricht **II U1,** 12
to **relive** [ˌri:'lɪv] wieder erleben **III U2,** 26
to **remember** [rɪ'membə] sich erinnern (an), sich merken **I U3,** 49
to **remind** [rɪ'maɪnd] erinnern °**III U3,** 56
to **reminisce** [ˌremɪ'nɪs] zurückdenken, in Erinnerungen schwelgen **IV U5,** 84
remote control [rɪˌməʊt kən'trəʊl] Fernbedienung, Fernsteuerung **IV U3,** 43
to **remove** [rɪ'mu:v] entfernen **IV U3,** 44
to **repair** [rɪ'peə] reparieren **IV U1,** 17
to **repeat** [rɪ'pi:t] wiederholen °**IV U4,** 66
to **replace** [rɪ'pleɪs] ersetzen **III U3,** 49
report [rɪ'pɔ:t] Bericht, Meldung; Zeugnis **IV U2,** 26
to **report** [rɪ'pɔ:t] berichten; (sich) melden **IV U3,** 51
reporter [rɪ'pɔ:tə] Reporter/Reporterin **I U7,** 92
rescue ['reskju:] Rettung **III U5,** 82
to **rescue** ['reskju:] retten **II U6,** 83
research [rɪ'sɜ:tʃ] **IV U3,** 43
reservation [ˌrezə'veɪʃn] Reservat; Reservierung **IV U4,** 60
respect [rɪ'spekt] Respekt **III U4,** 63
response [rɪ'spɒns] Reaktion, Antwort **III U4,** 63
rest [rest] Rest **III U1,** 17
rest area ['rest ˌeəriə] Rastplatz **IV U4,** 65
to **rest** [rest] sich entspannen, sich ausruhen **III U3,** 52
restaurant ['restrənt] Restaurant **II U4,** 55
restroom *(AE)* ['restrʊm] Toilette **IV U4,** 68
result [rɪ'zʌlt] Ergebnis, Resultat **IV U4,** 66
revision [rɪ'vɪʒn] Wiederholung °**I U2,** 32
*to **rewrite** [ˌri:'raɪt] noch einmal schreiben °**II U4,** 58
rhyme [raɪm] Reim °**I LUA,** 25
rhyming ['raɪmɪŋ] (sich) reimend °**II U4,** 58
rice [raɪs] Reis **II U4,** 49
rich [rɪtʃ] reich **III U2,** 29
ride [raɪd] Fahrt, Ritt **III U1,** 18; *hier:* Mitfahrgelegenheit **IV U4,** 69
*to **ride** [raɪd] fahren, reiten **I LUB,** 38
right [raɪt] richtig, korrekt **I U1,** 13; rechter/rechte/rechtes; rechts **I U4,** 55
right away [raɪt‿ə'weɪ] sofort, gleich **II U4,** 57

sis [sɪs] Schwesterchen °**III U4,** 65
sister ['sɪstə] Schwester **I LUA,** 25
half-sister ['hɑ:fˌsɪstə] Halbschwester **I U2,** 26
*to **sit** [sɪt] sitzen **I U3,** 48
to sit back [ˌsɪt 'bæk] sich zurücklehnen **IV U1,** 16
to sit down [sɪt 'daʊn] sich setzen, sich hinsetzen **I U1,** 19
to sit with ['sɪt wɪθ] sich setzen zu **I U5,** 74
sitcom ['sɪtkɒm] Situationskomödie **III U5,** 82
situation [ˌsɪtju'eɪʃn] Situation °**III U3,** 50
size [saɪz] Größe, Kleidergröße **III U5,** 90
to **skate** [skeɪt] Inlineskates fahren, skaten **I LUB,** 38
skateboard ['skeɪtbɔ:d] Skateboard **I U4,** 54
skates *(pl)* [skeɪts] Inlineskates **I U4,** 54
skiing ['ski:ɪŋ] Skifahren **IV U4,** 66
skill [skɪl] Fertigkeit; Geschick °**II U1,** 11
to **skim** [skɪm] überfliegen °**III U2,** 32
skimming ['skɪmɪŋ] Überfliegen °**III U2,** 32
skirt [skɜ:t] Rock **II U1,** 10
sky [skaɪ] Himmel **II U7,** 94
skyscraper ['skaɪˌskreɪpə] Wolkenkratzer **IV U1,** 9
poetry **slam** ['pəʊətri ˌslæm] Poetry Slam *(Gedichtwettbewerb)* **III U4,** 63
slamster ['slæmstə] Teilnehmer/Teilnehmerin an einem Poetry Slam **III U4,** 63
slang [slæŋ] Slang **IV U5,** 80
sleep [sli:p] Schlaf **IV U3,** 48
*to **sleep** [sli:p] schlafen **I U3,** 46
sleeping bag ['sli:pɪŋ ˌbæg] Schlafsack **I U6,** 84
sleepy ['sli:pi] schläfrig, verschlafen **II U7,** 94
slice [slaɪs] Scheibe **IV U1,** 12
slip [slɪp] Beleg, Schein **IV U2,** 27
slow [sləʊ] langsam **I U2,** 34
small [smɔ:l] klein **I U2,** 26
smart [smɑ:t] schlau, klug **IV U3,** 42
smell [smel] Geruch, Gestank **III U5,** 88
*to **smell** [smel] riechen **III U2,** 32
to **smile** [smaɪl] lächeln **I U3,** 43
smoke [sməʊk] Rauch **III U2,** 32
to **smoke** [sməʊk] rauchen **III U5,** 84
smuggler ['smʌglə] Schmuggler/Schmugglerin **III U3,** 45
snack [snæk] Imbiss, Snack **II U4,** 55
snack bar ['snæk bɑ:] Café, Imbissstube °**IV U1,** 13
snapshot ['snæpʃɒt] Schnappschuss **IV U1,** 16
to **sniff** [snɪf] schnüffeln, schnuppern **III U5,** 90
snow [snəʊ] Schnee **II U6,** 79
to **snow** [snəʊ] schneien **II U6,** 79
snowy ['snəʊi] verschneit **I U6,** 79
so [səʊ] so, also, deshalb **I U2,** 26
so far ['səʊ fɑ:] bis jetzt °**IV U1,** 17
soap [səʊp] Seifenoper, Seife **I U7,** 97
docu soap ['dɒkju ˌsəʊp] Dokusoap **III U5,** 80
soccer *(AE)* ['sɒkə] Fußball **IV U2,** 31
social ['səʊʃl] sozial, gesellschaftlich **IV U3,** 50
social security number [ˌsəʊʃl sɪ'kjʊərəti ˌnʌmbə] Sozialversicherungsnummer **IV U3,** 50
socket ['sɒkɪt] Steckdose **IV U3,** 46
sofa ['səʊfə] Sofa, Couch **I LUA,** 25
soft [sɒft] leise; weich, sanft **II U7,** 94
to **solve** [sɒlv] lösen **III U5,** 88
some [sʌm] einige; etwas **II U1,** 13
somebody ['sʌmbədi] jemand **III U5,** 83
somehow ['sʌmhaʊ] irgendwie **IV U4,** 69
someone ['sʌmwʌn] jemand **II U5,** 70
someone else [ˌsʌmwʌn‿'els] jemand anderes °**III U1,** 13
something ['sʌmθɪŋ] etwas **II U4,** 56
sometimes ['sʌmtaɪmz] manchmal **I U3,** 44
somewhere ['sʌmweə] irgendwo **II U4,** 57
son [sʌn] Sohn **III U5,** 86
song [sɒŋ] Lied **I U2,** 33
soon [su:n] bald **I U6,** 78
as soon as [əz 'su:n‿əz] sobald **III U4,** 66
sorry ['sɒri] Tut mir Leid. Entschuldigung. **I U1,** 12
I'm sorry about .... [aɪm 'sɒri‿əˌbaʊt] Es tut mir Leid wegen .... °**II U3,** 39
to feel sorry for [fi:l 'sɒri] Mitleid haben mit, bedauern **III U1,** 16
sort [sɔ:t] Art, Sorte **IV U1,** 16
to **sort** [sɔ:t] sortieren °**I U1,** 21
to sort out [sɔ:t‿'aʊt] klären, regeln *(ein Problem)* **I U2,** 30
soul [səʊl] Soulmusik; Seele **IV U5,** 77
sound [saʊnd] Ton, Geräusch, Klang **I U6,** 85
to **sound** [saʊnd] klingen, sich anhören **III U5,** 88
soup [su:p] Suppe **II U1,** 15
sour ['saʊə] sauer **II U4,** 49
south [saʊθ] Süden **I U4,** 55
southwest [ˌsaʊθ'west] Südwesten **II U6,** 78
souvenir [ˌsu:və'nɪə] Souvenir, Andenken **III U2,** 29
space [speɪs] Raum, Platz; Weltraum **IV U3,** 42
space station ['speɪs ˌsteɪʃn] Weltraumstation **IV U3,** 42
outer space [ˌaʊtə 'speɪs] Weltraum, Weltall **IV U3,** 42
spaceship ['speɪsʃɪp] Raumschiff **IV U3,** 43
spaghetti [spə'geti] Spaghetti **II U1,** 13
Spanish ['spænɪʃ] spanisch, Spanisch **IV U4,** 68
spark [spɑ:k] Funke(n) **III U2,** 32
*to **speak** [spi:k] sprechen **I U4,** 62
It's ... speaking. [ɪts ... 'spi:kɪŋ] Hier spricht .... **III U4,** 69
speaker ['spi:kə] Sprecher/Sprecherin **III U3,** 45
special ['speʃl] besonders, speziell **III U4,** 63; Spezialität **IV U1,** 12
spectacular [spek'tækjələ] spektakulär **III U2,** 26
speech bubble ['spi:tʃ ˌbʌbl] Sprechblase °**III U3,** 47
*to **spell** [spel] buchstabieren **I U4,** 60
spelling ['spelɪŋ] Orthographie, Rechtschreibung °**II U3,** 43
*to **spend** [spend] verbringen; ausgeben **I U6,** 83
spicy ['spaɪsi] würzig, pikant **II U4,** 49
spin-off ['spɪn‿ɒf] Nebenprodukt **IV U3,** 43
sponge [spʌndʒ] Schwamm **I U7,** 90
spooky ['spu:ki] unheimlich **I U2,** 35
spoon [spu:n] Löffel **II U4,** 50
sport [spɔ:t] Sport **I U1,** 12
sports day ['spɔ:ts deɪ] Sportfest **I U7,** 90
sports field ['spɔ:ts fi:ld] Sportplatz **I U7,** 92
sports shop ['spɔ:ts ʃɒp] Sportgeschäft **I U5,** 66
to do sports [du: 'spɔ:ts] Sport treiben **I U7,** 92
sporty ['spɔ:ti] sportlich **III U2,** 29
to **spot** [spɒt] entdecken, erkennen °**IV U4,** 67
to **spray** [spreɪ] (be)sprühen, lackieren **IV U4,** 68
spring [sprɪŋ] Frühling **I U6,** 78

stadium ['steɪdiəm] Stadion **III U1,** 8
staff [stɑ:f] Personal; Kollegium **IV U4,** 67
stairs *(pl)* [steəz] Treppe **III U3,** 52
stall [stɔ:l] Stand, Bude **I U7,** 90
stall holder ['stɔ:l ˌhəʊldə] Standbesitzer/Standbesitzerin **II U4,** 54
white elephant stall [ˌwaɪt 'elɪfənt stɔ:l] Trödelstand **I U7,** 96
stamp [stæmp] Briefmarke **III U3,** 47
stand [stænd] Tribüne **III U1,** 9
*to **stand** [stænd] stehen **III U3,** 49
star [stɑ:] Star; Stern **III U1,** 12
word star ['wɜ:d stɑ:] Wortstern °**I U1,** 22
start [stɑ:t] Anfang, Beginn, Start **II U1,** 10
to **start** [stɑ:t] anfangen, starten **I U3,** 44
to start up [stɑ:t‿'ʌp] eröffnen **IV U2,** 32
starter ['stɑ:tə] Vorspeise **II U4,** 49
state [steɪt] Staat, Land; staatlich; Zustand **III U4,** 67
to get into such a state [get‿ˌɪntə 'sʌtʃ‿ə 'steɪt] durchdrehen, (sich) verrückt machen **III U4,** 70
statement ['steɪtmənt] Aussage, Behauptung °**III U5,** 82
negative statement [ˌnegətɪv 'steɪtmənt] Verneinung °**III U5,** 82
station ['steɪʃn] Wache, Station, Bahnhof **I U6,** 87
space station ['speɪs ˌsteɪʃn] Weltraumstation **IV U3,** 42
statistics *(pl)* [stə'tɪstɪks] Statistik °**IV U4,** 66
statue ['stætʃu:] Statue, Standbild **IV U5,** 77
to **stay** [steɪ] bleiben **I U4,** 60
to stay out [steɪ‿'aʊt] wegbleiben **III U4,** 69
to stay with ['steɪ wɪð] wohnen bei **I U6,** 78
*to **steal** [sti:l] stehlen **II U4,** 57
steel band [ˌsti:l 'bænd] Steelband *(Band, deren Instrumente aus leeren Ölfässern bestehen)* **III U4,** 64
steelworker ['sti:lˌwɜ:kə] Stahlarbeiter/Stahlarbeiterin °**IV U1,** 15
step [step] Stufe, Schritt **IV U1,** 9
to **step** [step] treten, steigen, gehen **IV U2,** 33
stepdad ['stepdæd] Stiefvater **I U2,** 26
stick [stɪk] Stock **II U2,** 26
*to **stick** [stɪk] kleben; stecken **IV U4,** 68

still (picture) ['stɪl ˌpɪktʃə] Standfoto **IV U5,** 78
still [stɪl] noch, immer noch **II U1,** 21; dennoch **IV U2,** 28
stomach ['stʌmək] Magen, Bauch **II U3,** 41
stone [stəʊn] Stein **II U6,** 82; *brit. Gewichtseinheit* (= 6,35 kg) **III U1,** 11
stop [stɒp] Halt, Haltestelle **I LUC,** 52
bus stop ['bʌs ˌstɒp] Bushaltestelle **I LUC,** 52
to **stop** [stɒp] aufhören (mit), anhalten **I U3,** 42
to stop + -ing [stɒp] aufhören etw. zu tun **II U4,** 52
store [stɔ:] Kaufhaus, Geschäft, Laden **II U2,** 30
store detective ['stɔ: dɪˌtektɪv] Kaufhausdetektiv/Kaufhausdetektivin **II U2,** 30
department store [dɪ'pɑ:tmənt stɔ:] Kaufhaus **I LUC,** 52
storm [stɔ:m] Sturm **II U6,** 81
stormy ['stɔ:mi] stürmisch **II U6,** 78
story ['stɔ:ri] Geschichte, Erzählung **I U1,** 21
detective story [dɪ'tektɪv ˌstɔ:ri] Krimi **III U5,** 80
straight [streɪt] gerade, direkt **IV U2,** 27
stranded ['strændɪd] gestrandet **IV U4,** 65
strange [streɪndʒ] merkwürdig, seltsam **I U2,** 35
stranger ['streɪndʒə] Fremder/Fremde **III U3,** 47
straw [strɔ:] Stroh **III U2,** 32
strawberry ['strɔ:bri] Erdbeere **IV U1,** 12
stream [stri:m] Bach **II U6,** 82
street [stri:t] Straße **I LUC,** 52
stress [stres] Stress; Betonung **IV U3,** 48
to **stress** [stres] betonen °**III U5,** 86
strict [strɪkt] streng, strikt **III U4,** 62
string [strɪŋ] Schnur, Kordel, Bindfaden **IV U5,** 78
stroke [strəʊk] Schlag(anfall) **III U4,** 70
strong [strɒŋ] stark **III U5,** 86
student ['stju:dnt] Student/Studentin, Schüler/Schülerin **IV U2,** 24
studio ['stju:diəʊ] Studio **I U2,** 33
to **study** ['stʌdi] studieren; lernen **II U6,** 74
stuff [stʌf] Zeug, Sachen **IV U4,** 68
stupid ['stju:pɪd] dumm, blöd **I U2,** 35
style [staɪl] Stil; *hier:* Frisur **III U2,** 35
subject ['sʌbdʒɪkt] Schulfach; Thema **II U1,** 13

to **substitute** ['sʌbstɪtju:t] auswechseln, ersetzen **III U1,** 17
suburb ['sʌbɜ:b] Vorort **IV U5,** 80
success [sək'ses] Erfolg **III U5,** 80
such [sʌtʃ] solch **III U4,** 70
such as ['sʌtʃ‿æz] wie **IV U1,** 14
sudden ['sʌdn] plötzlich **III U4,** 70
suddenly ['sʌdnli] plötzlich, auf einmal **I U2,** 35
to **suggest** [sə'dʒest] vorschlagen **III U4,** 69
suggestion [sə'dʒestʃn] Vorschlag, Anregung **III U4,** 65
suit [su:t] Anzug **IV U2,** 33
summary ['sʌmri] Zusammenfassung °**III U3,** 49
summer ['sʌmə] Sommer **I U6,** 79
summer fair ['sʌmə ˌfeə] Sommerfest **I U7,** 90
sun [sʌn] Sonne **III U3,** 46
Sunday ['sʌndeɪ] Sonntag **I LUB,** 39
sunny ['sʌni] sonnig **I U6,** 79
sunny side up [ˌsʌni saɪd‿'ʌp] Spiegelei **IV U4,** 65
suntan ['sʌntæn] Sonnenbräune **II U1,** 14
superlative [su:'pɜ:lətɪv] Superlativ **II U4,** 50
supermarket ['su:pəˌmɑ:kɪt] Supermarkt **I LUC,** 52
supper ['sʌpə] Abendessen **I U3,** 44
for supper [fə 'sʌpə] zum Abendessen **II U3,** 38
to have supper [hæv 'sʌpə] zu Abend essen **I U3,** 44
to **support** [sə'pɔ:t] unterstützen, stützen **IV U5,** 84
supporter [sə'pɔ:tə] Anhänger/Anhängerin **IV U2,** 25
sure [ʃʊə] sicher **I U1,** 16
to make sure [meɪk 'ʃʊə] sichergehen **II U6,** 82
to **surf** [sɜ:f] (wind)surfen **II U1,** 14
to surf the Internet [ˌsɜ:f ðiˌ'ɪntənet] im Internet surfen **II U1,** 14
surfing ['sɜ:fɪŋ] Wellenreiten, Surfen **II U1,** 14
surprised [sə'praɪzd] überrascht, erstaunt **II U1,** 18
surprising [sə'praɪzɪŋ] überraschend **II U7,** 96
survey ['sɜ:veɪ] Umfrage **I U4,** 56
survival [sə'vaɪvl] Überleben **III U4,** 66
suspect ['sʌspekt] Verdächtigter/Verdächtigte **III U5,** 84
suspense [sə'spens] Spannung **IV U3,** 50

swap [swɒp] Tausch **II U7,** 88
to **swap** [swɒp] tauschen **I LUB,** 38
sweatshirt ['swetʃɜ:t] Sweatshirt **II U1,** 10
sweet [swi:t] süß **I LUA,** 24; Bonbon, Süßigkeit **II U4,** 53
to **swerve** [swɜ:v] ausweichen, ausscheren **III U4,** 70
*to **swim** [swɪm] schwimmen **I LUB,** 38
swimmer ['swɪmə] Schwimmer/ Schwimmerin **III U3,** 45
swimming pool ['swɪmɪŋ ˌpu:l] Schwimmbecken; Schwimmbad **III U1,** 12
swimsuit ['swɪmsu:t] Badeanzug **III U1,** 12
switch [swɪtʃ] Schalter **IV U3,** 46
to **switch off** [ˌswɪtʃ‿'ɒf] ausschalten **IV U1,** 17
to switch on [ˌswɪtʃ‿'ɒn] einschalten, anmachen **IV U3,** 44
symbol ['sɪmbl] Symbol, Sinnbild, Zeichen **IV U1,** 9
synonym ['sɪnənɪm] Synonym **IV U5,** 87
syrup ['sɪrəp] Sirup **IV U1,** 12
system ['sɪstəm] System **III U4,** 67

T

table ['teɪbl] Tisch **I U1,** 18
table-tennis ['teɪblˌtenɪs] Tischtennis **II U7,** 88
to set the table [ˌset ðə 'teɪbl] den Tisch decken **II U4,** 50
*to **take** [teɪk] nehmen, mitnehmen, wegnehmen, bringen **I U3,** 42; dauern, *(Zeit)* brauchen **III U3,** 45
to take a deep breath [ˌteɪk‿ə 'di:p ˌbreθ] tief Luft holen °**III U5,** 86
to take care [teɪk 'keə] aufpassen, sich kümmern **IV U2,** 31
to take home [ˌteɪk 'həʊm] nach Hause bringen **I U2,** 35
to take notes [teɪk 'nəʊts] sich Notizen machen °**II U4,** 55
to take off [ˌteɪk‿'ɒf] wegbringen, fortschaffen **III U1,** 17; ausziehen **III U3,** 52; abheben, starten, abfliegen **IV U1,** 16
to take out [teɪk‿'aʊt] herausnehmen **I U3,** 42
to take part in [teɪk 'pɑ:t‿ɪn] teilnehmen an **III U4,** 63
to take pictures [teɪk 'pɪktʃəz] fotografieren, Fotos machen **II U5,** 62
to take place [teɪk 'pleɪs] stattfinden **III U4,** 63
to take your chance [ˌteɪk jɔ: 'tʃɑ:ns] etwas wagen, etwas riskieren **III U3,** 53
takeaway ['teɪkəweɪ] Restaurant mit Straßenverkauf; Essen zum Mitnehmen **II U4,** 48
talk [tɔ:k] Vortrag, Rede **III U1,** 14
talk show ['tɔ:k ˌʃəʊ] Talkshow **III U5,** 80
to give a talk [ˌgɪv‿ə 'tɔ:k] einen Vortrag/eine Rede halten °**III U1,** 14
to **talk** [tɔ:k] sprechen, reden **I U1,** 10
to talk to ['tɔ:k tə] sprechen mit, reden mit **II U2,** 28
talkie ['tɔ:ki] Tonfilm **IV U5,** 78
tall [tɔ:l] groß, hoch **II U3,** 36
task [tɑ:sk] Aufgabe, Auftrag °**IV U3,** 48
to **taste** [teɪst] schmecken **I U7,** 94
tasty ['teɪsti] schmackhaft **II U4,** 50
Pizza is tastier. ['pi:tsə ɪz ˌteɪstɪə] Pizza schmeckt besser. **II U4,** 50
tattoo [tæt'u:] Tätowierung **III U4,** 62
taxi ['tæksi] Taxi **III U2,** 34
tea [ti:] Tee, Abendessen **I U7,** 94
afternoon tea [ˌɑ:ftənu:n 'ti:] Nachmittagstee **I U7,** 94
*to **teach** [ti:tʃ] unterrichten, lehren **I LUB,** 38
teacher ['ti:tʃə] Lehrer/Lehrerin **I U1,** 12
team [ti:m] Mannschaft, Team **II U2,** 23
technical ['teknɪkl] technisch °**II U7,** 96
Technology [tek'nɒlədʒi] Technik **II U1,** 10
teen [ti:n] Jugendlicher/Jugendliche **II U6,** 80
teenage ['ti:neɪdʒ] jugendlich **III U4,** 63
teenager ['ti:nˌeɪdʒə] Teenager, Jugendlicher/Jugendliche **III U2,** 28
*to **tell** [tel] erzählen, sagen **I U3,** 49
temperature ['temprətʃə] Temperatur **II U6,** 78
tennis ['tenɪs] Tennis **III U1,** 12
table-tennis ['teɪblˌtenɪs] Tischtennis **II U7,** 88
tense [tens] Zeit, Zeitform *(grammatisch)* °**III U2,** 39
tent [tent] Zelt **I U6,** 84
term [tɜ:m] Trimester *(Einteilung des englischen Schuljahrs)* °**II U1,** 10
terrible ['terəbl] schrecklich, furchtbar **I U2,** 35
test [test] Test, Klassenarbeit **II U3,** 44
to **test** [test] testen, prüfen °**I U2,** 31
text [tekst] Text °**I U2,** 27
text message ['tekst ˌmesɪdʒ] SMS **I U6,** 80
to **text** [tekst] Textnachricht (SMS) schicken, simsen **III U4,** 64
textbook ['teksbʊk] Schulbuch **IV U3,** 48
than [ðæn] als **I U4,** 55
to **thank** [θæŋk] danken **I U4,** 60
thank you ['θæŋk ju:] danke **I U1,** 12
thanks [θæŋks] danke **II U2,** 26
thanks to ['θæŋks tə] dank (dir/ ihnen), wegen **III U2,** 28
that [ðæt] das, jenes **I U1,** 12
That's what I call .... [ˌðæts wɒt‿'aɪ ˌkɔ:l] Das nenne ich .... **II U1,** 14
that (bad) ['ðæt bæd] so (schlimm) **II U2,** 24
that evening [ˌdæt‿'i:vnɪŋ] an diesem Abend **II U1,** 19
that's why ['ðæts ˌwaɪ] deshalb **II U1,** 18
to **thaw** [θɔ:] auftauen **IV U4,** 65
the [ðə; ði] der/die/das **I U1,** 11
theater *(AE)* ['θɪətə] Theater; Kino **IV U1,** 9
their [ðeə] ihr/ihre **I U2,** 30
them [ðem] sie, ihnen **I U4,** 60
theme park ['θi:m ˌpɑ:k] Freizeitpark **IV U2,** 24
then [ðen] dann **I LUB,** 38
there [ðeə] dort, da **I U2,** 26
there are [ðeər‿'ɑ:] da sind, es gibt **I U2,** 32
there is [ðeər‿'ɪz] da ist, es gibt **I U2,** 32
over there [ˌəʊvə 'ðeə] da drüben **I U5,** 66
these [ði:z] diese, diese hier **I U6,** 84
they [ðeɪ] sie *(Mehrzahl)* **I U1,** 16; man **III U1,** 8
thick [θɪk] dick *(nicht für Personen)*; dumm **III U1,** 16
thing [θɪŋ] Sache, Ding **I U3,** 40
*to **think** [θɪŋk] denken **I U3,** 49; glauben **II U4,** 50
think up [θɪŋk‿'ʌp] (sich) ausdenken **IV U2,** 26
to think about ['θɪŋk‿əˌbaʊt] nachdenken über, denken an °**II U7,** 95
to think of ['θɪŋk‿əv] denken an °**II U3,** 39
third [θɜ:d] dritte/dritter/drittes **I U5,** 70
this [ðɪs] dies; diese/dieser/dieses **I U1,** 12
this evening [ðɪs 'i:vnɪŋ] heute Abend **III U3,** 52

those [ðəʊz] diese dort, jene **I U6,** 84
though [ðəʊ] trotzdem, dennoch **IV U5,** 84
thought [θɔ:t] Gedanke **IV U3,** 50
thoughtful ['θɔ:tfl] aufmerksam, fürsorglich **IV U2,** 28
thousand ['θaʊznd] tausend **II U2,** 23
thread [θred] Zwirn, Garn, Faden **IV U1,** 10
thriller ['θrɪlə] Thriller **III U5,** 80
through [θru:] durch **II U4,** 57
throw [θrəʊ] Wurf **III U1,** 18
*to **throw** [θrəʊ] werfen **I U3,** 49
Thursday ['θɜ:zdeɪ] Donnerstag **I LUB,** 39
to **tick** [tɪk] abhaken °**II U5,** 65
ticket ['tɪkɪt] Ticket, Fahrschein, Eintrittskarte **I U7,** 90
tiger ['taɪgə] Tiger **I U2,** 26
till [tɪl] bis **IV U4,** 68
time [taɪm] Zeit **I U2,** 30; Mal **II U1,** 18
What's the time, please? [ˌwɒts ðə 'taɪm ˌpli:z] Wie viel Uhr ist es, bitte?; Wie spät ist es, bitte? **I U3,** 42
on time [ɒn 'taɪm] pünktlich **IV U3,** 48
to have a good time [ˌhæv‿ə gʊd 'taɪm] sich amüsieren **I U5,** 75
to **time** [taɪm] stoppen, die Zeit nehmen **I U7,** 92
timeline ['taɪmlaɪn] Zeitleiste °**I U4,** 63
timetable ['taɪmteɪbl] Stundenplan, Fahrplan **II U1,** 12
tin [tɪn] Dose, Büchse **III U2,** 34
tiny ['taɪni] winzig **I LUA,** 25
tip [tɪp] Tipp **II U4,** 52; Trinkgeld **IV U1,** 12
tired ['taɪəd] müde **II U3,** 38
dog-tired [ˌdɒg'taɪəd] hundemüde **I U3,** 49
title ['taɪtl] Titel, Überschrift **II U3,** 42
to [tʊ; tə] zu, nach, bis **I U1,** 19
toast [təʊst] Toast **IV U1,** 12
tobacco [tə'bækəʊ] Tabak **IV U2,** 27
today [tə'deɪ] heute **I U2,** 29
toe [təʊ] Zeh **II U3,** 41
together [tə'geðə] zusammen, miteinander **I LUB,** 38
toilet ['tɔɪlɪt] Toilette **I U1,** 19
tomato, tomatoes *(pl)* [tə'mɑ:təʊ; tə'mɑ:təʊz] Tomate **I U5,** 68
tomorrow [tə'mɒrəʊ] morgen **II U1,** 18
ton [tʌn] Tonne *(Gewicht)* **III U3,** 49
tongue [tʌŋ] Zunge **III U4,** 62
tongue twister ['tʌŋ ˌtwɪstə] Zungenbrecher °**II U4,** 55

tonight [tə'naɪt] heute Abend, heute Nacht **I U6,** 84
too [tu:] auch **I U1,** 10; zu **I U5,** 66
tooth, teeth *(pl)* [tu:θ; ti:θ] Zahn **III U5,** 86
toothache ['tu:θeɪk] Zahnschmerzen **IV U3,** 50
top [tɒp] Spitze, oberer Teil **III U1,** 14
at the top [ət ðə 'tɒp] oben, im oberen Teil **III U1,** 14
topic ['tɒpɪk] Thema **I U2,** 33
torch, torches *(pl)* [tɔ:tʃ; 'tɔ:tʃɪz] Taschenlampe, Fackel **I U6,** 84
to **touch** [tʌtʃ] berühren; antippen **III U3,** 53
tough [tʌf] hart, rau, zäh **III U5,** 80
tour [tʊə] Tour, Fahrt, Reise **IV U1,** 16
tourist ['tʊərɪst] Tourist/Touristin **III U2,** 28
towards [tə'wɔ:dz] in Richtung, auf … zu, darauf zu **III U5,** 90
tower ['taʊə] Turm **III U2,** 26
town [taʊn] Stadt **I U3,** 41
toy [tɔɪ] Spielzeug **III U2,** 28
track [træk] Spur; Gleis **IV U4,** 62
tractor ['træktə] Traktor **IV U3,** 43
tradition [trə'dɪʃn] Tradition **III U2,** 34
traffic ['træfɪk] Verkehr **III U2,** 26
traffic jam ['træfɪk ˌdʒæm] Stau **III U2,** 26
air traffic controller [ˌeə træfɪk kən'trəʊlə] Fluglotse/Fluglotsin **IV U3,** 51
train [treɪn] Zug **I U4,** 54
to **train** [treɪn] eine Ausbildung machen **III U2,** 34; trainieren **IV U2,** 32
training ['treɪnɪŋ] Training, Ausbildung **III U4,** 68
transport ['træntspɔ:t] Transport **I U4,** 57
to **transport** [træn'spɔ:t] transportieren **IV U4,** 61
*to be **trapped** [bi: 'træpt] in der Falle sitzen **II U6,** 83
travel ['trævl] Reise **III U5,** 82
to **travel** ['trævl] reisen **III U3,** 44
tree [tri:] Baum **I U1,** 20
family tree ['fæmli tri:] Familienstammbaum °**I U2,** 28
trendy ['trendi] modisch **III U2,** 26
tribe [traɪb] (Volks-)Stamm **IV U4,** 60
trick [trɪk] Trick, Streich **I U3,** 40
trip [trɪp] Ausflug, Reise **I U6,** 80
trolley ['trɒli] Gepäckwagen, Einkaufswagen, Handkarren **III U3,** 50
trophy ['trəʊfi] Trophäe, Preis **IV U5,** 77

trouble ['trʌbl] Schwierigkeiten, Ärger **I U2,** 30
trousers *(pl)* ['traʊzəz] Hose **II U1,** 10
truck *(AE)* [trʌk] Lastwagen, Truck **IV U4,** 61
trucker *(AE)* ['trʌkə] Lastwagenfahrer/Lastwagenfahrerin, Trucker **IV U4,** 61
true [tru:] wahr **II U1,** 18
to come true [kʌm 'tru:] wahr werden **III U2,** 30
trunk *(AE)* [trʌŋk] Kofferraum **IV U4,** 65
trust [trʌst] Vertrauen **III U5,** 88
to **trust** [trʌst] vertrauen **III U3,** 52
to **try** [traɪ] versuchen, probieren **II U1,** 10
to try hard [traɪ‿'hɑ:d] sich stark bemühen **III U4,** 70
tryout ['traɪaʊt] Auswahlverfahren **IV U2,** 24
T-shirt ['ti:ʃɜ:t] T-Shirt **I U2,** 30
tucker ['tʌkə] Essen *(australischer Ausdruck)* °**II U1,** 14
Tuesday ['tju:zdeɪ] Dienstag **I LUB,** 39
tug [tʌg] Ziehen, Zupfen **III U3,** 52
tumble drier ['tʌmbl ˌdraɪə] Wäschetrockner **IV U3,** 44
tunnel ['tʌnl] Tunnel, Unterführung **I U4,** 54
turkey ['tɜ:ki] Truthahn, Pute **IV U1,** 12
Turkish ['tɜ:kɪʃ] türkisch **I U2,** 29
It's your **turn.** [ɪts jɔ: 'tɜ:n] Du bist dran. **II U1,** 13
to **turn** [tɜ:n] drehen, sich umdrehen **III U5,** 86
to turn back [tɜ:n 'bæk] umkehren, zurückgehen **II U1,** 19
to turn left/right [tɜ:n 'left/'raɪt] links/rechts abbiegen **II U7,** 97
to turn off [tɜ:n‿'ɒf] abschalten, ausschalten **I U5,** 75
to turn on [ˌtɜ:n‿'ɒn] einschalten, anmachen **IV U3,** 46
to turn over [ˌtɜ:n‿'əʊvə] (sich) umdrehen **II U7,** 94
to turn round [tɜ:n 'raʊnd] (sich) umdrehen **II U1,** 18
TV [ˌti:'vi:] Fernsehen, Fernseher **I LUA,** 25
twice [twaɪs] zweimal **III U5,** 80
type [taɪp] Typ, Art, Sorte **IV U4,** 66

U

umbrella [ʌm'brelə] Regenschirm **II U6,** 81

English – German

umpire ['ʌmpaɪə] Schiedsrichter/Schiedsrichterin **III U1,** 12
uncle ['ʌŋkl] Onkel **I U2,** 28
under ['ʌndə] unter **I U1,** 18
undercover [ˌʌndə'kʌvə] geheim, verdeckt **IV U3,** 50
underground ['ʌndəgraʊnd] U-Bahn **III U2,** 27
to **underline** [ˌʌndə'laɪn] unterstreichen **II U1,** 18
underlined [ˌʌndə'laɪnd] unterstrichen °**I U7,** 98
*to **understand** [ˌʌndə'stænd] verstehen **III U3,** 53
underwater [ˌʌndə'wɔ:tə] Unterwasser- **IV U4,** 62
unfair [ʌn'feə] ungerecht, unfair °**III U4,** 62
unfriendly [ʌn'frendli] unfreundlich **IV U5,** 83
unhappy [ʌn'hæpi] unglücklich **I U2,** 33
unhealthy [ʌn'helθi] ungesund **II U4,** 53
uniform ['ju:nɪfɔ:m] Uniform **I U3,** 44
union ['ju:njən] Liga; Vereinigung, Union **III U1,** 11
unit ['ju:nɪt] Kapitel, Einheit °**III U5,** 93
university [ˌju:nɪ'vɜ:səti] Universität **III U2,** 31
unknown [ʌn'nəʊn] unbekannt °**IV U1,** 14
until [ʌn'tɪl; n'tɪl] bis **II U4,** 56
*to **unwind** [ʌn'waɪnd] sich abwickeln **IV U1,** 10
up [ʌp] auf, hinauf, oben **II U2,** 30
Hurry up! [ˌhʌri‿'ʌp] Beeil dich! **I U2,** 30
What's up? [ˌwɒts‿'ʌp] Was ist los? **I U1,** 16
up to ['ʌp tə] bis zu **III U3,** 49
to get up [get‿'ʌp] aufstehen **I U3,** 44
to give up [gɪv‿'ʌp] aufgeben **III U2,** 30
to go up [gəʊ‿'ʌp] hinaufgehen °**I U4,** 61
to wake up [weɪk‿'ʌp] aufwecken, aufwachen **I U3,** 48
to walk up to [wɔ:k‿'ʌp tə] hingehen, zugehen auf **III U5,** 87
to **update** [ʌp'deɪt] aktualisieren °**II U5,** 62
upper ['ʌpə] oberer/obere/oberes **IV U2,** 30
*to **upset** [ʌp'set] erschrecken, durcheinander bringen, umstoßen **III U4,** 64
*to be **upset** [bi: ʌp'set] aufgeregt sein, bestürzt sein **II U3,** 44
upstairs [ʌp'steəz] oben, im oberen Stock **I U2,** 27; (die Treppe) hinauf/herauf **III U5,** 85
to run upstairs [ˌrʌn‿ʌp'steəz] die Treppe hinaufrennen **III U3,** 53
us [ʌs] uns **I U4,** 60
use [ju:s] Verwendung, Nutzung °**II U5,** 63
to **use** [ju:z] benutzen, verwenden **I U4,** 54
useful ['ju:sfl] nützlich **IV U3,** 47
useless ['ju:sləs] nutzlos **III U4,** 64
usually ['ju:ʒli] normalerweise, gewöhnlich **II U4,** 53

V

vacation *(AE)* [və'keɪʃn] Ferien, Urlaub **IV U1,** 12
valuable ['væljuəbl] wertvoll **III U2,** 26
van [væn] Lieferwagen **I U6,** 86
vast [vɑ:st] riesig, ausgedehnt **IV U4,** 61
vegetable ['vedʒtəbl] Gemüse **II U1,** 15
vending machine ['vendɪŋ məˌʃi:n] Warenautomat **III U4,** 66
verb [vɜ:b] Verb °**II U1,** 20
modal auxiliary verb [ˌməʊdl‿ɔ:g'zɪljəri 'vɜ:b] modales Hilfsverb °**III U3,** 46
verse [vɜ:s] Vers, Strophe °**IV U5,** 82
very ['veri] sehr **I U1,** 20; aller- **IV U1,** 16
video ['vɪdiəʊ] Video **I LUB,** 38
view [vju:] Aussicht, Sicht **III U2,** 26
to **view** [vju:] anschauen, betrachten **IV U5,** 80
viewer ['vju:ə] Zuschauer/Zuschauerin **III U5,** 80
village ['vɪlɪdʒ] Dorf **III U4,** 64
virtual ['vɜ:tʃuəl] virtuell **IV U3,** 43
visa, visas *(pl)* ['vi:zə] Visum *(pl. Visa),* Einreisebewilligung **IV U3,** 50
visit ['vɪzɪt] Besuch **I U7,** 94
to **visit** ['vɪzɪt] besuchen, besichtigen **I U4,** 54
visitor ['vɪzɪtə] Besucher/Besucherin **I U4,** 55
vital ['vaɪtl] lebenswichtig, unerlässlich; Lebens- **IV U5,** 82
vital signs *(pl)* [ˌvaɪtl 'saɪnz] Lebenszeichen **IV U5,** 82
vocabulary [vəʊ'kæbjələri] Wortschatz, Vokabular °**II U1,** 20
voice [vɔɪs] Stimme **II U2,** 31
volleyball ['vɒlibɔ:l] Volleyball **I U3,** 40
volunteer [ˌvɒlən'tɪə] Freiwilliger/Freiwillige **IV U5,** 81
vote [vəʊt] Abstimmung; Stimme **IV U2,** 33
to **vote (for)** [vəʊt] abstimmen, wählen, stimmen (für) **IV U2,** 32
V-shaped ['vi:ˌʃeɪpt] V-förmig **IV U3,** 51

W

to **wait** [weɪt] warten **I U5,** 69
to wait for ['weɪt fɔ:] warten auf **I U6,** 86
waiter ['weɪtə] Kellner, Bedienung **II U4,** 55
*to **wake** [weɪk] (auf)wecken **II U7,** 94
to wake up [weɪk‿'ʌp] aufwecken, aufwachen **I U3,** 48
walk [wɔ:k] Spaziergang **III U1,** 12
to go for a walk [ˌgəʊ fər‿ə 'wɔ:k] spazieren gehen **III U5,** 88
to **walk** [wɔ:k] gehen, laufen **I U4,** 54
to walk the dog [wɔ:k ðə 'dɒg] mit dem Hund spazieren gehen **I U3,** 42
to walk up to [wɔ:k‿'ʌp tə] hingehen, zugehen auf **III U5,** 87
wall [wɔ:l] Wand, Mauer **I U1,** 18
wallet ['wɒlɪt] Brieftasche, Geldbeutel **II U4,** 56
to **want (to)** ['wɒnt tə] wollen, mögen **I U4,** 54
to want sb to do sth [wɒnt] wollen, dass jemand etwas tut **III U4,** 62
war [wɔ:] Krieg **IV U1,** 10
wardrobe ['wɔ:drəʊb] Kleiderschrank, Garderobe **I U2,** 30
to **warm up** [wɔ:m‿'ʌp] (sich) aufwärmen **IV U2,** 32
warm [wɔ:m] warm **II U2,** 25
to **warn** [wɔ:n] warnen, ermahnen °**IV U4,** 72
warning ['wɔ:nɪŋ] Warn-; Warnung **IV U3,** 48
to **wash** [wɒʃ] waschen, sich waschen **I U3,** 44
washing machine ['wɒʃɪŋ məˌʃi:n] Waschmaschine **IV U3,** 44
to **waste** [weɪst] verschwenden **IV U2,** 32
to **watch** [wɒtʃ] ansehen, beobachten **I LUB,** 38; achten auf **II U2,** 31
water ['wɔ:tə] Wasser **I U5,** 68
wave [weɪv] Welle **III U4,** 70
to **wave** [weɪv] winken, schwenken **II U6,** 83

way [weɪ] Weg **I U3,** 42; Art, Weise **III U3,** 49
He is on his way to .... [ˌhiː‿ɪz‿ɒn hɪz ˈweɪ tə] Er ist auf dem Weg zu .... **I U3,** 42
No way! [ˌnəʊ‿ˈweɪ] Auf keinen Fall! **IV U4,** 62
by the way [ˌbaɪ ðə ˈweɪ] übrigens **IV U4,** 65
we [wiː] wir **I U1,** 16
weak [wiːk] schwach **III U4,** 70
to go weak [gəʊ ˈwiːk] schwach werden **III U4,** 70
*to **wear** [weə] anhaben, tragen **I U3,** 45
weather [ˈweðə] Wetter **II U1,** 14
weatherman, weathermen *(pl)* [ˈweðəmən; ˈweðəmen] Meteorologe °**II U6,** 78
webcam [ˈwebkæm] Webcam °**II U5,** 63
website [ˈwebsaɪt] Website, Internetauftritt **II U5,** 64
Wednesday [ˈwenzdeɪ] Mittwoch **I LUB,** 39
week [wiːk] Woche **I LUB,** 39
a week [ə ˈwiːk] pro Woche, in der Woche **II U4,** 52
weekend [ˌwiːkˈend] Wochenende **I U3,** 45
weight [weɪt] Gewicht **III U1,** 11
Welcome to ... [ˈwelkəm tə] Willkommen in ... **III U4,** 67
to **welcome** [ˈwelkəm] willkommen heißen **I U7,** 90
You're **welcome.** [jʊə ˈwelkəm] Bitte sehr!, Gern geschehen! **I U1,** 19
well [wel] gut **III U1,** 16
Well done! [ˌwel ˈdʌn] Gut gemacht! **III U3,** 47
as well as [əz ˈwel‿əz] sowohl ... als auch **III U4,** 67
well [wel] also, na ja, nun gut **I U2,** 29
Welsh [welʃ] walisisch; Waliser/Waliserin **III U3,** 48
west [west] Westen **I U4,** 54
western [ˈwestən] Western **IV U5,** 78
wet [wet] nass **II U6,** 74
wet blanket [wet ˈblæŋkɪt] Miesmacher/Miesmacherin **II U6,** 74
what [wɒt] welche/welcher/welches **I LUA,** 25; was **I U1,** 11
What about ... ? [wɒt‿əˈbaʊt] Was ist mit ...?; Wie wäre es mit ...? **I U2,** 30
What a laugh! [ˌwɒt‿ə ˈlɑːf] Wie lustig! **III U1,** 17
What a week! [ˌwɒt‿ə ˈwiːk] Was für eine Woche! **II U2,** 22
What does it say? [ˌwɒt dʌz‿ɪt ˈseɪ] Was steht da? **II U3,** 44
What's the matter? [ˌwɒts ðə ˈmætə] Was ist los? **III U5,** 88
What's the time, please? [ˌwɒts ðə ˈtaɪm ˌpliːz] Wie viel Uhr ist es, bitte?; Wie spät ist es, bitte? **I U3,** 42
What's up? [ˌwɒts‿ˈʌp] Was ist los? **I U1,** 16
What's your name? [ˌwɒts jə ˈneɪm] Wie heißt du? **I U1,** 11
What the heck ... ? [ˌwɒt ðə ˈhek] Was zum Teufel ... ? **III U4,** 70
wheel [wiːl] Rad **III U2,** 30
when [wen] wenn, als; wann **I U2,** 33
where [weə] wo, wohin **I U1,** 11
Where are you from? [ˌweər‿ə jə ˈfrɒm] Woher kommst du? **I U1,** 11
Where's the fire? [ˌweəz ðə ˈfaɪə] Wo brennt's denn? **I U7,** 96
which [wɪtʃ] welche/welcher/welches **II U1,** 14; der/dem/den/die/das *(Relativpronomen)* **II U3,** 42
while [waɪl] während **III U5,** 85
to **whisper** [ˈwɪspə] flüstern, zuflüstern **II U1,** 18
whistle [ˈwɪsl] Trillerpfeife **III U1,** 12
white [waɪt] weiß **I LUA,** 24
white elephant stall [ˌwaɪt ˈelɪfənt stɔːl] Trödelstand **I U7,** 96
whitewater [ˈwaɪtwɔːtə] Wildwasser **IV U4,** 62
who [huː] wer, wem, wen **I U5,** 70; der/dem/den/die *(Relativpronomen)* **II U3,** 42
whole [həʊl] ganz **IV U3,** 51
whom [huːm] wem, wen **III U3,** 52
whose [huːz] wessen **II U5,** 68; dessen, deren *(Relativpronomen)* **III U3,** 48
why [waɪ] warum **I U5,** 70
wicked [ˈwɪkɪd] großartig **II U5,** 70
wife, wives *(pl)* [waɪf; waɪvz] Ehefrau **III U5,** 86
wig [wɪg] Perücke **II U2,** 28
wild [waɪld] wild **III U2,** 31
***will ('ll), won't** [wɪl; wəʊnt] werden/werden nicht *(futurisch)* **II U6,** 76
*to **win** [wɪn] gewinnen, siegen **II U7,** 91
wind [wɪnd] Wind **I U2,** 35
window [ˈwɪndəʊ] Fenster **I U1,** 18
to **windsurf** [ˈwɪndsɜːf] windsurfen **III U3,** 46
windy [ˈwɪndi] windig **I U6,** 79
winner [ˈwɪnə] Gewinner/Gewinnerin, Sieger/Siegerin **III U4,** 63
winter [ˈwɪntə] Winter **I U6,** 79
wish [wɪʃ] Wunsch **III U4,** 63
to **wish** [wɪʃ] wünschen **III U4,** 68
with [wɪð] mit **I U1,** 14; bei **II U1,** 11
to go (together) with [ˈgəʊ wɪð] passen zu **III U5,** 81
within [wɪˈðɪn] innerhalb **III U2,** 28
without [wɪˈðaʊt] ohne **I U4,** 54
to go without [ˌgəʊ wɪˈðaʊt] ohne ... auskommen **II U4,** 52
wizard [ˈwɪzəd] Zauberer **II U5,** 69
wolf, wolves *(pl)* [wʊlf; wʊlvz] Wolf **III U5,** 86
woman, women *(pl)* [ˈwʊmən; ˈwɪmɪn] Frau **I U4,** 62
wood [wʊd] Holz **III U2,** 32; *hier:* Wald **IV U4,** 62
wooden [ˈwʊdn] hölzern **III U3,** 49
Woof! [wʊf] Wau! °**I U2,** 27
word [wɜːd] Wort **I U1,** 15
word star [ˈwɜːd stɑː] Wortstern °**I U1,** 22
work [wɜːk] Arbeit **I U3,** 47
to **work** [wɜːk] arbeiten, funktionieren **I U3,** 48
worker [ˈwɜːkə] Arbeiter/Arbeiterin, Angestellter/Angestellte **IV U3,** 50
workman, workmen *(pl)* [ˈwɜːkmən; ˈwɜːkmen] Handwerker **IV U1,** 17
worksheet [ˈwɜːkʃiːt] Arbeitsblatt **I U4,** 58
workshop [ˈwɜːkʃɒp] Workshop, Werkstatt **III U4,** 63
world [wɜːld] Erde, Welt **III U2,** 26
*to be **worried** [biː ˈwʌrid] besorgt sein, beunruhigt sein **I U6,** 87
worry [ˈwʌri] Sorge °**III U4,** 64
to **worry** [ˈwʌri] sich Sorgen machen **I U6,** 82; ängstigen, beunruhigen **II U3,** 45
worse [wɜːs] schlimmer, schlechter **II U4,** 50
worst [wɜːst] schlimmste/schlimmster/schlimmstes, schlechteste/schlechtester/schlechtestes **II U4,** 50
***would** [wʊd] würde/würden **III U3,** 53
would like [wʊd ˈlaɪk] hätte gern, möchte gern **II U4,** 52
wow [waʊ] wow °**I U1,** 12
wreck [rek] Wrack **III U4,** 70
*to **write** [raɪt] schreiben **I U3,** 43
to write down [ˈraɪt ˌdaʊn] aufschreiben °**I LUB,** 38
writing [ˈraɪtɪŋ] Schreiben °**III U4,** 68
wrong [rɒŋ] falsch **I U1,** 16
to be wrong [biː ˈrɒŋ] Unrecht haben **III U3,** 53

to get … wrong [get … ˈrɒŋ] falsch machen **II U3,** 44; falsch verstehen °**II U3,** 47
to go wrong [gəʊ ˈrɒŋ] schief gehen **II U6,** 85

Y

yard [jɑːd] Elle *(Längenmaß: 0,914 m)* **III U3,** 48
yarn [jɑːn] Garn, Faden **IV U1,** 10
yeah *(slang)* [jeə] ja **IV U1,** 16
year [jɪə] Jahr, Jahrgangsstufe **I U1,** 10
year-old [ˌjɪər‿ˈəʊld] -jährig; -Jähriger/-Jährige **III U4,** 63
yearbook [ˈjɪəbʊk] Jahrbuch **IV U2,** 24
yellow [ˈjeləʊ] gelb **I LUA,** 24
yes [jes] ja **I U1,** 12
yesterday [ˈjestədeɪ] gestern **II U2,** 26
not … **yet** [jet] noch nicht **II U5,** 66
you [juː; jə] dich, dir, Sie, Ihnen, euch **I LUB,** 38; du, ihr **I U1,** 11; man **III U1,** 8
Here you are! [ˈhɪə juː‿ɑː] Bitte schön! **I U1,** 20
thank you [ˈθæŋk juː] danke **I U1,** 12
you'd better [jʊd ˈbetə] du solltest lieber **III U4,** 70
You're kidding. [ˌjə ˈkɪdɪŋ] Du machst Witze. **IV U2,** 32
you're lucky [jʊə ˈlʌki] du hast Glück **I U1,** 16
You're welcome. [jʊə ˈwelkəm] Bitte sehr!, Gern geschehen! **I U1,** 19
you see [jʊ ˈsiː] weißt du **III U1,** 12
young [jʌŋ] jung **I U3,** 45
your [jɔː] dein/deine, euer/eure, Ihr/Ihre **I U1,** 11
Yours [jɔːz] Dein …/Deine …/Euer …/Eure … *(in Briefen)* **II U3,** 36
yourself [jɔːˈself] dich selbst °**III U1,** 11
youth [juːθ] Jugend **II U3,** 38
Yuk! [jʌk] Igitt! **IV U2,** 32
yukky [ˈjʌki] ekelhaft **III U4,** 66

Z

zone [zəʊn] Zone **IV U2,** 27
zoo [zuː] Zoo, Tierpark **II U2,** 22
zookeeper [ˈzuːˌkiːpə] Tierpfleger/Tierpflegerin, Wärter/Wärterin **II U2,** 26

Boys' names

Andy [ˈændi] **III U4,** 69
Angus [ˈæŋgəs] **II FA,** 103
Arthur [ˈɑːθə] **III FA,** 100
Ben [ben] **I U2,** 27
Bob [bɒb] **I U6,** 78
Brad [bræd] **IV U2,** 26
Brandon [ˈbrændən] **IV U1,** 16
Burt [bɜːt] **II U4,** 55
Cal [kæl] **IV U2,** 32
Carly [ˈkɑːli] **IV U5,** 80
Chandler [ˈtʃændlə] **II U3,** 37
Charles [tʃɑːlz] **III U5,** 88
Charlie [ˈtʃɑːli] **I U2,** 33
Daniel [ˈdænjəl] **II U4,** 51
Dave [deɪv] **III U1,** 9
David [ˈdeɪvɪd] **I U2,** 28
Derek [ˈderɪk] **II U4,** 51
Dicken [ˈdɪkn] **II FA,** 110
Diego [diˈeɪgəʊ] **IV U1,** 12
Donny [ˈdɒni] **IV U4,** 68
Douglas [ˈdʌgləs] **II FA,** 102
Ector [ˈektə] **III FA,** 100
Eric [ˈerɪk] **I FA,** 102
Frank [fræŋk] **IV U1,** 16
Fred [fred] **III U3,** 47
Henry [ˈhenri] **II FA,** 114
Ian [ˈiːən] **III U5,** 87
Jack [dʒæk] **I FA,** 102
Jake [dʒeɪk] **II U1,** 14
Jamal [dʒəˈmɑːl] **III U4,** 65
James [dʒeɪmz] **I U2,** 28
Jamie [ˈdʒeɪmi] **III U1,** 12
Jay [dʒeɪ] **IV U2,** 32
Jim [dʒɪm] **I U5,** 73
Jo [dʒəʊ] **I FA,** 105
Joey [ˈdʒəʊi] **II U3,** 37
John [dʒɒn] **I U4,** 57
Jojo [ˈdʒəʊdʒəʊ] **IV U5,** 81
José [həʊˈzeɪ] **IV U1,** 12
Kay [keɪ] **III FA,** 100
Kit [kɪt] **IV U4,** 65
Larry [ˈlæri] **IV U2,** 26
Leo [ˈlɪːəʊ] **III U1,** 16
Leon [ˈliːɒn] **III U1,** 11
Leroy [ˈliːrɔɪ] **III U4,** 70
Llywelyn [ləˈwelɪn] **III U5,** 86
Marc [mɑːk] **III U4,** 63
Mark [mɑːk] **I U4,** 61
Matt [mæt] **II U2,** 31
Mike [maɪk] **III U4,** 72
Miles [maɪlz] **IV U2,** 32
Nelson [ˈnelsn] **I U1,** 13
Pablo [ˈpɑːbləʊ] **IV U4,** 67
Patrick [ˈpætrɪk] **II U7,** 88
Paul [pɔːl] **I U6,** 85
Pete [piːt] **II U1,** 11
Peter [ˈpiːtə] **I U4,** 61
Phil [fɪl] **I U2,** 28
Ray [reɪ] **III U4,** 68
Reece [riːs] **III U4,** 69
Reg [redʒ] **III U2,** 34
Richard [ˈrɪtʃəd] **I U2,** 27
Rick [rɪk] **IV U4,** 68
Rico [ˈriːkəʊ] **IV U3,** 55
Rob [rɒb] **I U2,** 26
Robert [ˈrɒbət] **II U4,** 51
Rodger [ˈrɒdʒə] **III U5,** 89
Roger [ˈrɒdʒə] **II U3,** 36
Ron [rɒn] **IV U2,** 29
Ross [rɒs] **II U3,** 37
Sam [sæm] **I U1,** 16
Steve [stiːv] **I U1,** 23
Stu [stuː] **IV U2,** 29
Ted [ted] **I U2,** 26
Terry [ˈteri] **I U1,** 10
Thomas [ˈtɒməs] **I LUA,** 25
Tim [tɪm] **I LUA,** 25
Todd [tɒd] **II U3,** 36
Tom [tɒm] **I U1,** 10
Tony [ˈtəʊni] **I LUA,** 25
Tyler [ˈtaɪlə] **IV U2,** 29
Uther [ˈjuːθə] **III FA,** 100

Girls' names

Abby [ˈæbi] **IV U4,** 62
Alison [ˈælɪsən] **II U5,** 67
Alysha [əˈlɪʃə] **IV U2,** 32
Amanda [əˈmændə] **III U5,** 87
Anna [ˈænə] **I U3,** 47
Barbara [ˈbɑːbrə] **III U1,** 12
Brenda [ˈbrendə] **IV U2,** 35
Carrie [ˈkæri] **III U4,** 64
Cindy [ˈsɪndi] **IV U4,** 65
Daisy [ˈdeɪzi] **III U4,** 64
Debbie [ˈdebi] **II U3,** 36
Denise [dəˈniːz] **IV U4,** 68
Donna [ˈdɒnə] **IV U2,** 32
Dorothy [ˈdɒrəθi] **II U5,** 68
Elena [ˈelɪnə] **I U2,** 28
Elizabeth [ɪˈlɪzəbəθ] **III U2,** 29
Em [em] **II FA,** 114
Emma [ˈemə] **I U1,** 12
Farah [ˈfɑːrə] **I U2,** 26
Fiona [fiˈəʊnə] **I U1,** 23
Glinda [ˈglɪndə] **II FA,** 114
Grace [greɪs] **I U2,** 26
Helen [ˈhelən] **II U7,** 88
Igraine [ɪˈgreɪn] **III FA,** 100

Germany ['dʒɜ:məni] Deutschland **I U2,** 29
Glasgow ['glɑ:zgəʊ] **II FA,** 102
Grand Canyon [ˌgrænd 'kænjən] **IV U4,** 60
Greece [gri:s] Griechenland **I U2,** 29
Greenwich ['grenɪdʒ] **I U1,** 10
Greenwich Village [ˌgrenɪdʒ 'vɪlɪdʒ] **IV U1,** 16
Hastings ['heɪstɪŋz] **III U3,** 44
Hawaii [hə'waɪ] **IV U4,** 66
Heathrow [ˌhi:θ'rəʊ] **III U3,** 45
Hollyoaks ['hɒliəʊks] **III U5,** 82
Hollywood ['hɒliwʊd] **III U5,** 80
Honolulu [ˌhɒn'lu:lu:] **IV U4,** 64
India ['ɪndiə] **III U1,** 13
Ireland ['aɪələnd] Irland **II U6,** 85
Irish Sea [ˌaɪrɪʃ 'si:] **III U3,** 44
Isle of Dogs [ˌaɪl‿əv 'dɒgz] **I U4,** 54
Isle of Wight [ˌaɪl‿əv 'waɪt] **III U3,** 44
Istanbul [ˌɪstæn'bʊl] **I U1,** 13
Italy ['ɪtəli] Italien **I U2,** 29
Jamaica [dʒə'meɪkə] Jamaica **IV U5,** 81
Kansas ['kænzəs] **II FA,** 114
Kent [kent] **III U3,** 57
Kilkenny [kɪl'keni] **II U7,** 93
Las Vegas [ˌlæs 'veɪgəs] **IV U4,** 61
Limerick ['lɪmrɪk] **II ZI,** 8
Little Oyster Island [ˌlɪtl‿ɔɪstər‿'aɪlənd] **IV U1,** 10
Loch Ness [ˌlɒx 'nes] **II ZI,** 8
London ['lʌndən] **I U1,** 10
Los Angeles (LA) [lɒs‿'ændʒəli:z] **IV U4,** 61
Madrid [mə'drɪd] **I U1,** 13
Manchester ['mæntʃɪstə] **III U2,** 39
Manhattan [mæn'hætn] **IV U1,** 8
Marble Arch ['mɑ:bl ˌɑ:tʃ] **III U2,** 28
Mexico ['meksɪkəʊ] Mexiko **IV U1,** 10
Mexico City [ˌmeksɪkəʊ 'sɪti] **IV U4,** 69
Miami [maɪ'æmi] **IV U4,** 64
Moher ['məʊhə] **II U7,** 93
Moscow ['mɒskəʊ] **III U3,** 52
Nairobi [naɪ'rəʊbi] **I U1,** 13
Neston ['nestn] **I U6,** 78
Nevada [nə'vɑ:də] Nevada **IV U3,** 51
New Amsterdam [ˌnju: æmstə'dæm] **IV U1,** 10
New Jersey [ˌnju: 'dʒɜ:zi] **IV U5,** 78
New Mexico [ˌnju: 'meksɪkəʊ] **IV U4,** 65
New York [ˌnju: 'jɔ:k] **I U4,** 55
New York City (NYC) [ˌnju: jɔ:k 'sɪti] **IV U1,** 8
New York Harbor [ˌnju: jɔ:k 'hɑ:bə] **IV U1,** 9
Northern Ireland [ˌnɔ:ðn‿'aɪələnd] **II U7,** 89
North Sea [ˌnɔ:θ 'si:] Nordsee **III U3,** 44
Nottingham ['nɒtɪŋəm] **II U2,** 25
Paris ['pærɪs] **I U1,** 13
Perth [pɜ:θ] °**II ZI,** 8
Philippines ['fɪlɪpi:nz] Philippinen **IV U1,** 10
Phoenix ['fi:nɪks] **IV U3,** 51
Piccadilly Circus [ˌpɪkədɪli 'sɜ:kəs] **III U2,** 28
Poland ['pəʊlənd] Polen **I U2,** 29
Prescott ['preskət] **IV U3,** 51
Queens [kwi:nz] **IV U1,** 9
Republic of Ireland [rɪˌpʌblɪk‿əv‿'aɪələnd] Republik Irland **II U7,** 88
Rome [rəʊm] **IV U1,** 18
Round Rock [ˌraʊnd 'rɒk] **IV U5,** 80
Russia ['rʌʃə] Russland **I U2,** 29
Sacramento [ˌsækrə'mentəʊ] **III U1,** 11
Salisbury ['sɔ:lzbri] **III U3,** 44
San Francisco [ˌsæn frən'sɪskəʊ] **IV U4,** 64
Scilly Isles ['sɪli ˌaɪlz] **II U6,** 78
Scotland ['skɒtlənd] Schottland **II ZI,** 8
Seattle [si'ætl] **IV U4,** 64
Shannon ['ʃænən] **II U7,** 93
Sherwood Forest [ˌʃɜ:wʊd 'fɒrɪst] **II FA,** 110
Shoreditch [ʃɔ:'dɪtʃ] **III U2,** 35
Southampton [saʊ'θæmtən] **III U3,** 44
South England [ˌsaʊθ 'ɪŋglənd] Südengland **III U3,** 44
Spain [speɪn] Spanien **III U1,** 15
Staten Island [ˌstætn‿'aɪlənd] **IV U1,** 9
Stonehenge [stəʊn'hendʒ] **III U3,** 45
Tarr Steps [tɑ: 'steps] **II U6,** 82
Texas ['teksəs] **IV U1,** 16
the **Thames** [temz] **I U4,** 54
Tokyo ['təʊkiəʊ] **I U1,** 13
Tucson ['tu:sɒn] **IV U3,** 51
Turkey ['tɜ:ki] Türkei **I U2,** 29
Twickenham ['twɪknəm] **III U1,** 8
UK [ju:'keɪ] **III U1,** 11
United Kingdom [ju:ˌnaɪtɪd 'kɪŋdəm] Vereinigtes Königreich von Großbritannien und Nordirland **III U3,** 44
US [ju:'es] **IV U1,** 9
the **USA** [ju:es'eɪ] **III U1,** 11
Utah ['ju:tɑ:] **IV U4,** 73
Valley of the Sun [ˌvæli‿əv‿ðə‿'sʌn] **IV U3,** 51
Wales [weɪlz] Wales **II ZI,** 8
Western Australia [ˌwestən ɒs'treɪliə] **II U1,** 14
Wildcroft ['waɪldkrɒft] **I FA,** 100
Wiltshire ['wɪltʃə] **I U6,** 78
Wimbledon ['wɪmbldn] **III U1,** 15

Other names

Academy Award [əˌkædəmi ə'wɔ:d] **IV U5,** 77
Alpha Centauri [ˌælfə sen'tɔ:ri] **IV U3,** 51
Angelina Jolie [ˌændʒ'li:nə 'dʒəʊli] **III U2,** 29
Annie Moore [ˌæni 'mɔ:] **IV U1,** 10
Apache Lake [əˌpætʃi 'leɪk] **IV U4,** 68
Aquarius [ə'kweəriəs] Wassermann **II U6,** 80
Arena [ə'ri:nə] **II U2,** 22
Arsenal ['ɑ:snl] **III U1,** 16
Arthur Conan Doyle [ˌɑ:θə ˌkəʊnən 'dɔɪl] **III U5,** 87
B Section ['bi: ˌsekʃn] **IV U5,** 84
Bakerloo Line [ˌbeɪkəl'u: ˌlaɪn] **III U2,** 28
Barker ['bɑ:kə] **I U2,** 27
Baskerville Hall [ˌbæskəvɪl 'hɔ:l] **III U5,** 88
Batman ['bætmæn] **III U5,** 87
BBC [ˌbi:bi:'si:] **III U5,** 82
Beatles ['bi:tlz] **IV U5,** 79
Big Ben [ˌbɪg 'ben] **III U2,** 26
Billabong ['bɪləbɒŋ] **IV U4,** 62
Blue Eagles [ˌblu: 'i:glz] **IV U2,** 24
Blugirl ['blu:gɜ:l] **IV U5,** 80
Boxing Day ['bɒksɪŋ ˌdeɪ] **I FA,** 114
British Airways (BA) [ˌbrɪtɪʃ 'eəweɪz] **III U2,** 30
Brooklyn Bridge [ˌbrʊklɪn 'brɪdʒ] **IV U1,** 9
Buckingham Bridge [ˌbʌkɪŋəm 'brɪdʒ] **III U2,** 33
Buckingham Palace [ˌbʌkɪŋəm 'pælɪs] **II U3,** 47
Cadillac ['kædɪlæk] **IV U4,** 68
Charlie Chaplin [ˌtʃɑ:li 'tʃæplɪn] **III U4,** 72
Chunnel ['tʃʌnl] Tunnel durch den Ärmelkanal **III U3,** 45
Circle Line ['sɜ:kl ˌlaɪn] **III U2,** 28
Concorde ['kɒŋkɔ:d] **III U2,** 38
Cutty Sark [ˌkʌti 'sɑ:k] **I U4,** 54
Cutty Sark Gardens [kʌti ˌsɑ:k 'gɑ:dnz] **I U4,** 54
Derrek Lee [ˌderɪk 'li:] **III U1,** 9
Discman ['dɪskmən] Discman **I U2,** 30
DLR [ˌdi:‿el‿'ɑ:] **I U4,** 55
Docklands Light Railway ['dɒkləndz ˌlaɪt 'reɪlweɪ] **I U4,** 55

Jade [dʒeɪd] **I U2,** 27
Jane [dʒeɪn] **III U2,** 33
Jenna ['dʒenə] **III U4,** 69
Jenny ['dʒeni] **I U4,** 57
Julia ['dʒu:liə] **III U2,** 30
Julie ['dʒu:li] **III U4,** 72
Kate [keɪt] **I U4,** 57
Kath [kæθ] **I U6,** 78
Kim [kɪm] **IV U1,** 16
Laura ['lɔ:rə] **II U1,** 11
Lauren ['lɔ:rən] **III U4,** 64
Lisa ['li:sə] **I U1,** 10
Lynn [lɪn] **IV U4,** 63
Marcia ['mɑ:siə] **III U1,** 12
Marg [mɑ:dʒ] **III U5,** 85
Maria [mə'ri:ə] **I U2,** 28
Marita [mə'ri:tə] **IV U4,** 68
Mariya [mə'ri:ə] **IV U2,** 35
Mary ['meəri] **I U4,** 57
Maxi ['mæksi] **IV U4,** 65
Monika ['mɒnɪkə] **II U3,** 37
Nadine [neɪ'di:n] **I U1,** 13
Nancy ['nænsi] **III U1,** 9
Nasreen [nʌs'ri:n] **I U2,** 26
Nicola ['nɪklə] **I FA,** 100
Nicole [nɪ'kəʊl] **II U3,** 36
Nina ['ni:nə] **IV U2,** 29
Nyla ['naɪlə] **III U4,** 64
Pat [pæt] **II U1,** 16
Paula ['pɔ:lə] **III U1,** 11
Paula-Jo [ˌpɔ:lə 'dʒəʊ] **IV U2,** 29
Phoebe ['fi:bi] **II U3,** 37
Polly ['pɒli] **III U5,** 85
Pru [pru:] **III U2,** 35
Rachel ['reɪtʃl] **II U3,** 37
Rebecca [rɪ'bekə] **IV U2,** 29
Ruby ['ru:bi] **III U4,** 65
Sally ['sæli] **I U6,** 85
Sandra ['sændrə] **IV U2,** 25
Sandy ['sændi] **IV U4,** 68
Sarah ['seərə] **I U2,** 28
Sharleen [ʃə'li:n] **IV U2,** 32
Sheila ['ʃi:lə] **III U1,** 15
Stella ['stelə] **II FA,** 104
Sue [su:] **I U2,** 27
Susan ['su:zn] **I U2,** 28
Suzanne [su:'zæn] **I U1,** 11
Tamara [tə mɑ:rə] **I LUA,** 25
Tammy ['tæmi] **IV U2,** 29
Terri ['teri] **IV U2,** 29
Tess [tes] **I U6,** 85
Tilly ['tɪli] **I LUA,** 25
Tina ['ti:nə] **I LUA,** 25
Tracy ['treɪsi] **I U2,** 28
Trina ['tri:nə] **III U1,** 15
Virginia [və'dʒɪnjə] **III FA,** 112

Surnames

Akodu [ə'kəʊdʊ] **III U4,** 68
Barnes ['bɑ:nz] **III U1,** 16
Barnfield ['bɑ:nfi:ld] **III U2,** 30
Barrymore ['bærimɔ:] **III U5,** 88
Baskerville ['bæskəvɪl] **III U5,** 82
Bell [bel] **II U4,** 52
Berry [beri] **III U1,** 9
Black [blæk] **II U1,** 11
Bland [blænd] **II FA,** 108
Brook [brʊk] **I U1,** 12
Brown [braʊn] **II U1,** 11
Burns [bɜ:nz] **III U5,** 83
Cage [keɪdʒ] **III U1,** 9
Canterville ['kæntəvɪl] **III FA,** 110
Carter ['kɑ:tə] **I U1,** 12
Cartwright ['kɑ:traɪt] **III U2,** 34
Clarke [klɑ:k] **III U3,** 52
Fox [fɒks] **IV U3,** 52
George [dʒɔ:dʒ] **III U1,** 11
Glenn [glen] **III U4,** 70
Gruntle ['grʌntl] **II FA,** 108
Gulch [gʌltʃ] **II FA,** 114
Gusman ['gʌzmən] **IV U4,** 67
Hall [hɔ:l] **III U5,** 87
Howard ['haʊəd] **II U1,** 14
Hunter ['hʌntə] **I U6,** 82
Jackson ['dʒæksn] **I U1,** 10
Jones [dʒəʊnz] **III U4,** 70
Lean [li:n] **I FA,** 104
MacDonald [mək'dɒnld] **IV U2,** 24
Mangold ['mæŋgəʊld] **III U5,** 85
Marco ['mɑ:kəʊ] **II U1,** 11
Marks [mɑ:ks] **III U2,** 30
Martin ['mɑ:tɪn] **I FA,** 106
McArthur [mək'ɑ:θə] **II FA,** 102
Monte ['mɒnteɪ] **I U2,** 28
Morley ['mɔ:li] **III U4,** 64
Muir [mjʊə] **II FA,** 103
Newitt ['nju:ɪt] **III U5,** 84
Newman ['nju:mən] **I U1,** 12
O'Brien [əʊ'braɪən] **II U7,** 88
Otis ['əʊtɪs] **III FA,** 110
Pilch [pɪltʃ] **I U2,** 28
Richards ['rɪtʃədz] **II U3,** 45
Robbins ['rɒbɪnz] **III U3,** 51
Rose [rəʊz] **I U4,** 60
Simpson ['sɪmpsən] **III U5,** 82
Smith [smɪθ] **III U4,** 63
Spencer ['spentsə] **I U2,** 28
Stapleton ['steɪpltən] **III U5,** 89
Stavros ['stʌvrəs] **I U2,** 28
Taylor ['teɪlə] **I U1,** 10
Tiny ['taɪni] **I LUA,** 25
Watson ['wɒtsn] **III U5,** 81
White [waɪt] **III U2,** 33
Wilkins ['wɪlkɪnz] **III U4,** 70
Willis ['wɪlɪs] **III U5,** 87

Place names

Abergavenny [ˌæbəgə'veni] **III U1,** 11
Acton ['æktən] **III U2,** 34
America [ə'merɪkə] **II U3,** 36
Anchorage ['æŋkrɪdʒ] **IV U4,** 64
Arizona [ˌærɪ'zəʊnə] **IV U3,** 51
Atlanta [ət'læntə] **IV U5,** 80
Austin ['ɒstɪn] **IV U5,** 80
Australia [ɒs'treɪliə] Australien **II ZI,** 8
Avondale ['eɪvndeɪl] **III U5,** 81
Baker Street ['beɪkə ˌstri:t] **III U5,** 88
Barcelona [ˌbɑ:sl'əʊnə] **III U1,** 15
Bath [bɑ:θ] **I U6,** 79
Belgium ['beldʒəm] Belgien **IV U1,** 10
Bollywood ['bɒliwʊd] **III U5,** 80
Boston ['bɒstn] **III U1,** 15
Brighton ['braɪtn] **III U3,** 44
Bristol ['brɪstl] **I U1,** 12
Britain ['brɪtn] **II FA,** 102
British Isles [ˌbrɪtɪʃ 'aɪlz] Britische Inseln **II ZI,** 8
Bronx [brɒŋks] **IV U1,** 9
Brooklyn ['brʊklɪn] **IV U1,** 9
California [ˌkælɪ'fɔ:niə] **III U1,** 11
Camden ['kæmdən] **II U2,** 22
Canada ['kænədə] Kanada **III U5,** 88
Castle Garden [ˌkɑ:sl 'gɑ:dn] **IV U1,** 10
Central Park [ˌsentrl 'pɑ:k] **IV U1,** 8
Chicago [ʃɪ'kɑ:gəʊ] **III U1,** 9
China ['tʃaɪnə] China **III U1,** 15
Chinatown ['tʃaɪnətaʊn] **IV U1,** 9
Colorado [ˌkɒlr'ɑ:dəʊ] **IV U4,** 65
Cornwall ['kɔ:nwɔ:l] **II U6,** 78
Covent Garden [ˌkɒvnt 'gɑ:dn] **III U2,** 28
Dartmoor ['dɑ:tmɔ:] **III U5,** 88
Denver ['denvə] **IV U4,** 64
Devon ['devn] **II U6,** 78
Dover ['dəʊvə] **III U3,** 44
Dublin ['dʌblɪn] **II U7,** 88
Eastbourne ['i:stbɔ:n] **III U3,** 44
Eastern Europe [ˌi:stn 'jʊərəp] Osteuropa **IV U1,** 10
Ellis Island [ˌelɪs 'aɪlənd] **IV U1,** 9
England ['ɪŋglənd] England **I U2,** 29
Europe ['jʊərəp] Europa **IV U1,** 10
Exmoor ['eksmɔ:] **II ZI,** 8
Florida ['flɒrɪdə] **IV U3,** 55
Folkestone ['fəʊkstən] **III U3,** 44
Forest Springs [ˌfɒrɪst 'sprɪŋz] **IV U4,** 62
France [frɑ:nts] Frankreich **IV U5,** 78

Germany [ˈdʒɜːməni] Deutschland **I U2,** 29
Glasgow [ˈglɑːzgəʊ] **II FA,** 102
Grand Canyon [ˌgrænd ˈkænjən] **IV U4,** 60
Greece [griːs] Griechenland **I U2,** 29
Greenwich [ˈgrenɪdʒ] **I U1,** 10
Greenwich Village [ˌgrenɪdʒ ˈvɪlɪdʒ] **IV U1,** 16
Hastings [ˈheɪstɪŋz] **III U3,** 44
Hawaii [həˈwaɪ] **IV U4,** 66
Heathrow [ˌhiːθˈrəʊ] **III U3,** 45
Hollyoaks [ˈhɒliəʊks] **III U5,** 82
Hollywood [ˈhɒliwʊd] **III U5,** 80
Honolulu [ˌhɒnˈluːluː] **IV U4,** 64
India [ˈɪndiə] **III U1,** 13
Ireland [ˈaɪələnd] Irland **II U6,** 85
Irish Sea [ˌaɪrɪʃ ˈsiː] **III U3,** 44
Isle of Dogs [ˌaɪl‿əv ˈdɒgz] **I U4,** 54
Isle of Wight [ˌaɪl‿əv ˈwaɪt] **III U3,** 44
Istanbul [ˌɪstænˈbʊl] **I U1,** 13
Italy [ˈɪtəli] Italien **I U2,** 29
Jamaica [dʒəˈmeɪkə] Jamaica **IV U5,** 81
Kansas [ˈkænzəs] **II FA,** 114
Kent [kent] **III U3,** 57
Kilkenny [kɪlˈkeni] **II U7,** 93
Las Vegas [ˌlæs ˈveɪgəs] **IV U4,** 61
Limerick [ˈlɪmrɪk] **II ZI,** 8
Little Oyster Island [ˌlɪtl‿ɔɪstər‿ˈaɪlənd] **IV U1,** 10
Loch Ness [ˌlɒx ˈnes] **II ZI,** 8
London [ˈlʌndən] **I U1,** 10
Los Angeles (LA) [lɒs‿ˈændʒɪliːz] **IV U4,** 61
Madrid [məˈdrɪd] **I U1,** 13
Manchester [ˈmæntʃɪstə] **III U2,** 39
Manhattan [mænˈhætn] **IV U1,** 8
Marble Arch [ˈmɑːbl ˌɑːtʃ] **III U2,** 28
Mexico [ˈmeksɪkəʊ] Mexiko **IV U1,** 10
Mexico City [ˌmeksɪkəʊ ˈsɪti] **IV U4,** 69
Miami [maɪˈæmi] **IV U4,** 64
Moher [ˈməʊhə] **II U7,** 93
Moscow [ˈmɒskəʊ] **III U3,** 52
Nairobi [naɪˈrəʊbi] **I U1,** 13
Neston [ˈnestn] **I U6,** 78
Nevada [nəˈvɑːdə] Nevada **IV U3,** 51
New Amsterdam [ˌnjuː æmstəˈdæm] **IV U1,** 10
New Jersey [ˌnjuː ˈdʒɜːzi] **IV U5,** 78
New Mexico [ˌnjuː ˈmeksɪkəʊ] **IV U4,** 65
New York [ˌnjuː ˈjɔːk] **I U4,** 55
New York City (NYC) [ˌnjuː jɔːk ˈsɪti] **IV U1,** 8
New York Harbor [ˌnjuː jɔːk ˈhɑːbə] **IV U1,** 9
Northern Ireland [ˌnɔːðn‿ˈaɪələnd] **II U7,** 89
North Sea [ˌnɔːθ ˈsiː] Nordsee **III U3,** 44
Nottingham [ˈnɒtɪŋəm] **II U2,** 25
Paris [ˈpærɪs] **I U1,** 13
Perth [pɜːθ] °**II ZI,** 8
Philippines [ˈfɪlɪpiːnz] Philippinen **IV U1,** 10
Phoenix [ˈfiːnɪks] **IV U3,** 51
Piccadilly Circus [ˌpɪkədɪli ˈsɜːkəs] **III U2,** 28
Poland [ˈpəʊlənd] Polen **I U2,** 29
Prescott [ˈpreskət] **IV U3,** 51
Queens [kwiːnz] **IV U1,** 9
Republic of Ireland [rɪˌpʌblɪk‿əv‿ˈaɪələnd] Republik Irland **II U7,** 88
Rome [rəʊm] **IV U1,** 18
Round Rock [ˌraʊnd ˈrɒk] **IV U5,** 80
Russia [ˈrʌʃə] Russland **I U2,** 29
Sacramento [ˌsækrəˈmentəʊ] **III U1,** 11
Salisbury [ˈsɔːlzbri] **III U3,** 44
San Francisco [ˌsæn frənˈsɪskəʊ] **IV U4,** 64
Scilly Isles [ˈsɪli ˌaɪlz] **II U6,** 78
Scotland [ˈskɒtlənd] Schottland **II ZI,** 8
Seattle [siˈætl] **IV U4,** 64
Shannon [ˈʃænən] **II U7,** 93
Sherwood Forest [ˌʃɜːwʊd ˈfɒrɪst] **II FA,** 110
Shoreditch [ʃɔːˈdɪtʃ] **III U2,** 35
Southampton [saʊˈθæmtən] **III U3,** 44
South England [ˌsaʊθ ˈɪŋglənd] Südengland **III U3,** 44
Spain [speɪn] Spanien **III U1,** 15
Staten Island [ˌstætn‿ˈaɪlənd] **IV U1,** 9
Stonehenge [stəʊnˈhendʒ] **III U3,** 45
Tarr Steps [tɑː ˈsteps] **II U6,** 82
Texas [ˈteksəs] **IV U1,** 16
the Thames [temz] **I U4,** 54
Tokyo [ˈtəʊkiəʊ] **I U1,** 13
Tucson [ˈtuːsɒn] **IV U3,** 51
Turkey [ˈtɜːki] Türkei **I U2,** 29
Twickenham [ˈtwiknəm] **III U1,** 8
UK [juːˈkeɪ] **III U1,** 11
United Kingdom [juːˌnaɪtɪd ˈkɪŋdəm] Vereinigtes Königreich von Großbritannien und Nordirland **III U3,** 44
US [juːˈes] **IV U1,** 9
the USA [ˌjuːesˈeɪ] **III U1,** 11
Utah [ˈjuːtɑː] **IV U4,** 73
Valley of the Sun [ˌvæli‿əv‿ðə‿ˈsʌn] **IV U3,** 51
Wales [weɪlz] Wales **II ZI,** 8
Western Australia [ˌwestən ɒsˈtreɪliə] **II U1,** 14
Wildcroft [ˈwaɪldkrɒft] **I FA,** 100
Wiltshire [ˈwɪltʃə] **I U6,** 78
Wimbledon [ˈwɪmbldn] **III U1,** 15

Other names

Academy Award [əˌkædəmi əˈwɔːd] **IV U5,** 77
Alpha Centauri [ˌælfə senˈtɔːri] **IV U3,** 51
Angelina Jolie [ˌændʒˈliːnə ˈdʒəʊli] **III U2,** 29
Annie Moore [ˌæni ˈmɔː] **IV U1,** 10
Apache Lake [əˌpætʃi ˈleɪk] **IV U4,** 68
Aquarius [əˈkweəriəs] Wassermann **II U6,** 80
Arena [əˈriːnə] **II U2,** 22
Arsenal [ˈɑːsnl] **III U1,** 16
Arthur Conan Doyle [ˌɑːθə ˌkəʊnən ˈdɔɪl] **III U5,** 87
B Section [ˈbiː ˌsekʃn] **IV U5,** 84
Bakerloo Line [ˌbeɪkəlˈuː ˌlaɪn] **III U2,** 28
Barker [ˈbɑːkə] **I U2,** 27
Baskerville Hall [ˌbæskəvɪl ˈhɔːl] **III U5,** 88
Batman [ˈbætmæn] **III U5,** 87
BBC [ˌbiːbiːˈsiː] **III U5,** 82
Beatles [ˈbiːtlz] **IV U5,** 79
Big Ben [ˌbɪg ˈben] **III U2,** 26
Billabong [ˈbɪləbɒŋ] **IV U4,** 62
Blue Eagles [ˌbluː ˈiːglz] **IV U2,** 24
Blugirl [ˈbluːgɜːl] **IV U5,** 80
Boxing Day [ˈbɒksɪŋ ˌdeɪ] **I FA,** 114
British Airways (BA) [ˌbrɪtɪʃ ˈeəweɪz] **III U2,** 30
Brooklyn Bridge [ˌbrʊklɪn ˈbrɪdʒ] **IV U1,** 9
Buckingham Bridge [ˌbʌkɪŋəm ˈbrɪdʒ] **III U2,** 33
Buckingham Palace [ˌbʌkɪŋəm ˈpælɪs] **II U3,** 47
Cadillac [ˈkædɪlæk] **IV U4,** 68
Charlie Chaplin [ˌtʃɑːli ˈtʃæplɪn] **III U4,** 72
Chunnel [ˈtʃʌnl] Tunnel durch den Ärmelkanal **III U3,** 45
Circle Line [ˈsɜːkl ˌlaɪn] **III U2,** 28
Concorde [ˈkɒŋkɔːd] **III U2,** 38
Cutty Sark [ˌkʌti ˈsɑːk] **I U4,** 54
Cutty Sark Gardens [kʌti ˌsɑːk ˈgɑːdnz] **I U4,** 54
Derrek Lee [ˌderɪk ˈliː] **III U1,** 9
Discman [ˈdɪskmən] Discman **I U2,** 30
DLR [ˌdiː‿el‿ˈɑː] **I U4,** 55
Docklands Light Railway [ˈdɒkləndz ˌlaɪt ˈreɪlweɪ] **I U4,** 55

Dynamo Moscow [ˌdaɪnəməʊ ˈmɒskəʊ] **III U1,** 16
Eadweard Muybridge [ˌedwəd ˈmaɪbrɪdʒ] **IV U5,** 78
Edwin Porter [ˌedwɪn ˈpɔːtə] **IV U5,** 78
Embankment [ɪmˈbæŋkmənt] **III U2,** 28
Emergency Room [ɪˈmɜːdʒnsi ˌrʊm] **III U5,** 82
Empire State Building [ˌempaɪə ˈsteɪt ˌbɪldɪŋ] **IV U1,** 9
European Union [ˌjʊərəˈpiːən ˈjuːnjən] **III U3,** 55
Fergie [ˈfɜːgi] **IV U5,** 84
Friar Tuck [ˌfraɪə ˈtʌk] **II FA,** 110
Gelert [ˈgelət] **III U5,** 81
Georges Méliès [ˌʒɔːʒ melˈjeɪ] **IV U5,** 78
GMT [ˈdʒiːemˈtiː] **I U4,** 55
GPS [ˌdʒiːpiːˈes] GPS *(globales Positionsbestimmungssystem)* **IV U3,** 43
Grammy Award [ˌgræmi əˈwɔːd] **IV U5,** 77
Great Fire [ˌgreɪt ˈfaɪə] **III U2,** 26
Great Tower [ˌgreɪt ˈtaʊə] **III U2,** 31
Green Day [ˈgriːn ˌdeɪ] **IV U5,** 77
Greenwich Mean Time [ˌgrenɪdʒ ˈmiːn taɪm] **I U4,** 55
Harland Club Teen Center [ˌhɑːlənd ˈklʌb ˌtiːn ˈsentə] **IV U5,** 80
Harrods [ˈhærədz] **II U2,** 23
Harry Potter [ˌhæri ˈpɒtə] **II U1,** 11
HIP Bar [ˌhɪp ˈbɑː] **IV U5,** 81
Houses of Parliament [ˌhaʊzɪz‿əv ˈpɑːləmənt] **I FA,** 114
Hualapai [ˌhʊələˈpeɪ] **IV U4,** 60
James Bond [ˌdʒeɪmz ˈbɒnd] **I FA,** 104
Jennifer Hudson [ˌdʒenɪfə ˈhʌdsn] **IV U5,** 76
Led Zeppelin [ˌled ˈzeplɪn] **IV U5,** 80
Leeds Castle [ˌliːdz ˈkɑːsl] **III U3,** 57
Lil Jon [ˌlɪl ˈdʒɒn] **IV U5,** 80
London Dungeon [ˌlʌndən ˈdʌndʒn] **III U2,** 26
London Bridge [ˌlʌndən ˈbrɪdʒ] **III U2,** 32
London Eye [ˌlʌndən‿ˈaɪ] **III U2,** 26
London Knights [ˌlʌndən ˈnaɪts] **II U2,** 22
Lord of the Rings [ˌlɔːd‿əv ðə‿ˈrɪŋz] **IV U5,** 79
Ludacris [ˈluːdəkrɪs] **IV U5,** 84
Madonna [məˈdɒnə] **III U2,** 29
Man U [ˈmæn juː] **III U5,** 82
Meridian Line [məˈrɪdiən ˈlaɪn] **I U4,** 54
MiB [ˌem‿aɪ ˈbiː] *(Men in Black)* **IV U3,** 50
Mohawk [ˈməʊhɔːk] **IV U1,** 9
Monument [ˈmɒnjəmənt] **III U2,** 28
MTV [ˌemtiːˈviː] **I U6,** 82
Mustang [ˈmʌstæŋ] **IV U5,** 84
Naomi Campbell [ˌneɪəmiː ˈkæmbl] **III U2,** 29
Napoleon [nəˈpəʊliən] **II U5,** 62
NASA [ˈnæsə] NASA *(US-Weltraumbehörde)* **IV U3,** 43
Nelly Furtado [ˌneli fəˈtɑːdəʊ] **IV U5,** 77
Nessie [ˈnesi] **II FA,** 103
Neuralizer [ˈnjuːrəˌlaɪzə] **IV U3,** 50
New Stone Age [ˈnjuː ˌstəʊn ˌeɪdʒ] Jungsteinzeit **III U3,** 49
Nicole Kidman [nɪˌkəʊl ˈkɪdmən] **IV U5,** 76
Oscar [ˈɒskə] **IV U5,** 77
OutKast [ˈaʊtkɑːst] **IV U5,** 80
Oz [ɒz] **II FA,** 114
Palace of Westminster [ˌpælɪs‿əv ˈwesmɪnstə] **III U2,** 26
Paradise Valley High School (PVHS) [ˈpærədaɪs væli ˈhaɪ ˌskuːl] **IV U2,** 24
Queen Elizabeth [ˌkwiːn‿ɪˈlɪzəbəθ] **I U5,** 73
Robbie Williams [ˌrɒbi ˈwɪljəmz] **II U1,** 14
Robin Hood [ˌrɒbɪn ˈhʊd] **II FA,** 110
Robin Leach [ˌrɒbɪn ˈliːtʃ] **IV U5,** 84
Route 66 [ruːt] **IV U4,** 61
Royal Family [ˈrɔɪəl ˈfæmli] **III U2,** 26
Royal Observatory [ˌrɔɪəl əbˈzɜːvətri] **I U4,** 55
Rugby School [ˌrʌgbi ˈskuːl] **III U1,** 8
Samuel Ellis [ˌsæmjʊəl‿ˈelɪs] **IV U1,** 10
Sean Paul [ˌʃɔːn ˈpɔːl] **IV U5,** 77
Shake-A-Break [ˌʃeɪk‿ə ˈbreɪk] **IV U1,** 16
Shakespeare [ˈʃeɪkspɪə] **II U5,** 62
Sherlock Holmes [ˌʃɜːlɒk ˈhəʊmz] **III U5,** 82
Shrove Tuesday [ˌʃrəʊv ˈtjuːzdeɪ] **I FA,** 115
Skywalk [ˈskaɪwɔːk] **IV U4,** 60
Spiderman [ˈspaɪdəmæn] **II U6,** 85
Statue of Liberty [ˌstætʃuː‿əv ˈlɪbəti] **IV U1,** 8
St James's Park [snt ˌdʒeɪmzɪz ˈpɑːk] **III U2,** 28
St Paul's Cathedral [snt ˌpɔːlz ˈkəθiːdrl] **III U2,** 28
Sunrise NY [ˌsʌnraɪz njuːˈjɔːk] **IV U1,** 15
Superman [ˈsuːpəmæn] **III U5,** 87
Taco Bell [ˌtɑːkəʊ ˈbel] **IV U5,** 84
Taj Mahal [ˌtɑːdʒ məˈhɑːl] **II U4,** 48
Teen Center [ˌtiːn ˈsentə] **IV U5,** 81
Teentalk [ˈtiːntɔːk] **IV U5,** 80
Thanksgiving [ˌθæŋksˈgɪvɪŋ] **IV U4,** 64
The Great Train Robbery [ðə ˌgreɪt ˈtreɪn ˌrɒbri] **IV U5,** 78
The Jazz Singer [ðə ˌdʒæz ˈsɪŋə] **IV U5,** 78
The Philosopher's Stone [ˌðə fɪˈlɒsəfəz ˌstəʊn] **IV U5,** 79
Thomas Edison [ˌtɒməs‿ˈedɪsn] **IV U5,** 78
Thomas Tallis School [ˌtɒməs tælɪs ˈskuːl] **I U1,** 10
Times Square [ˌtaɪmz ˈskweə] **IV U1,** 9
Titanic [taɪˈtænɪk] **III U3,** 45
Tower of London [ˌtaʊər‿əv ˈlʌndən] **III U2,** 26
Tube [tjuːb] **III U2,** 26
Tuzie [ˈtuːzi] **IV U5,** 80
UFO *(Unidentified Flying Object)* [ˈjuːefˈəʊ] **IV U3,** 51
Urquhart Castle [ˌɜːkət ˈkɑːsl] **II FA,** 102
Valentine [ˈvæləntaɪn] **II U6,** 85
We are the Champions [ˈtʃæmpiənz] **IV U5,** 79
Wembley Stadium [ˈwembli ˈsteɪdiəm] **III U1,** 12
William the Conqueror [ˌwɪljəm ðə ˈkɒŋkrə] **III U2,** 31
Wizard of Oz [ˌwɪzəd əv‿ˈɒz] °**II U5,** 64
Zandra Rhodes [ˌzændrə ˈrəʊdz] **IV U5,** 76

German – English

A

ab off [ɒf]
Abc alphabet ['ælfəbet]
Abend evening ['i:vnɪŋ]; night [naɪt]
am Abend in the evening [ˌɪn ði: 'i:vnɪŋ]
an diesem Abend that evening [ˌdæt‿'i:vnɪŋ]
heute Abend this evening [ðɪs 'i:vnɪŋ]; tonight [tə'naɪt]
zu Abend essen to have supper [hæv 'sʌpə]
Abendessen dinner ['dɪnə]; supper ['sʌpə]; tea [ti:]
zum Abendessen for supper [fə 'sʌpə]
Abendkleid evening dress ['i:vnɪŋ ˌdres]
abends in the evening [ˌɪn ði: 'i:vnɪŋ]
Abenteuer adventure [əd'ventʃə]
aber but [bʌt]
abfahren to leave [li:v]
Abfall rubbish ['rʌbɪʃ]
Abfälle rubbish ['rʌbɪʃ]
abfliegen to take off [ˌteɪk‿'ɒf]
Abflug departure [dɪ'pɑ:tʃə]
Abgang exit ['eksɪt]
abgebrannt broke [brəʊk]
abheben to take off [ˌteɪk‿'ɒf]
abholen to collect [kə'lekt]; to pick up [pɪk‿'ʌp]
Abitur A-levels *(pl)* ['eɪlevlz]
ablaufen *(Wasser)* to run away [rʌn‿ə'weɪ]
ablaufen *(Zeit)* to run out [rʌn‿'aʊt]
Abreise departure [dɪ'pɑ:tʃə]
abschalten to turn off [tɜ:n‿'ɒf]
abschicken to post [pəʊst]
abschließen to lock [lɒk]
abschneiden to cut (off) [kʌt‿'ɒf]
abschrecken to frighten away [ˌfraɪtn‿ə'weɪ]
abschreiben to copy ['kɒpi]
absolut absolutely [ˌæbsə'lu:tli]
Abstand distance ['dɪstnts]
abstimmen to vote (for) [vəʊt]
Abstimmung vote [vəʊt]
abwesend absent ['æbsnt]
Abwesenheit absence ['æbsns]
sich **abwickeln** to unwind [ʌn'waɪnd]
achten auf to watch [wɒtʃ]
Achtung attention [ə'tentʃn]
Acker field [fi:ld]
Adapter adaptor [ə'dæptə]
addieren to add [æd]
Adresse address [ə'dres]
Aftershave aftershave ['ɑ:ftəʃeɪv]
Agent/Agentin agent ['eɪdʒnt]
Agentur agency ['eɪdʒnsi]
Ahorn maple ['meɪpl]
Akku battery ['bætri]
Aktion action ['ækʃn]
aktiv active ['æktɪv]
Aktivität activity [æk'tɪvəti]
Akzent accent ['æksnt]
Alarm alarm [ə'lɑ:m]
Album album ['ælbəm]
Alkohol alcohol ['ælkəhɒl]
alle everybody ['evribɒdi]
alle/alles all [ɔ:l]
aller- very ['veri]
alleine alone [ə'ləʊn]
alles everything ['evriθɪŋ]
alles klar all right [ɔ:l 'raɪt]
Alphabet alphabet ['ælfəbet]
alphabetisch alphabetical [ˌælfə'betɪkl]
als as [æz; əz]
als *(Vergleich)* than [ðæn]
als *(zeitlich)* when [wen]
also so [səʊ]; well [wel]
alt ancient ['eɪnʃnt]; old [əʊld]
Alter age [eɪdʒ]
im Alter von of age [əv‿'eɪdʒ]
Amerikaner American [ə'merɪkən]
Hispano-Amerikaner/-Amerikanerin Hispanic [hɪ'spænɪk]
amerikanisch American [ə'merɪkən]
sich **amüsieren** to have a good time [ˌhæv‿ə gʊd 'taɪm]; to have fun [ˌhæv 'fʌn]
an at [æt; ət]; on [ɒn]
an sein to be on [bi:‿'ɒn]
anbieten to offer ['ɒfə]
Anblick sight [saɪt]
anbringen to attach [ə'tætʃ]; to fix (to) [fɪks]
andauern to go on [gəʊ‿'ɒn]
Andenken souvenir [ˌsu:və'nɪə]
andere/anderer/anderes other ['ʌðə]
ein anderer/eine andere/ein anderes another [ə'nʌðə]
ändern to change [tʃeɪndʒ]
anders different ['dɪfrnt]
Änderung change [tʃeɪndʒ]
Anfang beginning [bɪ'gɪnɪŋ]; start [stɑ:t]
anfangen to begin [bɪ'gɪn]; to start [stɑ:t]
anfügen to attach [ə'tætʃ]
Anführer/Anführerin leader ['li:də]
Angebot offer ['ɒfə]
Angelegenheit matter ['mætə]
angeln to fish [fɪʃ]
Angeln fishing ['fɪʃɪŋ]
Angestellter/Angestellte worker ['wɜ:kə]
angreifen to attack [ə'tæk]
Angriff raid [reɪd]
Angst haben (vor) to be frightened (of) [bi: 'fraɪtnd]
Angst machen to scare ['skeə]
Ich habe Angst. I'm scared. [aɪm 'skeəd]
ängstigen to worry ['wʌri]
anhaben to wear [weə]
anhalten to stop [stɒp]
anhängen to attach [ə'tætʃ]
Anhänger/Anhängerin supporter [sə'pɔ:tə]
anhören to listen ['lɪsn]
sich anhören to sound [saʊnd]
fest **anklopfen** to bang [bæŋ]
ankommen to arrive [ə'raɪv]
Ankündigung announcement [ə'naʊntsmənt]
anmachen to switch on [ˌswɪtʃ‿'ɒn]; to turn on [ˌtɜ:n‿'ɒn]
anmalen to paint [peɪnt]
(sich) **anmelden** to register ['redʒɪstə]
Anmerkung note [nəʊt]
annähernd nearly ['nɪəli]
Anorak anorak ['ænəræk]
Anregung suggestion [sə'dʒestʃn]
Anrufbeantworter answerphone ['ɑ:nsəfəʊn]
anrufen to call [kɔ:l]; to phone [fəʊn]; to ring [rɪŋ]
anschauen to have a look (at) [ˌhæv‿ə 'lʊk]; to view [vju:]
sich **anschließen** to join [dʒɔɪn]
ansehen to look at ['lʊk‿ət]; to watch [wɒtʃ]
sich ansehen to look at ['lʊk‿ət]
Anstandswauwau chaperon ['ʃæprəʊn]
anstatt instead of [ɪn'sted‿əv]
Anstieg rise [raɪz]
anstreichen to paint [peɪnt]
antippen to touch [tʌtʃ]
Antwort answer ['ɑ:nsə]; response [rɪ'spɒns]
Anweisung instruction [ɪn'strʌkʃn]
Anzeige advert ['ædvɜ:t]
anziehen to attract [ə'trækt]; to put on [pʊt‿'ɒn]
sich anziehen to dress [dres]
Anzug suit [su:t]
Apartment apartment *(AE)* [ə'pɑ:tmənt]

Apfel apple ['æpl]
Apparat machine [mə'ʃi:n]
April April ['eɪprl]
Arbeit work [wɜ:k]
arbeiten to work [wɜ:k]
Arbeiter/Arbeiterin worker ['wɜ:kə]
Arbeitsblatt worksheet ['wɜ:kʃi:t]
Arbeitsgemeinschaft club [klʌb]
Arbeitsstelle job [dʒɒb]
Architekt/Architektin architect ['ɑ:kɪtekt]
Arena arena [ə'ri:nə]
Ärger trouble ['trʌbl]
Argument argument ['ɑ:gjəmənt]
argumentieren to argue ['ɑ:gju:]
arm poor [pɔ:; pʊə]
Arm arm [ɑ:m]
Ärmel arm [ɑ:m]
Armut poverty ['pɒvəti]
Arsch ass *(AE)* [æs]
Art kind [kaɪnd]; sort [sɔ:t]; type [taɪp]; way [weɪ]
Artikel article ['ɑ:tɪkl]
Arzt/Ärztin doctor ['dɒktə]
  zum Arzt gehen to see a doctor [si: ə 'dɒktə]
Assistent/Assistentin assistant [ə'sɪstnt]
Astronaut/Astronautin astronaut ['æstrənɔ:t]
Attraktion attraction [ə'trækʃn]
attraktiv attractive [ə'træktɪv]
auch also ['ɔ:lsəʊ]; too [tu:]
  sowohl … als auch as well as [əz 'wel‿əz]
auf at [æt; ət]; on [ɒn]; onto ['ɒntu:; 'ɒntə]; up [ʌp]
  auf … zu towards [tə'wɔ:dz]
  auf dem Land in the country [ˌɪn ðə 'kʌntri]
  auf einmal suddenly ['sʌdnli]
  auf Sendung on the air [ˌɒn ði‿'eə]
  auf Wiedersehen goodbye [gʊd'baɪ]
  (auf …) hinauf onto ['ɒntu:; 'ɒntə]
aufbauen to put up [pʊt‿'ʌp]; to set up [set‿'ʌp]
  wieder aufbauen to rebuild [ˌri:'bɪld]
aufbewahren to keep [ki:p]
Aufblinken flash [flæʃ]
aufbrechen to set off [set‿'ɒf]
aufführen to perform [pə'fɔ:m]
Aufführung performance [pə'fɔ:məns]
Aufgabe exercise ['eksəsaɪz]
aufgeben to give up [gɪv‿'ʌp]
  aufgeben *(einen Brief)* to post [pəʊst]
aufgehen to open ['əʊpn]
aufgeregt excited [ɪk'saɪtɪd]; nervous ['nɜ:vəs]
  aufgeregt sein to be upset [bi: ʌp'set]
aufheben to pick up [pɪk‿'ʌp]
aufhören to finish ['fɪnɪʃ]; to stop [stɒp]
  aufhören etw. zu tun to stop + -ing [stɒp]
  aufhören mit to stop [stɒp]
aufmachen to open ['əʊpn]
aufmerksam thoughtful ['θɔ:tfl]
Aufmerksamkeit attention [ə'tentʃn]
Aufnahme recording [rɪ'kɔ:dɪŋ]
aufnehmen to include [ɪn'klu:d]; to record [rɪ'kɔ:d]
aufpassen to take care [teɪk 'keə]
  aufpassen auf to look after [lʊk‿'ɑ:ftə]
sich **aufregen** to panic ['pænɪk]
aufregend exciting [ɪk'saɪtɪŋ]
Aufregung fuss [fʌs]
aufschauen to look up [lʊk‿'ʌp]
aufsetzen to put on [pʊt‿'ɒn]
aufspringen to jump up [dʒʌmp‿'ʌp]
aufstehen to get out of bed [ˌget‿aʊt‿əv 'bed]; to get up [get‿'ʌp]
aufsteigen to get on [get‿'ɒn]
aufstellen to put up [pʊt‿'ʌp]
Aufstieg rise [raɪz]
auftauen to thaw [θɔ:]
auftragen *(Make-up)* to put on [pʊt‿'ɒn]
auftreten to perform [pə'fɔ:m]
aufwachen to wake up [weɪk‿'ʌp]
(sich) **aufwärmen** to warm up [wɔ:m‿'ʌp]
aufwecken to wake [weɪk]; to wake up [weɪk‿'ʌp]
aufzeichnen to record [rɪ'kɔ:d]
Aufzeichnung recording [rɪ'kɔ:dɪŋ]
Auge eye [aɪ]
Augenblick moment ['məʊmənt]
  im Augenblick at the moment [æt ðə 'məʊmənt]
  in diesem Augenblick right now [ˌraɪt 'naʊ]
Augenbraue eyebrow ['aɪbraʊ]
August August ['ɔ:gəst]
aus from [frɒm]
  aus … heraus out of ['aʊt‿əv]
Ausbildung training ['treɪnɪŋ]
  eine Ausbildung machen to train [treɪn]
auschecken to check out [tʃek‿'aʊt]
ausdenken think up [θɪŋk‿'ʌp]
  sich ausdenken think up [θɪŋk‿'ʌp]; to make up [meɪk‿'ʌp]
Ausdruck phrase [freɪz]
Ausfahrt exit ['eksɪt]
Ausflug trip [trɪp]
ausfüllen to fill in [fɪl‿'ɪn]
Ausgang exit ['eksɪt]
ausgeben to spend [spend]
ausgedehnt vast [vɑ:st]
ausgefallen outrageous [aʊt'reɪdʒəs]
ausgehen to go out [gəʊ‿'aʊt]
  ausgehen *(Zeit)* to run out [ˌrʌn‿'aʊt]
ausgraben to dig up [dɪg‿'ʌp]
ohne … **auskommen** to go without [ˌgəʊ wɪ'ðaʊt]
auslachen to laugh at ['lɑ:f‿ət]
im/ins **Ausland** abroad [ə'brɔ:d]
ausländisch alien ['eɪliən]; foreign ['fɒrɪn]
auslaufen to leak [li:k]
auslösen *(Alarm)* to set off [set‿'ɒf]
Auslöser button ['bʌtn]
ausmachen to matter ['mætə]; to put out [pʊt‿'aʊt]
ausradieren to erase [ɪ'reɪz]
ausrauben to rob [rɒb]
Ausreißer/Ausreißerin runaway ['rʌnəˌweɪ]
sich **ausruhen** to relax [rɪ'læks]; to rest [rest]
Ausrüstung equipment [ɪ'kwɪpmənt]
ausschalten to switch off [ˌswɪtʃ‿'ɒf]; to turn off [tɜ:n‿'ɒf]
ausscheren to swerve [swɜ:v]
aussehen to look [lʊk]
Aussehen look [lʊk]
außer beside [bɪ'saɪd]; but [bʌt]; except [ɪk'sept]
außerhalb outside [aʊt'saɪd]
Außerirdischer/Außerirdische alien ['eɪliən]
Aussicht view [vju:]
Ausstattung equipment [ɪ'kwɪpmənt]
aussteigen to get out [get‿'aʊt]
  aussteigen aus to get off [get‿'ɒf]
Ausstellung exhibition [ˌeksɪ'bɪʃn]
Austausch exchange [ɪks'tʃeɪndʒ]
Australier Australian [ɒs'treɪliən]
australisch Australian [ɒs'treɪliən]
Auswahl choice [tʃɔɪs]
auswählen to choose [tʃu:z]
Auswahlverfahren tryout ['traɪaʊt]
auswandern to emigrate ['emɪgreɪt]
auswechseln to substitute ['sʌbstɪtju:t]
ausweichen to swerve [swɜ:v]
Auszeichnung award [ə'wɔ:d]

ausziehen to take off [teɪk‿'ɒf]
Auto car [kɑ:]
Autobahn Interstate *(AE)* [ˌɪntə'steɪt]; motorway ['məʊtəweɪ]
Autogramm autograph ['ɔ:təgrɑ:f]
Autopanne breakdown ['breɪkdaʊn]

B

Baby baby, babies *(pl)* ['beɪbi; 'beɪbiz]
Bach stream [stri:m]
Bäcker/Bäckerin baker ['beɪkə]
Backofen oven ['ʌvn]
Badeanzug swimsuit ['swɪmsu:t]
Badezimmer bathroom ['bɑ:θrʊm]
Badminton badminton ['bædmɪntən]
Bagel bagel ['beɪgl]
Bahnhof station ['steɪʃn]
Bahnsteig platform ['plætfɔ:m]
bald soon [su:n]
Ball ball [bɔ:l]
Ballkönigin homecoming queen [ˌhəʊmkʌmɪŋ 'kwi:n]
Ballsaal ballroom ['bɔ:lrʊm]
Banane banana [bə'nɑ:nə]
Band band [bænd]
Bande band [bænd]; gang [gæŋ]
Bank bank [bæŋk]
Bar bar [bɑ:]
Bär/Bärin bear [beə]
Barkeeper barman, barmen *(pl)* ['bɑ:mən, 'bɑ:men]
Barmann barman, barmen *(pl)* ['bɑ:mən, 'bɑ:men]
Bart beard [bɪəd]
Base base [beɪs]
Baseball baseball ['beɪsbɔ:l]
Basketball basketball ['bɑ:skɪtbɔ:l]
Bass bass [beɪs]
Batterie battery ['bætri]
Bauch stomach ['stʌmək]
bauen to build [bɪld]; to construct [kən'strʌkt]
Bauer/Bäuerin farmer ['fɑ:mə]
Bauernhaus farmhouse ['fɑ:mhaʊs]
Bauernhof farm [fɑ:m]
Baum tree [tri:]
Bazillus bug [bʌg]
Beamter/Beamtin officer ['ɒfɪsə]; official [ə'fɪʃl]
beängstigend frightening ['fraɪtnɪŋ]
bearbeiten to edit ['edɪt]
bedauerlich sad [sæd]
bedauern to feel sorry for [fi:l 'sɒri]
bedeuten to mean [mi:n]
Bedeutung meaning ['mi:nɪŋ]; sense [sens]
von Bedeutung sein to matter ['mætə]
bedienen to operate ['ɒpəreɪt]; to serve [sɜ:v]
Bedienung waiter ['weɪtə]
Beeil dich! Hurry up! [ˌhʌri‿'ʌp]
beenden to end [end]; to finish ['fɪnɪʃ]
beerdigen to bury ['beri]
Beerdigung funeral ['fju:nrəl]
befestigen to fix (to) [fɪks]
befolgen to follow ['fɒləʊ]
befördern to carry ['kæri]
Beginn beginning [bɪ'gɪnɪŋ]; start [stɑ:t]
beginnen to begin [bɪ'gɪn]
Begleitperson chaperon ['ʃæprəʊn]
begraben to bury ['beri]
behalten to keep [ki:p]
Behörde agency ['eɪdʒnsi]
bei at [æt; ət]; with [wɪð]
beide both [bəʊθ]
Beifahrer/Beifahrerin passenger ['pæsndʒə]
Bein leg [leg]
beinahe almost ['ɔ:lməʊst]
beinhalten to include [ɪn'klu:d]
zum **Beispiel** for example [ˌfər‿ɪg'zɑ:mpl]
beitreten to join [dʒɔɪn]
sich **beklagen** to moan [məʊn]
bekommen to get [get]
belebt busy ['bɪzi]
Beleg slip [slɪp]
beleidigen to diss *(slang)* [dɪs]
Belgier/Belgierin Belgian ['beldʒən]
belgisch Belgian ['beldʒən]
beliebt popular ['pɒpjələ]
bellen to bark [bɑ:k]
Bellen barking ['bɑ:kɪŋ]
bemerken to notice ['nəʊtɪs]
sich stark **bemühen** to try hard [traɪ‿'hɑ:d]
benennen to name [neɪm]
benötigen to need [ni:d]
benutzen to use [ju:z]
beobachten to watch [wɒtʃ]
bequem comfortable ['kʌmpftəbl]
Berater/Beraterin counselor ['kaʊnsələ]
bereit ready ['redi]
Berg mountain ['maʊntɪn]
Bericht report [rɪ'pɔ:t]
berichten to report [rɪ'pɔ:t]
berühmt famous ['feɪməs]
berühren to touch [tʌtʃ]
Besatzung crew [kru:]
beschädigen to damage ['dæmɪdʒ]
beschäftigt busy ['bɪzi]
beschreiben to describe [dɪ'skraɪb]
besichtigen to visit ['vɪzɪt]
besiegen to beat [bi:t]
besitzen to have got [hæv 'gɒt]
Besitzer/Besitzerin owner ['əʊnə]
besonders special ['speʃl]
besorgen to get [get]
besorgt sein to be worried [bi: 'wʌrid]
Besprechung meeting ['mi:tɪŋ]
besprühen to spray [spreɪ]
besser better ['betə]
beste/bester/bestes best [best]
bestehen to pass [pɑ:s]
besteigen to climb ['klaɪm]
bestellen to order ['ɔ:də]
am **besten** best [best]
bestimmt definitely ['defɪnətli]
bestraft werden to get it ['get‿ɪt]
bestürzt sein to be upset [bi: ʌp'set]
Besuch visit ['vɪzɪt]
besuchen to see [si:]; to visit ['vɪzɪt]
Besucher/Besucherin visitor ['vɪzɪtə]
sich **beteiligen an** to enter ['entə]
Betonung stress [stres]
betrachten to view [vju:]
betreten to enter ['entə]
Betreuer/Betreuerin counselor ['kaʊnsələ]
Bett bed [bed]
beunruhigen to worry ['wʌri]
beunruhigt sein to be worried [bi: 'wʌrid]
Bevölkerung population [ˌpɒpjə'leɪʃn]
bevor before [bɪ'fɔ:]
bewachen to guard [gɑ:d]
bewegen to move [mu:v]
sich bewegen to move [mu:v]
Bewegung motion ['məʊʃn]; move [mu:v]
bezahlen to pay for [peɪ]
Bezirk borough ['bʌrə]
Bild picture ['pɪktʃə]
bilden to form [fɔ:m]
Bildschirm screen [skri:n]
Bildung education [edʒʊ'keɪʃn]
Bildunterschrift caption ['kæpʃn]
billig cheap [tʃi:p]
Bindeglied link [lɪŋk]
Bindfaden string [strɪŋ]
Birne pear [peə]
bis to [tʊ; tə]; until [ʌn'tɪl; n'tɪl]; till [tɪl]

bis zu up to ['ʌp tə]
Bis .... See you around! [ˌsi: jə ə'raʊnd]
Bis dann! See you! ['si: jə]; See you around! [ˌsi: jə ə'raʊnd]
ein **bisschen** a bit [ə 'bɪt]
bitte please [pli:z]
Bitte schön! Here you are! ['hɪə ju:ˌɑ:]
Bitte sehr! You're welcome. [jʊə 'welkəm]
bitten um to ask (for) ['ɑ:sk fə]
blasen to blow [bləʊ]
Blatt leaf, leaves *(pl)* [li:f; li:vz]
blau blue [blu:]
Blei lead [led]
bleiben to stay [steɪ]
Bleistift pencil ['pensl]
Blende shutter ['ʃʌtə]
Blick look [lʊk]
einen Blick werfen (auf) to have a look (at) [ˌhæv‿ə 'lʊk]
einen vernichtenden Blick zuwerfen to give ... a dirty look [ˌgɪv‿ə dɜ:ti 'lʊk]
blind blind [blaɪnd]
blinken to flash [flæʃ]
blitzen to flash [flæʃ]
Blitzen flash [flæʃ]
blöd stupid ['stju:pɪd]
blond blond [blɒnd]; blond(e)-haired ['blɒndˌheəd]; fair [feə]
bloß only ['əʊnli]
Blume flower ['flaʊə]
Blut blood [blʌd]
Boden bottom ['bɒtəm]; ground [graʊnd]
Bogen bow [bəʊ]
Bohne bean [bi:n]
Bohrer drill [drɪl]
Bohrmaschine drill [drɪl]
Bombe bomb [bɒm]
Bonbon sweet [swi:t]
Boot boat [bəʊt]
an **Bord** on board [ɒn 'bɔ:d]
borgen to borrow ['bɒrəʊ]
bösartig fierce [fɪəs]
böse angry ['æŋgri]
böse sein auf to be angry with [bi: 'æŋgri wɪð]
Boss boss [bɒs]
Boulevard boulevard ['bu:ləvɑ:d]
Branche business ['bɪznɪs]
brand- brand [brænd]
Brand fire [faɪə]
brauchen to need [ni:d]
(Zeit) brauchen to take [teɪk]
braun brown [braʊn]
Breakdance tanzen to break-dance ['breɪkdɑ:nts]
brechen to break [breɪk]
breit across [ə'krɒs]
brennen to burn [bɜ:n]
brennen *(Licht)* to be on [bi:‿'ɒn]
schwarzes **Brett** notice board ['nəʊtɪs bɔ:d]
Brief letter ['letə]
Briefmarke stamp [stæmp]
Brieftasche wallet ['wɒlɪt]
Briefumschlag envelope ['envələʊp]
Brille glasses *(pl)* ['glɑ:sɪz]
bringen to bring [brɪŋ]; to take [teɪk]
nach Hause bringen to take home [ˌteɪk 'həʊm]
britisch British ['brɪtɪʃ]
Brot bread [bred]
belegtes Brot sandwich ['sænwɪdʒ]
Brücke bridge [brɪdʒ]
Bruder brother ['brʌðə]
Buch book [bʊk]
Büchse tin [tɪn]
Buchstabe letter ['letə]
buchstabieren to spell [spel]
Bude stall [stɔ:l]
bügeln to iron [aɪən]
Bumm! Crash! [kræʃ]
Bundesstraße highway *(AE)* ['haɪweɪ]
bunt colourful ['kʌləfl]
Burg castle ['kɑ:sl]
Büro office ['ɒfɪs]
bürsten to brush [brʌʃ]
Bus bus, buses *(pl)* [bʌs; 'bʌsɪz]
im Bus on the bus [ˌɒn ðə 'bʌs]
Busch bush [bʊʃ]
Bushaltestelle bus stop ['bʌs ˌstɒp]
Butter butter ['bʌtə]

C

Café café ['kæfeɪ]
Café latte latte ['lɑ:teɪ]
Cafeteria cafeteria [ˌkæfə'tɪəriə]
Camp camp [kæmp]
Camper/Camperin camper ['kæmpə]
Camping camping ['kæmpɪŋ]
Canyon canyon ['kænjən]
Cartoon cartoon [kɑ:'tu:n]
Casino casino [kə'si:nəʊ]
CD CD [ˌsi:'di:]
CD-Player CD player [ˌsi:'di: ˌpleɪə]
Celsius Celsius (C) ['selsiəs]
Cent *(Währung)* cent [sent]
Champagner champagne [ʃæm'peɪn]
Chaos chaos ['keɪɒs]
Charts charts *(pl)* [tʃɑ:ts]
Chatroom *(Internetforum, wo man sich online unterhalten kann)* chat room ['tʃæt rʊm]
Cheerleader *(Mädchen, das in einer Gruppe eine Sportmannschaft anfeuert)* cheerleader ['tʃɪəˌli:də]
Cheerleading cheerleading ['tʃɪəˌli:dɪŋ]
Chef/Chefin boss [bɒs]
chillen to chill out [tʃɪl‿'aʊt]
chinesisch Chinese [tʃaɪ'ni:z]
circa about [ə'baʊt]
Code code [kəʊd]
Cola coke [kəʊk]
College college ['kɒlɪdʒ]
Comic comic ['kɒmɪk]
Comicheft comic ['kɒmɪk]
Computer computer [ˌkəm'pju:tə]
cool cool [ku:l]
Cornflakes cornflakes ['kɔ:nfleɪks]
aus **Cornwall** Cornish ['kɔ:nɪʃ]
Couch couch [kaʊtʃ]; sofa ['səʊfə]
Countdown countdown ['kaʊntdaʊn]
Countrymusik country ['kʌntri]
Cousin/Cousine cousin ['kʌzn]
Cowboy cowboy ['kaʊbɔɪ]
Creme cream [kri:m]
Crew crew [kru:]
Curry *(Gewürz oder Gericht)* curry ['kʌri]

D

da there [ðeə]
da drüben over there [ˌəʊvə 'ðeə]
da ist there is [ðeər‿'ɪz]
da sind there are [ðeər‿'ɑ:]
Dach roof [ru:f]
Dancehall *(Musikrichtung)* dancehall ['dɑ:nshɔ:l]
dänisch Danish ['deɪnɪʃ]
dank thanks to ['θæŋks tə]
danke thanks [θæŋks]; thank you ['θæŋk ju:]
danken to thank [θæŋk]
dann then [ðen]
darauf zu towards [tə'wɔ:dz]
darstellen to pose [pəʊz]
sich darstellen to pose [pəʊz]
quer **darüber** across [ə'krɒs]
das the [ðə; ði]; that [ðæt]
Das nenne ich .... That's what I call .... [ˌðæts wɒt‿'aɪ ˌkɔ:l]

Datum date [deɪt]
dauern to last [lɑ:st]; to take [teɪk]
Decke blanket ['blæŋkɪt]
definitiv definitely ['defɪnətli]
dein/deine your [jɔ:]
Dein ... *(in Briefen)* Yours [jɔ:z]
Deine ... *(in Briefen)* Yours [jɔ:z]
Dekoration decoration [ˌdek'reɪʃn]
Deli deli *(AE)* ['deli]
denken to think [θɪŋk]
dennoch still [stɪl]
dennoch though [ðəʊ]
der the [ðə; ði]
der/dem/den/die *(Relativpronomen)* who [hu:]
der/dem/den/die/das *(Relativpronomen)* which [wɪtʃ]
deren whose [hu:z]
derselbe/dieselbe/dasselbe the same [seɪm]
Desaster disaster [dɪ'zɑ:stə]
deshalb that's why ['ðæts ˌwaɪ]
Designer/Designerin designer [dɪ'zaɪnə]
dessen whose [hu:z]
Dessert dessert [dɪ'zɜ:t]
Detektiv/Detektivin detective [dɪ'tektɪv]
deuten (auf) to point (to) [pɔɪnt]
deutsch German ['dʒɜ:mən]
Deutscher/Deutsche German ['dʒɜ:mən]
Dezember December [dɪ'sembə]
Dialog dialogue ['daɪəlɒg]
Diamant diamond ['daɪəmənd]
Diät diet [daɪət]
eine Diät machen to go on a diet [ˌgəʊ‿ɒn‿ə 'daɪət]
dich you [ju:; jə]
Dichter/Dichterin poet ['pəʊɪt]
dick thick [θɪk]
die the [ðə; ði]
dienen to serve [sɜ:v]
Diener/Dienerin servant ['sɜ:vnt]
Dienst service ['sɜ:vɪs]
Dienstag Tuesday ['tju:zdeɪ]
dies this [ðɪs]
diese these [ði:z]
diese/dieser/dieses this [ðɪs]
an diesem Abend that evening [ˌdæt‿'i:vnɪŋ]
diese dort those [ðəʊz]
diese hier these [ði:z]
digital digital ['dɪdʒɪtl]
Ding thing [θɪŋ]
dir you [ju:; jə]

direkt direct [dɪ'rekt]; straight [streɪt]; right [raɪt]
Direktor/Direktorin director [dɪ'rektə]
Disko disco ['dɪskəʊ]
Distanz distance ['dɪstnts]
DJ DJ [ˌdi:'dʒeɪ]
Dokument paper ['peɪpə]
Dokumentarfilm documentary [ˌdɒkjə'mentri]
dokumentiert on record [ɒn 'rekɔ:d]
Dokusoap docu soap ['dɒkju ˌsəʊp]
Dollar *(Währung)* dollar ['dɒlə]
Dom cathedral [kə'θi:drl]
Donnerstag Thursday ['θɜ:zdeɪ]
Doppelgänger double ['dʌbl]
das **Doppelte** double ['dʌbl]
Dorf village ['vɪlɪdʒ]
dort there [ðeə]
Dose tin [tɪn]
Drache dragon ['drægn]
Drama drama ['drɑ:mə]
dramatisch dramatic [drə'mætɪk]
draußen outside [aʊt'saɪd]
Drehbuch script [skrɪpt]
drehen to turn [tɜ:n]
drin inside [ɪn'saɪd]
dritte/dritter/drittes third [θɜ:d]
Droge drug [drʌg]
dröhnen to roar [rɔ:]
drücken to press [pres]
drucken to print [prɪnt]
drücken to push [pʊʃ]
du you [ju:; jə]
Du bist dran. It's your turn. [ɪts jɔ: 'tɜ:n]
dumm silly ['sɪli]; stupid ['stju:pɪd]; thick [θɪk]
Dummkopf idiot ['ɪdiət]; silly ['sɪli]
dunkel dark [dɑ:k]
Dunkelheit dark [dɑ:k]
durch through [θru:]
quer durch across [ə'krɒs]
durchdrehen to get into such a state [get‿ɪntə 'sʌtʃ‿ə 'steɪt]; to go bananas [ˌgəʊ bə'nɑ:nəz]
Durcheinander mess [mes]
durcheinander bringen to upset [ʌp'set]
Durcheinander chaos ['keɪɒs]
im **Durchmesser** across [ə'krɒs]
Durchsage announcement [ə'naʊntsmənt]
durchschnittlich average ['ævrɪdʒ]
dürfen can [kæn]; may [meɪ]; to be allowed to (do sth) [bi:‿ə'laʊd]
nicht dürfen mustn't ['mʌsnt]

Dusche shower ['ʃaʊə]
DVD DVD [di:vi:'di:]
DVD-Player DVD player [ˌdi:vi:'di: 'pleɪə]

E

Ebene level ['levl]
echt real [rɪəl]
Es ist mir **egal.** I don't care. [aɪ dəʊnt 'keə]
Ehefrau wife, wives *(pl)* [waɪf; waɪvz]
ehrlich honest ['ɒnɪst]
Ei egg [eg]
eifersüchtig (auf) jealous (of) ['dʒeləs]
eigener/eigene/eigenes own [əʊn]
eigentlich actually ['æktʃuəli]
es **eilig haben** to be in a hurry [bi:‿ɪn‿ə 'hʌri]
ein/eine a, an [ə; ən]
ein paar a few [ə 'fju:]
einander each other [ˌi:tʃ‿'ʌðə]
Einband cover ['kʌvə]
Einbrecher/Einbrecherin burglar ['bɜ:glə]
einfach easy ['i:zi]; simple ['sɪmpl]
Einfall idea [aɪ'dɪə]
einflussreich important [ɪm'pɔ:tnt]
eingängig catchy ['kætʃi]
eingeboren native ['neɪtɪv]
einheimisch native ['neɪtɪv]
einige a few [ə 'fju:]; any ['enɪ]; some [sʌm]
Einkauf shopping ['ʃɒpɪŋ]
Einkaufen shopping ['ʃɒpɪŋ]
Einkaufspassage (shopping) mall [mɔ:l]
Einkaufswagen trolley ['trɒli]
Einkaufszentrum (shopping) mall [mɔ:l]
einladen to invite [ɪn'vaɪt]
Einladung invitation [ˌɪnvɪ'teɪʃn]
einmal once [wʌnts]
Einreisebewilligung visa, visas *(pl)* ['vi:zə]
einrichten to set up [set‿'ʌp]
einsam lonely ['ləʊnli]
einschalten to switch on [ˌswɪtʃ‿'ɒn]; to turn on [ˌtɜ:n‿'ɒn]
einschicken to send in [send‿'ɪn]
einschieben to put in [pʊt‿'ɪn]
einsetzen to put in [pʊt‿'ɪn]
einst once [wʌnts]
einsteigen *(in Zug, Bus ...)* to get on [get‿'ɒn]

einsteigen *(Bus)* to get onto [get‿'ɒntə]
einsteigen in *(Auto)* to get into [get‿'ɪntə]
einstellen to set [set]
eintreten to enter ['entə]
Eintritt verboten! Keep out! [ki:p‿'aʊt]
Eintrittskarte ticket ['tɪkɪt]
Einwanderer/Einwanderin immigrant ['ɪmɪgrənt]
Einwanderung immigration [ˌɪmɪ'greɪʃn]
Einzelkind only child ['əʊnli ˌtʃaɪld]
einzige/einziger/einziges only ['əʊnli]
Eis ice [aɪs]; ice-cream [aɪs'kri:m]
Eisbahn ice rink ['aɪs rɪŋk]
Eiscreme ice-cream [aɪs'kri:m]
Eishockey ice hockey ['aɪs ˌhɒki]
ekelhaft yukky ['jʌki]
Elefant elephant ['elɪfənt]
elektrisch electric [ɪ'lektrɪk]; electrical [ɪ'lektrɪkl]
Elektrizität electricity [ˌelɪk'trɪsəti]
Ellbogen elbow ['elbəʊ]
Elle *(Längenmaß: 0,914 m)* yard [jɑ:d]
Eltern parents ['peərənts]
Elternteil parent ['peərnt]
E-Mail e-mail ['i:meɪl]
E-Mail schreiben to e-mail ['i:meɪl]
per E-Mail schicken to mail [meɪl]
emigrieren to emigrate ['emɪgreɪt]
Empfang reception [rɪ'sepʃn]
empfangen to receive [rɪ'si:v]
Empfangschef/Empfangschefin receptionist [rɪ'sepʃnɪst]
empörend outrageous [aʊt'reɪdʒəs]
Ende end [end]
enden to end [end]; to end up [ˌend‿'ʌp]
endlich finally ['faɪnli]
Engländer/Engländerinnen English ['ɪŋglɪʃ]
englisch English ['ɪŋglɪʃ]
enorm enormous [ɪ'nɔ:məs]
entdecken to discover [dɪ'skʌvə]
entfernen to remove [rɪ'mu:v]
Entfernung distance ['dɪstnts]
entkommen to escape (from) [ɪ'skeɪp]; to get out [get‿'aʊt]
entlang along [ə'lɒŋ]
Geh … entlang. Go down …. ['gəʊ daʊn]
entlanggehen to go down [gəʊ 'daʊn]
entschärfen to defuse [ˌdi:'fju:z]
entscheiden to decide [dɪ'saɪd]
Entschuldigung! Excuse me! [ɪk'skju:z mi:]
sich **entspannen** to chill out [tʃɪl‿'aʊt]; to relax [rɪ'læks]; to rest [rest]
enttäuscht disappointed [ˌdɪsə'pɔɪntɪd]
entwerfen to design [dɪ'zaɪn]
Entzücken glee [gli:]
er he [hi:]
Erbe/Erbin inheritor [ɪn'herɪtə]
Erbse pea [pi:]
Erdbeere strawberry ['strɔ:bri]
Erde earth [ɜ:θ]
Erdkunde Geography [dʒi'ɒgrəfi]
Ereignis event [ɪ'vent]
erfahren to learn [lɜ:n]
Erfahrung experience [ɪk'spɪəriənts]
Erfassung registration [ˌredʒɪ'streɪʃn]
erfinden to invent [ɪn'vent]; to make up [meɪk‿'ʌp]
Erfindung fiction ['fɪkʃn]; invention [ɪn'ventʃn]
Erfolg success [sək'ses]
erforschen to explore [ɪk'splɔ:]
sich **erfreuen** to enjoy [ɪn'dʒɔɪ]
Ergebnis result [rɪ'zʌlt]
erhalten to receive [rɪ'si:v]
sich **erinnern (an)** to remember [rɪ'membə]
Erinnerung memory ['memri]
in Erinnerungen schwelgen to reminisce [ˌremɪ'nɪs]
erkennen to identify [aɪ'dentɪfaɪ]
erklären to explain [ɪk'spleɪn]
erkunden to explore [ɪk'splɔ:]
Erlaubnis permission [pə'mɪʃn]
erläutern to explain [ɪk'spleɪn]
wieder **erleben** to relive [ˌri:'lɪv]
Erlebnis experience [ɪk'spɪəriənts]
erledigen to finish ['fɪnɪʃ]
erlöschen to go out [gəʊ‿'aʊt]
Ermittler/Ermittlerin investigator [ɪn'vestɪgeɪtə]
ermorden to murder ['mɜ:də]
ernst serious ['sɪəriəs]
ernsthaft serious ['sɪəriəs]
eröffnen to start up [stɑ:t‿'ʌp]
erreichen to catch [kætʃ]; to reach [ri:tʃ]
erschrecken to scare ['skeə]; to upset [ʌp'set]
ersetzen to replace [rɪ'pleɪs]; to substitute ['sʌbstɪtju:t]
erst only ['əʊnli]
erstaunt surprised [sə'praɪzd]
erste/erster/erstes first [fɜ:st]
ersticken to choke [tʃəʊk]
Erwachsener/Erwachsene adult ['ædʌlt]
erwarten to expect [ɪk'spekt]
erzählen to tell [tel]
Erzählung story ['stɔ:ri]
Erziehung education [edʒʊ'keɪʃn]
es it [ɪt]
es gibt there are [ðeər‿'ɑ:]; there is [ðeər‿'ɪz]
Es lautete …. It said …. [ɪt 'sed]
essen to eat [i:t]
Essen food [fu:d]
Essen zum Mitnehmen takeaway ['teɪkəweɪ]
Esszimmer dining room ['daɪnɪŋ rʊm]
et cetera etc. [ɪt'setrə]
etliche many ['meni]
etwa about [ə'baʊt]; around [ə'raʊnd]
etwas any ['enɪ]; anything ['eniθɪŋ]; some [sʌm]; something ['sʌmθɪŋ]
euch you [ju:; jə]
euer/eure your [jɔ:]
Euer … *(in Briefen)* Yours [jɔ:z]
Eure … *(in Briefen)* Yours [jɔ:z]
Euro *(Währung)* euro ['jʊərəʊ]
europäisch European [ˌjʊərə'pi:ən]
Examen exam [ɪg'zæm]
existieren to exist [ɪg'zɪst]
Experiment experiment [ɪk'sperɪmənt]

F

fabelhaft fabulous ['fæbjələs]
Fabrik factory ['fæktri]
Fackel torch, torches *(pl)* [tɔ:tʃ; 'tɔ:tʃɪz]
Faden thread [θred]; yarn [jɑ:n]
Fahne flag [flæg]
Fähre ferry ['feri]
fahren to drive [draɪv]; to ride [raɪd]
fahren *(Schiff)* to sail [seɪl]
Fahrenheit Fahrenheit (F) ['færnhaɪt]
Fahrer/Fahrerin driver ['draɪvə]
Fahrplan timetable ['taɪmteɪbl]
Fahrrad bike [baɪk]
mit dem Fahrrad by bike [baɪ 'baɪk]
Fahrschein ticket ['tɪkɪt]
Fahrspur lane [leɪn]
Fahrt journey ['dʒɜ:ni]; ride [raɪd]; tour [tʊə]
fair fair [feə]
Fakt fact [fækt]
in der **Falle sitzen** to be trapped [bi: 'træpt]
fallen to fall [fɔ:l]; to drop [drɒp]
fallen lassen to drop [drɒp]
falls if [ɪf]
falsch wrong [rɒŋ]

falsch machen to get … wrong [get … 'rɒŋ]
Familie family ['fæmli]
Fan fan [fæn]
fangen to catch [kætʃ]
Fänger/Fängerin catcher ['kætʃə]
fantastisch fabulous ['fæbjələs]; fantastic [fæn'tæstɪk]
Farbe colour ['kʌlə]; paint [peɪnt]
färben to dye [daɪ]
farbig colourful ['kʌləfl]
Farm farm [fɑ:m]
fast almost ['ɔ:lməʊst]; nearly ['nɪəli]
Fastfood-Restaurant burger bar ['bɜ:gə ˌbɑ:]
Februar February ['februəri]
Federball badminton ['bædmɪntən]
fehlen to be missing [bi: 'mɪsɪŋ]; to miss [mɪs]
Fehler mistake [mɪ'steɪk]
Feier party ['pɑ:ti]
eine Party **feiern** to have a party [ˌhæv‿ə 'pɑ:ti]
Feiertag holiday ['hɒlədeɪ]
fein fine [faɪn]
Feind/Feindin enemy ['enəmi]
Feld field [fi:ld]
Felsen rock [rɒk]
Fenster window ['wɪndəʊ]
Ferien holiday(s) ['hɒlədeɪ(z)]; vacation *(AE)* [və'keɪʃn]
Ferienhaus cottage ['kɒtɪdʒ]
Fernbedienung remote control [rɪˌməʊt kən'trəʊl]
Fernsehen TV [ˌti:'vi:]
Fernseher TV [ˌti:'vi:]
Fernsteuerung remote control [rɪˌməʊt kən'trəʊl]
fertig ready ['redi]
Fest festival ['festɪvl]
festhalten to hold [həʊld]
Festival festival ['festɪvl]
festnehmen to arrest [ə'rest]
Festung fortress ['fɔ:trəs]
Feuer fire [faɪə]
Feuerstelle fire [faɪə]
Feuerwehr fire brigade ['faɪə brɪˌgeɪd]
Feuerwerk firework ['faɪəwɜ:k]
Feuerwerkskörper firework ['faɪəwɜ:k]
Figur figure ['fɪgə]
Fiktion fiction ['fɪkʃn]
Film film [fɪlm]; movie *(AE)* ['mu:vi]; picture ['pɪktʃə]
filmen to film [fɪlm]
finden to find [faɪnd]
Finger finger ['fɪŋgə]

Firma firm [fɜ:m]; company ['kʌmpəni]
Fisch fish, fish *(pl)* [fɪʃ]
fischen to fish [fɪʃ]
Fischen fishing ['fɪʃɪŋ]
fit fit [fɪt]
flach flat [flæt]
Fläche area ['eəriə]
Flagge flag [flæg]
Flamme flame [fleɪm]
Flasche bottle ['bɒtl]
Fleck mark [mɑ:k]
Fleisch meat [mi:t]
fliegen to fly [flaɪ]
flüchten (vor) to escape (from) [ɪ'skeɪp]
Flug flight [flaɪt]
Flugblatt leaflet ['li:flət]
Flughafen airport ['eəpɔ:t]
Fluglotse/Fluglotsin air traffic controller [ˌeə træfɪk kən'trəʊlə]
Flugzeug plane [pleɪn]
Flur corridor ['kɒrɪdɔ:]; hall [hɔ:l]
Fluss river ['rɪvə]
flüstern to whisper ['wɪspə]
flutartige Überschwemmung flash flood ['flæʃ ˌflʌd]
folgen to follow ['fɒləʊ]
folgend/folgender/folgende/folgendes following ['fɒləʊɪŋ]
Fön hairdryer ['heəˌdraɪə]
Football American football [əˌmerɪkən 'fʊtbɔ:l]
Form form [fɔ:m]
formal formal ['fɔ:ml]
formell formal ['fɔ:ml]
formen to form [fɔ:m]
förmlich formal ['fɔ:ml]
Formular form [fɔ:m]
Forschung research [rɪ'sɜ:tʃ]
fortgeschritten advanced [əd'vɑ:nst]
fortschaffen to take off [teɪk‿'ɒf]
Forum forum ['fɔ:rəm]
Foto photo ['fəʊtəʊ]
Fotos machen to take pictures [teɪk 'pɪktʃəz]
Fotoapparat camera ['kæmrə]
Fotograf/Fotografin photographer [fə'tɒgrəfə]
Fotografie photo ['fəʊtəʊ]; photography [fə'tɒgrəfi]
fotografieren to take pictures [teɪk 'pɪktʃəz]
Frage matter ['mætə]; question ['kwestʃn]
fragen to ask [ɑ:sk]
fragen nach to ask for ['ɑ:sk fə]
französisch French [frentʃ]

Frau woman, women *(pl)* ['wʊmən; 'wɪmɪn]
Frau *(Anrede)* Miss [mɪs]; Mrs ['mɪsɪz]
frei free [fri:]
Freiheit freedom ['fri:dəm]
Freitag Friday [fraɪdeɪ]
Freiwilliger/Freiwillige volunteer [ˌvɒlən'tɪə]
Freizeitpark theme park ['θi:m ˌpɑ:k]
fremd alien ['eɪliən]; foreign ['fɒrɪn]
Fremder/Fremde alien ['eɪliən]; stranger ['streɪndʒə]
fressen to eat [i:t]
Freund/Freundin friend [frend]
Freund *(in einer Paarbeziehung)* boyfriend ['bɔɪfrend]
Freundin *(in einer Paarbeziehung)* girlfriend ['gɜ:lfrend]
freundlich friendly ['frendli]; kind [kaɪnd]
Freundschaft schließen (mit) to make friends (with) [ˌmeɪk 'frendz]
Friede peace [pi:s]
frieren to be cold [bi: 'kəʊld]
frisch fresh [freʃ]
Frischkäse cream cheese [ˌkri:m 'tʃi:z]
Friseur/Friseurin hairdresser ['heəˌdresə]
Frisur style [staɪl]
froh glad [glæd]; happy ['hæpi]
Frucht fruit [fru:t]
früh early ['ɜ:li]
Frühling spring [sprɪŋ]
Frühstück breakfast ['brekfəst]
frustriert frustrated [frʌs'treɪtɪd]
fühlen to feel [fi:l]
sich fühlen to feel [fi:l]
Führer/Führerin leader ['li:də]
Führerschein driver's license *(AE)* ['draɪvəz ˌlaɪsnts]
füllen to fill [fɪl]
Füller pen [pen]
Fünftel fifth [fɪfθ]
Funk *(Musikrichtung)* funk [fʌŋk]
Funke(n) spark [spɑ:k]
funktionieren to work [wɜ:k]
für for [fɔ:; fə]
Für und Wider pros and cons [ˌprəʊz‿ənd 'kɒnz]
furchtbar awful ['ɔ:fl]; frightening ['fraɪtnɪŋ]; horrible ['hɒrəbl]; terrible ['terəbl]
fürsorglich thoughtful ['θɔ:tfl]
Fuß foot, feet *(pl)* [fʊt; fi:t]
Fuß *(Längenmaß: 30,48 cm)* foot, feet *(pl)* [fʊt; fi:t]
zu Fuß on foot [ɒn 'fʊt]

Fußball football ['fʊtbɔ:l]; soccer *(AE)* ['sɒkə]
Fußboden floor [flɔ:]
füttern to feed [fi:d]

G

Gabel fork [fɔ:k]
gälisch Gaelic ['geɪlɪk]
Gang corridor ['kɒrɪdɔ:]
Gang *(Menü)* course [kɔ:s]
Gang gang [gæŋ]
Gangster/Gangsterin gangster ['gæŋkstə]
ganz all [ɔ:l]; full (of) [fʊl]; whole [həʊl]
ganz schön pretty ['prɪti]
im Ganzen in all [ɪn‿'ɔ:l]
Garderobe wardrobe ['wɔ:drəʊb]
Garn thread [θred]; yarn [jɑ:n]
Garten garden ['gɑ:dn]
Gärtner/Gärtnerin gardener ['gɑ:dnə]
Gasse lane [leɪn]
Gast guest [gest]
Gastgeber host [həʊst]
Gate gate [geɪt]
Gebäude building ['bɪldɪŋ]
geben to give [gɪv]
Gebiet area ['eəriə]
gebrochen broken ['brəʊkn]
Geburt birth [bɜ:θ]
gebürtig native ['neɪtɪv]
Geburtstag birthday ['bɜ:θdeɪ]
Gedächtnis memory ['memri]
Gedanke thought [θɔ:t]
Gedicht poem ['pəʊɪm]
gefährlich dangerous ['deɪndʒrəs]
Gefängnis prison ['prɪzn]
gefroren frozen ['frəʊzn]
Gefühl feeling ['fi:lɪŋ]
gegen against [ə'genst]
Gegensatz contrast ['kɒntrɑ:st]
im Gegensatz zu in contrast to [ɪn 'kɒntrɑ:st tə]
sich **gegenseitig** each other [ˌi:tʃ‿'ʌðə]
Gegenstand object ['ɒbdʒɪkt]
geheim secret ['si:krət]
Geheimnis mystery ['mɪstri]; secret ['si:krət]
gehen to go [gəʊ]; to leave [li:v]; to step [step]; to walk [wɔ:k]
... gehen to go + -ing [gəʊ]
Geh ... entlang. Go down .... ['gəʊ daʊn]
gehören (zu) to belong (to) [bɪ'lɒŋ]
Geist ghost [gəʊst]; mind [maɪnd]
gelangweilt bored [bɔ:d]
gelb yellow ['jeləʊ]
Geld money ['mʌni]
Geldbeutel wallet ['wɒlɪt]
Geldbuße fine [faɪn]
Geldstrafe fine [faɪn]
geloben to pledge [pledʒ]
Gemälde painting ['peɪntɪŋ]
gemein mean [mi:n]
Gemüse vegetable ['vedʒtəbl]
genannt called [kɔ:ld]
genau exact [ɪg'zækt]; exactly [ɪg'zæktli]; right [raɪt]
genau genommen in fact [ɪn 'fækt]
genießen to enjoy [ɪn'dʒɔɪ]
genug enough [ɪ'nʌf]
genügend enough [ɪ'nʌf]
geöffnet open ['əʊpn]
Geografie Geography [dʒi'ɒgrəfi]
Gepäck luggage ['lʌgɪdʒ]
Gepäckwagen trolley ['trɒli]
Geplauder chat [tʃæt]
gerade straight [streɪt]
Geräusch noise [nɔɪz]; sound [saʊnd]
gerecht fair [feə]
Gern geschehen! You're welcome. [jʊə 'welkəm]
gern haben to like [laɪk]
gern mögen to love [lʌv]
Geruch smell [smel]
Gesamtschule comprehensive school [kɒmprɪ'hensɪv ˌsku:l]
Geschäft business ['bɪznɪs]; shop [ʃɒp]; store [stɔ:]
Geschäftsmann businessman, businessmen *(pl)* ['bɪznɪsmən; 'bɪznɪsmen]
geschehen to happen ['hæpn]
Geschenk present ['preznt]
Geschichte History ['hɪstəri]; story ['stɔ:ri]
geschieden von divorced from [dɪ'vɔ:st frəm]
geschlossen closed [kləʊzd]
geschockt shocked [ʃɒkt]
Gesellschaft company ['kʌmpəni]
gesellschaftlich social ['səʊʃl]
Gesellschaftstanz ballroom dancing [ˌbɔ:lrʊm 'dɑ:nsɪŋ]
Gesicht face [feɪs]
Gespenst ghost [gəʊst]
Gespräch dialogue ['daɪəlɒg]
Gestalt figure ['fɪgə]
Gestank smell [smel]
gestern yesterday ['jestədeɪ]
gestern Abend last night [lɑ:st 'naɪt]
gestern Nacht last night [lɑ:st 'naɪt]
gestrandet stranded ['strændɪd]
gesund healthy ['helθi]
Getränk drink [drɪŋk]
Gewächshaus greenhouse ['gri:nhaʊs]
gewagt outrageous [aʊt'reɪdʒəs]
gewaltig huge [hju:dʒ]
Gewicht weight [weɪt]
gewinnen to win [wɪn]
Gewinner/Gewinnerin winner ['wɪnə]
gewöhnlich usually ['ju:ʒli]
Gitarre guitar [gɪ'tɑ:]
Gitter grid [grɪd]
glamourös glamorous ['glæmrəs]
Glas glass [glɑ:s]
glauben to believe [bɪ'li:v]; to think [θɪŋk]
gleich the same [seɪm]; right away [raɪt‿ə'weɪ]
Gleis track [træk]
Glocke bell [bel]
Glück luck [lʌk]
Glück haben to get lucky *(AE)* [get 'lʌki]
du hast Glück you're lucky [ˌjʊə 'lʌki]
Viel Glück! Good luck! [ˌgʊd 'lʌk]
glücklich happy ['hæpi]; lucky ['lʌki]
glücklicherweise luckily ['lʌkɪli]
Glühbirne light bulb ['laɪt bʌlb]
Gold gold [gəʊld]
Mein **Gott!** My God! [maɪ 'gɒd]
Grab grave [greɪv]
Grabstein gravestone ['greɪvstəʊn]
Grad degree (°) [dɪ'gri:]
Gramm gramme (g) [græm]
Gras grass [grɑ:s]
grau grey [greɪ]
greifen to grab [græb]
Grenze border ['bɔ:də]
Grieche/Griechin Greek [gri:k]
griechisch Greek [gri:k]
grob raw [rɔ:]
groß big [bɪg]; great [greɪt]; large [lɑ:dʒ]; tall [tɔ:l]
großartig fantastic [fæn'tæstɪk]; great [greɪt]; wicked ['wɪkɪd]
Größe height [haɪt]; size [saɪz]
Großstadt city ['sɪti]
größtenteils mostly ['məʊstli]
grün green [gri:n]
Grund bottom ['bɒtəm]
gründen to found [faʊnd]; to set up [set‿'ʌp]
Grundlinie back line [ˌbæk 'lain]; base [beɪs]

Grundschule elementary school *(AE)* [elɪ'mentri ˌsku:l]; primary school ['praɪməri ˌsku:l]
Gruppe group [gru:p]
gruselig scary ['skeəri]
Gummi rubber ['rʌbə]
Gummistiefel rubber boots *(pl)* [ˌrʌbə 'bu:ts]
gut all right [ɔ:l 'raɪt]; fine [faɪn]; good [gʊd]; well [wel]
Es geht uns gut. We're OK. [ˌwɪər‿əʊ'keɪ]
Guten Morgen! Good morning! [ˌgʊd 'mɔ:nɪŋ]
gut mit … umgehen können to be good with … [bi: 'gʊd wɪð]
ich bin gut in … I'm good at … [aɪm 'gʊd‿ət]
Güter goods *(pl)* [gʊdz]
Gymnasium grammar school ['græmə ˌsku:l]

H

Haar, Haare hair [heə]
haben to have [hæv]; to have got [hæv 'gɒt]
keine Ahnung haben to have no clue [ˌhæv nəʊ 'klu:]
Hafen harbor *(AE)* ['hɑ:bə]; port [pɔ:t]
Hähnchen chicken ['tʃɪkɪn]
halb half [hɑ:f]
zum halben Preis half-price [ˌhɑ:f'praɪs]
eine halbe Stunde half an hour [ˌhɑ:f‿ən‿'aʊə]
halb (drei) half past (two) ['hɑ:f pɑ:st]
Halbschwester half-sister ['hɑ:fˌsɪstə]
Halbzeit half-time [ˌhɑ:f'taɪm]
Hälfte half [hɑ:f]
Halle hall [hɔ:l]
Hallo! Hello! [he'ləʊ]; Hi, there! ['haɪ ðeə]
halten to hold [həʊld]; to keep [ki:p]
Haltestelle stop [stɒp]
Hand hand [hænd]
Hände weg! Hands off! [hændz‿'ɒf]
Handkarren trolley ['trɒli]
Handlung action ['ækʃn]
Handschuh glove [glʌv]
Handtasche handbag ['hænbæg]
Handwerker workman, workmen *(pl)* ['wɜ:kmən; 'wɜ:kmen]
Handy cell phone *(AE)* ['sel fəʊn]; mobile ['məʊbaɪl]
hart hard [hɑ:d]; tough [tʌf]
Hass hate [heɪt]
hassen to hate [heɪt]
hätte gern would like [wʊd 'laɪk]
Haupt- main [meɪn]
hauptsächlich mostly ['məʊstli]
Haus house [haʊs]
zu Hause at home [ət 'həʊm]
Hausaufgabe/Hausaufgaben homework ['həʊmwɜ:k]
Hausmeister/Hausmeisterin caretaker ['keəˌteɪkə]
Haustier pet [pet]
Heft exercise book ['eksəsaɪz ˌbʊk]
heilig sacred ['seɪkrɪd]
Heim home [həʊm]
Heimat home [həʊm]
heimlich secret ['si:krət]
Heimweh haben to feel homesick [ˌfi:l 'həʊmsɪk]
heiraten to marry ['mæri]
heiß hot [hɒt]
Ich heiße …. My name is …. [maɪ 'neɪm‿ɪz]
Heizung heating ['hi:tɪŋ]
Held hero, heroes *(pl)* ['hɪərəʊ; 'hɪərəʊz]
Heldin heroine ['herəʊɪn]
helfen to help [help]
Helikopter helicopter ['helɪˌkɒptə]
hell fair [feə]
Helm helmet ['helmət]
Hemd shirt [ʃɜ:t]
(die Treppe) **herauf** upstairs [ʌp'steəz]
heraus out [aʊt]
herausfinden to find out [faɪnd‿'aʊt]
herausnehmen to take out [teɪk‿'aʊt]
Herbst autumn ['ɔ:təm]
herein in [ɪn]
hereinkommen to come in [kʌm‿'ɪn]
Herr *(Anrede)* Mr ['mɪstə]
herstellen to produce [prə'dju:s]
Herstellung production [prə'dʌkʃn]
herüberkommen to come over [kʌm‿'əʊvə]
herüberreichen to pass [pɑ:s]
(um …) **herum** round [raʊnd]
um … herum around [ə'raʊnd]
herumfummeln (an) to fiddle (with) ['fɪdl]
herumlungern to hang around *(AE)* [ˌhæŋ‿ə'raʊnd]
herumreisen to go places [ˌgəʊ 'pleɪsɪz]
herumspringen to jump about [ˌdʒʌmp‿ə'baʊt]
sich **herumtreiben** to hang out [hæŋ‿'aʊt]
herunter down [daʊn]; off [ɒf]
(die Treppe) herunter downstairs [ˌdaʊn'steəz]
herunterfallen to fall off [fɔ:l‿'ɒf]; to fall [fɔ:l]
herunterkommen to come down [kʌm 'daʊn]
herunterladen to download [ˌdaʊn'ləʊd]
Herz heart [hɑ:t]
Herzliche Grüße love [lʌv]
Herzschrittmacher pacemaker ['peɪsˌmeɪkə]
heute today [tə'deɪ]
heute Abend tonight [tə'naɪt]
heute Nacht tonight [tə'naɪt]
Hi! Hi! [haɪ]
hier here [hɪə]
high-tech high-tech [ˌhaɪ'tek]
Highway highway *(AE)* ['haɪweɪ]
Hilfe help [help]
hilflos helpless ['helpləs]
hilfreich helpful ['helpfəl]
Himmel sky [skaɪ]
hinauf up [ʌp]
(die Treppe) hinauf upstairs [ʌp'steəz]
die Treppe **hinaufrennen** to run upstairs [ˌrʌn‿ʌp'steəz]
hinaufschauen to look up [lʊk‿'ʌp]
hinaus out [aʊt]
hinausgehen to go out [gəʊ‿'aʊt]
hinauslehnen to lean out [li:n‿'aʊt]
sich hinauslehnen to lean out [li:n‿'aʊt]
hinausstellen to put out [pʊt‿'aʊt]
hineingehen to go in [gəʊ 'ɪn]
hinfallen to fall [fɔ:l]
hingehen to walk up to [wɔ:k‿'ʌp tə]
hinlegen to lie down [laɪ 'daʊn]
sich hinlegen to lie down [laɪ 'daʊn]
sich **hinsetzen** to sit down [sɪt 'daʊn]
hinten at the back [ət ðə 'bæk]
hinter behind [bɪ'haɪnd]
Hinter- back [bæk]
Hintergrund background ['bækgraʊnd]
hinterhergehen to follow ['fɒləʊ]
Hintern ass *(AE)* [æs]
hinüber across [ə'krɒs]
hinübergehen to go over [gəʊ‿'əʊvə]
hinunter down [daʊn]
(die Treppe) hinunter downstairs [ˌdaʊn'steəz]
hinuntergehen to go down [gəʊ 'daʊn]
Hinweis clue [klu:]
hinzufügen to add [æd]; to put in [pʊt‿'ɪn]

hispanisch Hispanic [hɪ'spænɪk]
Hit hit [hɪt]
Hitparade charts *(pl)* [tʃɑ:ts]
Hitze heat [hi:t]
Hobby hobby, hobbies *(pl)* ['hɒbi; 'hɒbiz]
hoch high [haɪ]; tall [tɔ:l]
hochheben to lift [lɪft]
Hochmoor moor [mɔ:]
hochspringen to jump up [dʒʌmp‿'ʌp]
Hochwasser flood [flʌd]
hochziehen to lift [lɪft]
Hockey hockey ['hɒki]
hoffen to hope [həʊp]
Hoffnung hope [həʊp]
höflich polite [pə'laɪt]
Höhe height [haɪt]
holen to get [get]
Hölle hell [hel]
Holz wood [wʊd]
hölzern wooden ['wʊdn]
Homecoming *(Schulfest an amerikanischen High Schools)* homecoming ['həʊmkʌmɪŋ]
hören to hear [hɪə]
Horoskop horoscope ['hɒrəskəʊp]
Hose trousers *(pl)* ['traʊzəz]
kurze Hose shorts *(pl)* [ʃɔ:ts]
Hosentasche pocket ['pɒkɪt]
Hotel hotel [həʊ'tel]
Hotline hotline ['hɒtlaɪn]
Hubschrauber helicopter ['helɪˌkɒptə]
Huhn chicken ['tʃɪkɪn]
Hund dog [dɒg]
mit dem Hund spazieren gehen to walk the dog [wɔ:k ðə 'dɒg]
hundemüde dog-tired [ˌdɒg'taɪəd]
hundert hundred ['hʌndrəd]
Hunger bekommen to get hungry [get 'hʌŋgri]
Hungersnot famine ['fæmɪn]
hungrig hungry ['hʌŋgri]
Hut hat [hæt]
Hütte cabin ['kæbɪn]

I

ich I [aɪ]
Ich heiße … . My name is … . [maɪ 'neɪm‿ɪz]
Ich nehme … . I'm having … . [aɪm 'hævɪŋ]
ich würde gern I'd like to [ˌaɪd 'laɪk tə]
ich würde lieber I'd rather [aɪd 'rɑ:ðə]
Idee idea [aɪ'dɪə]
identifizieren to identify [aɪ'dentɪfaɪ]
Idiot idiot ['ɪdɪət]
Igitt! Yuk! [jʌk]
ihm him [hɪm]
ihn him [hɪm]
ihnen them [ðem]
Ihnen you [ju:; jə]
ihr you [ju:; jə]
ihr/ihre her [hɜ:]; its [ɪts]; their [ðeə]
Ihr/Ihre your [jɔ:]
Ikone icon ['aɪkɒn]
illegal illegal [ɪ'li:gl]
im Gange sein to be on [bi:‿'ɒn]
Imbiss snack [snæk]
Imbissstube deli *(AE)* ['deli]; diner *(AE)* ['daɪnə]
immer always ['ɔ:lweɪz]
immer noch still [stɪl]
Immigrant/Immigrantin immigrant ['ɪmɪgrənt]
Immigration immigration [ˌɪmɪ'greɪʃn]
improvisieren to freestyle *(slang)* ['fri:staɪl]
im unteren Teil at the bottom [ət ðə 'bɒtəm]
in at [æt; ət]; in [ɪn]; into ['ɪntə]
in … hinein into ['ɪntə]
Indianer/Indianerin Native American [ˌneɪtɪv‿ə'merɪkən]
Indie *(Musikrichtung)* indie ['ɪndi]
indisch Indian ['ɪndiən]
Industrie industry ['ɪndəstri]
Information/Informationen information [ˌɪnfə'meɪʃn]
Informationszentrum information centre [ɪnfə'meɪʃn ˌsentə]
Inhalt content ['kɒntent]
alles inklusive all inclusive [ˌɔ:l‿ɪŋ'klu:sɪv]
Inlineskates skates *(pl)* [skeɪts]
Inlineskates fahren to skate [skeɪt]
innen inside [ɪn'saɪd]
innerhalb within [wɪ'ðɪn]
Insel island ['aɪlənd]
insgesamt in all [ɪn‿'ɔ:l]
Inspektor inspector [ɪn'spektə]
Institut college ['kɒlɪdʒ]
Instruktion instruction [ɪn'strʌkʃn]
inszenieren to produce [prə'dju:s]
intelligent intelligent [ɪn'telɪdʒnt]
interessant interesting ['ɪntrəstɪŋ]
sich **interessieren** to get interested [get 'ɪntrəstɪd]
interessiert interested ['ɪntrəstɪd]
interessiert sein an to be into [bi:‿'ɪntə]
international international [ˌɪntə'næʃnl]
Internet Internet ['ɪntənet]
im Internet surfen to surf the Internet [ˌsɜ:f ði‿'ɪntənet]
Internetauftritt website ['websaɪt]
Interview interview ['ɪntəvju:]
interviewen to interview ['ɪntəvju:]
Iren/Irinnen Irish ['aɪrɪʃ]
irgendetwas anything ['eniθɪŋ]
irgendjemand anybody ['eniˌbɒdi]; anyone ['eniwʌn]
irgendwie somehow ['sʌmhaʊ]
irgendwo anywhere ['eniweə]; somewhere ['sʌmweə]
irisch Irish ['aɪrɪʃ]
Italiener/Italienerin Italian [ɪ'tæliən]
italienisch Italian [ɪ'tæliən]

J

ja yeah *(slang)* [jeə]; yes [jes]
Jacke jacket ['dʒækɪt]
Jackentasche pocket ['pɒkɪt]
Jagdhund hound [haʊnd]
Jagen hunting ['hʌntɪŋ]
Jahr year [jɪə]
Jahrbuch yearbook ['jɪəbʊk]
Jahreszeit season ['si:zn]
Jahrgangsstufe year [jɪə]
Jahrhundert century ['sentʃri]
Jahrmarkt fair [feə]
Jahrtausend millennium [mɪ'leniəm]
Jamsession jam [dʒæm]
Januar January ['dʒænjuəri]
Jazz jazz [dʒæz]
je each [i:tʃ]
Jeans jeans *(pl)* [dʒi:nz]
jede/jeder/jedes each [i:tʃ]; every ['evri]
jedenfalls anyway ['eniweɪ]
jeder everybody ['evribɒdi]; everyone ['evriwʌn]
jeder (beliebige) anybody ['eniˌbɒdi]; anyone ['eniwʌn]
jemals ever ['evə]
jemand somebody ['sʌmbədi]; someone ['sʌmwʌn]
jene those [ðəʊz]
jenes that [ðæt]
jetzt now [naʊ]
jetzt gleich right now [ˌraɪt 'naʊ]
jeweils each [i:tʃ]
Job job [dʒɒb]
joggen to jog [dʒɒg]
Jogger/Joggerin jogger ['dʒɒgə]

Jugend youth [ju:θ]
jugendlich teenage ['ti:neɪdʒ]
Jugendlicher/Jugendliche teenager ['ti:nˌeɪdʒə]; teen [ti:n]
Jugendtreffen rally ['ræli]
Juli July [dʒʊ'laɪ]
jung young [jʌŋ]
Junge boy [bɔɪ]; lad [læd]
Juni June [dʒu:n]
Juwel jewel ['dʒu:əl]

K

Kabel cord *(AE)* [kɔ:d]
Kabinett cabinet ['kæbɪnət]
Käfer bug [bʌg]
Kaffee coffee ['kɒfi:]
Kalender calendar ['kæləndə]
kalt cold [kəʊld]
Kamera camera ['kæmrə]
Kamin fireplace ['faɪəpleɪs]
Kaminfeuer fire [faɪə]
Kampf fight [faɪt]; battle ['bætl]
kämpfen to battle ['bætl]; to fight [faɪt]
Kampfrichter judge [dʒʌdʒ]
Kanal channel ['tʃænl]
Kante edge [edʒ]
Kanu fahren to canoe [kə'nu:]
Kapelle band [bænd]
Kapitän captain ['kæptɪn]
Kappe cap [kæp]
Kapsel capsule ['kæpsju:l]
kaputt broken ['brəʊkn]
kaputtmachen to break [breɪk]
Karotte carrot ['kærət]
Karte card [kɑ:d]
Kartoffel potato, potatoes *(pl)* [pə'teɪtəʊ]
Kartoffelchip crisp [krɪsp]
Käse cheese [tʃi:z]
Kasten box, boxes *(pl)* [bɒks; 'bɒksɪz]; cabinet ['kæbɪnət]
Katastrophe disaster [dɪ'zɑ:stə]
Kategorie category ['kætəgri]
Kathedrale cathedral [kə'θi:drl]
Katze cat [kæt]
kaufen to buy [baɪ]
Kaufhaus department store [dɪ'pɑ:tmənt stɔ:]; store [stɔ:]
Kaufhausdetektiv/Kaufhausdetektivin store detective ['stɔ: dɪˌtektɪv]
Kautschuk rubber ['rʌbə]
Kaviar caviar ['kæviɑ:]
kein/keine no [nəʊ]
keine Ahnung no idea [ˌnəʊ‿aɪ'dɪə]
keiner/keine none [nʌn]
Keks biscuit ['bɪskɪt]
Kelch cup [kʌp]
Kellergeschoss basement ['beɪsmənt]
Kellner waiter ['weɪtə]
kennen to know [nəʊ]
Kerl bloke [bləʊk]; guy [gaɪ]
Kette chain [tʃeɪn]
Kick kick [kɪk]
Kickboard kickboard ['kɪkbɔ:d]
kicken to kick [kɪk]
Kilo(gramm) kilo (kg) ['kɪləʊ]
Kilometer kilometre ['kɪləʊˌmi:tə; kɪ'lɒmɪtə]
Kind child, children *(pl)* [tʃaɪld; 'tʃɪldrɪn]; kid [kɪd]
Kino cinema ['sɪnəmə]; movies *(AE)* ['mu:viz]; theater *(AE)* ['θɪətə]
Kirche church [tʃɜ:tʃ]
Kirsche cherry ['tʃeri]
Kiste box, boxes *(pl)* [bɒks; 'bɒksɪz]
klagen to moan [məʊn]
Klamm gorge [gɔ:dʒ]
Klang sound [saʊnd]
Klappe shutter ['ʃʌtə]
klar clear [klɪə]
klären *(ein Problem)* to sort out [sɔ:t‿'aʊt]
Klasse class [klɑ:s]; grade *(AE)* [greɪd]
Klassenarbeit test [test]
Klassenzimmer classroom ['klɑ:srʊm]
Klatsch gossip ['gɒsɪp]
klatschen to clap [klæp]
kleben to stick [stɪk]
Kleid dress [dres]
Kleider clothes *(pl)* [kləʊθs]
Kleidergröße size [saɪz]
Kleiderschrank wardrobe ['wɔ:drəʊb]
Kleidung clothes *(pl)* [kləʊθs]; dress [dres]
klein little [lɪtl]; small [smɔ:l]
klettern to climb ['klaɪm]
klicken to click [klɪk]
Klingel bell [bel]
klingeln to ring [rɪŋ]
Es klingelt. The bell rings. [ðə 'bel rɪŋz]
klingen to sound [saʊnd]
Klippe cliff [klɪf]
klopfen to knock [nɒk]
fest klopfen to bang [bæŋ]
Klopfen knock [nɒk]
Kloster monastery ['mɒnəstri]
Klub club [klʌb]
klug intelligent [ɪn'telɪdʒnt]; smart [smɑ:t]
Klunker bling bling *(slang)* [ˌblɪŋ 'blɪŋ]
knallen to pop [pɒp]
knallen lassen to pop [pɒp]
knarren to creak [kri:k]
Knäuel ball [bɔ:l]
Kneipe bar [bɑ:]
Knie knee [ni:]
Knopf button ['bʌtn]
Kobold goblin ['gɒblɪn]
Koch/Köchin cook [kʊk]
kochen to cook [kʊk]
Kochen cooking ['kʊkɪŋ]
Kofferraum trunk *(AE)* [trʌŋk]
Kollegium staff [stɑ:f]
komfortabel comfortable ['kʌmpftəbl]
komisch funny ['fʌni]
kommen to come [kʌm]; to get [get]
Komm./Kommt. Come on. [kʌm‿'ɒn]
Komödie comedy ['kɒmədi]
Kompanie company ['kʌmpəni]
Komparativ comparative [kəm'pærətɪv]
komplex complex ['kɒmpleks]
kompliziert complex ['kɒmpleks]
König king [kɪŋ]
Königin queen [kwi:n]
königlich royal ['rɔɪəl]
Konkurrent/Konkurentin rival ['raɪvl]
können can [kæn]
könnte/könnten could [kʊd]; might [maɪt]
konnte/konnten could [kʊd]
kann/könnte(n) vielleicht may [meɪ]
konstruieren to construct [kən'strʌkt]
kontaktieren to contact ['kɒntækt]
Kontext context ['kɒntekst]
Kontrast contrast ['kɒntrɑ:st]
Kontrolle control [kən'trəʊl]
kontrollieren to check [tʃek]; to control [kən'trəʊl]
Konzert concert ['kɒnsət]
Kopf head [hed]
Kopfhörer headphones *(pl)* ['hedfəʊnz]
Kopfsalat lettuce ['letɪs]
kopieren to copy ['kɒpi]
Kordel string [strɪŋ]; cord *(AE)* [kɔ:d]
kornisch Cornish ['kɔ:nɪʃ]
Körper body ['bɒdi]
körperlich physical ['fɪzɪkl]
korrekt correct [kə'rekt]; right [raɪt]
Korridor corridor ['kɒrɪdɔ:]
Kosten cost [kɒst]
kostenlos free [fri:]
krabbeln to crawl [krɔ:l]
Krach! Crash! [kræʃ]
Kraft power ['paʊə]

krank sick [sɪk]
Krankenhaus hospital ['hɒspɪtl]
Krankenpfleger nurse [nɜ:s]
Krankenschwester nurse [nɜ:s]
Krankenwagen ambulance ['æmbjələnts]
Krankmeldung sick note ['sɪk ˌnəʊt]
Kreis circle ['sɜ:kl]
kreuzen to cross [krɒs]
Kreuzfahrt cruise [kru:z]
Kricket cricket ['krɪkɪt]
kriechen to crawl [krɔ:l]
Krieg war [wɔ:]
Krimi detective story [dɪ'tektɪv ˌstɔ:ri]
Kriminalität crime [kraɪm]
Krone crown [kraʊn]
Küche kitchen ['kɪtʃɪn]
Kuchen cake [keɪk]
Küchenschrank cupboard ['kʌbəd]
Kuh cow [kaʊ]
kühl cool [ku:l]
Kühlschrank fridge [frɪdʒ]; refrigerator [rɪ'frɪdʒreɪtə]
sich **kümmern** to care [keə]; to take care [teɪk 'keə]
  sich kümmern um to look after [lʊk‿'ɑ:ftə]
Kumpel homie *(slang)* ['həʊmi]
Kunde/Kundin customer ['kʌstəmə]
Kunst Art [ɑ:t]
Kurier courier ['kʊriə]
Kurs class [klɑ:s]; course [kɔ:s]
Kurve curve [kɜ:v]
kurz short [ʃɔ:t]
  zu kurz kommen (mit) to miss out (on) [mɪss‿'aʊt]
Kuss kiss [kɪs]
küssen to kiss [kɪs]
Küste coast [kəʊst]; seaside ['si:saɪd]
Küstenlinie coastline ['kəʊstlaɪn]

L

Labor lab(oratory) [læb; lə'bɒrətri]
lächeln to smile [smaɪl]
lachen to laugh [lɑ:f]
lackieren to spray [spreɪ]
Laden shop [ʃɒp]; store [stɔ:]
Lager camp [kæmp]
Lagerfeuer campfire ['kæmpfaɪə]
Lamm lamb [læm]
Lammfleisch lamb [læm]
Lampe lamp [læmp]
Land country, countries *(pl)* ['kʌntri; 'kʌntriz]; land [lænd]; state [steɪt]
landen to end up [ˌend‿'ʌp]; to land [lænd]
landesweit national ['næʃnl]
Landkarte map [mæp]
Landschaft scenery ['si:nri]
Landstraße road [rəʊd]
Landwirt/Landwirtin farmer ['fɑ:mə]
lang long [lɒŋ]
Länge length [leŋkθ]
langsam slow [sləʊ]
langweilig boring ['bɔ:rɪŋ]
Laptop laptop ['læptɒp]
Lärm noise [nɔɪz]
lassen to leave [li:v]; to let [let]
  Lasst uns .... Let's .... [lets]
Lassi *(Jogurtgetränk)* lassi ['lasɪ]
Lastwagen truck *(AE)* [trʌk]
Lastwagenfahrer/Lastwagenfahrerin trucker *(AE)* ['trʌkə]
lateinamerikanisch Hispanic [hɪ'spænɪk]
Laterne lantern ['læntən]
Latino Latino [lə'ti:nəʊ]
Latinomusik Latino [lə'ti:nəʊ]
Lauf run [rʌn]
laufen to be on [bi:‿'ɒn]; to run [rʌn]; to walk [wɔ:k]
  laufen gegen to run into [rʌn‿'ɪntə]
Läufer/Läuferin runner ['rʌnə]
laut loud [laʊd]
Es **lautete ....** It said .... [ɪt 'sed]
leben to live [lɪv]
Leben life, lives *(pl)* [laɪf; laɪvz]
  am Leben alive [ə'laɪv]
lebendig alive [ə'laɪv]
Lebens- vital ['vaɪtl]
Lebensart lifestyle ['laɪfstaɪl]
Lebensmittel food [fu:d]
lebenswichtig vital ['vaɪtl]
Lebenszeichen vital signs *(pl)* [ˌvaɪtl 'saɪnz]
leer dead [ded]; empty ['empti]
legal legal ['li:gl]
legen to put [pʊt]
  sich legen to come down [kʌm 'daʊn]
lehnen to lean [li:n]
  sich lehnen to lean [li:n]
lehren to teach [ti:tʃ]
Lehrer/Lehrerin teacher ['ti:tʃə]
Lehrplan curriculum [kə'rɪkjələm]
leicht easy ['i:zi]
Tut mir **Leid.** sorry ['sɒri]
leihen to borrow ['bɒrəʊ]; to lend [lend]
Leinwand screen [skri:n]
leise quiet ['kwaɪət]; soft [sɒft]
leiten to control [kən'trəʊl]
Leiter ladder ['lædə]
lernen to learn [lɜ:n]; to study ['stʌdi]
lesen to read [ri:d]
letzte/letzter/letztes last [lɑ:st]; final ['faɪnl]
Leuchte lamp [læmp]
leuchten to glow [gləʊ]
leuchtend brilliant ['brɪljənt]
Leuchtfeuer flare [fleə]
Leute people ['pi:pl]
Licht light [laɪt]
Lichtschein flare [fleə]
lieb dear [dɪə]
Liebe love [lʌv]
  Liebe ... *(Anrede in Briefen)* Dear [dɪə]
  Lieber ... *(Anrede in Briefen)* Dear [dɪə]
lieben to love [lʌv]
ich würde **lieber** I'd rather [aɪd 'rɑ:ðə]
Liebling pet [pet]
Lieblings- favourite ['feɪvrɪt]
Lied song [sɒŋ]
liefern to deliver [dɪ'lɪvə]
Lieferwagen van [væn]
liegen to lie [laɪ]
Liga union ['ju:njən]
lila purple ['pɜ:pl]
Limonade lemonade [ˌlemə'neɪd]
Limousine limousine [ˌlɪmə'zi:n]
Lineal ruler ['ru:lə]
Linie line [laɪn]
linke/linker/linkes left [left]
links left [left]; on the left [ɒn ðə 'left]
  links abbiegen to turn left [tɜ:n 'left]
Lippenpflegestift lip balm ['lɪp bɑ:m]
Liste list [lɪst]
live live [laɪv]
Loch dump [dʌmp]
Löffel spoon [spu:n]
lokal local ['ləʊkl]
löschen *(Text)* to delete [dɪ'li:t]
  löschen to erase [ɪ'reɪz]
  löschen *(Feuer)* to put out [pʊt‿'aʊt]
lösen to solve [sɒlv]
losgehen *(Alarm)* to go off [gəʊ‿'ɒf]
Löwe lion ['laɪən]
Luft air [eə]
lügen to lie [laɪ]
lustig funny ['fʌni]
  sich lustig machen über to laugh at ['lɑ:f‿ət]
Lyrik poetry ['pəʊətri]

M

machen to do [du:]; to make [meɪk]
eine Diät machen to go on a diet [ˌgəʊ‿ɒn‿ə 'daɪət]
sich lustig machen über to laugh at ['lɑ:f‿ət]
Spaß machen to be fun [bi: 'fʌn]
Macht power ['paʊə]
Mädchen girl [gɜ:l]
Magazin magazine [mægə'zi:n]
Magen stomach ['stʌmək]
Mahlzeit meal [mi:l]
Mai May [meɪ]
mailen to mail [meɪl]
makellos pristine ['prɪsti:n]
Make-up make-up ['meɪkʌp]
Mal *(zeitlich)* time [taɪm]
malen to paint [peɪnt]
Mama mom *(AE)* [mɒm]; mum [mʌm]
man they [ðeɪ]; you [ju:; jə]
Manager/Managerin manager ['mænɪdʒə]
manchmal sometimes ['sʌmtaɪmz]
manipulieren to fix [fɪks]
Mann man, men *(pl)* [mæn; men]
Mannschaft crew [kru:]; team [ti:m]
Mantel coat [kəʊt]
Mäppchen pencil case ['pensl ˌkeɪs]
Mappe folder ['fəʊldə]
Markstein landmark ['lændmɑ:k]
Markt market ['mɑ:kɪt]
Marmelade jam [dʒæm]
März March [mɑ:tʃ]
Maschine engine ['endʒɪn]; machine [mə'ʃi:n]
Mast post [pəʊst]
Material material [mə'tɪəriəl]
Mathematik Maths [mæθs]
Mauer wall [wɔ:l]
Maus mouse [maʊs]
Mechaniker/Mechanikerin mechanic [mə'kænɪk]
Medikament drug [drʌg]
Meer sea [si:]
Meeresküste seaside ['si:saɪd]
mehr more [mɔ:]
Mehrzahl plural ['plʊrəl]
Meile *(brit. Längenmaß)* mile [maɪl]
meilenweit for miles [fə‿'maɪlz]
mein/meine my [maɪ]
Mein Gott! My God! [maɪ 'gɒd]
Meinung opinion [ə'pɪnjən]
einer Meinung sein to agree [ə'gri:]
das **meiste** most [məʊst]
die meisten most [məʊst]

melden to report [rɪ'pɔ:t]
sich melden (bei) to get back (to) [get 'bæk tə]
sich melden to report [rɪ'pɔ:t]
Meldung report [rɪ'pɔ:t]
Menagerie menagerie [mə'nædʒri]
eine **Menge** a lot of [ə 'lɒt‿əv]
Mensch human ['hju:mən]
Menschen people ['pi:pl]
Menschenmenge crowd [kraʊd]
menschlich human ['hju:mən]
Menü menu ['menju:]
sich **merken** to remember [rɪ'membə]
merkwürdig strange [streɪndʒ]
Messe fair [feə]
Messer knife, knives *(pl)* [naɪf; naɪvz]
Metal *(Musikrichtung)* metal ['metl]
Metall metal ['metl]
Meter metre ['mi:tə]
Mexikaner/Mexikanerin Mexican ['meksɪkən]
mexikanisch Mexican ['meksɪkən]
mich me [mi:]
Miesmacher/Miesmacherin wet blanket [wet 'blæŋkɪt]
Mikrofon microphone ['maɪkrəfəʊn]
Mikrowelle microwave ['maɪkrəʊweɪv]
Milch milk [mɪlk]
Milchmann milkman, milkmen *(pl)* ['mɪlkmən; 'mɪlkmen]
Milchshake milkshake ['mɪlkʃeɪk]
Million million ['mɪlɪən]
mindestens at least [ət 'li:st]
Mineral- mineral ['mɪnərəl]
Minestrone minestrone [ˌmɪnɪ'strəʊni]
Minimum minimum ['mɪnɪməm]
Minute minute ['mɪnɪt]
mir me [mi:]
mit with [wɪð]
mitbringen to bring [brɪŋ]
miteinander together [tə'geðə]
Mitfahrgelegenheit ride [raɪd]
Mitglied member ['membə]
mitnehmen to take [teɪk]
zum Mitnehmen to go [tə‿'gəʊ]
Mitspieler/Mitspielerin player ['pleɪə]
Mittagessen dinner ['dɪnə]; lunch [lʌntʃ]
Mittagszeit lunchtime ['lʌntʃtaɪm]
Mitte middle ['mɪdl]
mittel medium ['mi:diəm]
Mittel- middle ['mɪdl]
Mittelpunkt centre ['sentə]; hub [hʌb]
Mittelschule *(weiterführende Schule in den USA, Mittelstufe)* middle school *(AE)* ['mɪdl ˌsku:l]

Mitternacht midnight ['mɪdnaɪt]
Mittwoch Wednesday ['wenzdeɪ]
Möbel furniture ['fɜ:nɪtʃə]
Mobiltelefon cell phone *(AE)* ['sel fəʊn]; mobile ['məʊbaɪl]
möchte gern would like [wʊd 'laɪk]
Mode fashion ['fæʃn]
Model model ['mɒdl]
Modell model ['mɒdl]
modern modern ['mɒdn]
modisch trendy ['trendi]
mögen to like [laɪk]
gern mögen to love [lʌv]
möglich possible ['pɒsəbl]
Mohrrübe carrot ['kærət]
Molkerei dairy ['deəri]
Moment moment ['məʊmənt]
Moment mal! Hang on! ['hæŋ‿ɒn]
momentan at the moment [æt ðə 'məʊmənt]
Monat month [mʌnθ]
Mond moon [mu:n]
Monster monster ['mɒnstə]
Montag Monday ['mʌndeɪ]
montags on Mondays [ɒn 'mʌndeɪz]
morgen tomorrow [tə'mɒrəʊ]
Morgen morning ['mɔ:nɪŋ]
am Morgen in the morning [ˌɪn ðə 'mɔ:nɪŋ]
am nächsten Morgen the next morning [ðə ˌnekst 'mɔ:nɪŋ]
Guten Morgen! Good morning! [ˌgʊd 'mɔ:nɪŋ]
Morgenappell assembly [ə'sembli]
morgens in the morning [ˌɪn ðə 'mɔ:nɪŋ]
Motor engine ['endʒɪn]
Motorrad motorbike ['məʊtəbaɪk]
MP3 MP3 [ˌempi:'θri:]
MP3-Player MP3 player [ˌempi:'θri: ˌpleɪə]
müde tired ['taɪəd]
Müll rubbish ['rʌbɪʃ]
Mülleimer bin [bɪn]
Müllkippe dump [dʌmp]
Mülltonne bin [bɪn]
Mund mouth [maʊθ]
Museum museum [mju:'zi:əm]
Musical musical ['mju:zɪkl]
Musik music ['mju:zɪk]
Musiker/Musikerin musician [mju:'zɪʃn]
müssen must [mʌst]; to have to ['hæv tə]; to need [ni:d]
wieder guten **Mutes sein** to cheer up [tʃɪer‿'ʌp]

mutig brave [breɪv]
Mutter mother ['mʌðə]
Mutti mom *(AE)* [mɒm]; mum [mʌm]
Mütze cap [kæp]
Mythos myth [mɪθ]

N

nach after ['ɑ:ftə]
nach *(Uhrzeit)* past [pɑ:st]
nach to [tʊ; tə]
nach draußen outside [aʊt'saɪd]
nach drinnen inside [ɪn'saɪd]
nach Hause home [həʊm]
nach Hause bringen to take home [ˌteɪk 'həʊm]
nach unten down [daʊn]
Nachbar/Nachbarin neighbour ['neɪbə]
Nachbarschaft neighborhood *(AE)* ['neɪbəhʊd]
nachdem after ['ɑ:ftə]
Nachmittag afternoon [ˌɑ:ftə'nu:n]
am Nachmittag in the afternoon [ˌɪn ði: ˌɑ:ftə'nu:n]
nachmittags in the afternoon [ˌɪn ði: ˌɑ:ftə'nu:n]
Nachmittagstee afternoon tea [ˌɑ:ftənu:n 'ti:]
Nachricht message ['mesɪdʒ]; news *(sg.)* [nju:z]
Nachrichten news *(sg.)* [nju:z]
neueste Nachrichten breaking news [ˌbreɪkɪŋ 'nju:z]
nachschlagen to look up [lʊk‿'ʌp]
nächste/nächster/nächstes next [nekst]
am nächsten Morgen the next morning [ðə ˌnekst 'mɔ:nɪŋ]
Nacht night [naɪt]
heute Nacht tonight [tə'naɪt]
nachts at night [ət 'naɪt]
Nachtisch dessert [dɪ'zɜ:t]; pudding ['pʊdɪŋ]
Nachtschwester night nurse ['naɪt nɜ:s]
nahe close [kləʊs]; near [nɪə]
in der **Nähe von** near [nɪə]
Nahrung food [fu:d]
Name name [neɪm]
Nase nose [nəʊz]
die Nase voll haben to be fed up [bi: ˌfed‿'ʌp]
nass wet [wet]
national national ['næʃnl]
Nationalpark national park [ˌnæʃnl 'pɑ:k]
Natur nature ['neɪtʃə]
natürlich of course [əv 'kɔ:s]
Naturwissenschaft Science ['saɪəns]
Nebel fog [fɒg]
neben beside [bɪ'saɪd]; next to ['nekst tə]
nebenan next door [ˌnekst 'dɔ:]
Nebenprodukt spin-off ['spɪn‿ɒf]
neblig foggy ['fɒgi]
Neffe nephew ['nefju:]
nehmen to take [teɪk]
Ich nehme .... I'm having .... [aɪm 'hævɪŋ]
neidisch (auf) jealous (of) ['dʒeləs]
nein no [nəʊ]
nennen to call [kɔ:l]; to name [neɪm]
Das nenne ich .... That's what I call .... [ˌðæts wɒt‿'aɪ ˌkɔ:l]
neonfarben neon ['ni:ɒn]
nervös nervous ['nɜ:vəs]
nett friendly ['frendli]; kind [kaɪnd]; nice [naɪs]
Netz net [net]
neu new [nju:]
Neuigkeit news *(sg.)* [nju:z]
Neuigkeiten news *(sg.)* [nju:z]
nicht no [nəʊ]; not [nɒt]
nicht einmal not even [nɒt‿'i:vn]
auch nicht not ... either [ˌnɒt ... 'aɪðə]
noch nicht not ... yet [jet]
nichts nothing ['nʌθɪŋ]
Nickel *(Währung)* nickel ['nɪkl]
nie never ['nevə]
nieder down [daʊn]
Niederländer/Niederländerinnen Dutch [dʌtʃ]
niederländisch Dutch [dʌtʃ]
niederlegen to lie down [laɪ 'daʊn]
niedrig low [ləʊ]
niemals never ['nevə]
niemand nobody ['nəʊbədi]; no one ['nəʊwʌn]
nirgendwo nowhere ['nəʊweə]
nirgendwohin nowhere ['nəʊweə]
Niveau level ['levl]
noch still [stɪl]
noch ein/noch eine another [ə'nʌðə]
noch nicht not ... yet [jet]
Norden north [nɔ:θ]
normal normal ['nɔ:ml]
normalerweise usually ['ju:ʒli]
Note grade *(AE)* [greɪd]; mark [mɑ:k]
Notfall emergency [ɪ'mɜ:dʒnsi]
Notiz note [nəʊt]; notice ['nəʊtɪs]
Notlage emergency [ɪ'mɜ:dʒnsi]
November November [nəʊ'vembə]
Nummer number ['nʌmbə]
nun now [naʊ]
nur only ['əʊnli]
nützlich useful ['ju:sfl]
nutzlos useless ['ju:sləs]

O

ob if [ɪf]
obere, oberer, oberes upper ['ʌpə]
oben above [ə'bʌv]; at the top [ət ðə 'tɒp]; up [ʌp]; upstairs [ʌp'steəz]
oberer/obere/oberes upper ['ʌpə]
oberer Teil top [tɒp]
oberhalb above [ə'bʌv]
Objekt object ['ɒbdʒɪkt]
obligatorisch compulsory [kəm'pʌlsri]
Observatorium observatory [əb'zɜ:vətri]
Obst fruit [fru:t]
obwohl although [ɔ:l'ðəʊ]
oder or [ɔ:]
offen open ['əʊpn]
öffentlich public ['pʌblɪk]
offiziell official [ə'fɪʃl]
öffnen to open ['əʊpn]
sich öffnen to open ['əʊpn]
Öffnungszeiten hours ['aʊəz]
oft often ['ɒfn]
ohne without [wɪ'ðaʊt]
ohne ... auskommen to go without [ˌgəʊ wɪ'ðaʊt]
ohnmächtig werden to faint [feɪnt]
Ohr ear [ɪə]
o.k. OK [əʊ'keɪ]
Oktober October [ɒk'təʊbə]
Oma grandma ['grændmɑ:]
Onkel uncle ['ʌŋkl]
Opa grandad ['grændæd]
operieren to operate ['ɒpəreɪt]
Orange orange ['ɒrɪndʒ]
Ordner folder ['fəʊldə]
in **Ordnung** all right [ɔ:l 'raɪt]
Organisator/Organisatorin organizer ['ɔ:gənaɪzə]
organisieren to organize ['ɔ:gənaɪz]
Ort place [pleɪs]
örtlich local ['ləʊkl]
Osten east [i:st]
Ozean ocean ['əʊʃn]
Ozeandampfer ocean liner ['əʊʃn ˌlaɪnə]

P

ein **paar** a few [ə 'fju:]
Paar couple ['kʌpl]
Päckchen packet ['pækɪt]
packen to pack [pæk]
Paket packet ['pækɪt]
Palast palace ['pælɪs]
paniken to panic ['pænɪk]
Panter panther ['pænθə]
Papa dad [dæd]
Papier paper ['peɪpə]
Parade parade [pə'reɪd]
Paradies paradise ['pærəˌdaɪs]
Park park [pɑ:k]
Parkplatz parking lot *(AE)* ['pɑ:kɪŋ ˌlɒt]
Partitur (music) score [skɔ:]
Partner/Partnerin partner ['pɑ:tnə]
Party party ['pɑ:ti]
eine Party feiern to have a party [ˌhæv‿ə 'pɑ:ti]
Pass passport ['pɑ:spɔ:t]
Passagier/Passagierin passenger ['pæsndʒə]
passen to fit [fɪt]
passen zu to match [mætʃ]; to go (together) with ['gəʊ wɪð]
Passkontrolle passports *(pl)* ['pɑ:spɔ:ts]
Pastrami pastrami [pəs'trɑ:mi]
Patient/Patientin patient ['peɪʃnt]
Pause break [breɪk]; recess *(AE)* ['rɪses]
PC PC [ˌpi:'si:]
Pech bad luck [ˌbæd 'lʌk]
peinlich embarrassing [ɪm'bærəsɪŋ]
Pence *(Währung)* pence *(pl)* [pents]
Periode period *(AE)* ['pɪəriəd]
Person person ['pɜ:sn]
Personal staff [stɑ:f]
Perücke wig [wɪg]
Pfad path [pɑ:θ]
Pfannkuchen pancake ['pænkeɪk]
Pfeife pipe [paɪp]
Pfeil arrow ['ærəʊ]
Pferd horse [hɔ:s]
Pflanze plant [plɑ:nt]
pflücken to pick [pɪk]
Pflücker/Pflückerin picker ['pɪkə]
pflügen to plough [plaʊ]
Pforte gate [geɪt]
Pfosten post [pəʊst]
Pfund *(Währung)* pound (£) [paʊnd]
Pfund *(Gewicht)* pound (lb) [paʊnd]
physisch physical ['fɪzɪkl]
pikant spicy ['spaɪsi]
Pilot/Pilotin pilot ['paɪlət]
pink pink [pɪŋk]
Pizza pizza ['pi:tsə]
Plakat poster ['pəʊstə]
Plan plan [plæn]
planen to plan [plæn]
Planet planet ['plænɪt]
platt flat [flæt]
Plattform platform ['plætfɔ:m]
Platz place [pleɪs]; room [ru:m; rʊm]; space [speɪs]
pleite broke [brəʊk]
plötzlich at once [ət 'wʌnts]; sudden ['sʌdn]; suddenly ['sʌdnli]
Plundergebäck Danish ['deɪnɪʃ]
Plural plural ['plʊrəl]
plus plus [plʌs]
Poet/Poetin poet ['pəʊɪt]
Poetry Slam *(Gedichtwettbewerb)* poetry slam ['pəʊətri ˌslæm]
Pokal cup [kʌp]
politisch political [pə'lɪtɪkl]
Polizei police [pə'li:s]
Polizist policeman, policemen *(pl)* [pə'li:smən; pə'li:smen]
Polizist/Polizistin cop *(AE)* [kɒp]
polnisch Polish ['pəʊlɪʃ]
Pommes frites French fries *(AE)* ['frentʃ ˌfraɪz]; chips *(pl)* [tʃɪps]
Pompon *(bunte Quaste der Cheerleader)* pompom ['pɒmpɒm]
Pony pony ['pəʊni]
Popmusik pop [pɒp]
populär popular ['pɒpjələ]
posieren to pose [pəʊz]
Position position [pə'zɪʃn]
Postamt post office ['pəʊst‿ɒfɪs]
posten *(im Internetforum)* to post [pəʊst]
Poster poster ['pəʊstə]
Postkarte postcard ['pəʊstkɑ:d]
Prachtstraße boulevard ['bu:ləvɑ:d]
praktizieren to practise ['præktɪs]
präsentieren to present [prɪ'zent]
Preis award [ə'wɔ:d]; cost [kɒst]; price [praɪs]; prize [praɪz]; trophy ['trəʊfi]
zum halben Preis half-price [ˌhɑ:f'praɪs]
Presse press [pres]
pressen to press [pres]
prima brilliant ['brɪljənt]; cool [ku:l]
Prinz prince [prɪns]
privat private ['praɪvɪt]
Privatschule (GB) public school [ˌpʌblɪk 'sku:l]
pro per [pɜ:]
Pro und Kontra pros and cons [ˌprəʊz‿ənd 'kɒnz]
proben to practise ['præktɪs]
proben *(ein Theaterstück)* to rehearse [rɪ'hɜ:s]
probieren to try [traɪ]
Problem problem ['prɒbləm]
Produktion production [prə'dʌkʃn]
produzieren to produce [prə'dju:s]
Programm channel ['tʃænl]; programme ['prəʊgræm]
Projekt project ['prɒdʒekt]
Prospekt leaflet ['li:flət]
Prozent per cent (%) [pə 'sent]
Prüfung exam [ɪg'zæm]
Publikum audience ['ɔ:diəns]
publizieren to publish ['pʌblɪʃ]
Pudding pudding ['pʊdɪŋ]
Puder powder ['paʊdə]
Pulver powder ['paʊdə]
Punk punk [pʌŋk]
Punkt point [pɔɪnt]
punkten to score [skɔ:]
Punktestand score [skɔ:]
pünktlich on time [ɒn 'taɪm]
Pute turkey ['tɜ:ki]
putzen to brush [brʌʃ]
Putzkraft cleaner ['kli:nə]

Q

quietschen to creak [kri:k]
Quote quota ['kwəʊtə]

R

Rad wheel [wi:l]
Rad fahren to cycle ['saɪkl]
Radiergummi rubber ['rʌbə]
Radio radio ['reɪdiəʊ]
Radiosendung radio show ['reɪdiəʊ ˌʃəʊ]
Radkranz rim [rɪm]
Rafting rafting ['rɑ:ftɪŋ]
Rakete rocket ['rɒkɪt]
Rallye rally ['ræli]
Ranch ranch [ræntʃ]
Rand edge [edʒ]
Rap rap [ræp]
rappen to rap [ræp]
Rapper/Rapperin rapper ['ræpə]
Rasierwasser aftershave ['ɑ:ftəʃeɪv]
Rastplatz rest area ['rest ˌeəriə]
raten to advise [əd'vaɪz]; to guess [ges]
Rätsel mystery ['mɪstri]
rau tough [tʌf]

rauben to rob [rɒb]
Räuber/Räuberin robber ['rɒbə]
Rauch smoke [sməʊk]
rauchen to smoke [sməʊk]
Raum room [ru:m; rʊm]; space [speɪs]
Raumfähre shuttle ['ʃʌtl]
Raumpfleger/Raumpflegerin cleaner ['kli:nə]
Raumschiff spaceship ['speɪsʃɪp]
Razzia raid [reɪd]
R&B R&B [ˌɑ:r‿n'bi:]
Reaktion response [rɪ'spɒns]
Realität reality [ri'æləti]
Realityshow reality show [ri'æləti ˌʃəʊ]
Recherche research [rɪ'sɜ:tʃ]
Recht haben to be right [bi: 'raɪt]
rechte/rechter/rechtes right [raɪt]
rechtlich legal ['li:gl]
rechts on the right [ɒn ðə 'raɪt]; right [raɪt]
rechts abbiegen to turn right [tɜ:n 'raɪt]
Rechts- legal ['li:gl]
rechtswidrig illegal [ɪ'li:gl]
Rede talk [tɔ:k]
reden to talk [tɔ:k]
reden mit to talk to ['tɔ:k tə]
Redewendung phrase [freɪz]
Refrain chorus ['kɔ:rəs]
Regal shelf, shelves *(pl)* [ʃelf; ʃelvz]
Regalbrett shelf, shelves *(pl)* [ʃelf; ʃelvz]
Regel rule [ru:l]
regeln *(ein Problem)* to sort out [sɔ:t‿'aʊt]
Regen rain [reɪn]
Regenguss shower ['ʃaʊə]
Regenschirm umbrella [ʌm'brelə]
Reggae reggae ['regeɪ]
Regisseur/Regisseurin director [dɪ'rektə]
registrieren to register ['redʒɪstə]
sich registrieren to register ['redʒɪstə]
Registrierung registration [ˌredʒɪ'streɪʃn]
regnen to rain [reɪn]
regnerisch rainy ['reɪni]
reich rich [rɪtʃ]
Reihe row [rəʊ]
Reihenfolge order ['ɔ:də]
rein pristine ['prɪsti:n]
reinigen to clean [kli:n]
Reis rice [raɪs]
Reise journey ['dʒɜ:ni]; tour [tʊə]; trip [trɪp]; travel ['trævl]
reisen to travel ['trævl]
Reisepass passport ['pɑ:spɔ:t]
reiten to ride [raɪd]
Religionsunterricht Religious Education (RE) [rɪˌlɪdʒəs‿edʒʊ'keɪʃn]
religiös religious [rɪ'lɪdʒəs]
Renn- racing ['reɪsɪŋ]
rennen to run [rʌn]
Rennen race [reɪs]
reparieren to fix (to) [fɪks]; to repair [rɪ'peə]
Reporter/Reporterin reporter [rɪ'pɔ:tə]
Reservat reservation [ˌrezə'veɪʃn]
Reservierung reservation [ˌrezə'veɪʃn]
Respekt respect [rɪ'spekt]
Respektlosigkeit disrespect [ˌdɪsrɪ'spekt]
Rest rest [rest]
Restaurant restaurant ['restrɒnt]
Restaurant mit Straßenverkauf takeaway ['teɪkəweɪ]
Resultat result [rɪ'zʌlt]
retten to rescue ['reskju:]; to save [seɪv]
Rettung rescue ['reskju:]
Rettungsschwimmer/ Rettungsschwimmerin lifeguard ['laɪfgɑ:d]
Rezept recipe ['resɪpi:]
Rezeption reception [rɪ'sepʃn]
Richter judge [dʒʌdʒ]
richtig correct [kə'rekt]; right [raɪt]
richtig machen to get … right [get … 'raɪt]
in **Richtung** towards [tə'wɔ:dz]
riechen to smell [smel]
riesig enormous [ɪ'nɔ:məs]; huge [hju:dʒ]; large [lɑ:dʒ]; vast [vɑ:st]
Rinderhirte cowboy ['kaʊbɔɪ]
Ring ring [rɪŋ]
Risiko risk [rɪsk]
riskieren to dare [deə]
etwas riskieren to take your chance [ˌteɪk jɔ: 'tʃɑ:ns]
Ritt ride [raɪd]
Ritter knight [naɪt]
Rivale/Rivalin rival ['raɪvl]
Roboter robot ['rəʊbɒt]
Robotertechnik robotics [rə'bɒtɪks]
Rock skirt [skɜ:t]
rocken to rock [rɒk]
Rockmusik rock [rɒk]
Rodeo rodeo [rəʊ'deɪəʊ; 'rəʊdiəʊ]
roh raw [rɔ:]
Rolle part [pɑ:t]; role [rəʊl]
Roller kickboard ['kɪkbɔ:d]
rosa pink [pɪŋk]
rot red [red]
rot werden to go red [gəʊ 'red]
Rücken back [bæk]
rückenfrei backless ['bækləs]
Rucksack rucksack ['rʌksæk]
rückwärtig back [bæk]
rufen to call [kɔ:l]; to cry [kraɪ]; to shout [ʃaʊt]
rufen *(Eule)* to hoot [hu:t]
rhythmisch rufen to chant [tʃɑ:nt]
Rugby rugby ['rʌgbi]
Rugbyschuh rugby boot ['rʌgbi bu:t]
Ruhe quiet [kwaɪət]
ruhig calm [kɑ:m]; quiet ['kwaɪət]
rumhängen to hang around *(AE)* [ˌhæŋ‿ə'raʊnd]
Run run [rʌn]
Runde round [raʊnd]; run [rʌn]
Russe/Russin Russian ['rʌʃn]
russisch Russian ['rʌʃn]

S

Saal hall [hɔ:l]
Sache thing [θɪŋ]
Safe safe [seɪf]
Saft juice [dʒu:s]
sagen to say [seɪ]; to tell [tel]
Sahne cream [kri:m]
Saison season ['si:zn]
Salat salad ['sæləd]
sammeln to collect [kə'lekt]
Samstag Saturday ['sætədeɪ]
Sand sand [sænd]
sandig sandy ['sændɪ]
Sandwich sandwich ['sænwɪdʒ]
sanft soft [sɒft]
Sänger/Sängerin singer ['sɪŋə]
Satellit satellite ['sætlaɪt]
sauber clean [kli:n]
säubern to clean [kli:n]
sauer sour ['saʊə]
Sauerkraut sauerkraut ['saʊəkraʊt]
Säugling baby, babies *(pl)* ['beɪbi; 'beɪbiz]
Schachtel box, boxes *(pl)* [bɒks; 'bɒksɪz]
Schaden harm [hɑ:m]
Schaf sheep, sheep *(pl)* [ʃi:p]
Schallplatte record ['rekɔ:d]
Schalter desk [desk]; switch [swɪtʃ]
scharf hot [hɒt]
Schatten shadow ['ʃædəʊ]
Schatz *(Anrede)* dear [dɪə]
Schau show [ʃəʊ]

schauen to look [lʊk]
schaukeln to rock [rɒk]
Schauplatz scene [si:n]
Schauspieler actor ['æktə]
Schauspielerin actress ['æktrəs]
Scheibe slice [slaɪs]
Schein slip [slɪp]
schenken to give [gɪv]
scherzen to joke [dʒəʊk]
Scheune barn [bɑ:n]
schicken to send [send]
  Textnachricht schicken to text [tekst]
schieben to push [pʊʃ]
Schiedsrichter/Schiedsrichterin umpire ['ʌmpaɪə]; referee [ˌrefr'i:]
schief gehen to go wrong [gəʊ 'rɒŋ]
ein Tor **schießen** to score [skɔ:]
Schiff boat [bəʊt]
Schild sign [saɪn]
Schinken ham [hæm]
Schinkenspeck bacon ['beɪkn]
Schlacht battle ['bætl]
Schlaf sleep [sli:p]
schlafen to be asleep [ˌbi:‿ə'sli:p]; to sleep [sli:p]
schläfrig sleepy ['sli:pi]
Schlafsack sleeping bag ['sli:pɪŋ ˌbæg]
Schlafzimmer bedroom ['bedrʊm]
Schlag knock [nɒk]; shot [ʃɒt]; stroke [strəʊk]
Schlaganfall stroke [strəʊk]
schlagen to bang [bæŋ]; to bat [bæt]; to beat [bi:t]; to hit [hɪt]; to knock [nɒk]
  k.o. schlagen to knock out [nɒk‿'aʊt]
Schläger bat [bæt]
Schlagmann/Schlagfrau batter ['bætə]
Schlagzeug drums *(pl)* [drʌmz]
Schlagzeuger/Schlagzeugerin drummer ['drʌmə]
Schlange queue [kju:]
schlau smart [smɑ:t]
schlecht bad [bæd]
  schlechter worse [wɜ:s]
  schlechteste/schlechtester/schlechtestes worst [wɜ:st]
schleichen to crawl [krɔ:l]
Schleiereule barn owl ['bɑ:n‿aʊl]
schließen to close [kləʊz]
Schließfach locker ['lɒkə]
schließlich finally ['faɪnli]; in the end [ɪn ði:‿'end]
schlimmer worse [wɜ:s]
  schlimmste/schlimmster/schlimmstes worst [wɜ:st]

Schlittschuhbahn ice rink ['aɪs rɪŋk]
Schloss castle ['kɑ:sl]
Schlucht canyon ['kænjən]; gorge [gɔ:dʒ]
schlürfen to sip [sɪp]
Schluss end [end]
  zum Schluss in the end [ɪn ði:‿'end]
Schlüssel key [ki:]
schmackhaft tasty ['teɪsti]
schmecken to taste [teɪst]
Schmerz pain [peɪn]
Schminke make-up ['meɪkʌp]
Schmuck jewellery ['dʒu:əlri]
Schmuggler/Schmugglerin smuggler ['smʌglə]
schmutzig dirty ['dɜ:ti]
schnappen to grab [græb]
Schnappschuss snapshot ['snæpʃɒt]
Schnee snow [snəʊ]
schneiden to cut (off) [kʌt‿'ɒf]
schneien to snow [snəʊ]
schnell fast [fɑ:st]; quick [kwɪk]
schnüffeln to sniff [snɪf]
schnuppern to sniff [snɪf]
Schnur cord *(AE)* [kɔ:d]; string [strɪŋ]
schockiert shocked [ʃɒkt]
Schokolade chocolate ['tʃɒklət]
schön beautiful ['bju:tɪfl]; fine [faɪn]; nice [naɪs]
schon already [ɔ:l'redi]
schottisch Scottish ['skɒtɪʃ]
Schrank cabinet ['kæbɪnət]; cupboard ['kʌbəd]
einen **Schrecken einjagen** to scare ['skeə]
schrecklich awful ['ɔ:fl]; frightening ['fraɪtnɪŋ]; horrible ['hɒrəbl]; terrible ['terəbl]
Schrei cry [kraɪ]
schreiben to write [raɪt]
  E-Mail schreiben to e-mail ['i:meɪl]
Schreibtisch desk [desk]
schreien to cry [kraɪ]; to shout [ʃaʊt]
  schreien *(Eule)* to hoot [hu:t]
Schritt footstep ['fʊtstep]; move [mu:v]; step [step]
schüchtern shy [ʃaɪ]
Schuh shoe [ʃu:]
den **Schulabschluss machen** to graduate ['grædjueɪt]
Schulbuch textbook ['teksbʊk]
Schule school [sku:l]
  staatliche Schule (USA) public school [ˌpʌblɪk 'sku:l]
Schüler/Schülerin pupil ['pju:pl]; student *(AE)* ['stju:dnt]

Schulfach subject ['sʌbdʒɪkt]
Schulhof playground ['pleɪgraʊnd]
Schulklasse class [klɑ:s]
Schulranzen school bag ['sku:l bæg]
Schultasche school bag ['sku:l bæg]
Schulter shoulder ['ʃəʊldə]
Schuppen shed [ʃed]
Schuss gunshot ['gʌnʃɒt]; shot [ʃɒt]
Schüssel bowl [bəʊl]
Schusswaffe gun [gʌn]
schütteln to shake [ʃeɪk]
schwach weak [wi:k]
  schwach werden to go weak [gəʊ 'wi:k]
Schwamm sponge [spʌndʒ]
schwarz black [blæk]
schwatzen to gossip ['gɒsɪp]
Schwein pig [pɪg]
Schweinefleisch pork [pɔ:k]
schwenken to wave [weɪv]
schwer heavy ['hevi]
Schwester sister ['sɪstə]
schwierig difficult ['dɪfɪklt]; hard [hɑ:d]
Schwierigkeit problem ['prɒbləm]
Schwimmbad swimming pool ['swɪmɪŋ ˌpu:l]
Schwimmbecken pool [pu:l]; swimming pool ['swɪmɪŋ ˌpu:l]
schwimmen to swim [swɪm]
Schwimmer/Schwimmerin swimmer ['swɪmə]
Schwimmreifen rubber ring [ˌrʌbə 'rɪŋ]
schwindelig dizzy ['dɪzi]
Sciencefiction science fiction [ˌsaɪəns 'fɪkʃn]
Scone *(Gebäck)* scone [skɒn]
Screenshot screen shot ['skri:n ˌʃɒt]
See lake [leɪk]
seekrank seasick ['si:sɪk]
Seele soul [səʊl]
segeln to sail [seɪl]
sehen to look [lʊk]; to see [si:]
Sehenswürdigkeit attraction [ə'trækʃn]; sight [saɪt]
sehr very ['veri]
Seife soap [səʊp]
Seifenoper soap [səʊp]
sein to be [bi:]
  an der Reihe sein to be on [bi:‿'ɒn]
  an sein to be on [bi:‿'ɒn]
sein his [hɪz]
  sein/seine its [ɪts]
seit for [fɔ:; fə]; since [sɪnts]
seitdem since [sɪnts]
Seite page [peɪdʒ]; side [saɪd]
Sekretär/Sekretärin secretary ['sekrətri]

Sekunde second ['seknd]
selbst gemacht home-made [ˌhəʊm'meɪd]
selbstverständlich of course [əv 'kɔ:s]
selten seldom ['seldəm]
seltsam strange [streɪndʒ]
Sendung programme ['prəʊgræm]; show [ʃəʊ]
auf Sendung on the air [ˌɒn ði‿'eə]
September September [sep'tembə]
Serie series, series *(pl)* ['sɪəri:z]
Service service ['sɜ:vɪs]
servieren to serve [sɜ:v]
sich **setzen** to sit down [sɪt 'daʊn]
sich setzen zu to sit with ['sɪt wɪθ]
Shorts shorts *(pl)* [ʃɔ:ts]
Show show [ʃəʊ]
sicher safe [seɪf]; sure [ʃʊə]
sichergehen to make sure [meɪk 'ʃʊə]
Sicherheit security [sɪ'kjʊərəti]
Sicherungskasten fuse-box ['fju:zbɒks]
Sicht sight [saɪt]; view [vju:]
sie her [hɜ:]; she [ʃi:]
sie *(Mehrzahl)* they [ðeɪ]; them [ðem]
siegen to win [wɪn]
Sieger/Siegerin winner ['wɪnə]
Siegtreffer winning goal ['wɪnɪŋ gəʊl]
Signal signal ['sɪgnl]
signalisieren to signal ['sɪgnl]
simpel simple ['sɪmpl]
simsen to text [tekst]
singen to sing [sɪŋ]; to chant [tʃɑ:nt]
Sinn sense [sens]
Sinnbild symbol ['sɪmbl]
Sintflut flash flood ['flæʃ ˌflʌd]
Sirup syrup ['sɪrəp]
Situationskomödie sitcom ['sɪtkɒm]
Sitz seat [si:t]
sitzen to sit [sɪt]
in der Falle sitzen to be trapped [bi: 'træpt]
Sitzplatz seat [si:t]
Skateboard skateboard ['skeɪtbɔ:d]
skaten to skate [skeɪt]
Skifahren skiing ['ski:ɪŋ]
Slang slang [slæŋ]
SMS text message ['tekst ˌmesɪdʒ]
Snack snack [snæk]
so so [səʊ]
so … wie … as … as [æz … æz; əz … əz]
so (schlimm) that (bad) ['ðæt bæd]
sobald as soon as [əz 'su:n‿əz]
Sofa couch [kaʊtʃ]; sofa ['səʊfə]
sofort at once [ət 'wʌnts]; right away [raɪt‿ə'weɪ]

sogar even ['i:vn]
Sohn son [sʌn]
solange as long as [əz 'lɒŋ‿əz]
solch such [sʌtʃ]
sollte/sollten should [ʃʊd]
Sommer summer ['sʌmə]
Sommerfest summer fair ['sʌmə ˌfeə]
Sonne sun [sʌn]
Sonnenbräune suntan ['sʌntæn]
sonnig sunny ['sʌni]
Sonntag Sunday ['sʌndeɪ]
sonst else [els]
sich **Sorgen machen** to worry ['wʌri]
sorgfältig careful ['keəfl]
Sorte kind [kaɪnd]; sort [sɔ:t]; type [taɪp]
Soulmusik soul [səʊl]
Souvenir souvenir [ˌsu:və'nɪə]
sowieso anyway ['eniweɪ]
sozial social ['səʊʃl]
Sozialversicherungsnummer social security number [ˌsəʊʃl sɪ'kjʊərəti ˌnʌmbə]
Spaghetti spaghetti [spə'geti]
spanisch Spanish ['spænɪʃ]
Spanisch Spanish ['spænɪʃ]
spannend exciting [ɪk'saɪtɪŋ]
Spannung suspense [sə'spens]
sparen to save [seɪv]
Sparschwein piggy bank ['pɪgi bæŋk]
Spaß fun [fʌn]
Spaß haben to have fun [ˌhæv 'fʌn]
Spaß machen to be fun [bi: 'fʌn]
Viel Spaß! Have fun! [ˌhæv 'fʌn]
spät late [leɪt]
zu spät late [leɪt]
spazieren gehen to go for a walk [ˌgəʊ fər‿ə 'wɔ:k]
Spaziergang walk [wɔ:k]
Speisekarte menu ['menju:]
Speisesaal dining room ['daɪnɪŋ rʊm]
spektakulär spectacular [spek'tækjələ]
Spezialität special ['speʃl]
speziell special ['speʃl]
Spiegel mirror ['mɪrə]
Spiegelei sunny side up [ˌsʌni saɪd‿'ʌp]
Spiel game [geɪm]; match [mætʃ]; play [pleɪ]
spielen to play [pleɪ]
spielen *(Theater)* to act [ækt]
Spieler/Spielerin player ['pleɪə]
Spielfeld court [kɔ:t]; pitch [pɪtʃ]
Spielplatz playground ['pleɪgraʊnd]
Spielstand score [skɔ:]
Spielzeug toy [tɔɪ]
Spitze top [tɒp]

Spitzname nickname ['nɪkneɪm]
Sport sport [spɔ:t]
Sport *(Schulfach)* Physical Education (PE) [ˌfɪzɪkl‿edʒʊ'keɪʃn]
Sport machen to exercise ['eksəsaɪz]
Sport treiben to do sports [du: 'spɔ:ts]
Sportfest sports day ['spɔ:ts deɪ]
Sportgeschäft sports shop ['spɔ:ts ʃɒp]
sportlich sporty ['spɔ:ti]
Sportplatz sports field ['spɔ:ts fi:ld]
Sportzeug PE kit [ˌpi:‿'i: kɪt]
Sprache language ['læŋgwɪdʒ]
sprechen to say [seɪ]; to speak [spi:k]; to talk [tɔ:k]
sprechen mit to talk to ['tɔ:k tə]
Sprecher/Sprecherin speaker ['spi:kə]
Sprechgesang chant [tʃɑ:nt]
springen to jump [dʒʌmp]
sprühen to spray [spreɪ]
Spülbecken sink [sɪŋk]
Spur track [træk]
Staat state [steɪt]
staatlich state [steɪt]
staatliche Schule (USA) public school [ˌpʌblɪk 'sku:l]
Stadion stadium ['steɪdiəm]; arena [ə'ri:nə]
Stadt city ['sɪti]; town [taʊn]
Stadtplan map [mæp]
Stadtteil borough ['bʌrə]
Stamm tribe [traɪb]
Stammkunde/Stammkundin regular ['regjələ]
Stand stall [stɔ:l]
Standbesitzer/Standbesitzerin stall holder ['stɔ:l ˌhəʊldə]
Standbild statue ['stætʃu:]
Standfoto still (picture) ['stɪl ˌpɪktʃə]
ständig always ['ɔ:lweɪz]
Star star [stɑ:]
stark hard [hɑ:d]; strong [strɒŋ]
Stärke power ['paʊə]
Start start [stɑ:t]
starten to launch [lɔ:nʃ]; to start [stɑ:t]; to take off [ˌteɪk‿'ɒf]
Station station ['steɪʃn]
statt instead of [ɪn'sted‿əv]
stattfinden to take place [teɪk 'pleɪs]
Statue statue ['stætʃu:]
Stau traffic jam ['træfɪk ˌdʒæm]
Steckdose socket ['sɒkɪt]
stecken to stick [stɪk]
Stecker plug [plʌg]
stehen to stand [stænd]
stehlen to steal [sti:l]

steigen to climb ['klaɪm]; to rise [raɪz]; to step [step]
Stein rock [rɒk]; stone [stəʊn]
Stelle place [pleɪs]
stellen *(Uhr)* to set [set]
sterben to die [daɪ]
Stern star [stɑ:]
Sternwarte observatory [əb'zɜ:vətri]
Stiefel boot [bu:t]
Stiefvater stepdad ['stepdæd]
Stil style [staɪl]
still quiet ['kwaɪət]
Stille quiet [kwaɪət]
Stimme voice [vɔɪs]
stimmen für to vote (for) [vəʊt]
Stock stick [stɪk]
im oberen Stock upstairs [ʌp'steəz]
im unteren Stock downstairs [ˌdaʊn'steəz]
Stoff material [mə'tɪəriəl]
Stollenschuh rugby boot ['rʌgbi bu:t]
stolz auf proud of ['praʊd‿əv]
Stöpsel plug [plʌg]
stoßen to knock [nɒk]; to push [pʊʃ]
stoßen gegen to run into [rʌn‿'ɪntə]
Strand beach [bi:tʃ]
Straße road [rəʊd]; street [stri:t]
Straßenrand roadside ['rəʊdsaɪd]
Strauch bush [bʊʃ]
Streich trick [trɪk]
streichen to paint [peɪnt]
Streit argument ['ɑ:gjəmənt]
streiten to argue ['ɑ:gju:]; to fight [faɪt]
sich streiten to have an argument [ˌhæv‿ən‿'ɑ:gjəmənt]
streng strict [strɪkt]
Stress stress [stres]
strikt strict [strɪkt]
Stroh straw [strɔ:]
Strom electricity [ˌelɪk'trɪsəti]
Stromausfall blackout *(AE)* ['blækaʊt]
Stubenhocker couch potato ['kaʊtʃ pəˌteɪtəʊ]
Stück piece [pi:s]
Student/Studentin student ['stju:dnt]
studieren to study ['stʌdi]
Studio studio ['stju:diəʊ]
Stufe step [step]
Stuhl chair [tʃeə]
Stunde hour ['aʊə]
eine halbe Stunde half an hour [ˌhɑ:f‿ən‿'aʊə]
stundenlang for hours [fər‿'aʊəz]
Stundenplan curriculum [kə'rɪkjələm]; timetable ['taɪmteɪbl]
Sturm storm [stɔ:m]
stürmisch stormy ['stɔ:mi]
stützen to support [sə'pɔ:t]
suchen to look for ['lʊk fə]
Süden south [saʊθ]
Südwesten southwest [ˌsaʊθ'west]
Superlativ superlative [su:'pɜ:lətɪv]
Supermarkt supermarket ['su:pəˌmɑ:kɪt]
Suppe soup [su:p]
surfen to surf [sɜ:f]
im Internet surfen to surf the Internet [ˌsɜ:f ði‿'ɪntənet]
Surfen surfing ['sɜ:fɪŋ]
süß sweet [swi:t]
Süßigkeit sweet [swi:t]
Süßigkeiten candy *(AE)* ['kændi]
Sweatshirt sweatshirt ['swetʃɜ:t]
Symbol symbol ['sɪmbl]
Synonym synonym ['sɪnənɪm]
System system ['sɪstəm]
Szene scene [si:n]

T

Tabak tobacco [tə'bækəʊ]
Tabelle grid [grɪd]
Tafel board [bɔ:d]
Tag day [deɪ]
Einen schönen Tag noch. Have a nice day. [ˌhæv‿ə naɪs 'deɪ]
eines Tages one day [wʌn 'deɪ]
jeden Tag any day ['eni deɪ]
Tagebuch diary ['daɪəri]
täglich daily ['deɪli]
Talkmaster host [həʊst]
Talkshow talk show ['tɔ:k ˌʃəʊ]
Tante aunt [ɑ:nt]
Tanz dance [dɑ:nts]
tanzen to dance [dɑ:nts]
Breakdance tanzen to break-dance ['breɪkdɑ:nts]
Tanzen dancing ['dɑ:ntsɪŋ]
Tanzfläche dance floor ['dɑ:nts flɔ:]
tapfer brave [breɪv]
Tasche bag [bæg]
Taschendieb/Taschendiebin pickpocket ['pɪkˌpɒkɪt]
Taschengeld pocket money ['pɒkɪt ˌmʌni]
Taschenlampe torch, torches *(pl)* [tɔ:tʃ; 'tɔ:tʃɪz]
Taschenmesser penknife, penknives *(pl)* ['pennaɪf; 'pennaɪvz]
Tasse cup [kʌp]
tasten nach to feel for ['fi:l fə]
in der **Tat** in fact [ɪn 'fækt]
Tätowierung tattoo [tæt'u:]
Tatsache fact [fækt]
tatsächlich actually ['æktʃuəli]
tauchen to dive [daɪv]
Tausch exchange [ɪks'tʃeɪndʒ]; swap [swɒp]
tauschen to change [tʃeɪndʒ]; to swap [swɒp]
tausend thousand ['θaʊznd]
Taxi taxi ['tæksi]
Team team [ti:m]
Technik Technology [tek'nɒlədʒi]
Tee tea [ti:]
Teenager teenager ['ti:nˌeɪdʒə]
Teil part [pɑ:t]
teilen to share [ʃeə]
teilnehmen an to take part in [teɪk 'pɑ:t‿ɪn]
Telefon phone [fəʊn]
telefonieren to phone [fəʊn]
Telefonnummer phone number ['fəʊn ˌnʌmbə]
Telefonzelle phone box ['fəʊn ˌbɒks]
Teller plate [pleɪt]
Temperatur temperature ['temprətʃə]
Tennis tennis ['tenɪs]
Teppichboden carpet ['kɑ:pɪt]
Terminkalender diary ['daɪəri]
Test test [test]
teuer expensive [ɪk'spentsɪv]
Textnachricht schicken to text [tekst]
Theater theater *(AE)* ['θɪətə]
Theaterstück play [pleɪ]
Thema subject ['sʌbdʒɪkt]; topic ['tɒpɪk]
Thriller thriller ['θrɪlə]
Ticket ticket ['tɪkɪt]
tief low [ləʊ]
tief ausgeschnitten low-cut ['ləʊkʌt]
Tier animal ['ænɪml]
Tierpark zoo [zu:]
Tierpfleger/Tierpflegerin zookeeper ['zu:ˌki:pə]
Tiger tiger ['taɪgə]
Tipp tip [tɪp]
Tisch table ['teɪbl]
den Tisch decken to set the table [ˌset ðə 'teɪbl]
Tischtennis table-tennis ['teɪblˌtenɪs]
Titel title ['taɪtl]
Titelseite cover ['kʌvə]
Toast toast [təʊst]
Tochter daughter ['dɔ:tə]
Toilette restroom *(AE)* ['restrʊm]; toilet ['tɔɪlɪt]

toll awesome ['ɔ:səm]; brilliant ['brɪljənt]; great [greɪt]; hot [hɒt]
tollpatschig clumsy ['klʌmzi]
Tomate tomato, tomatoes *(pl)* [tə'mɑ:təʊ; tə'mɑ:təʊz]
Ton sound [saʊnd]
Tonfilm talkie ['tɔ:ki]
Tonne (*Gewicht*) ton [tʌn]
Topf pot [pɒt]
Tor gate [geɪt]; goal [gəʊl]
ein Tor schießen to score [skɔ:]
Torpfosten goal post ['gəʊl pəʊst]
Torwart goalkeeper ['gəʊl,ki:pə]
tot dead [ded]
töten to kill [kɪl]
Tour tour [tʊə]
Tourist/Touristin tourist ['tʊərɪst]
Tradition tradition [trə'dɪʃn]
tragen to carry ['kæri]
trainieren to train [treɪn]
Training practice ['præktɪs]; training ['treɪnɪŋ]
Traktor tractor ['træktə]
Transport transport ['træntspɔ:t]
transportieren to transport [træn'spɔ:t]
Tratsch gossip ['gɒsɪp]
tratschen to gossip ['gɒsɪp]
Traum dream [dri:m]
traurig sad [sæd]
treffen to hit [hɪt]; to meet [mi:t]
sich treffen to meet [mi:t]
Treffen meeting ['mi:tɪŋ]
Treppe stairs *(pl)* [steəz]
die Treppe hinaufrennen to run upstairs [,rʌn‿ʌp'steəz]
Tresor safe [seɪf]
treten to kick [kɪk]; to step [step]
Treue allegiance [ə'li:dʒns]
Tribüne platform ['plætfɔ:m]; stand [stænd]
Trick trick [trɪk]
Trikot jersey ['dʒɜ:zi]
Trillerpfeife whistle ['wɪsl]
trinken to drink [drɪŋk]
schluckweise trinken to sip [sɪp]
Trinkgeld tip [tɪp]
trocknen to dry [draɪ]
Trödelstand white elephant stall [,waɪt 'elɪfənt stɔ:l]
tröpfeln to drip [drɪp]
tropfen (lassen) to drip [drɪp]
Trophäe trophy ['trəʊfi]
Trottel jerk *(slang)* [dʒɜ:k]
trotzdem though [ðəʊ]
Truck truck *(AE)* [trʌk]
Trucker trucker *(AE)* ['trʌkə]
Truthahn turkey ['tɜ:ki]
tschüss bye [baɪ]
T-Shirt T-shirt ['ti:ʃɜ:t]
tun to do [du:]; to make [meɪk]
Tunnel tunnel ['tʌnl]
Tür door [dɔ:]
türkisch Turkish ['tɜ:kɪʃ]
Türklingel doorbell ['dɔ:bel]
Turm tower ['taʊə]
Turnhalle gym [dʒɪm]
Turnier competition [,kɒmpə'tɪʃn]
Türstufe doorstep ['dɔ:step]
Tüte bag [bæg]
Typ bloke [bləʊk]; guy [gaɪ]; type [taɪp]
tyrannisieren to bully ['bʊli]

U

U-Bahn underground ['ʌndəgraʊnd]
Übelkeit verspüren to feel sick [fi:l 'sɪk]
üben to exercise ['eksəsaɪz]; to practise ['præktɪs]
über above [ə'bʌv]; across [ə'krɒs]; over ['əʊvə]; about [ə'baʊt]
überall all over [,ɔ:l‿'əʊvə]; anywhere ['eniweə]; everywhere ['evriweə]
überfluten to flood [flʌd]
überhaupt (nicht) (not ...) at all [,nɒt ... ət‿'ɔ:l]
Überleben survival [sə'vaɪvl]
überprüfen to check [tʃek]
überqueren to cross [krɒs]
überraschend surprising [sə'praɪzɪŋ]
überrascht surprised [sə'praɪzd]
Überschrift title ['taɪtl]
überschwemmen to flood [flʌd]
Überschwemmung flood [flʌd]
flutartige Überschwemmung flash flood ['flæʃ ,flʌd]
übertreiben to overdo [,əʊvə'du:]
überwachen to control [kən'trəʊl]; to monitor ['mɒnɪtə]
überwältigend overwhelming [,əʊvə'welmɪŋ]
überwiegend mostly ['məʊstli]
übrig left [left]
übrigens by the way [,baɪ ðə 'weɪ]
Übung exercise ['eksəsaɪz]
Übungsheft exercise book ['eksəsaɪz ,bʊk]
Uhr clock [klɒk]
Uhr *(Zeitangabe)* o'clock [ə'klɒk]
Wie viel Uhr ist es, bitte? What's the time, please? [,wɒts ðə 'taɪm ,pli:z]
umdrehen to turn [tɜ:n]
(sich) umdrehen to turn over [,tɜ:n‿'əʊvə]; to turn round [tɜ:n 'raʊnd]
Umfrage survey ['sɜ:veɪ]
Umgebung environment [ɪn'vaɪərnmənt]
umhauen to knock out [nɒk‿'aʊt]
umher around [ə'raʊnd]
umkehren to turn back [tɜ:n 'bæk]
Umschlag envelope ['envələʊp]
sich **umsehen** to look round [lʊk 'raʊnd]
umsonst free [fri:]
umsteigen to change [tʃeɪndʒ]
umstoßen to upset [ʌp'set]
Umwelt environment [ɪn'vaɪərnmənt]
Umweltverschmutzung pollution [pə'lu:ʃn]
umziehen to move [mu:v]
Umzug parade [pə'reɪd]
unabhängig independent [,ɪndɪ'pendənt]
und and [ænd]
unerlässlich vital ['vaɪtl]
Unfall accident ['æksɪdnt]
unfreundlich unfriendly [ʌn'frendli]
ungefähr about [ə'baʊt]; around [ə'raʊnd]
ungeschickt clumsy ['klʌmzi]
ungesund unhealthy [ʌn'helθi]
unglücklich unhappy [ʌn'hæpi]
unheimlich scary ['skeəri]; spooky ['spu:ki]
Uniform uniform ['ju:nɪfɔ:m]
Union union ['ju:njən]
Universität university [,ju:nɪ'vɜ:səti]
unrechtmäßig illegal [ɪ'li:gl]
uns us [ʌs]
unser/unsere our ['aʊə]
Unsinn rubbish ['rʌbɪʃ]
unten at the bottom [ət ðə 'bɒtəm]; below [bɪ'ləʊ]; downstairs [,daʊn'steəz]
(nach) unten down [daʊn]
unterer Teil bottom ['bɒtəm]
unter under ['ʌndə]
Unterdrückung oppression [ə'preʃn]
untere/unterer/unteres lower ['ləʊə]
Unterführung tunnel ['tʌnl]
Untergeschoss basement ['beɪsmənt]
unterhalb below [bɪ'ləʊ]
sich **unterhalten** to chat [tʃæt]
Unterhaltung chat [tʃæt]
Unterricht class [klɑ:s]
unterrichten to teach [ti:tʃ]

Unterrichtsstunde lesson ['lesn]; period *(AE)* ['pɪəriəd]
Unterschied difference ['dɪfrnts]
unterschreiben to sign [saɪn]
unterstreichen to underline [ˌʌndə'laɪn]
unterstützen to support [sə'pɔ:t]
untersuchen to check [tʃek]
Untersuchung research [rɪ'sɜ:tʃ]
Untertitel caption ['kæpʃn]
Unterwasser- underwater [ˌʌndə'wɔ:tə]
Ureinwohner/Ureinwohnerin Amerikas Native American [ˌneɪtɪv‿ə'merɪkən]
Urlaub holiday(s) ['hɒlədeɪ(z)]; vacation *(AE)* [və'keɪʃn]
usw. etc. [ɪt'setrə]

V

Vater father ['fɑ:ðə]
Vati dad [dæd]
sich **verabreden** to date [deɪt]
Verabredung date [deɪt]
Verachtung disrespect [ˌdɪsrɪ'spekt]
verändern to change [tʃeɪndʒ]
verängstigt scared [skeəd]
Veranstalter/Veranstalterin organizer ['ɔ:gənaɪzə]
Veranstaltung event [ɪ'vent]; session ['seʃn]
verärgert angry ['æŋgri]
verbinden to join [dʒɔɪn]
Verbindung link [lɪŋk]
sich in Verbindung setzen mit to contact ['kɒntækt]
Verbrechen crime [kraɪm]
Verbrecher/Verbrecherin gangster ['gæŋkstə]
verbrennen to burn [bɜ:n]
verbringen to spend [spend]
Verdächtigter/Verdächtigte suspect ['sʌspekt]
verdammt damn [dæm]
verdeckt undercover [ˌʌndə'kʌvə]
Verein club [klʌb]
Vereinigung union ['ju:njən]
verfehlen to miss [mɪs]
Vergangenheit past [pɑ:st]
vergessen to forget [fə'get]
vergleichen to compare [kəm'peə]
verhaften to arrest [ə'rest]
verheiratet mit married to ['mærid tə]
sich **verirren** to get lost [get 'lɒst]
sich **verirrt haben** to be lost [bi: 'lɒst]
verkaufen to sell [sel]
Verkäufer/Verkäuferin shop assistant ['ʃɒp‿əˌsɪstnt]
Verkehr traffic ['træfɪk]
verlassen to leave [li:v]
verlegen embarrassed [ɪm'bærəst]
verleihen to present [prɪ'zent]
verletzen to hurt [hɜ:t]
verletzend hurtful ['hɜ:tfl]
verletzt hurt [hɜ:t]
Verletzung harm [hɑ:m]
verlieren to lose [lu:z]
verloren gehen to get lost [get 'lɒst]
vermissen to miss [mɪs]; to miss out (on) [mɪss‿'aʊt]
vermuten to guess [ges]
vernünftig intelligent [ɪn'telɪdʒnt]; sensible ['sensɪbl]
veröffentlichen to publish ['pʌblɪʃ]
verpassen to miss [mɪs]
verregnet rainy ['reɪni]
verrückt crazy ['kreɪzi]; mad [mæd]
verrückt machen to drive crazy [draɪv 'kreɪzi]
verrückt nach ... sein to be nuts about [bi: ˌnʌts‿ə'baʊt]
verrückt werden to go bananas [ˌgəʊ bə'nɑ:nəz]
Versammlung assembly [ə'sembli]; rally ['ræli]
verschieden different ['dɪfrnt]
verschlafen sleepy ['sli:pi]
Verschluss shutter ['ʃʌtə]
Verschlüsselung code [kəʊd]
Verschmutzung pollution [pə'lu:ʃn]
verschneit snowy ['snəʊi]
verschwenden to waste [weɪst]
verschwinden to disappear [ˌdɪsə'pɪə]
verspätet delayed [dɪ'leɪd]; late [leɪt]
versprechen to promise ['prɒmɪs]
Verstand mind [maɪnd]
verstecken to hide [haɪd]
sich verstecken to hide [haɪd]
verstehen to understand [ˌʌndə'stænd]
Versuch experiment [ɪk'sperɪmənt]
versuchen to try [traɪ]
es versuchen to give it a go [ˌgɪv‿ɪt‿ə 'gəʊ]
vertrauen to trust [trʌst]
Vertrauen trust [trʌst]
Vertreter/Vertreterin agent ['eɪdʒnt]
vervollständigen to complete [kəm'pli:t]
verwenden to use [ju:z]
verzeichnet on record [ɒn 'rekɔ:d]
verzögert delayed [dɪ'leɪd]
V-förmig V-shaped ['vi:ˌʃeɪpt]
Video video ['vɪdiəʊ]
viel a lot [ə 'lɒt]; much [mʌtʃ]
viele many ['meni]; loads of ['ləʊdz‿əv]
viel/viele a lot of [ə 'lɒt‿əv]; lots (of) ['lɒts‿əv]
Viel Glück! Good luck! [ˌgʊd 'lʌk]
vielleicht maybe ['meɪbi]; perhaps [pə'hæps]
Viertel neighborhood *(AE)* ['neɪbəhʊd]; quarter ['kwɔ:tə]
Viertel nach quarter past ['kwɔ:tə pɑ:st]
Viertel vor quarter to ['kwɔ:tə tə]
Vierteldollar *(Währung)* quarter ['kwɔ:tə]
violett purple ['pɜ:pl]
virtuell virtual ['vɜ:tʃuəl]
Visum *(pl. Visa)* visa, visas *(pl)* ['vi:zə]
Vogel bird [bɜ:d]
Volksmusik folk [fəʊk]
Volksstamm tribe [traɪb]
voll (von) full (of) [fʊl]
Volleyball volleyball ['vɒlibɔ:l]
völlig absolutely [ˌæbsə'lu:tli]
von by [baɪ]; from [frɒm]; of [ɒv; əv]
vor before [bɪ'fɔ:]; in front of [ɪn 'frʌnt‿əv]
vor *(zeitlich)* ago [ə'gəʊ]
vorbei over ['əʊvə]
vorbeigehen an to pass [pɑ:s]
sich **vorbereiten** to get ready [get 'redi]
Vordergrund foreground ['fɔ:graʊnd]
Vorderseite front [frʌnt]
Vorführung exhibition [ˌeksɪ'bɪʃn]
Vorhang curtain ['kɜ:tn]
Vorhersage *(Wetter)* forecast ['fɔ:kɑ:st]
vorhersagen *(Wetter)* to forecast ['fɔ:kɑ:st]
Vormittag morning ['mɔ:nɪŋ]
vormittags *(Uhrzeit)* a.m. [ˌeɪ'em]
vormittags in the morning [ˌɪn ðə 'mɔ:nɪŋ]
vorne at the front [ət ðə 'frʌnt]
nach vorne forward ['fɔ:wəd]
Vorort suburb ['sʌbɜ:b]
Vorschlag suggestion [sə'dʒestʃn]
vorschlagen to suggest [sə'dʒest]
Vorschrift rule [ru:l]
vorsichtig careful ['keəfl]
Vorsingen audition [ɔ:'dɪʃn]
Vorspeise starter ['stɑ:tə]
Vorsprechen audition [ɔ:'dɪʃn]
sich (etwas) **vorstellen** to imagine [ɪ'mædʒɪn]
Vorstellung performance [pə'fɔ:məns]

Vortanzen audition [ɔ:'dɪʃn]
Vor- und Nachteile pros and cons [ˌprəʊz‿ənd 'kɒnz]
Vortrag talk [tɔ:k]
vorüber over ['əʊvə]
vorwärts forward ['fɔ:wəd]

W

Wache guard [gɑ:d]
wachsen to rise [raɪz]
Wächter/Wächterin guard [gɑ:d]
wagen to dare [deə]
etwas wagen to take your chance [ˌteɪk jɔ: 'tʃɑ:ns]
Wahl choice [tʃɔɪs]
wählen to choose [tʃu:z]; to vote (for) [vəʊt]
wahr true [tru:]
wahr werden to come true [kʌm 'tru:]
während *(+ Nomen)* during *(+ noun)* ['djʊərɪŋ]
während while [waɪl]
wahrscheinlich probably ['prɒbəbli]
Wahrzeichen landmark ['lændmɑ:k]
Wald forest ['fɒrɪst]; wood [wʊd]
Waliser/Waliserin Welsh [welʃ]
walisisch Welsh [welʃ]
Wand wall [wɔ:l]
Wandtafel board [bɔ:d]
wann when [wen]
Wanze bug [bʌg]
Waren goods *(pl)* [gʊdz]
Warenautomat vending machine ['vendɪŋ məˌʃi:n]
warm warm [wɔ:m]
Warn- warning ['wɔ:nɪŋ]
Warnung warning ['wɔ:nɪŋ]
warten to wait [weɪt]
warten auf to wait for ['weɪt fɔ:]
Warte mal! Hang on! ['hæŋ‿ɒn]
Wärter/Wärterin zookeeper ['zu:ˌki:pə]
Warteschlange queue [kju:]
warum why [waɪ]
was what [wɒt]
Was ist los? What's up? [ˌwɒts‿'ʌp]
Was ist mit …? What about … ? [wɒt‿ə'baʊt]
Was steht da? What does it say? [ˌwɒt dʌz‿ɪt 'seɪ]
Waschbecken *(im Amerikanischen)* sink [sɪŋk]
waschen to wash [wɒʃ]
sich waschen to wash [wɒʃ]
Wäschetrockner tumble drier ['tʌmbl ˌdraɪə]
Waschmaschine washing machine ['wɒʃɪŋ məˌʃi:n]
Wasser water ['wɔ:tə]
Wasserhahn faucet *(AE)* ['fɔ:sɪt]
Website website ['websaɪt]
Wechselgeld change [tʃeɪndʒ]
wechseln to change [tʃeɪndʒ]
wecken to wake [weɪk]
Wecker alarm clock [ə'lɑ:m ˌklɒk]
weg away [ə'weɪ]
Weg path [pɑ:θ]; way [weɪ]
sich auf den Weg machen to set off [set‿'ɒf]
Er ist auf dem Weg zu …. He is on his way to …. [ˌhi:‿ɪz‿ɒn hɪz 'weɪ tə]
wegbleiben to stay out [steɪ‿'aʊt]
wegbringen to take off [teɪk‿'ɒf]
weggehen to leave [li:v]
wegnehmen to take [teɪk]
wegräumen von to get off [get‿'ɒf]
wegrennen to run away [rʌn‿ə'weɪ]
weh tun to hurt [hɜ:t]
wehen to fly [flaɪ]
weich soft [sɒft]
weil because [bɪ'kɒz]
weinen to cry [kraɪ]
Weise way [weɪ]
weit far [fɑ:]
weiter farther ['fɑ:ðə]
immer weiter farther and farther ['fɑ:ðə]
es weit bringen to go far [gəʊ 'fɑ:]
weit kommen to go far [gəʊ 'fɑ:]
weiter- to … on [ɒn]
weitergeben to pass [pɑ:s]
weitermachen to go on [gəʊ‿'ɒn]
Weitsprung long jump ['lɒŋ ˌdʒʌmp]
welche/welcher/welches what [wɒt]; which [wɪtʃ]
Welle wave [weɪv]
Wellenreiten surfing ['sɜ:fɪŋ]
Welt world [wɜ:ld]
Weltall outer space [ˌaʊtə 'speɪs]
Weltraum outer space [ˌaʊtə 'speɪs]; space [speɪs]
Weltraumstation space station ['speɪs ˌsteɪʃn]
wem who [hu:]; whom [hu:m]
wen who [hu:]; whom [hu:m]
wenig little ['lɪtl]
wenige few [fju:]
weniger less [les]
wenigstens at least [ət 'li:st]
wenn if [ɪf]; when [wen]
wer who [hu:]
Werbespot advert ['ædvɜ:t]
werden to become [bɪ'kʌm]; to get [get]
werden/werden nicht *(futurisch)* will ('ll), won't [wɪl; wəʊnt]
werfen to throw [θrəʊ]
Werfer/Werferin pitcher ['pɪtʃə]
Werk factory ['fæktri]
Werkstatt workshop ['wɜ:kʃɒp]
wertvoll valuable ['væljuəbl]
wessen whose [hu:z]
Westen west [west]
Western western ['westən]
Wettbewerb competition [ˌkɒmpə'tɪʃn]
wetten to bet [bet]
Wetter weather ['weðə]
Wettkampf match [mætʃ]
Wettlauf race [reɪs]
einen Wettlauf machen to run a race [ˌrʌn‿ə 'reɪs]
wichtig important [ɪm'pɔ:tnt]
widerhallen to echo ['ekəʊ]
wie *(Vergleich)* like [laɪk]
wie as [æz; əz]; such as ['sʌtʃ‿æz]
wie how [haʊ]
Wie alt bist du? How old are you? [haʊ‿'əʊld‿ɑ: ju:]
Wie geht es dir/Ihnen/euch? How are you? [ˌhaʊ‿'ɑ: ju:]
Wie heißt du? What's your name? [ˌwɒts jə 'neɪm]
Wie spät ist es, bitte? What's the time, please? [ˌwɒts ðə 'taɪm ˌpli:z]
wie viele how many [haʊ 'meni]
Wie viel kosten … ? How much are … ? [ˌhaʊ 'mʌtʃ‿ɑ:]
Wie viel kostet … ? How much is … ? [ˌhaʊ 'mʌtʃ‿ɪz]
Wie viel Uhr ist es, bitte? What's the time, please? [ˌwɒts ðə 'taɪm ˌpli:z]
Wie wäre es mit …? What about … ? [wɒt‿ə'baʊt]
wieder again [ə'gen]
wieder erleben to relive [ˌri:'lɪv]
wiederherstellen to rebuild [ˌri:'bɪld]
auf **Wiedersehen** goodbye [gʊd'baɪ]
wild wild [waɪld]
Wildwasser whitewater ['waɪtwɔ:tə]
willkommen heißen to welcome ['welkəm]
Willkommen in … Welcome to … ['welkəm tə]
Wind wind [wɪnd]
windig windy ['wɪndi]

windsurfen to surf [sɜ:f]; to windsurf ['wɪndsɜ:f]
winken to wave [weɪv]
Winter winter ['wɪntə]
winzig tiny ['taɪni]
wir we [wi:]
Wirbel fuss [fʌs]
wirklich real [rɪəl]; really ['rɪəli]
Wirklichkeit reality [ri'æləti]
wissen to know [nəʊ]
Wissenschaft Science ['saɪəns]
Wissenschaftler/Wissenschaftlerin scientist ['saɪəntɪst]
wissenschaftlich scientific [ˌsaɪən'tɪfɪk]
Witz joke [dʒəʊk]
Witze machen to joke [dʒəʊk]
Du machst Witze. You're kidding. [ˌjə 'kɪdɪŋ]
wo where [weə]
Woche week [wi:k]
in der Woche a week [ə 'wi:k]
pro Woche a week [ə 'wi:k]
Wochenende weekend [ˌwi:k'end]
wohin where [weə]
Wohltätigkeit charity ['tʃærɪti]
Wohltätigkeitsverein charity ['tʃærɪti]
wohnen to live [lɪv]
wohnen bei to stay with ['steɪ wɪð]
Wohnung apartment *(AE)* [ə'pɑ:tmənt]; flat [flæt]
Wohnzimmer living room ['lɪvɪŋ rʊm]
Wolf wolf, wolves *(pl)* [wʊlf; wʊlvz]
Wolke cloud [klaʊd]
Wolkenkratzer skyscraper ['skaɪˌskreɪpə]
wolkig cloudy ['klaʊdi]
Wolldecke blanket ['blæŋkɪt]
wollen to want (to) ['wɒnt tə]
Workshop workshop ['wɜ:kʃɒp]
Wort word [wɜ:d]
Wrack wreck [rek]
wunderschön beautiful ['bju:tɪfl]
Wunsch wish [wɪʃ]
wünschen to wish [wɪʃ]
würde/würden would [wʊd]
Wurf throw [θrəʊ]
Wurst sausage ['sɒsɪdʒ]
Würstchen sausage ['sɒsɪdʒ]
würzig spicy ['spaɪsi]
wütend furious ['fjʊəriəs]; mad [mæd]

Z

zäh tough [tʌf]
Zahl number ['nʌmbə]
zahlen to pay [peɪ]
Zahn tooth, teeth *(pl)* [tu:θ; ti:θ]
Zahnarzt/Zahnärztin dentist ['dentɪst]
Zahnschmerzen toothache ['tu:θeɪk]
Zauberer wizard ['wɪzəd]
Zeh toe [təʊ]
Zehncentstück *(Währung)* dime [daɪm]
Zeichen sign [saɪn]; signal ['sɪgnl]; symbol ['sɪmbl]
ein Zeichen geben to signal ['sɪgnl]
Zeichentrickfilm cartoon [kɑ:'tu:n]
zeichnen to design [dɪ'zaɪn]; to draw [drɔ:]
zeigen to show [ʃəʊ]
zeigen (auf) to point (to) [pɔɪnt]
Zeile line [laɪn]
Zeit time [taɪm]
Du liebe Zeit! Good grief! [gʊd 'gri:f]
Zeitabschnitt period *(AE)* ['pɪəriəd]
Zeitalter age [eɪdʒ]
Zeitschrift magazine [mægə'zi:n]
Zeitschriftenhändler/ Zeitschriftenhändlerin newsagent ['nju:sˌeɪdʒənt]
Zeitung newspaper ['nju:sˌpeɪpə]; paper ['peɪpə]
Zelt tent [tent]
Zelten camping ['kæmpɪŋ]
Zentimeter centimetre ['sentɪˌmi:tə]
Zentrum centre ['sentə]; hub [hʌb]
zerbrechen to break [breɪk]
zerbrochen broken ['brəʊkn]
Zeremonie ceremony ['serɪməni]
zerstören to destroy [dɪ'strɔɪ]
Zeug stuff [stʌf]
Zeugnis report [rɪ'pɔ:t]
ziehen to pull [pʊl]
Ziehen tug [tʌg]
Ziel goal [gəʊl]
ziemlich pretty ['prɪti]; quite [kwaɪt]
Zimmer room [ru:m; rʊm]
zirka around [ə'raʊnd]
zittern to shake [ʃeɪk]
Zoll customs *(pl)* ['kʌstəmz]
Zoll *(Längenmaß: 2,54 cm)* inch [ɪnʃ]
Zone zone [zəʊn]
Zoo zoo [zu:]
zu closed [kləʊzd]
zu to [tʊ; tə]
zuallererst first of all [ˌfɜ:st‿ɒf‿'ɔ:l]
zuerst at first [ət 'fɜ:st]; first [fɜ:st]; first of all [ˌfɜ:st‿ɒf‿'ɔ:l]
zuflüstern to whisper ['wɪspə]
zufrieden sein mit to be pleased with [bi: 'pli:zd wɪð]
Zug train [treɪn]
Zugang access ['ækses]
zugehen auf to walk up to [wɔ:k‿'ʌp tə]
Zuhause home [həʊm]
zuhören to listen ['lɪsn]
zumachen to close [kləʊz]
zunächst at first [ət 'fɜ:st]; first of all [ˌfɜ:st‿ɒf‿'ɔ:l]
zunehmen to rise [raɪz]
Zunge tongue [tʌŋ]
zuordnen to match [mætʃ]
Zupfen tug [tʌg]
zurück back [bæk]
zurückdenken to reminisce [ˌremɪ'nɪs]
zurückgehen to turn back [tɜ:n 'bæk]
zurückkommen (zu/nach) to get back (to) [get 'bæk tə]
sich **zurücklehnen** to sit back [ˌsɪt 'bæk]
zusammen together [tə'geðə]
Zusammenbruch breakdown ['breɪkdaʊn]
zusammenfügen to match [mætʃ]
Zusammenhang context ['kɒntekst]
Zusatz extra ['ekstrə]
zusätzlich extra ['ekstrə]
Zuschauer/Zuschauerin viewer ['vju:ə]
Zustand state [steɪt]
zustimmen to agree [ə'gri:]
zuzüglich plus [plʌs]
zweimal twice [twaɪs]
zweitens secondly ['sekndli]
zwingend compulsory [kəm'pʌlsri]
Zwirn thread [θred]
zwischen between [bɪ'twi:n]

In the classroom

What you can say ...

... when you arrive and leave:

Good morning, Mrs/Mr	Guten Morgen, Frau/Herr ... .
I'm sorry, I'm late.	Tut mir Leid, dass ich mich verspätet habe.
I'm sorry, I've forgotten my exercise book.	Tut mir Leid, ich habe mein Heft vergessen.
What's for homework, please?	Was haben wir als Hausaufgabe auf?
Goodbye./Bye.	Auf Wiedersehen./Tschüs.

... if you want to be polite:

I'm sorry (to bother you), but could I please borrow your mobile/... ?	Entschuldige, (dass ich dich störe,) aber kann ich bitte dein Handy/... ausleihen?
I'm sorry about my homework/... .	Es tut mir Leid wegen meiner Hausaufgaben/... .
I'm sorry (that) I'm late.	Entschuldigung, dass ich zu/so spät komme.
Oh, I'm sorry!	Oh, Entschuldigung/Verzeihung!
That's OK./ No problem.	Macht nichts./Nichts passiert.
Wait, I'll help you.	Warte mal! Ich helfe dir.
Thanks./Thank you (very much).	Danke! Vielen Dank!

... if there is a problem:

How are you?	Wie geht es dir?
Are you feeling sick?	Ist dir schlecht?
I'm fine, thank you.	Gut, danke.
I'm not feeling well.	Ich fühle mich nicht gut.
Can I open the window, please?	Darf ich bitte das Fenster öffnen?
Can I go to the toilet, please?	Darf ich bitte auf die Toilette gehen?

... if you want to ask for help:

Can you help me, please?	Können Sie mir bitte helfen?
I don't understand this.	Ich verstehe das nicht.
What's that in English/German?	Was heißt das auf Englisch/Deutsch?
Can I say: ...?/What does ... mean?	Kann ich sagen: ...?/Was bedeutet ...?
How do you do this exercise?	Wie macht man diese Übung?
Is this right? I'm not sure.	Ist das richtig? Ich bin nicht sicher.
Sorry, I don't know.	Tut mir Leid, das weiß ich nicht.
Can you write it on the board, please?	Können Sie das bitte an die Tafel schreiben?
Can I ask a question, please?	Kann ich bitte eine Frage stellen?
Pardon? Can you repeat the question/sentence, please?	Wie bitte? Können Sie die Frage/den Satz bitte wiederholen?
Can you play the CD again, please?	Können Sie die CD bitte nochmal abspielen?
Can we do another example, please?	Können wir noch ein Beispiel machen?

... if you have a discussion:

What do you think?	Was meinst du?
In my opinion	Meiner Meinung nach ... .
I think you are right/wrong.	Ich denke, du hast recht/Unrecht.
On the one hand ... , on the other hand	Einerseits ... , andererseits ... .

... if you give a talk:

Today I'd like to talk about	Heute möchte ich über ... reden.
Here you can see	Hier seht ihr ... .
On the left/right	Auf der linken/rechten Seite ... .
I hope you liked the talk.	Ich hoffe, euch hat mein Vortrag gefallen.
Are there any questions?	Habt ihr Fragen dazu?

... if you work together:

Can I work with ... ?	Kann ich mit ... zusammenarbeiten?
Can I have your ... ?	Kann ich mal dein/e/n ... haben?
Whose turn is it?	Wer ist dran?
What are we going to do first?	Was machen wir als Erstes?
Let's write ... on our poster.	Schreiben wir ... auf unser Poster.
Let's put this picture here.	Setzen/Kleben wir das Bild hier hin.
You can be ... and I'll be	Du kannst ... spielen und ich werde ... spielen.
Let's act the story/play a game.	Lasst uns die Geschichte/ein Spiel spielen.
I don't understand what you mean.	Ich verstehe nicht, was du meinst.
Can you repeat that, please?	Könntest du das bitte wiederholen?
I think we should ... first.	Ich denke, wir sollten zuerst ... .
What did you find on the Internet?	Was hast du im Internet gefunden?
I really like your idea.	Mir gefällt deine Idee sehr gut.
What do you suggest?	Was schlägst du vor?
Where shall we start?	Wo sollen wir anfangen?
I think we need	Ich denke, wir brauchen ... .

... if you want to talk about stories/poems/songs:

I like/don't like this story/poem/song/game.	Diese Geschichte/Dieses Gedicht/Lied/Spiel gefällt m gefällt mir nicht.
I think it's good/interesting/brilliant/funny/really exciting.	Ich finde sie/es gut/interessant/toll/ witzig/wirklich spannend.
I think it's sad/boring/terrible.	Ich finde sie/es traurig/langweilig/schrecklich.
It was OK but I've read better ones.	Sie/Es ist ganz nett, aber ich habe schon bessere gele
I don't think this is right/wrong.	Ich glaube nicht, dass dies richtig/falsch ist.

What the teacher says to you

Questions

Excuse me. Could you ... ?	Entschuldigung, könntest du ... ?
Could you help me, please?	Könntest du mir bitte helfen?
What's the problem?	Was ist das Problem?/Was ist los?
What's happening in the picture?	Was passiert (gerade) im Bild?
What do you know about poetry slams/... ?	Was wisst ihr über 'poetry slams'/... ?
What do you think of ... ?	Was haltet ihr von ... ?
Have you got any other ideas?	Habt ihr andere/sonstige Ideen?
Can you find the mistakes?	Könnt ihr die Fehler entdecken?
What does ... mean?	Was bedeutet ... ?

Instructions

Be careful with the word order/... .	Achtet auf die Satzstellung/... .
Make a grid (like this).	Macht eine Tabelle (wie diese).
Match the questions/pictures with the answers/ sentences.	Ordnet den Fragen/Bildern die Antworten/Sätze zu.
Read the definitions.	Lest die Definitionen.
Define these jobs/... .	Erklärt diese Berufe/... .
Discuss with a partner.	Diskutiert mit einem Partner/einer Partnerin.
Give three reasons.	Nenne drei Gründe.
Find the places on the map.	Sucht die Orte auf der Karte.
Close your books, please.	Macht eure Bücher zu.
Don't forget to check your spelling.	Vergesst nicht, die Rechtschreibung zu prüfen.
Give your talk to the class.	Halte dein Referat vor der Klasse.
Present your poster/DVD to the class.	Präsentiere dein Poster/deine DVD vor der Klasse.

List of irregular verbs

to **be** [bi:]	**was/were** [wɒz/wɜ:]	**been** [bi:n]	sein
to **beat** [bi:t]	**beat** [bi:t]	**beaten** [bi:tn]	besiegen, schlagen
to **become** [bɪ'kʌm]	**became** [bɪ'keɪm]	**become** [bɪ'kʌm]	werden
to **begin** [bɪ'gɪn]	**began** [bɪ'gæn]	**begun** [bɪ'gʌn]	beginnen, anfangen
to **bet** [bet]	**bet** [bet]	**bet** [bet]	wetten
to **build** [bɪld]	**built** [bɪlt]	**built** [bɪlt]	bauen
to **blow** [bləʊ]	**blew** [blu:]	**blown** [bləʊn]	blasen
to **break** [breɪk]	**broke** [brəʊk]	**broken** ['brəʊkn]	(zer)brechen; kaputtmachen
to **bring** [brɪŋ]	**brought** [brɔ:t]	**brought** [brɔ:t]	bringen, mitbringen
to **burn** [bɜ:n]	**burnt** [bɜ:nt]	**burnt** [bɜ:nt]	(ver)brennen
to **buy** [baɪ]	**bought** [bɔ:t]	**bought** [bɔ:t]	kaufen
to **catch** [kætʃ]	**caught** [kɔ:t]	**caught** [kɔ:t]	fangen
to **choose** [tʃu:z]	**chose** [tʃəʊz]	**chosen** ['tʃəʊzn]	wählen, auswählen
to **come** [kʌm]	**came** [keɪm]	**come** [kʌm]	kommen
to **cut** [kʌt]	**cut** [kʌt]	**cut** [kʌt]	schneiden
to **dig up** [dɪg‿'ʌp]	**dug up** [dʌg‿'ʌp]	**dug up** [dʌg‿'ʌp]	ausgraben
to **do** [du:]	**did** [dɪd]	**done** [dʌn]	machen, tun
to **draw** [drɔ:]	**drew** [dru:]	**drawn** [drɔ:n]	zeichnen
to **drink** [drɪŋk]	**drank** [dræŋk]	**drunk** [drʌŋk]	trinken
to **drive** [draɪv]	**drove** [drəʊv]	**driven** ['drɪvn]	fahren
to **eat** [i:t]	**ate** [et/eɪt]	**eaten** ['i:tn]	essen, fressen
to **fall** [fɔ:l]	**fell** [fel]	**fallen** ['fɔ:ln]	fallen, herunterfallen, hinfallen
to **feed** [fi:d]	**fed** [fed]	**fed** [fed]	füttern
to **feel** [fi:l]	**felt** [felt]	**felt** [felt]	fühlen, sich fühlen
to **fight** [faɪt]	**fought** [fɔ:t]	**fought** [fɔ:t]	kämpfen
to **find** [faɪnd]	**found** [faʊnd]	**found** [faʊnd]	finden
to **fly** [flaɪ]	**flew** [flu:]	**flown** [fləʊn]	fliegen
to **forecast** ['fɔ:kɑ:st]	**forecast** ['fɔ:kɑ:st]	**forecast** ['fɔ:kɑ:st]	vorhersagen *(Wetter)*
to **forget** [fə'get]	**forgot** [fə'gɒt]	**forgotten** [fə'gɒtn]	vergessen
to **get** [get]	**got** [gɒt]	**got** [gɒt]	kommen, bekommen; werden
to **give** [gɪv]	**gave** [geɪv]	**given** ['gɪvn]	geben, schenken
to **go** [gəʊ]	**went** [went]	**gone** [gɒn]	gehen
to **hang out** [hæŋ‿'aʊt]	**hung out** [hʌŋ‿'aʊt]	**hung out** [hʌŋ‿'aʊt]	sich herumtreiben
to **hear** [hɪə]	**heard** [hɜ:d]	**heard** [hɜ:d]	hören
to **hide** [haɪd]	**hid** [hɪd]	**hidden** ['hɪdn]	verstecken, sich verstecken
to **hit** [hɪt]	**hit** [hɪt]	**hit** [hɪt]	schlagen, treffen
to **hold** [həʊld]	**held** [held]	**held** [held]	halten
to **hurt** [hɜ:t]	**hurt** [hɜ:t]	**hurt** [hɜ:t]	verletzen, weh tun
to **keep** [ki:p]	**kept** [kept]	**kept** [kept]	(be)halten
to **know** [nəʊ]	**knew** [nju:]	**known** [nəʊn]	wissen, kennen
to **lay** [leɪ]	**laid** [leɪd]	**lain** [leɪn]	legen
to **lead** [li:d]	**led** [led]	**led** [led]	führen
to **lean** [li:n]	**leant** [lent]	**leant** [lent]	(sich)lehnen
to **learn** [lɜ:n]	**learnt** [lɜ:nt]	**learnt** [lɜ:nt]	lernen
to **leave** [li:v]	**left** [left]	**left** [left]	lassen, verlassen, abfahren
to **lend** [lend]	**lent** [lent]	**lent** [lent]	leihen

to **let** [let]	**let** [let]	**let** [let]	lassen
to **lie** [laɪ]	**lay** [leɪ]	**lain** [leɪn]	liegen
to **lose** [lu:z]	**lost** [lɒst]	**lost** [lɒst]	verlieren
to **mean** [mi:n]	**meant** [ment]	**meant** [ment]	bedeuten, meinen
to **meet** [mi:t]	**met** [met]	**met** [met]	treffen, sich treffen
to **overdo** [ˌəʊvə'du:]	**overdid** [ˌəʊvə'dɪd]	**overdone** [ˌəʊvə'dʌn]	übertreiben
to **pay** [peɪ]	**paid** [peɪd]	**paid** [peɪd]	(be)zahlen
to **put** [pʊt]	**put** [pʊt]	**put** [pʊt]	setzen, stellen, legen
to **read** [ri:d]	**read** [red]	**read** [red]	lesen
to **rebuild** [ˌri:'bɪld]	**rebuilt** [ˌri:'bɪlt]	**rebuilt** [ˌri:'bɪlt]	wieder aufbauen, wiederherstellen
to **ride** [raɪd]	**rode** [rəʊd]	**ridden** ['rɪdn]	fahren, reiten
to **ring** [rɪŋ]	**rang** [ræŋ]	**rung** [rʌŋ]	klingeln; anrufen
to **rise** [raɪz]	**rose** [rəʊz]	**risen** ['rɪzn]	steigen, wachsen, zunehmen
to **run** [rʌn]	**ran** [ræn]	**run** [rʌn]	rennen, laufen
to **say** [seɪ]	**said** [sed]	**said** [sed]	sagen, sprechen
to **see** [si:]	**saw** [sɔ:]	**seen** [si:n]	sehen; besuchen
to **sell** [sel]	**sold** [səʊld]	**sold** [səʊld]	verkaufen
to **send** [send]	**sent** [sent]	**sent** [sent]	schicken
to **set** [set]	**set** [set]	**set** [set]	stellen, einstellen
to **shake** [ʃeɪk]	**shook** [ʃʊk]	**shaken** ['ʃeɪkn]	schütteln, zittern
to **show** [ʃəʊ]	**showed** [ʃəʊd]	**shown** [ʃəʊn]	zeigen
to **sing** [sɪŋ]	**sang** [sæŋ]	**sung** [sʌŋ]	singen
to **sit** [sɪt]	**sat** [sæt]	**sat** [sæt]	sitzen
to **sleep** [sli:p]	**slept** [slept]	**slept** [slept]	schlafen
to **smell** [smel]	**smelt** [smelt]	**smelt** [smelt]	riechen
to **speak** [spi:k]	**spoke** [spəʊk]	**spoken** ['spəʊkn]	sprechen
to **spell** [spel]	**spelt** [spelt]	**spelt** [spelt]	buchstabieren
to **spend** [spend]	**spent** [spent]	**spent** [spent]	verbringen, ausgeben
to **stand** [stænd]	**stood** [stʊd]	**stood** [stʊd]	stehen
to **steal** [sti:l]	**stole** [stəʊl]	**stolen** ['stəʊln]	stehlen
to **stick** [stɪk]	**stuck** [stʌk]	**stuck** [stʌk]	kleben, stecken
to **swim** [swɪm]	**swam** [swæm]	**swum** [swʌm]	schwimmen
to **take** [teɪk]	**took** [tʊk]	**taken** ['teɪkn]	nehmen, mitnehmen, bringen
to **teach** [ti:tʃ]	**taught** [tɔ:t]	**taught** [tɔ:t]	lehren
to **tell** [tel]	**told** [təʊld]	**told** [təʊld]	erzählen, sagen
to **think** [θɪŋk]	**thought** [θɔ:t]	**thought** [θɔ:t]	denken, glauben
to **throw** [θrəʊ]	**threw** [θru:]	**thrown** [θrəʊn]	werfen
to **understand** [ˌʌndə'stænd]	**understood** [ˌʌndə'stʊd]	**understood** [ˌʌndə'stʊd]	verstehen
to **unwind** [ʌn'waɪnd]	**unwound** [ʌn'waʊnd]	**unwound** [ʌn'waʊnd]	sich abwickeln
to **upset** [ʌp'set]	**upset** [ʌp'set]	**upset** [ʌp'set]	erschrecken, durcheinander bringen, umstoßen
to **wake** [weɪk]	**woke** [wəʊk]	**woken** ['wəʊkn]	(auf)wecken
to **wear** [weə]	**wore** [wɔ:]	**worn** [wɔ:n]	anhaben, tragen
to **win** [wɪn]	**won** [wɒn]	**won** [wɒn]	gewinnen, siegen
to **write** [raɪt]	**wrote** [rəʊt]	**written** ['rɪtn]	schreiben

Lösungen/Lösungsvorschläge Check-out

Unit 1 – Seite 20–21

1 A day in NYC

a) 1. They ate at a deli.
2. They climbed to the top of the ESB.
3. They didn't walk through Central Park.
4. They didn't ride on a kickboard.
5. They took lots of photos.
6. They didn't buy (any) souvenirs.
7. They visited Chinatown.
8. They didn't write (any) postcards.
9. They went to Ellis Island.
10. They didn't fly in a helicopter.

2 Yesterday in Central Park

a)	b)
2. A horse played football with some kids.	F Before that the horse had escaped.
3. A woman lay down on a sofa.	D Before that she had found the sofa.
4. Two boys picked up some rubbish.	C Before that they had thrown it everywhere.
5. The trees lost all their leaves.	A Before that a helicopter had landed.
6. A man ate a meal.	B Before that he had felt hungry.

3 Mixed bag: The history of Central Park

came/had lived; had been/started; wanted; could; had argued/decided; had drawn/talked/lived/had chosen; had left/destroyed/started; changed; worked; was; started; took

4 Cloze text: Day one in NYC!

1. in	2. they	3. huge	4. expected
5. crowds	6. hot	7. shower	8. had rested
9. where	10. Building	11. had walked	12. hotel
13. ate	14. missed	15. started	16. loved

Unit 2 – Seite 36–37

1 On Make a Difference Day

a) **Sharleen** has already bought (the) paper. And she has already made the cards. She has also drawn the pictures. She hasn't written the text or made the envelopes yet.
Cal and Alysha have already collected (the) old books. They've already repaired the covers and they have washed some/the old plates. But they haven't written (the) prices on them yet. And they haven't fixed the broken toys yet.
Miles has already bought (the) paint and he has borrowed a ladder. But he hasn't cleaned the windows. He hasn't painted the wood yet. And he hasn't taken the ladder back yet.

b) **Sharleen** sold different cards. **Cal and Alysha** sold old things. **Miles** painted windows.

2 Things they should do

a) 2. Terri hasn't changed her T-shirt yet.
3. Paula-Jo and Tammy haven't put their boots on yet.
4. Sue hasn't finished her lunch/food yet.
5. Brad and Larry haven't picked up the rubbish yet.
6. Stu hasn't done his homework yet.

b) 1. I should organize my birthday party, but I haven't organized it yet.
2. I should learn my English vocabulary, but I haven't learnt it yet.
3. I should clean my room, but I haven't cleaned it yet.

3 Different school rules

a) should; should; may; must not (mustn't); may; must not (mustn't); must not (mustn't); should; should

b) I **may** wear my own clothes but I **mustn't** wear T-shirts with adverts on them for things like drugs of alcohol. I **may** also wear jewellery to school but I **mustn't** smoke in the school or on my way there. I **mustn't** wear jeans to the homecoming dance because dress is formal. So I **should** take a long dress with me.

4 Cloze text: A great start to the year

1. started	2. homecoming	3. success	4. thank
5. helped	6. football	7. before	8. cheerleader
9. chose	10. organized	11. Difference	12. prize
13. Grade	14. competition	15. students	16. Wizard
17. agree	18. help	19. address	

Unit 3 – Seite 54–55

1 Short forms

a) 2. is written 3. are called 4. are shown 5. are used
6. is discovered 7. are launched 8. is forecast

b) 1. In our family supper **is usually eaten** at 6 p.m.
2. In the US pop songs **are often sung** in English.
3. Lots of CDs **are recorded** in LA.

2 Every year

a) 2. isn't reported 3. aren't noticed 4. isn't drawn
5. aren't given 6. aren't sent 7. aren't told
8. aren't killed 9. aren't destroyed 10. aren't damaged

b) 2. the national weather stations 3. experts 4. phone
5. the TV stations 6. teachers 7. police
8. trees which fall on their cars 9. flash floods 10. the strong winds

3 Your own robot

is done; aren't washed/are washed; aren't put/are dried; aren't done/are organized; are put away; are cleaned; is fixed; isn't switched on/is done; are done; are done

4 Things that are done

a) 2. Experiments are planned by scientists.
3. The scientific equipment is checked by assistants.
4. VR activities are practised by astronauts.
5. Special clothes are designed by high-tech companies.
6. Meals are made by cooks.
7. TV screens are watched by guards.
8. The weather is forecast by weathermen.

b) 2. Experiments aren't planned by scientists.
3. The scientific equipment isn't checked by assistants.
4. VR activities aren't practised by astronauts.
5. Special clothes aren't designed by high-tech companies.
6. Meals aren't made by cooks.
7. TV screens aren't watched by guards.
8. The weather isn't forecast by weathermen.

c) Cars are repaired by mechanics with the help of computers. Planes are flown by pilots with the help of high-tech equipment. Luggage is checked by customs officers with the help of special screens.

5 Cloze text: The new boy

a)

1. immigrated	2. an alien	3. English	4. ones
5. a lot of	6. hundreds	7. intelligent	8. Science
9. experiments	10. space	11. scientists	12. kids

b) American English, clothes, much, lots, smart, Technology, tests, science, experts, students

Unit 4 – Seite 72–73

1 Family promises and warnings

a) 2. If you drive me to the station, I'll cook dinner.
3. If you wash my sports clothes, I'll do the shopping.
4. If you lend me the digital camera, I'll clean the windows.
5. If you buy (me) a new computer, I'll make a family website.

b) 2. If you don't clean your room, we won't drive you to the station.
3. If you don't help us in the garden, we won't wash your sports clothes.
4. If you don't take those bottles back to the shop, we won't lend you the digital camera.
5. If you don't do better in your next test, we won't buy (you) a new computer.

2 Warnings

1. If you try to carry too much wood, you'll drop it.
2. What will happen if we walk over the bridge? – If you walk over the bridge, you'll fall in the river.
3. … if we eat lots of chocolates? – If you eat lots of chocolates, you'll be sick.
4. … if we put wet wood on the fire? – If you put wet wood on the fire, it'll go out.

5. … if we go into the forest alone? – If you go into the forest alone, you'll get lost.
6. … if we walk over here/on the flowers? – If you walk over there/on the flowers, you'll damage them.

3 Vacations

1. If it rained on vacation, I'd visit a museum.
2. If I lost my cell phone, I'd buy another one.
3. If someone stole my bags, I'd tell the police.
4. If I got lost, I'd use my map/ask someone for help.
5. If I felt bored, I'd visit a friend/go swimming/go to the cinema.
6. If I missed my flight home, I'd have a longer holiday!

4 Imagine

a)
1. If a trucker saw something strange in the sky, I think he would call the police and follow it.
2. If an astronaut met an alien, I think he or she would wait and talk to it.
3. If a farmer found a box of money, I think he would pick it up and tell the police.
4. If a tourist saw a bear, I think he would turn round and run away.
5. If a driver found a turkey, I think he would stop and put it on the side of the road.
6. If they/people saw a star, I think they'd would look at her and take (lots of) photos.

b)
1. If I saw something strange in the sky, I'd take some photos.
2. If I met an alien, I'd say hello to it.
3. If I found a box of money, I'd take it home.
4. If I saw a bear, I'd be very scared.
5. If I found a turkey, I'd throw it away.
6. If I saw a star, I'd ask for a date.

5 Cloze text: Abby's friend

1. question	2. lived	3. city	4. would	5. bored	6. far
7. miles	8. was	9. cabin	10. would	11. are	12. I'll
13. smart	14. country				

Unit 5 – Seite 88–89

1 What happened when?

1. … wasn't produced in 1911. It was produced in 1877.
2. The first movie wasn't seen in New York in 1877. It was seen in 1894.
3. The first western movie wasn't made in 1927. It was made in 1903.
4. The first film studio wasn't built in 1894 in Hollywood. It was built in 1911.
5. The first talkie wasn't shown in 1903. It was shown in1927.

2 More 'firsts'

1. The first Westerns weren't seen in Europe. They were seen in the US.
2. The first telephone wasn't used in the 1970s. It was used in the 1870s.
3. The first television wasn't produced in Hollywood. It was produced in London.
4. The first space shuttle wasn't built in the 19th century. It was built in the 20th century.
5. The first book wasn't printed by Shakespeare. It was printed by Gutenberg.
6. The first Oscar wasn't given for videos. It was given for movies.
7. The first hip hop music wasn't made by pop groups. It was made by DJs.
8. The first car wasn't driven in New York. It was driven in Mannheim.
9. The first DVDs weren't sold in the 1890s. They were sold in the 1990s.

3 The history of break dancing

1. was invented	2. was played	3. were put	4. was started	5. weren't seen
6. wasn't called	7. were given	8. weren't performed	9. were used	10. was won

4 Cloze text: A dangerous job

1. didn't	2. police	3. dangerous	4. given
5. took	6. the	7. were	8. his
9. vacation	10. family	11. was	12. beach
13. playing	14. filming	15. threw	16. blown
17. hit	18. water	19. camera	20. rescued
21. more	22. policeman		

Lösungen/Lösungsvorschläge Try it out!

Try it out! 1 – Seite 22–23

A Reading

1 a. 2 Poland b. 1 an au-pair c. 1 in LA d. 2 a Green Card e. 2 in England

B Language

a. I immigrated to the US … .
b. No one could spell it.
c. It was my dream to go to America.
d. It took a few months to organize my visa.
e. He worked in the same office.

C Listening

a. She has a job/a home/a family/friends and she feels safe there.
b. Some immigrants have lost their job/are sick and have no money for a doctor.
c. They can't get good jobs. If the cops find them, they send them back to Mexico.

D Mediation and communication

You: What exactly is a Green Card?
You: Wenn man als Immigrant/in in die USA kommt und dort leben und arbeiten möchte, braucht man eine Green Card.
You: Why do people immigrate to the US?
You: Viele immigrieren, weil sie dort Arbeit suchen oder eine bessere Zukunft für ihre Kinder wollen.

E Writing

1

1972	– born in Poland
1999	– au-pair job in London
2000	– new computer job in London
6 months later	– job offered in LA
	– met Jaroslaw
	– married
	– went to LA alone
2004	– husband moved to LA, too

2 I was new in London and I felt alone. But I had a good job and could send money home. Then I met a really nice woman at work. Eva was from Poland, too! We married but she had a new job in LA. It took four years to get my visa so I could be with her there.

Try it out! 2 – Seite 40–41

A Listening

1 Part a) 1 Carly 2 Jason 3 Ramon 4 Marie

2 Part b) a. 3 from a company b. 1 in the company c. 3 deliver parts of bikes d. 3 five dollars an hour

3 Part c) a. true b. false c. true d. true e. true f. false g. false

4 All parts a. Ramon b. Ramon c. Ramon d. Jason e. Jason f. Carly g. Ramon h. Marie

B Speaking

1 You: We go home for lunch/meet friends/do our homework/play football (basketball, …).
You: Yes, I get some pocket money. I get about … euros a week/month. Yes, I have to help in the kitchen/clean my own room./I sometimes look after kids.
You: Yes, I can./No, I can't.
You: We can look after kids/deliver newspapers/wash cars/take the neighbour's dog for a walk/go shopping for people.

2 We wanted to play basketball together. But Ramon looked so tired. He's got a job in his uncle's bike company and he has to work hard there. He delivers parts or writes letters for his uncle. Sometimes he even cleans the workshop! And he only gets five dollars an hour! Marie gets more when she looks after kids! Ramon thinks his uncle wants to worry him so that he'll work harder at school and get good grades. He wants Ramon to have a better job one day.

C Writing

1

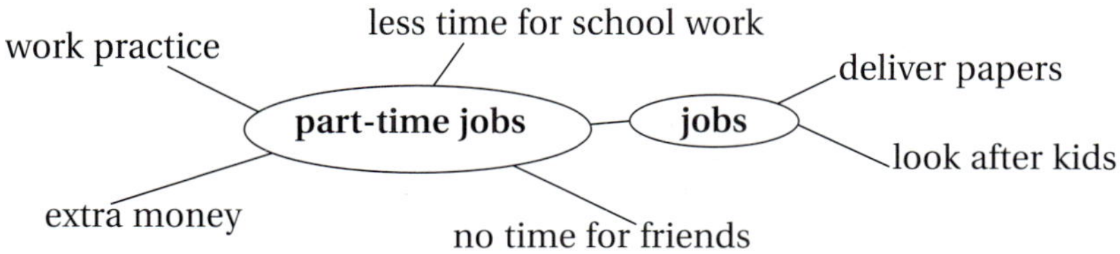

2

FOR

I don't agree. I think it's OK for kids to work when they are at school. It gives you practice for jobs later. You learn not to be late and how to work with other people. It's great to have more money than just your pocket money. If you have worked for the money, it feels different when you spend it. Maybe that's because you understand better what 'money' means.

AGAINST

I agree. A school kid with a part-time job probably doesn't have enough time to do homework. It's hard when you have to learn for tests. And you can't see you friends as often as you like or just stay in bed longer on a Saturday morning. Most school kids live and eat at home and their parents buy them their clothes, etc. Extra money is perhaps nice, but you don't really need it!

Try it out! 3 – Seite 58–59

A Reading

1 a. climate ['klaɪmət] b. air-conditioning ['eəˌkəndɪʃnɪŋ] c. ranger ['reɪndʒə]
d. gases ['gæsɪz] e. polar bear [ˌpəʊlə 'beə] f. storms [stɔ:mz]
g. tornado [tɔ:'nɑ:dəʊ]

2 a. 2 park ranger b. 3 the climate c. 2 easier d. 1 tornados
e. 1 rain and floods f. 2 change the way we live g. 3 under a tree

B Language

a. in nature b. the climate c. the most modern countries in the world
d. technology makes life e. drought to many of the countries

C Mediation and communication

You: What's the weather like where you come from?
You: Ich komme aus Florida. Wir haben schreckliche Tornados dort.
You: Do you also have floods?
You: Ja, aber andere Staaten haben schon schlimmere Überschwemmungen gehabt.
You: Are a lot of Americans worried about these storms?
You: Oh, ja. Viele haben (deswegen) angefangen, anders zu leben/zu ändern, wie sie leben.

D Listening

a. 3 information b. 3 It opens again after lunch.

E Writing

1 FOR: I think we really need new technologies. It's important that these new technologies help us to solve the climate problem on Earth. I'm sure we can make cars that don't produce any gases. Maybe we can get most of our electricity from the wind or the sun. In places where there is drought perhaps a new technology could make sea water OK for us to drink and for the farmers' fields.
AGAINST: No, we don't need new technologies because most of the ones which we have are bad for us and the Earth. We must stop these gases. I think it would be better, for example, to find ways for people to live near their work or school. They could then walk, go by bike or use public transport. It would be better for us and for nature.

2 Dear …,
The Earth is getting warmer very fast and this is dangerous for our lives so I think we should all use less electricity. And we must remember to switch off equipment and lights when we aren't using them. And shop windows in town don't need all those lights on all night!
Of course you feel safer in the streets if it's not too dark. But the town could put up lamps which use very little electricity or which collect it from the sun.
Also we need better and cheaper public transport so that people don't need their own cars. We must all change to stop the climate change! NOW!
Yours,
…

Try it out! 4 – Seite 74–75

A Reading

1 a. 2 a new platform b. 2 a member of a tribe c. 3 be bad for his tribe
d. 2 the tribe's water e. 3 sacred to the Hualapai

2

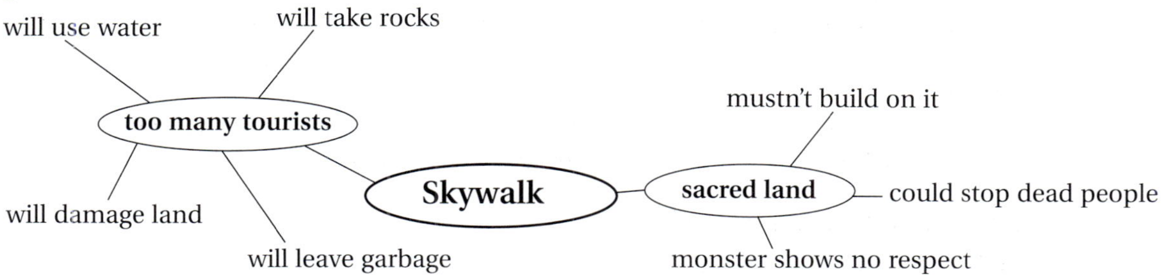

B Language

a. article b. look after c. tourists d. rocks e. garbage f. ground

C Listening

1 Part a) a. right b. wrong c. wrong d. right e. right f. wrong
2 Part b) a. She is for it.
b. 1 The Hualapai need money. 3 It's beautiful.
4 It gives work to her people. 5 Visitors can learn about her tribe.
c. Route 66

D Speaking

1 A Reading
CONS: too many tourists: will use water, will take rocks, will damage land, will leave garbage;
sacred land: mustn't build on it, monster shows no respect, could stop dead people
C Listening
CONS: could stop ancestors, past is important, peace and quiet and beautiful scenery will disappear
PROS: our children are more important, people on reservation need money, it gives jobs, visitors learn about the Hualapai, share beautiful canyon with others, the Earth belongs to everyone, beautiful piece of technology, tourists don't have to use it

2
Rory: I am really worried about the Skywalk.
Louisa: But why, Grandad? It's a beautiful piece of technology.
Rory: It's on sacred ground, Louisa! We mustn't build there. It could stop our ancestors.
Louisa: But our children are more important. They need money and their parents need jobs.
Rory: But we must respect the past, too, Louisa.
Louisa: But we can still do that with the Skywalk. Tourists will come and we can tell them all about our tribe and its history.

Rory: That's what I mean. There will be too many tourists. They will use our water, take our rocks and leave their garbage.

Louisa: Grandad, they aren't all bad people. Many respect the Earth as we respect our land. Remember the Earth belongs to everyone not just to the Hualapai tribe.

Rory: You are right about that, Louisa.

E Writing

1 FOR: I think the Skywalk is a good idea because it will help the Hualapai people. The tourists who come to see it will respect the land and will learn more about the tribe. Tourists who don't want to walk on the Skywalk can see the Grand Canyon from other places.
AGAINST: I think the Skywalk is a bad idea because it won't really help the Hualapai people. The tourists who come to see it won't respect the land. They will damage it and use all the tribe's water.

2 DON'T AGREE:
Dear Newtech,
I read the letter from Rory Quasala and I want to say that I don't agree with him. I think the future is more important than the past. Rory should think about the children and the young people on the reservation.
Yours …

AGREE:
Dear Newtech,
I read the letter from Rory Quasala and I want to say that I agree with him. I think the ancestors and the tribal land are important. There are too many tourists and they won't think about the people who live on the reservation.
Yours …

Lösungen Grammatik

Unit 1

G 1

1. Jack and Jane arrived in the jungle some time ago.
2. Why did they leave their country? – They wanted to go on a trip/see the jungle.
3. What didn't they have at home? – They didn't have a jungle.

G 3

After (a) famine had broken out/had started in Ireland, a lot of people went to America.

Unit 2

G 4

1. They have (already) collected wood.
2. They haven't started the fire yet.
3. Jane hasn't written all the cards yet.
4. Jack hasn't found enough chairs yet.
5. They have (already) set the tables.
6. They haven't prepared the food yet.
7. They have (already) put up the decorations.
8. They haven't brought the drinks yet.

G 5

a) 1. You mustn't leave bottles (here).
2. You must leave the panther alone.
3. You mustn't swim in the lake at night.
4. You must ask Jack for help.

b) 1. My friend should go to the doctor.
2. He/She should take it back to the shop.
3. He/She should go to the police.

Unit 3

G 6

a) 1. The shopping is done by Nutty.
2. The clothes are washed by the elephant.
3. The sandwiches are made by the tiger.
4. The floor is cleaned by the mouse.

b) 1. The shopping isn't done by Nutty.
2. The clothes aren't washed by the elephant.
3. The sandwiches aren't made by the tiger.
4. The floor isn't cleaned by the mouse.

Unit 4

G 7

1. If it rains this afternoon, they'll play computer games together.
2. If the weather is nice tomorrow, we'll go to the park.
3. If I go to the shops on Saturday, I'll buy a present for my friend.

G 8

1. If I had lots of money, I'd go on a trip around the world/buy a new computer/… .
2. If I had holidays now, I'd be in bed/go to the pool/meet my friends … .
3. If I worked on the moon, it would be exciting/I'd be famous/I'd feel lonely/… .
4. If I didn't live in Germany, I wouldn't speak German/I'd have different friends … .

Unit 5

G 9

a) 2. The clothes were washed by the elephant.
3. The sandwiches were made by the tiger.
4. The floor was cleaned by the mouse.

b) 1. The shopping wasn't done by Nutty.
2. The clothes weren't washed by the elephant.
3. The sandwiches weren't made by the tiger.
4. The floor wasn't cleaned by the mouse.

Textquellen:
S.15: Madonna/Stuart David Price © Darkdancer Ltd./Neue Welt Musikverlag GmbH & Co. KG; S.31: Travis L. Barker/Thomas DeLonge/Mark Hoppus © Fun with Goats/ EMI Music Publishing Germany GmbH & Co. KG; S.67: Johan K. Fransson/Niklas R. Johnsson/Tim M. Larsson/Tobias L. Lundgren © Warner-Chappell Music Scand AB/ Neue Welt Musikverlag GmbH & Co. KG; S.84: William Adams/Christopher Brian Bridges/Stacy Ferguson/Jamal F. Jones/Elvis Williams Jr © Cherry River Music Co/ Cherry Lane Music Publishing Co. Inc.

Bildquellen:
Cover: Getty Images (Clarissa Leahy/stone+), München; S.4: (1) iStockphoto (RF/ Sami Suni), Calgary, Alberta; (2) laif (Sasse), Köln; (3) JupiterImages (RF/Photos. com), Tucson, AZ; S.5: (1) laif (Kurt Henseler), Köln; (2) Corbis (George Logan/zefa), Düsseldorf; (3) Corbis (Jon Hicks), Düsseldorf; (4) Alamy Images RM (Douglas Fisher), Abingdon, Oxon; S.6: (1) Corbis (Lucas Jackson/Reuter), Düsseldorf; (2) Cinetext, Frankfurt; (3) Corbis (Tim Mosenfelder), Düsseldorf; (4) GOODSHOOT (Goodshoot), Annecy-Le-Vieux; S.7: (1) Corbis (Bettmann), Düsseldorf; (2) Alamy Images RM (Justin Leighton), Abingdon, Oxon; (3) Getty Images (Botanica/Jack O`La), München; S.8: (1) Corbis (David Ball), Düsseldorf; S.9: (1) iStockphoto (RF/ Sami Suni), Calgary, Alberta; (2) Alamy Images RM (SHOTFILE), Abingdon, Oxon; (3) laif (Sasse), Köln; (4) laif (Jonkmanns), Köln; S.10: (1) Alamy Images RM (Visual Arts Library), Abingdon, Oxon; 10.2: laif (Sasse), Köln; S11: (1) Corbis (Bettmann), Düsseldorf; S.12: (1) iStockphoto (RF/Liv Friis-Larsen), Calgary, Alberta; (2) iStock-photo (RF/aaron holbrough), Calgary, Alberta; (3) iStockphoto (RF/Lori Sparkia), Calgary, Alberta; (4) iStockphoto (RF/Greg Nicholas), Calgary, Alberta; (5) iStock-photo (RF/Jennifer Andal), Calgary, Alberta; (6) iStockphoto (RF/Cathleen Clapper), Calgary, Alberta; (7) iStockphoto (RF), Calgary, Alberta; (8) iStockphoto (RF/George Bailey), Calgary, Alberta; S.13: (1) Klett-Archiv (Hamida Aziz), Stuttgart; S.14: (1) Alamy Images RM (eStockPhoto), Abingdon, Oxon; S.15: (1) Corbis (Nathan Benn), Düsseldorf; (2) Alamy Images RM (Rodolfo Arpia), Abingdon, Oxon; (3) Alamy Images RM (Frances Roberts), Abingdon, Oxon; (4) Picture-Alliance (Landov Laura Cavanaugh), Frankfurt; S.18: (1) JupiterImages (RF/Photos.com), Tucson, AZ; S.19: (1) iStockphoto (RF/Lee Pettet), Calgary, Alberta; S.21: (1) The Library of Congress, Washington, D.C.; S.22: (1) iStockphoto (RF/Kathye Killer), Calgary, Alberta; S.24: (1) iStockphoto (Greg Nicholas), Calgary, Alberta; (2) Fotofinder (Visum/ImageWorks), Berlin; (3) iStockphoto (RF/Do Hoai), Calgary, Alberta; S.25: (1) Alamy Images RM (Jim West), Abingdon, Oxon; (2) Alamy Images RM (Dennis MacDonald), Abingdon, Oxon; (3) Avenue Images GmbH (Corbis RF), Hamburg; S.26: (1) iStockphoto (RF/Eileen Hart), Calgary, Alberta; (2) Avenue Images GmbH (Alamy RF), Hamburg; S.27: (1) Tim Dolighan, Dolighan Cartoons; S.30: (1) Getty Images (stone/Blasius Erlinger), München; S.31: (1) Fotofinder (Visum/Kalle Singer), Berlin; (2) JupiterImages (RF/Photos.com), Tucson, AZ; S.32: (1) Alamy Images RF (RF/David Davis Photoproductions), Abingdon, Oxon; (2) Alamy Images RM (Ted Horowitz), Abingdon, Oxon; (3) Corbis (ROB & SAS), Düsseldorf; (4) Alamy Images RM (Picture Partners), Abingdon, Oxon; (5) Alamy Images RM (Picture Partners), Abingdon, Oxon; (6) Avenue Images GmbH (Corbis RF), Hamburg; (7) Avenue Images GmbH (Creatas RF), Hamburg; S.37: (1) iStockphoto (Jim Jurica), Calgary, Alberta; S.39: (1) AP (Eckehard Schulz), Frankfurt am Main; (2) Picture-Alliance (Ingo Wagner), Frankfurt; S.40: (1) Avenue Images GmbH (Banana Stock), Hamburg; (2) Avenue Images GmbH (Photo Alto RF), Hamburg; (3) Avenue Images GmbH (Alamy RF/Blend Images), Hamburg; (4) iStockphoto (RF/Thomas Gordon), Calgary, Alberta; S.42: (1) laif (Kurt Henseler), Köln; S.43: (1) Fotofinder (PHONE Thiriet Claudius), Berlin; (2) Avenue Images GmbH (Brand X Pictures), Hamburg; (3) Corbis (George Logan/zefa), Düsseldorf; (4) Corbis (NOGUES ALAIN/CORBIS SYGMA), Düsseldorf; S.44: (1) Corbis (Javier Pierini), Düsseldorf; S.45: (1) iStockphoto (RF/Tom Tomczyk), Calgary, Alberta; (2) Avenue Images GmbH (Brand X Pictures), Hamburg; (3) iStockphoto (RF/Lukasz Witczak), Calgary, Alberta; (4) iStockphoto (RF/Grafissimo), Calgary, Alberta; (5) Alamy Images RM (Medical-on-Line), Abingdon, Oxon; (6) Alamy Images RM (Leslie Garland Picture), Abingdon, Oxon; S.47: (1) iStockphoto (RF/Galina Barskaya), Calgary, Alberta; S.49: (1) iStockphoto (RF/Dave Pilibosian), Calgary, Alberta; (2) iStockphoto (RF/starfotograf), Calgary, Alberta; (3) iStockphoto (RF/ Sandra O'Claire), Calgary, Alberta; (4) iStockphoto (RF/George Cairns), Calgary, Alberta; (5) iStockphoto (RF/Christopher Pattberg), Calgary, Alberta; (6) iStockphoto (RF/Spectral-Design), Calgary, Alberta; S.50: (1) picturemaxx AG (RM/defd movies), München; (2) Alamy Images RM (Rob Walls), Abingdon, Oxon; S.51: (1) Alamy Images RM (Alan Campbell), Abingdon, Oxon; (2) iStockphoto (RF/michael harvey), Calgary, Alberta; S.53: (1) iStockphoto (RF/Emrah Turudu), Calgary, Alberta; (2) iStockphoto (RF/Jeff Metzger), Calgary, Alberta; (3) iStockphoto (RF/Melissa King), Calgary, Alberta; (4) iStockphoto (RF/Karim Hesham), Calgary, Alberta; (5) iStock-photo (RF/DSGpro), Calgary, Alberta; (6) iStockphoto (RF/Ivan Cholakov), Calgary, Alberta; S.54: (1) iStockphoto (RF/ngirish), Calgary, Alberta; (2) Avenue Images GmbH (Alamy RF/Radius Images), Hamburg; S.55: (1) NASA Goddard Space Flight Center (PD), Greenbelt, Maryland; S.56: (1) Internet/Screenshot; (2) Internet/ Screenshot; (3) Internet/Screenshot; (4) Corbis (David Ball), Düsseldorf; (5) iStock-photo (RF/Daniel Stein), Calgary, Alberta; (6) iStockphoto (RF/Ivan Cholakov), Calgary, Alberta; S.58: (1) Alamy Images RM (Danita Delimont), Abingdon, Oxon; S.60: (1) Corbis (David Kadlubowski), Düsseldorf; S.61: (1) Corbis (Chris SattlbergerChris Sattlberger), Düsseldorf; (2) Corbis (Jon Hicks), Düsseldorf; (3) Alamy Images RM (Chad Ehlers), Abingdon, Oxon; S.62: (1) Alamy Images RM (Douglas Fisher), Abingdon, Oxon; (2) iStockphoto (RF/Danny Warren), Calgary, Alberta; S.64: (1) http: //wwp.greenwich-meantime.com/time-zone/usa/usa-time-zone-converters/; (2) MEV, Augsburg; S.67: (1) Getty Images (Sean Gallup), München; S.71: (1) iStockphoto (RF/Clint Spencer), Calgary, Alberta; (2) Corbis (Chris SattlbergerChr), Düsseldorf; (3) iStockphoto (RF/Roger Branch), Calgary, Alberta; (4) iStockphoto (RF/Sieto Verver), Calgary, Alberta; (5) Alamy Images RM (Hideo Kurihara), Abingdon, Oxon; (6) iStockphoto (RF/gocosmonaut), Calgary, Alberta; S.74: (1) Alamy Images RM (Lee Foster), Abingdon, Oxon; S.76: (1) Corbis (Lucas Jackson/Reuters), Düsseldorf; (2) Corbis (Frank Trapper), Düsseldorf; (3) Alamy Images RM (Allstar Pict. Library), Abingdon, Oxon; S.77: (1) Corbis (Mario Anzuoni/Reuters), Düsseldorf; (2) Corbis (Stephane Cardinale/People Avenue), Düsseldorf; (3) Corbis (Frank Trapper), Düsseldorf; S.78: (1) Alamy Images RM (Mary Evans), Abingdon, Oxon; (2) Corbis (Bettmann), Düsseldorf; (3) Cinetext, Frankfurt; (4) Corbis (Bettmann), Düsseldorf; (5) Corbis (Bettmann), Düsseldorf; S.82: (1) GOODSHOOT (Goodshoot), Annecy-Le-Vieux; S.83: (1) CartoonStock (Mike Baldwin), Bath; S.84: (1) Corbis, Düsseldorf; (2) Corbis (Tim Mosenfelder), Düssel-dorf; S.85: (1) iStockphoto (RF/Shane Thompson), Calgary, Alberta; (2) iStockphoto (RF/Andrew Dernie), Calgary, Alberta; (3) iStockphoto (RF/Libby Chapman), Calgary, Alberta; (4) Corbis (Fred Greaves/Reuters), Düsseldorf; (5) iStockphoto (RF/Dave Aspinall), Calgary, Alberta; (6) shutterstock, New York, NY; (7) iStockphoto (RF/Krista Weber), Calgary, Alberta; (8) iStockphoto (RF/Christopher O Driscoll), Calgary, Alberta; (9) iStockphoto (RF/Albert Campbell), Calgary, Alberta; (10) iStockphoto (RF/Wayne Stadler), Calgary, Alberta; (11) iStockphoto (RF/Hedda Gjerpen), Calgary, Alberta; (12) iStockphoto (RF/Madeleine Abrahamsson), Calgary, Alberta; S.87: (1) Corbis (Bettmann), Düsseldorf; (2) iStockphoto (Pascal Genest), Calgary, Alberta; (3) Corbis (Marc Serota/Reuters), Düsseldorf; S.88: (1) Alamy Images RM (Mary Evans), Abingdon, Oxon; (2) Corbis (Bettmann), Düsseldorf; (3) Cinetext, Frankfurt; (4) Corbis (Bettmann), Düsseldorf; (5) Corbis (Bettmann), Düsseldorf; (6) Corbis (Sunset Boulevard/Sygma), Düsseldorf; (7) iStockphoto (RF/Serega), Calgary, Alberta; (8) iStockphoto (RF/Andreas Guskos), Calgary, Alberta; (9) iStock-photo (RF/Ivan Cholakov), Calgary, Alberta; (10) iStockphoto (RF/Joe McCormick), Calgary, Alberta; (11) Corbis (Brendan McDermid/Reuters), Düsseldorf; (12) iStockphoto (RF/ nicolas hansen), Calgary, Alberta; (13) iStockphoto (RF/MACIEJ NOSKOWSKI), Calgary, Alberta; (14) Avenue Images GmbH (stock disc), Hamburg; S.90: (1) iStockphoto (RF/Peeter Viisimaa), Calgary, Alberta; (2) iStockphoto (RF/ Denise Ritchie), Calgary, Alberta; (3) Wikimedia Foundation Inc. (Public Domain), St. Petersburg FL; (4) Alamy Images RF (RF/Alecstewart), Abingdon, Oxon; (5) shutterstock (RF/Stephen coburn), New York, NY; S.99: (1) Image 100, Berlin; S.100: (1) Getty Images (Botanica/Jack O'La), München; (2) Picture-Alliance (ipol code), Frankfurt; (3) AKG, Berlin; (4) Corbis (Joseph Sohm; ChromoS), Düsseldorf; S.101: (1) Fotosearch RF, Waukesha, WI; (2) iStockphoto (RF/tness74), Calgary, Alberta; (3) Alamy Images RM (Justin Leighton), Abingdon, Oxon; (4) Getty Images RF (PhotoDisc), München; S.102: (1) Alamy Images RM (North Wind Picture Archives), Abingdon, Oxon; (2) Süddeutscher Verlag (Rue des Archives), München; (3) AKG, Berlin; (4) Corbis (Leonard de Selva), Düsseldorf; S.103: (1) BPK, Berlin; (2) Picture-Alliance (ipol code), Frankfurt; (3) Alamy Images RM (Visual Arts Library), Abingdon, Oxon; (4) The Sealed Knot Ltd, Nottingham NG2 5LH; S.104: (1) Rockwell Museum of Western Art, Corning, New York; (2) Süddeutscher Verlag, München; (3) The Granger Collection, New York; (4) Corbis (David Stoecklein), Düsseldorf; (5) Süddeutscher Verlag, München; (6) Corbis (Bettmann), Düsseldorf; S.105: (1) iStockphoto (appleuzr), Calgary, Alberta; S.106 (1) iStockphoto (RF/Geoffrey Hammond), Calgary, Alberta; (2) Avenue Images GmbH (Corbis RF), Hamburg; S.108: (1) iStockphoto (RF/Mark Stay), Calgary, Alberta; S.123: (1) MEV, Augsburg; S.127: (1) MEV, Augsburg; S.128: (1) Ingram Publishing, Tattenhall Chester; S.133: (1) NASA, Washington, D.C.; S.139: (1) Corbis (RF), Düsseldorf; S.143: (1) MEV, Augsburg; S.144: (1) Creativ Collection Verlag GmbH, Freiburg; S.148: (1) Klett-Archiv (Silberzahn), Stuttgart

ALASKA
WASHINGTON
Seattle
OREGON
IDAHO
MONTANA
NORTH DAKOTA
SOUTH DAKOTA
WYOMING
ROCKY MOUNTAINS
NEBRASKA
CALIFORNIA
San Francisco
NEVADA
UTAH
COLORADO
Denver
KANSAS
Grand Canyon
PACIFIC OCEAN
Los Angeles
San Diego
NEW MEXICO
USA
ARIZONA
TEXAS
HAWAII
MEXICO

1. How many states are there in the United States?
2. Write them on cards. Take two cards each and find out two things about each state on your cards.
3. Which state is the Grand Canyon in?

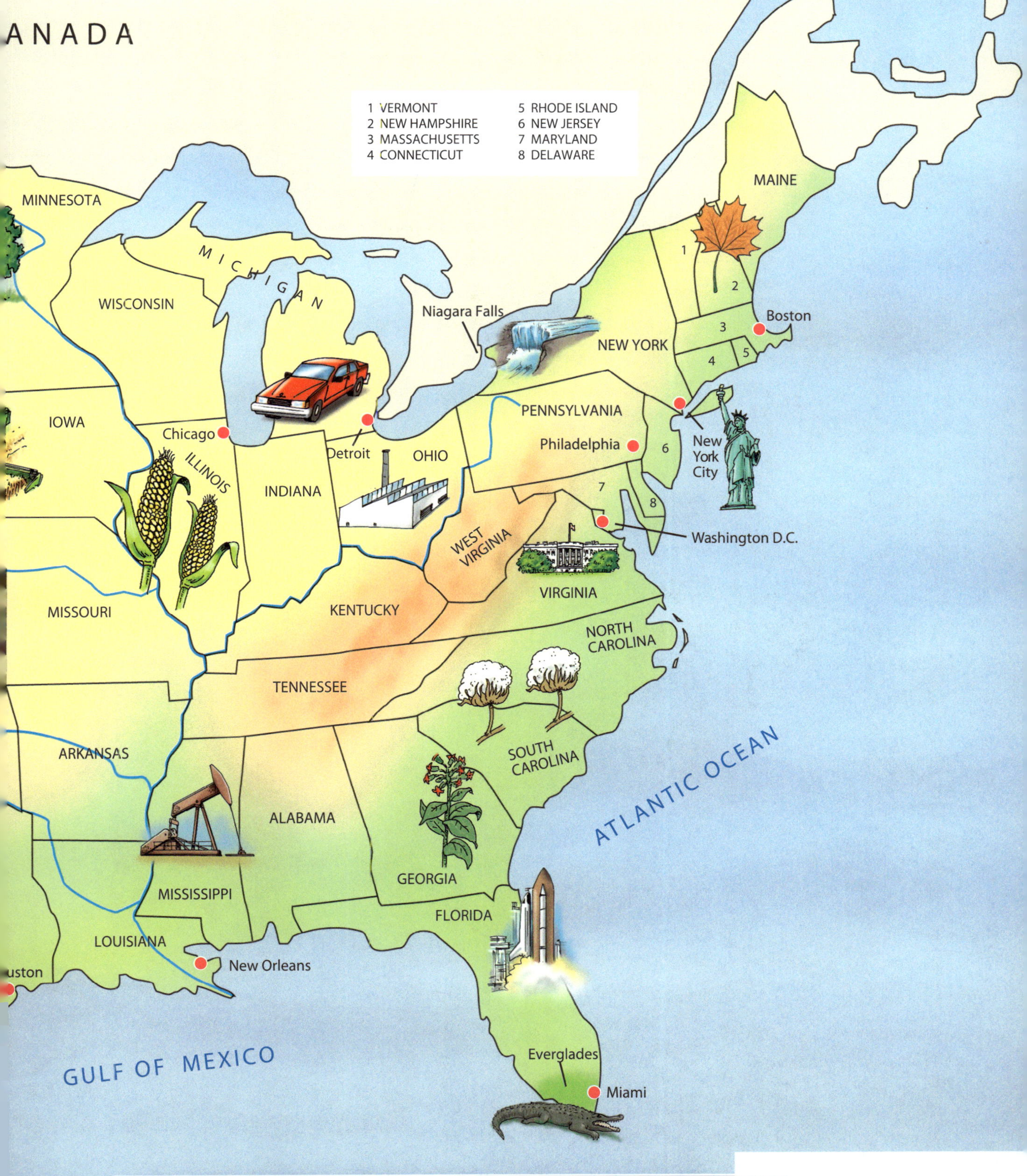

THE UNITED STATES OF AMERICA